FENTON

GLASS MADE for OTHER COMPANIES

ENCORE
GRACIOUS TOUCH
LENOX
ROSSO
TIARA
AND MORE...

VOLUME II
1970 – 2005

*Identification
&
Value Guide*

cb
COLLECTOR BOOKS
A Division of Schroeder Publishing Co., Inc.

Carrie and Gerald Domitz

On the front cover: Rosalene Tiger paperweight, $125.00 – 150.00; Avon vase, $125.00 – 150.00; Burmese child-size pitcher & tumbler, $425.00 – 500.00, 6-pc. set; Royal Blue Carnival vintage miniature epergne, $85.00 – 95.00; Provincial Blue Carnival Wild Rose & Bow Knot vase, $85.00 – 100.00.

On the back cover: Petal Pink Carnival Fisherman mug, $65.00 – 75.00; Purple Carnival Grape & Cable vase, $150.00 – 175.00; Light Aqua Wild Rose goblet, $14.50; Red Carnival Cactus 10" cracker basket, $200.00 – 250.00; Milk Glass Satin Butterfly Frango box, $75.00 – 95.00.

Cover design: Beth Summers
Book design: Lisa Henderson

COLLECTOR BOOKS
P.O. Box 3009
Paducah, Kentucky 42002–3009

www.collectorbooks.com

Copyright © 2007 Carrie & Gerald Domitz

The current values in this book should be used only as a guide. They are not intended to set prices, which vary from one section of the country to another. Auction prices, as well as dealer prices, vary greatly and are affected by condition as well as demand. Neither the authors nor the publisher assumes responsibility for any losses that might be incurred as a result of consulting this guide.

SEARCHING FOR A PUBLISHER?

We are always looking for people knowledgeable within their fields. If you feel that there is a real need for a book on your collectible subject and have a large comprehensive collection, contact Collector Books.

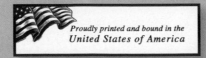

Proudly printed and bound in the **United States of America**

Contents

Dedication 4
Acknowledgments 5
Introduction 7
The Fenton Family History 8
Special Order Department 9
Advertising Bells 11
Aladdin Lamp 14
Alexander Julian 19
Army & Air Force Exchange Service 20
Avon 22
Candle-Land 23
Carolyn's Collectibles 26
Chesapeake & Ohio Railroad Historical Society 29
Collectors' Clubs 31
    Carnival Glass Clubs 31
    Duncan Glass Collectors Club 53
    Fenton Art Glass Collectors of America 54
    Fenton Finders of Kansas City 88
    National Fenton Glass Society 89
    Heisey Collectors of America 101
Cosmetics N Glass 110
Coyne's Parade of Gifts 111
Cracker Barrel 117
Crescent & Sprague 125
Danbury Mint 126
David Leo — The Jillian Collection 127
Doris Lechler 133
Douglas Parks 140
Encore — Dorothy Taylor 143
Eric Weber 153
Ethan Allen 156
Frederick Atkins 158
Gift Shop, FAGCO 159
Gift Shop, Limited Offer to the Antique Trade 177
Glass Press — Glass Collector's Digest 189
Gracious Touch 194
Hallmark Stores 215
Harger Lightning Protection 218
Heartlights 219
Heinz Company 222
Hershey's Chocolate World 223
Holophane — Verlys of America 225
House Warmings 232
John Infurna 234
Kaleidoscope 235
Lamp Shade Catalogs 239
Lenox Catalog Sales 243
Levay Glass — Gary and Dodie Levay 253
L.G. Wright Company 310
Lois Radcliff — Elemar Glass 334
Longaberger Baskets 337

Madonna Inn of San Luis Obispo, CA 339
Marshall Fields, Frederick & Nelson 342
Martha Stewart 345
Mary Walrath and Daughters 357
    Mary Jachim 364
    Joyce Colella & Mary Jachim 366
    Joyce Colella 373
    Carol's Antiques and Art 374
McMillen & Husband 375
Memories in Glass 379
Metropolitan Museum of Art 383
MIMI 386
Minerva, Ohio, Sesquicentennial 387
Miscellaneous 390
Monongehela Power Company 395
Nationwide Insurance 395
Nestlé Research & Development 396
Northwood Art Glass Company 396
Oglebay Institute Glass Museum 398
Ohio River Sternwheeler Festival 400
Olde Virginia Glass 401
Pascal 408
Pharmacy Items 416
Publishers Clearing House 417
A.L. Randall Company 420
RCA 423
Rejuvenators, Inc. 424
Rose Presznick 424
    Jim Myers and Kim Myers George 425
Rosso Glass 426
Sandwich Historical Society 450
Showcase Dealers 453
    Classic Glass 454
    Collectables Unlimited 458
    Collectors' Showcase 458
    Dreams & Rainbows 467
    Randy's Antiques and Gifts 467
Singleton Bailey 470
Snyder's Vaughn-Haven 490
Sports Awards 490
Stephenson's Apple Orchard Restaurant 491
Telephone Company Advertising 492
Tiara 493
Tom Collins and Audrey & Joe Humphrey 504
VIP Antiques 504
Virginia's Gift Shop, Knott's Berry Farm 505
Westlake Ruby Glass Works 505
West Virginia Parkway Authority 507
Wheaton Village 508
Zeta & Charles Todd 509

Back row: *Randy Fenton, Mike Fenton, George Fenton, Tom Fenton, Scott Fenton.* **Front row:** *Shelley Fenton Ash, Christine Fenton, Nancy Fenton, Lynn Fenton Erb.*

This book is dedicated to the third and fourth generation of Fentons, who continue to make the beautiful glassware we collect. Frank told me years ago that as long as there is a Fenton who wants to make glass, there will be a Fenton Art Glass Company. I know the company has been passed down to very capable men and women.

It is also written to honor the three Fenton men we have lost in the last few years.

Frank M. Fenton, 1915 – 2005

Bill Fenton, 1923 – 2002

The last several years have been sad years for the family of Bill Fenton. Bill's wife, Elinor, passed away February 13, 2002. They had been married for 58 years and were the very best of friends as well as husband and wife. Elinor was a sweet, gracious woman, and Bill lost his heart when she died. He followed her, dying of what must have been a broken heart, on December 11, 2002. It was almost more than their family could bear, but it would soon be worse. On February 3, 2003, at the young age of 52, their son, Don Fenton, died as a result of a heart attack suffered after a sports accident. Don was his father's son; he was a gregarious, funny man. He loved his family very much, and was so happy to be following in his father's footsteps. Everyone who knew Don loved him and he will always be missed.

Don Fenton, 1951 – 2003

ACKNOWLEDGMENTS

No one author can do a good research book on the American glass industry without the help and knowledge of others. I have been very blessed to have the help of the dealers, collectors, and the Fenton Art Glass Company employees past and present.

Many of the photographs in this book came from the Fenton archive catalogs that have been kept for recent special order glass. I thank Chris Benson for taking these pictures, because without these photographs, I wouldn't have been able to include as much information in this book. Nancy Fenton, Scott Fenton, Don Cunningham, Pam Dick, Terry Nutter, Jennifer Maston, Chris Benson, and Jim Measell came to my rescue when I was having difficulties finding information I couldn't find elsewhere.

In California, Barbara and Ed Nunes made taking pictures at their house a lot of fun. Ed has such a great sense of humor that he kept me laughing through all the work. They have a beautiful collection of blue glass, and a lot of it is in this book. They also have pieces for sale. Agnes Allison, a longtime Fenton collector, was nice enough to bring glass from her home so that I could add it to this book. Bill Harmon, who gives me a place to stay when I'm in San Jose, also gave me a lot of glass to photograph. I also photographed the glass of Ethel Bock, Virginia Domingo, Leota McLean, Sue and Chester Lightle, Paula Spencer, Jerry McCracken, Patrick Mayberry, Penny Parisi, and John Ojeda.

In West Virginia, Ohio, Indiana, Washington, and

Oregon, the following people were contributors. Eileen, Cheryl, and Dale Robinson shared an enormous collection of Fenton with me. Eileen passed away in 2005 and she is missed by many Fenton collectors. Ike and Betty Hardman have a fantastic collection of Fenton that they allowed me to photograph. Art and Ellen Gilbert sent me many pictures of their beautiful and rare glass. The Wisconsin Fenton collectors were also a great help. Without Arvin and Betty Wolfgram, I wouldn't have been able to add information about Parade of Gifts. Kay and Forest Kenworthy and Ferill and Otis Rice gave me information and encouragement. Jim and Sue Stage, Bill Cottenmyre, Ed Radcliffe, Doug and Cindy Coyle, Carolyn Coyle, Mary Clapper, John Rodger Holfinger, Bill Crowl, Audrey and Joe Humphrey, Patti Love, Marianne Lower, Jeffrey Greenlees, Mike and Kathy Wear, Howard and Shirley Hays, Carolyn Kriner, Don and Gladys Snyder, Kay and Swede Larsson, Dean and Doris Howard, Mark Howard, Bill and Kathy Etcheson, Sheila Pankratz, Lisa's Collectibles, Tom Gorz, George Higby, Becki Ray, Bev Franzen, Cindy David, Cindy Thomas, Nadine and Jay Downham, Larry and Kathy Eckert, Carolyn Crow, Barbara Coleman, Janice Ahl, Marian Carroll, Ron and Donna Miller, Judy Knoyle, Sharon Dennis, Dick Ponti, Kim Chetto, Mildred Coty, Jessica Snow, Mark Dreyer, and Norma Hill were all either willing to allow me to photograph their glass or furnished me with photographs.

Jerry's mother, Vera Dean Domitz, was a huge help. She contributed her collection of cup plates and gave me her neatly kept past Butterfly Nets to use for information I couldn't find elsewhere.

My daughter in law, Lynette Bottroff, was left out of the acknowledgments in the first book by accident. She owns many of the DeVilbiss atomizers that are in that book. My daughter, Greta Ross, taught me to photograph glass. My grandchildren, Sydnee and Jacob Galusha, loaned their collections of glass animals to be photographed.

The Williamstown Antique Mall in Williamstown, WV, has been very cooperative about allowing me to take pictures in their mall. While I gave credit to Ed Radcliff and Jim Stage, the person who spent the most time opening cases for me was Sue Stage. They were often very busy while I was photographing, so it was a distraction for them to have me there. Their contributions made both this and the first Fenton books possible. The Dexter City An-

tique Mall in Dexter City, Ohio, also allowed me to take photos in the mall. That mall has been moved to Marietta, OH, and is now the River City Antique Mall. The FAGCA allowed me to take photographs of pieces in its office as well as gave me permission to use some photos from the club's website. The National Fenton Glass Society answered all my questions and shared information with me.

Shows and clubs that allowed me the space to set up my lights and take pictures: Heavenly Productions, San Jose, CA; Palmer Wirf, Portland, OR; Green River DG club and E K Shows, Kent, WA; and Rain of Glass, Portland, OR.

Many of the photographs and information came from the internet, some by e-mail and some from websites. Singleton Bailey not only sent me information about the glass made for him, but also the glass made for Levay. Without the large file he has kept, I would have missed a lot of items made for Levay, pieces I have never seen or photographed.

Joyce Colella shared photos and information about her sister Carol Woods and her mother, Mary Walrath, as well as her own glass designs and information about the production of the pieces that were sold under their names. I found a great deal of information about Mary Walrath and her daughters on a website ran by Barbara Colligan.

Kim George, great granddaughter of Rose Presznick, sent the photo of Rose and one of the lamp made for herself. David Doty, who has a website for carnival glass, allowed me to use a few of his photos.

Randy Bradshaw of Randy's Antiques, Marion Thornton and her daughter Jenni Halverson of Collectors' Showcase, Steve and Kelli Tonelis of Classic Glass, Glen and Steve Thistlewood of the Woodsland World Wide Carnival Glass Association, and David McKinley and Arleen Buzzard of Northwood Art Glass Company also all deserve thanks for their contributions.

I also want to give credit where it is due. Everyone at Collector Books has worked hard on this book and they have done a wonderful job. Gail Ashburn and Amy Sullivan, my editors, must have had a great deal of patience to teach me how to do this right. Beth Summers, cover designer, and Lisa Henderson, book designer, spent many hours producing a beautiful book. Without these four people, this would be a very different book.

I can't begin this book without a few words about my friend Frank Fenton. Just days after collectors left West Virginia, where we celebrated Fenton's 100 years of glass-making, Frank passed away, leaving an enormous hole in the heart of every collector. It was a terrible personal loss for me. Frank had helped me, had argued with me, and had given me more encouragement than anyone other than my family. I loved and respected this giant of a man who had a giant heart. I am not alone in this feeling. Everyone who knew him will miss him but will never forget him. We are all blessed to have had him in our lives.

When Jerry and I decided to write a book covering all the special-order glass made by Fenton, we thought we could do it in just one book. It only took a month or two for us to realize that it simply wouldn't be possible to fit everything in one book unless we made it so thick and heavy that a reader would have to carry it around in a wheelbarrow. It took a little time to convince our publisher that we needed to expand our project, but eventually, the company agreed with us. Unfortunately, I discovered that I really couldn't get everything into just two books either, but we will do our best to cover the largest part of Fenton special order business.

This book covers the years of 1970 – 2005. There are a few dealers, such as Randall, who began buying items not in the general Fenton line in the 1950s. Some of those fit better into this book than the book that covers the years 1907 to 1980. Please bear with us, and I think you will be happy with our choices. We also made a decision to include some of the glass made for and sold by the Fenton Art Glass Gift Shop. It is a separate entity from the glassmaking part of Fenton, so it isn't much of a reach to include it. I'm not sure that it's well known that the gift shop deals in more than just second-quality glass. It does a great deal of business in specialty items like Black Crest and the leaded glass hangings. When Fenton is testing a mould or a product, samples are made so that it can market test them or decide if production costs will make it economically feasible to add it to the catalog. Many of those pieces go into the FAGCA Special Glass Room, which is an extension of the gift shop. The Santa Claus candy jar, pictured in the gift shop chapter, is one of those items. It was made by using an old Fostoria mould. The Fostoria Santa is very hard to find, and now Fenton can tell us the reason for that rarity. It was almost impossible to get the base and lid to match.

The next problem we faced was our inability to get pictures and information for this newer glass. That doesn't seem to make sense, but it was the case. We found that many of Fenton's Showcase dealers ordered pieces made in different colors or decorations than the general line and sold them in their areas of the country. If you don't live in the general region of that store, it is hard to find those pieces. Luckily, Fenton began to photograph special orders and keep the pictures in notebooks. We were able to use many of those pictures, but this was a recent practice, so there are large holes in the information available to us. While we were unable to get many details about some of those dealers, many of them were quick to respond to my inquiries and were very helpful with their pictures. We are including contact information when we have it so that you, as a collector, will be able to buy pieces that may be available when this book is printed.

You will undoubtedly notice a gap in our coverage of glass made for other companies. When I began to write this book, Frank Fenton asked me to not put QVC glass into it. Fenton writes and sells its own book covering glass made for QVC, so it was a reasonable and understandable request. Reasonable or not, I would honor any such request from Frank. Fenton's QVC book can be purchased from the FAGCO website.

After the deaths of Frank L. Fenton and Robert Fenton, the company was put into the inexperienced hands of Frank L. Fenton's sons, Frank M. and Wilmer (Bill) C. Fenton. Frank and Bill faced the difficulties of learning to run the glass factory without the help of their father and uncles. While they accomplished more than anyone would have expected of the two inexperienced glassmakers, it was difficult. Frank and Bill decided that their children would be brought into the business sooner rather than later. Their children, Tom, Mike, George, Don, Randy, Shelley, and Christine, learned the business from the bottom up during their high school and college years, beginning in the mid-1960s. Even Frank's daughter-in-law, Nancy, was trained early. Frank and his wife, Elizabeth, took Nancy with them to antique shows, where they would look for glass that could be adapted to the Fenton line. It isn't hard to see that Nancy's ability was well suited to that part of the business.

In 1978, Elizabeth was diagnosed with amyotropic lateral sclerosis, Lou Gehrig's disease. Frank wanted to spend as much time as possible with his ill wife, so he decided to step down from his post as president. Bill assumed that position and a new position for Frank, that of chairman of the board, was created. It seemed to be the time to decide who would follow them as president of the company.

George Fenton had worked full time at Fenton since he graduated from college in 1972. He had held several positions and was the manager of manufacturing from 1979 until 1985. It seemed clear that he would be the person who would follow Bill as president. In 1986, Frank retired as chairman of the board and Bill assumed that position, leaving the job of president to George. Nancy Fenton, George's wife, moved into the job that Frank had always planned for her, manager of new product development. George and Nancy have two sons, Benjamin and David, and two grandchildren, Audrey and Tyler.

Tom Fenton, Frank's second son, became vice president of manufacturing and plant manager, and his brother, Mike, became safety director and purchasing manager. Tom has two children and four grandchildren. Mike has three children, Kerry, Meredith, and Natalie, and two grandchildren, Isaiah and Mason.

Frank's oldest son, Frank R. Fenton, works in the field of animal husbandry. He has three children, Lynn, Frank D., and Matthew, and six grandchildren, Elissa, Isabelle, Zachery, Brady, Kass, and Delaney.

Bill's son Don was a natural to follow in his father's footsteps. He had a natural good humor that served him well in sales. I don't think I have ever met someone who knew him that didn't feel a great deal of affection for him. Don left three children, Greer, Craig, and Brice.

When the QVC home shopping channel became a major account for Fenton, Bill became a household name, quite a star to everyone who watched him. His youngest daughter, Shelley, was appointed assistant sales manager in 1985 and traveled to regional and national gift shows. Shelley inherited her father's good humor, so the job was a good fit for her. She worked closely with her father on the QVC account developing new products for the show. She lightened her schedule when she had her children, Amanda and Alex, in the mid-1990s, but she continues to be active in the company and with QVC.

Randy Fenton, Bill's second son, manages the Fenton Gift Shop, which is a separate business from Fenton Art Glass. He has expanded the gift shop, adding experimentals and exclusives to the shop, which began as a way to sell discontinued glassware and glass seconds. Now the gift shop carries many non-Fenton collectibles. The gift shop also has merchandise from the factory that has never been sold through Fenton's regular catalog sales. Randy has three children, Danielle, Cassandra, and Justin.

Christine Fenton, Bill's older daughter, began as a tour guide during her high school and college days. She worked at Union Carbide for several years before returning to Fenton to be a full-time employee of the gift shop. She worked in customer service for several years and now she does data processing.

Frank and Bill's sister, Lillian, was the mother of Craig Archer, Frank L. Fenton's grandson. He is a sales representative in New York.

THE FOURTH GENERATION

Lynn Fenton, daughter of Frank's oldest son, Frank, joined the company in 1994. Lynn worked on the sales and marketing team. She created the *Glass Messenger*, a newsletter for collectors, which has been a great success. She supervises the decorating department and develops new management support for that department. As hard as she works, she finds time to raise two young children, Elissa and Isabelle. I remember the first time I saw Frank with Isabelle, Lynn's oldest daughter. He just couldn't hide his affection for this tiny little girl.

Scott Fenton, son of Tom Fenton, followed Bill and Don into the sales field. They left large shoes to fill, but Scott has stepped up to the challenge and has been very successful. Like most of the fourth generation, he began working in the gift shop and as a tour guide when he was only 16. He held several other positions and worked for his father before he moved on to work with his cousin, Don Fenton. His present job is managing the distribution channel and the Fenton sales force. It doesn't leave

him a lot of time to spend with his wife, Grace, and their adorable baby boy, Jackson, but he makes sure he spends quality time with them.

Jennifer E. Fenton Hukill, daughter of Tom Fenton, can't be found at the Fenton factory, but she is still involved in the company. She is a sales representative for the Kentucky sales region. Jennifer has three children, Ray, Emily, and Kirsten.

It is easy to see that there is no shortage of glassmakers in the Fenton family. The FAGCO is in the capable hands of those sons, grandsons, daughters, and granddaughters of Frank and Bill Fenton.

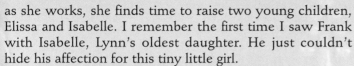

SPECIAL ORDER DEPARTMENT

PAT CLARK, DON CUNNINGHAM & CHRIS BENSON

In the 1980s, Fenton's special order department branched out from private mould work and acquired the licensing rights of several different companies, including Campbell's, Anheuser-Busch, and Jack Daniels. Most Fenton collectors are familiar with the Clydesdale items made by Fenton. For the most part, most of the glass made under those licenses required sand carving, often on imported glassware not made by Fenton. The image of Spuds Mackenzie was sandcarved on mugs and other items, most of which were sold in the stores owned by the company, but some were sold in the Fenton Gift Shop. Pat Clark, head of the special order department in the early 1980s, and Richard Delaney, Fenton artist, designed a Christmas scene with Spuds, but due to the concern of parents who found that Spuds had become too popular with their children, these pieces were never sold outside of the few that were sold in the gift shop. Of course, these bring very high prices now.

Fenton was also looking into the premium business, selling glass with a company name either sandcarved, pad printed, or hand painted onto the piece. Companies, colleges, college book stores, as well as cities celebrating special occasions were easy sells for the beautiful glass decorated just for them or for their occasions. The International Harvester's fifth annual toy show bought items that were hand painted with "Green Toy Tractor." West Virginia University bought a grouping of royal blue glass with slogans; its "Mountaineer" likeness was sandcarved in baskets, bells, ashtrays, plates, and vases. Bells sandcarved with names or images were very popular. The 1980s was not a profitable time for any glass company, and Fenton was no exception. This premium business kept the factory busy and the workers employed during a time when the Imperial, Westmoreland, and Fostoria glass companies closed their doors forever.

Don Cunningham, who had worked for the L. E. Smith Glass and the Viking Glass companies (he had handled Viking's private mould work), was hired to work with Pat Clark. Don handled more and more of the special order accounts, although Frank Fenton continued to work with the glass clubs who were buying souvenirs, and Don and Shelley worked with QVC. Pat

Clark left Fenton in 1989. Don continued to work with companies or individuals looking for glass that could be added to their product lines. Princess House, a party plan company, ordered 115,000 crystal bears and birds during the summer and fall of 1986. Don worked closely with Tiara Exclusives, a home party company that had been associated with the Indiana Glass Company and was, at that time, a part of the Lancaster Colony Corporation. Candle-Land was another home party plan company that worked closely with Fenton to add glass to its product lines. Don's philosophy was, "If you want it, Fenton can make it." He was always willing to go the extra mile to bring business into the Fenton factory.

Don retired in the late 1990s, but was very willing to drive back to the factory when Frank Fenton told him that Jerry and I were writing what we thought was one book. He spent most of the day with us and answered all our questions. That was before I knew how much I didn't know. I've spent a great deal of time on the phone with him, and I simply couldn't have written this without his help. We enjoyed the time we spent with him and feel very lucky that he was willing to answer the same questions twice when I couldn't find my notes.

Chris Benson is in charge of Fenton's special order department now. She has worked closely with some of the collector clubs that are looking for Fenton's more unique glassware. She is also responsible for photographing all the special order items produced. I depended heavily on her pictures for this book and for information I wasn't able to find on my own.

The flat surface of Fenton's #7566 bell is perfect for companies, clubs, or other organizations to buy decorated and with their names added. These are just a few of the many bells with this type of message. They range in price from $45.00 to $65.00, depending on where they are sold or the circumstance of the advertiser. If the advertiser no longer exists or has changed names, the value seems to rise. I would suspect that one of those bells with an advertisement of a store in New Orleans would sell for a great deal of money. Prices on eBay have become the final word on value.

Ice Blue #7566 bell, "Ring in the Millennium! January 1, 2000, The Marietta Times," $75.00 – 80.00.

Royal Blue #7566 bell, "American Flint Glass Workers Union, AFL-CIO, Local 121," $75.00 – 80.00.

Celeste Blue #7566 bell, "Ohio Bicentennial 1803 – 2003, Monroe County Bicentennial Barn," $75.00 – 80.00.

Spruce Green #7566 bell, painting of the Wood County Courthouse, $75.00 – 80.00.

Back side of #7566 bell, "Wood County Courthouse, Cornerstone Laid: October 5, 1899, Completed: 1901, 'Second in series,' 2000."

The Blennerhassett Collection®

presents

the Blennerhassett Mansion Bell

a limited edition collectors series.

This beautiful bell is sand carved in cobalt blue by Fenton

Send $23

MAIL TO: BLENNERHASSETT GALLERY
1606 36TH ST., PARKERSBURG, W. VA. 26101
SHIP TO:
NAME _____
ADDRESS _____
CITY _____ STATE _____ ZIP _____
□ CHECK □ M.O. □ VISA
VISA NUMBER _____
EXP. DATE _____ SIGNATURE _____
QUANTITY _____ TOTAL AMOUNT _____
Please! Allow 6 Weeks For Delivery

Blennerhassett Gallery

Featuring Limited Edition Prints and Custom Framing

1606 36th St.   MON.-FRI. 4:30-9:00
Parkersburg, WV   SAT. 10:00-5:00   Tom Corbitt 428-2343

Advertisement for a bell made for the Blennerhassett Collection. Blennerhassett Mansion is sand carved on the Cobalt Blue bell. The mansion is located in Parkersburg, WV. $85.00 – 95.00.

The Aladdin Lamp Company was formed in 1908 in Chicago, Illinois, under the name of the Mantle Lamp Company of America. It became Aladdin Industries in 1949 and moved to Tennessee. Almost every family owns or has owned one of the practical versions of this lamp, one that is used for those stormy nights when the electricity fails, but the company also made very beautiful versions of its standard lamp. As has happened for other decorative items, a club was formed, and the number of collectors grew. The club is called the Aladdin Knights.

In 1991, the American Lamp Supply Company, located in Clarksville, Tennessee, ordered a Cranberry Opalescent version of an Aladdin lamp. It was signed both "Fenton" and "Aladdin," numbered, and dated. Every year another lamp was produced in a new color. In 1999, a group of Aladdin Knights purchased the lamp division from Aladdin Industries and formed the Aladdin Mantle Lamp Company. I believe that the owners of the new company also owned the American Lamp Supply Company, but I may be wrong. The last Aladdin lamps made by Fenton were the 2001 short Lincoln Drapes in a satin ivory color, one with a floral-decorated shade and one that features an old covered bridge.

Cranberry short Lincoln Drape lamp with the Cranberry Opalescent Hobnail shade, $675.00 – 750.00.

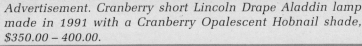

Advertisement. Cranberry short Lincoln Drape Aladdin lamp made in 1991 with a Cranberry Opalescent Hobnail shade, $350.00 – 400.00.

Grand Vertique lamp, Cased Twilight Blue with Blue Crest, 1994, $675.00 – 750.00.

Ruby Iridized short Lincoln Drape lamp with a Hobnail shade, 1993, $650.00 – $700.00.

Rosalene Grand Vertique lamp, shade decorated with roses, 1995, $800.00 – 875.00.

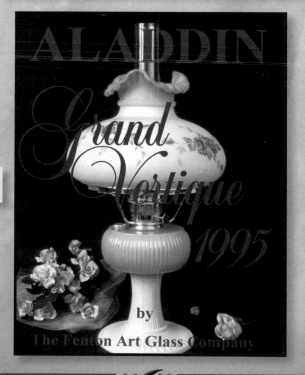

Golden Ruby

New Aladdin Crested Chimney for 1996 Beautiful Quality

Aladdin-Fenton Grand Vertique Special Limited Edition of Only 500 Lamps

Newly Designed Grand Vertique Shade for 1996

Cased Ruby over Milk Glass

Each Lamp Signed Aladdin-Fenton and dated 1996

Combination Kero-Electric Models include both oil and electric burners

Lamps are individually Numbered at Fenton factory 1 through 500

Overall Height to top of chimney is 25 1/4"

Overall Width is 12"

1996 Aladdin Fenton

Special Limited Edition

The Aladdin 1996 Grand Vertique in Golden Ruby Glass has been exquisitely hand crafted by America's most famous colored glass factory - The Fenton Art Glass Co. of Williamstown, West Virginia.

Fenton's ruby is the ultimate in beauty. The glass seems almost alive with a dazzeling red color that will take your breath away.

Aladdin-Fenton Grand Vertique lamps are complete with brass burner and shade (as pictured left) with your choice of either kerosene or electric models. For those that desire to own both burners, a combination kerosene-electric model is also available.

The '96 Aladdin-Fenton Grand Vertique lamp comes with a beautiful new shade that has been especially designed to compliment the classic base. The shade is expertly hand blown by the Fenton craftsmen with a ruby overlay (cased) on milk glass. The results are simply stunning and will be forever treasured by those fortunate owners.

Order the wonderful Aladdin-Fenton Grand Vertique Lamps UPS Prepaid for "Christmas '96 Gift Giving" as follows:

GV2396-K	Kerosene Only	$429.98
GV2396-E	Electric Only	429.98
GV2396-KE	Comb. Kero-Elec.	458.98

Great Christmas Gift!

Ruby Overlay Grand Vertique lamp, 1996, $675.00 – 750.00.

Burmese Grand Vertique lamp, 1997, could be bought with a decorated shade. With the shade, $950.00 – 1,000.00. Without the shade, $750.00 – 800.00.

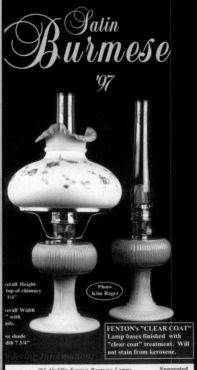

Satin Burmese '97

Overall Height to top of chimney 1/4"

Overall Width " with shade.

less shade th 7 3/4"

Photo Kim Rager

FENTON's "CLEAR COAT" Lamp bases finished with "clear coat" treatment. Will not stain from kerosene.

ALADDIN-FENTON GRAND VERTIQUE

Aladdin's 1997 Grand Vertique Lamp has been produced in beautiful Satin Burmese Glass by The Fenton Art Glass Company of Williamstown, West Virginia. Fenton's Burmese is a gold and uranium based glass with elegant shading from a soft, pale, lemon yellow to mauve pink.

Lamps are available either with or without shade in kerosene or electric models. Those desiring both burners can order a combination kerosene - electric unit.

HANDPAINTED SHADE

Sue Jackson, who did the beautiful hand decorating on the 1995 Rosalene shade, is again painting the shade for 1997. The design flows gracefully with soft, petit, pink florals on a natural pale yellow Burmese background. Each shade is signed on the bottom inside rim, "Aladdin/Fenton. Handpainted by Sue Jackson. 1997."

SPECIAL LIMITED EDITION

The Aladdin-Fenton '97 Grand Vertique in Satin Burmese Glass is a Special Limited Edition of 750 total lamps. In January and February, 500 lamps with handpainted shades were produced by Fenton. An additional 250 lamps without shades were also made. If sales demand warrant, then additional shades will be produced in August or September to balance orders. No more than 250 lamps without shades will be available.

The number of each lamp is individually handpainted on the bottom of the foot. Each lamp based is marked in raised embossed letters, "ALADDIN - FENTON 1997."

Your Aladdin-Fenton Dealer

Ordering Information

Model No.	'97 Aladdin-Fenton Burmese Lamps	Suggested
	Description	Retail Price
GV2397-827	Kerosene Only with Shade	$ 995.98
GV2397-827	Electric Only with Shade	995.98
EGV2397-827	Kero. - Elec. with Shade	1,057.98
GV2397	Kerosene Only less Shade	653.98
GV2397	Electric Only less Shade	653.98

Grand Vertique Lamp, Topaz cased with Opal, Blue Crest, 2000, $750.00 – 825.00.

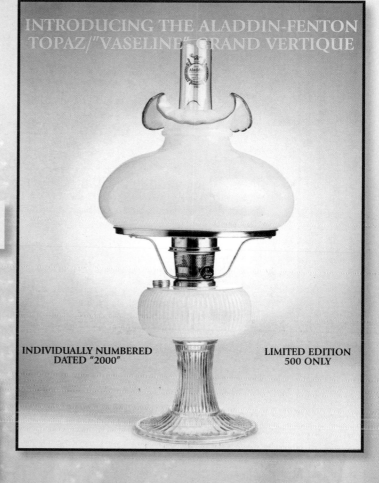

INTRODUCING THE ALADDIN-FENTON TOPAZ/"VASELINE" GRAND VERTIQUE

INDIVIDUALLY NUMBERED
DATED "2000"

LIMITED EDITION
500 ONLY

2001 Aladdin-Fenton

Ivory Grand Vertique Lamp

Ivory Grand Vertique lamp, shade decorated with a covered bridge, 2001, $550.00 – 625.00.

2001

 – Fenton

Limited Edition Short Lincoln Drape Lamps
Exclusively for Aladdin Knights
One of the most beautiful lamps ever made by Aladdin—Larry Alley

CALL FOR INFORMATION

Only 250 lamps produced, thus making them highly collectible. Now is the time to get your lamps, if you have not ordered them previously. If you have ordered two (2) lamps earlier, but want additional lamps, they are available now for you to purchase. We still have a limited number of these lamps available.

The frosted ivory glass made by Fenton gives the appearance of Alacite. The lamp and shade are in excellent balance and harmony reminiscent of Short Lincoln Drapes sold in 1939.

Signed *Aladdin-Fenton* and dated 2001.

Only a few are left, so get your order in today.

The price of each lamp is $395.00 each plus $10.00 shipping, handling and insurance. These lamps can be ordered with electric burners, as a replacement for the kerosene burner at the same price. If you want both burners, you can order either the N186B – Heel-less Electric Burner for $34.00 each, or the N186-3B – Heel-less Electric Burner with Nite Lite for $38.00 each (upper right picture). These will be packed in with your lamp(s). Please note: The pink ring was not applied at the foot as shown on this sample.

<u>Call today!!!</u> You do not want to miss this opportunity to own one or more of these beautiful lamps made exclusively for the Aladdin Knights. You can contact us at:

Aladdin Mantle Lamp Company
681 International Blvd.
Clarksville, TN 37040
Telephone: (800) 457-5267
Email: sales@aladdinlamps.com

Frosted Ivory short Lincoln Drape Aladdin Lamp, shade decorated with purple flowers, 2001, $450.00 – 500.00.

In 1999, Fenton made two sizes of bottles to be filled with perfume by Alexander Julian. The Fenton collectors rushed to buy this expensive perfume, which many poured out, to add to their collections. Both bottles are Crystal Iridescent similar to Fenton's Persian Pearl. The bottle filled with perfume was expensive. The perfume bottles will sell for between $100.00 and $125.00.

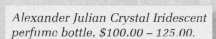

Alexander Julian Crystal Iridescent perfume bottle, $100.00 – 125.00.

Alexander Julian Crystal Iridescent perfume bottle in the original box, $125.00 – 150.00.

In 1996, a series of Fenton's #5146 eggs were made for the Army & Air Force Exchange Service to be sold in its post exchanges, stores that can only be used by military personnel and their families. There is no record of another purchase by the organization.

Sea Mist Green #5740 footed egg decorated with Florals, $42.00 – 46.00.

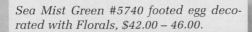

Sea Mist Green #5740 footed egg decorated with Florals, $42.00 – 46.00.

Sea Mist Green #5740 egg decorated with flower on top, $45.00 – 48.00.

Top view of decoration.

Favrene #5740 egg decorated with Florals, $55.00 – 58.00

Ruby #5740 egg, White flowers, $45.00 – 48.00.

Iridized French Opalescent #5740 egg with Scenic decoration, $50.00 – 54.00.

Iridized French Opalescent #5740 egg with Purple flowers, $44.00 – 46.00.

In 1983, Avon contacted Bill Fenton about a project that would be the much bigger than expected. It wanted a facsimile of an 1880 Stevens and Williams cameo vase that resided in the Cincinnati Museum, Cincinnati, Ohio. While the project seemed straightforward and easy to do, it took almost a year for Fenton to be able to recreate the cameo effect to match the old vase. The company's chemists, Subodh Gupta and Wayne King, worked on the formula that would match the original aqua blue. Paste moulds were used to make the 30,000 vases and, as you can imagine, it took two blow shops almost six months to finish this project. The next step was to match the soft satin finish of the original. This was done with an acid bath. An acid bath leaves a softer finish than the process of sand blasting. The decoration was done by applying special decals that came from the Instar Supply Com-

pany. An artist applied the white bands and then used the pointed tip of the brush to remove a tiny band of paint. It was this small detail that gave the vase the important cameo look of the original. The vase was introduced at a press party held at the Cincinnati Art Museum, where the Fenton vase and the original were placed side by side. They matched so well that Bill had a difficult time telling one from the other.

Fenton made bells for Avon, but for these, Fenton used wine glasses from France instead of its own glass. Fenton did the finishing and the pad printing, a process that simulated an etching that read "Avon 100." Because we have no way of guessing what the Fenton-decorated, non-Fenton bells would retail, I am not pricing them in this book.

No other glassware has been made for Avon to date.

Description	Color	Value
Cameo style	Avon Blue Satin	$125.00 – 150.00

Avon Blue Cameo-style vase, $125.00 – 150.00.

Avon catalog with the vase on the cover, $25.00 – 30.00.

CANDLE-LAND

Candle-Land is a party plan that features "hand-crafted, high quality, decorative gift items." Some of those items are "candles, rings, collectable things, wood and glass with a touch of class." Its catalog states, "Proudly featuring FENTON ART GLASS. In fact, 95% of our line is made with pride in the USA."

January of 1977 was the beginning of Fenton's association with Candle-Land Parties. The deal was de-veloped by Fred and Linda Strobel with the help of Don Fenton and the sales representative for Myerstown, PA, Tom Stork. Fenton provides its current catalog to Candle-Land, but the catalog is personalized by adding the company name and information to it. On occasion, Fenton has made special order glass for Candle-Land, but the bulk of Candle-Land's business comes straight from Fenton's catalog.

23

Special Order Limited Edition Lamps

Handpainted and Signed by the Artist

Light up your living with hand-made and handpainted lamps from Fenton. "A special pride of ownership" is felt by the possessor because you know you are one of a very few people who will own a lamp like this.

Due to limited quantities, lamps may not be shipped on delivery date. Allow 60-90 days for delivery.

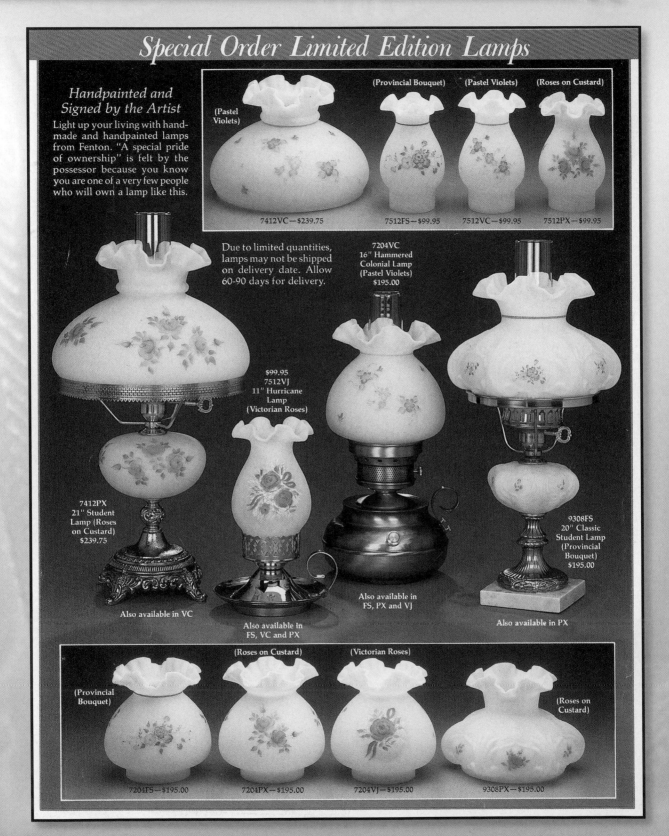

(Pastel Violets)

(Provincial Bouquet)

(Pastel Violets)

(Roses on Custard)

7412VC — $239.75

7512FS — $99.95

7512VC — $99.95

7512PX — $99.95

7204VC
16" Hammered
Colonial Lamp
(Pastel Violets)
$195.00

$99.95
7512VJ
11" Hurricane
Lamp
(Victorian Roses)

7412PX
21" Student
Lamp (Roses
on Custard)
$239.75

9308FS
20" Classic
Student Lamp
(Provincial
Bouquet)
$195.00

Also available in VC

Also available in
FS, VC and PX

Also available in
FS, PX and VJ

Also available in PX

(Provincial
Bouquet)

(Roses on Custard)

(Victorian Roses)

(Roses on
Custard)

7204FS — $195.00

7204PX — $195.00

7204VJ — $195.00

9308PX — $195.00

Row 1: *(None of the shades were sold separately, so only the full lamps are priced.)* Shades: 7412VX Pastel Violets on Custard, 7512FS Provincial Bouquet on Opal Satin, 7512VC Pastel Violets on Custard, 7512PX Roses on Custard.
Row 2: Lamps: A-7412PX 21" student lamp Roses on Custard, $300.00 – 350.00; 7412VC Pastel Violets on Custard, $300.00 – 350.00; B- 7512VJ 11" Hurricane lamp, Victorian Roses on Opal Satin *(also available as 7512FS Provincial Bouquet on Opal Satin, 7512VC Pastel Violets on Custard Satin, and 7512PX Roses on Custard Satin)*, $150.00 – 175.00 for any decoration; C-7204VC 16" Pastel Violets on Custard Hammered Colonial Lamp *(also available as 7204FS Provincial Bouquet on Opal Satin, 7204PX Roses on Custard, and 7204VJ Victorian Rose on Opal Satin)*, $250.00 – 275.00 for any decoration; D-9308FS 20" Provincial Bouquet on Opal Satin classic student lamp *(also available on 9308PX Roses on Custard Satin)*, $250.00   275.00.
Row 3: Shades: 7204FS Provincial Bouquet on Opal Satin, 7204PX Roses on Custard Satin, 7204VJ Victorian Rose on Opal Satin, 9308PX Roses on Custard Satin.

Special Order Limited Edition Lamps

Handpainted and Signed by the Artist

Light up your living with handmade and handpainted lamps from Fenton. "A special pride of ownership" is felt by the possessor because you know you are one of a very few people who will own a lamp like this.

(Pastel Violets)
(Provincial Bouquet)
(Pastel Violets)
(Roses on Custard)

7412VC — $239.75   7512FS — $99.95   7512VC — $99.95   7512PX — $99.95

Due to limited quantities, lamps may not be shipped on delivery date. Allow 60-90 days for delivery.

7204VC
16" Hammered Colonial Lamp
(Pastel Violets)
$195.00

$99.95
7512VJ
11" Hurricane Lamp
(Victorian Roses)

7412PX
21" Student Lamp (Roses on Custard)
$239.75

9308FS
20" Classic Student Lamp
(Provincial Bouquet)
$195.00

Also available in VC

Also available in FS, VC and PX

Also available in FS, PX and VJ

Also available in PX

(Provincial Bouquet)
(Roses on Custard)
(Victorian Roses)
(Roses on Custard)

7204FS — $195.00   7204PX — $195.00   7204VJ — $195.00   9308PX — $195.00

Left: *Cobalt Blue, White Floral #9035 paneled basket, $85.00 – 95.00.*
Center: *Cobalt Blue, White Floral #7463 bell, $65.00 – 75.00.*
Right: *Cobalt Blue, White Floral #7300 fairy light, $100.00 – 120.00.*

Carolyn's Collectibles

Carolyn Grable is the daughter of Jim Fenton. She has a computer-based business selling special-order items made by Fenton.

Description	Item #	Siamese,* all types	Calico black & white Tabby	Tye Dye	Rose or blue spongewear
Alley Cat	5177	$150.00 – 175.00	$125.00 – 150.00	$85.00 -100.00	
Bear	5151	$45.00 – 50.00	$45.00 – 50.00		
Cat, sitting	5165	$55.00 – 65.00	$45.00 – 55.00	$45.00 – 50.00	$45.00 – 50.00
Elephant	5058	$45.00 – 50.00			
Hippo	5063	$45.00 – 50.00			
Kitten	5365	$40.00 – 45.00	$40.00 – 45.00		
Mouse	5248	$45.00 – 50.00			
Puppy	5085	$45.00 – 50.00			
Rabbit	5293	$45.00 – 50.00			
Squirrel	5215	$45.00 – 50.00			
Turtle	5266	$45.00 – 50.00			
Fox**	5226	$50.00 – 60.00			

*Siamese types: Blue Point, Seal Point, and Lilac.
**Arctic, Gray, Red, Silver.

PLUM OPALESCENT

Description	Item #	Pattern	Value
Bowl, 10"		Hobnail	$65.00 – 85.00
Decanter		Hobnail	$275.00 – 350.00
Plate, 12"		Hobnail	$95.00 – 120.00
Salt & pepper		Hobnail	(set) $75.00 – 90.00
Kissing Kids			(set) $100.00 – 120.00
Kitten	5119		$55.00 – 65.00
Puppy	5225		$55.00 – 65.00
Scotty	5214		$55.00 – 65.00

Plum Opalescent Hobnail #3806 shaker, $75.00 – 90.00 pair.

Plum Opalescent Hobnail #3761 decanter with an opalescent handle, $375.00 50.00. (Old decanter has a crystal handle.)

Plum Opalescent Hobnail #3924 9" bowl, $65.00 – 85.00.

Plum Opalescent Kissing Kids, $100.00 – 120.00.

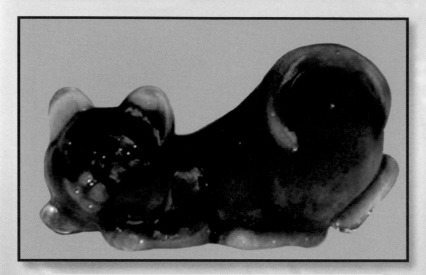

Plum Opalescent #5119 Crouching Kitten, $55.00 – 65.00.

Natural Red #5226 Fox, $50.00 – 60.00.

Natural Siamese #5165 Cat, $55.00 – 65.00.

Tye Dye #5063 Hippo, $45.00 – 50.00.

What could be sweeter than a picture of a kitten resting its head on a pillow and with a paw sticking out of the covers? Not much, thought L. C. Probert, an official of the Chesapeake & Ohio Railroad, when he saw a picture of the kitten in a newspaper. He developed a complete advertising campaign around the cat, dubbed Chessie. He wrote the ad for the railroad's new sleeper car: "Sleep Like a Kitten and Wake Up Fresh as a Daisy in Air-Conditioned Comfort." The company slogan became "Sleep Like a Kitten," and it was used in every newspaper, calendar, and magazine ad place by the Chesapeake & Ohio Railroad. Chessie became the darling of the Depression era, something that made people smile in the face of the poverty and hunger that held the country in its palm.

In advertising during WWII, Chessie became "America's Sleep Warden" and gave up her Pullman Berth for traveling soldiers. This advertising became more and more popular, so Chessie was given a mate, Peake, and two look-alike kittens. Eventually the railroad began using pictures of real cats, but only Chessie caught the imagination of the country.

In 1969, Fenton was asked by the railroad to design a candy box in the Chessie image. The railroad planned to give the boxes as gifts to its employees. That candy box was made in 1970 in dark carnival glass and has the date and "Chessie by Fenton." Fenton used other colors for this mould, and they were sold in Fenton's catalog. Those pieces still have the name "Chessie by Fenton" on the bases, but not the date. In 1986, The C&O Railroad asked for another box to be made. It was done in White Carnival. The second-quality pieces sold in Fenton's gift shop with an "S" on the bottom designating them as seconds. That year, in the FAGCA special glass room, many whimseys were sold. It is not possible to value or list those at this time. In 2005, an Emerald Green candy was sold on the website of the Chesapeake and Ohio Historical Society.

Color	Value
Dark Carnival	$225.00 – 250.00
White Carnival	$150.00 – 175.00
Emerald Green Carnival	$75.00 – 100.00

Old Chessie ad, $22.00 – 24.00.

Base of the Dark Carnival Chessie.

Dark Carnival Chessie candy box, $225.00 – 250.00.

Emerald Green Chessie box, 2005, $75.00 – 100.00.

1938 Chessie ad featuring the real cat that replaced the original drawing, $18.50 – 22.00.

Collectors' Clubs

CARNIVAL GLASS CLUBS

AMERICAN CARNIVAL GLASS ASSOCIATION

The American Carnival Glass Association was formed in the 1960s, when collectors were just finding an appreciation for this beautiful rainbow glass. It publishes a quarterly newsletter with information that will help the new and the experienced collector. It is a non-profit educational group that promotes interest in and enthusiasm for carnival glass.

In 1976, when the ACGA members found new pieces of carnival marked with the "N" of the Northwood Company, they went to court to register that trademark and prevent any glass company or importer from using it on new glass. It was a remarkable thing to do and has been a huge benefit to the carnival glass collecting world. Every year the ACGA holds a convention for collectors to trade glass and stories of their conquests in collecting. The convention also promotes the education of collectors. Souvenirs are made every year to be sold to ACGA members, and many of the souvenirs have been made by the Fenton Art Glass Company. Those are listed here, with the year, color, and value of each piece. The money realized from the glass sales goes to produce educational material for association members and for general yearly expenses.

Mould	Year	Color	Value
Beaded Shell mug	1971	Amber	$45.00 – 55.00
Beaded Shell mug	1978	Ice blue opalescent	$55.00 – 65.00
Beaded Shell mug	1979	Red	$55.00 – 65.00
Beaded Shell mug	1980	Ice	$45.00 – 55.00
Beaded Shell mug	1981	Vaseline green	$50.00 – 60.00
Seacoast cuspidor	1982	Peach Opalescent	$65.00 – 75.00
Seacoast cuspidor	1983	Green	$65.00 – 75.00
Seacoast cuspidor	1984	Red	$75.00 – 85.00
Seacoast cuspidor	1985	Teal Blue	$70.00 – 80.00
Seacoast cuspidor	1998	Lotus Mist Green	$65.00 – 75.00
Seacoast cuspidor	1999	Cobalt Blue	$65.00 – 75.00
Seacoast cuspidor	2000	Violet	$65.00 – 75.00
Seacoast cuspidor	2001	Topaz Opalescent	$75.00 – 85.00
Seacoast cuspidor	2002	Willow Green Opalescent	$75.00 – 80.00

Mould	Year	Color	Value
Morning Glory mini tankard	1986	Marigold	$45.00 – 50.00
Morning Glory mini tankard	1987	Green	$50.00 – 55.00
Morning Glory mini tankard	1988	Purple	$50.00 – 55.00
Morning Glory mini tankard	1989	Red	$55.00 – 60.00
Inverted Strawberry fairy lamp	1990	Red	$85.00 – 100.00
Basket	1991	Red	$75.00 – 95.00
Bell	1992	Red	$45.00 – 55.00
Spittoon	1993	Red	$75.00 – 95.00
Salt & pepper	1994	Red	$65.00 – 75.00
Covered sugar	1995	Red	$50.00 – 65.00
Creamer	1996	Red	$50.00 – 60.00
Hobstar & Feather mini punch bowl set	1997	Amethyst	$100.00 – 125.00
Hummingbird heart-shaped box	2003	Blue Topaz Iridized	$65.00 – 75.00

1982 Peach Opalescent Sea Coast spittoon, $65.00 – 75.00.

1983 Green Sea Coast spittoon, $65.00 – 75.00.

1985 Azure Blue Sea Coast spittoon, $70.00 – 80.00.

1984 Ruby Sea Coast spittoon, $75.00 – 85.00.

1086 Marigold Morning Glory mini tankard, $45.00 – 50.00.

1987 Green Morning Glory mini tankard, $50.00 – 55.00.

1988 Amethyst Morning Glory mini tankard, $50.00 – 55.00.

1989 Ruby Morning Glory mini tankard, $55.00 – 60.00.

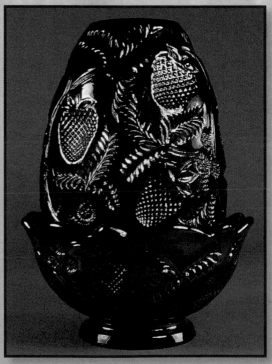

1990 Ruby Inverted Strawberry fairy light, $85.00 – 100.00.

1991 Ruby Inverted Strawberry #9537 basket, $75.00 – 95.00.

1992 Ruby Inverted Strawberry bell, $45.00 – 55.00.

1993 Ruby Inverted Strawberry ruffled cuspidor, $75.00 – 95.00.

1994 Ruby Inverted Strawberry salt & pepper, $65.00 – 75.00 pair.

1995 Ruby Inverted Straw-berry creamer, $50.00 – 60.00; covered sugar, $50.00 – 65.00.

1997 Amethyst Hobstar & Feather punch set, $100.00 – 125.00.

1998 Sea Mist Green Sea Coast spittoon, $65.00 – 75.00.

1999 Cobalt Blue Sea Coast spittoon, $65.00 – 75.00.

2000 Violet Sea Coast spittoon, $65.00 – 75.00.

2001 Topaz Opalescent Sea Coast spittoon, $75.00 – 85.00.

2002 Willow Green Opalescent Sea Coast spittoon, $75.00 – 80.00.

2003 Blue Topaz #5786 Hummingbird trinket box, $65.00 – 75.00.

Cobalt Blue Sea Coast flattened plate, whimsey, $75.00 – 85.00.

HEART OF AMERICA CARNIVAL GLASS ASSOCIATION

The Heart of America Carnival Glass Association was the brainchild of Bill and Dorothy Taylor of Kansas City, Kansas, and Davis and Viola Shikles of Independence, Missouri. They, along with seven other couples, formed this club. HOACGA is one of the first carnival glass clubs formed in the 1960s. Its trademark is the upside-down horseshoe, and it appears on all the commemorative glass made for it.

COMMEMORATIVE GLASS

Year	Color	Pattern	Shape	Value
1976	Red	Bicentennial design	Whiskey set, 6 shots	$175.00 – 225.00
1978	red	Corn	Vase	$100.00 – 125.00
1979	Red	Orange Tree	Loving cup	$100.00 – 125.00
1980	Ice Green	Good Luck	Hatpin holder	$100.00 – 125.00
1981	Red	Grape & Cable	Candle lamp	$150.00 – 175.00
1982	Ice Blue	Corn	Vase	$120.00 – 135.00
1983	Marigold over Milk Glass	Orange Tree	Loving cup	$75.00 – 95.00
1984	Red	Butterfly & Berry	Fernery	$125.00 – 150.00
1985	Red	Circle Scroll/Northwood	Bell	$75.00 – 85.00
1986	Green Opal	Circle Scroll/Fenton	Bell	$65.00 – 75.00
1987	Cobalt	Circle Scroll/Millersburg	Bell	$65.00 – 75.00
1988	Marigold	Circle Scroll/Imperial	Bell	$65.00 – 75.00
1989	Teal	Circle Scroll/Dugan	Bell	$65.00 – 75.00
1991	Red	Peacock & Dahlia	Plate, 6"	$55.00 – 70.00
1993	Red	Good Luck	Plate, 6"	$55.00 – 70.00
1995	Plum	Good Luck	Hatpin holder	$50.00 – 65.00
1998	White	Orange Tree	Loving cup	$75.00 – 85.00
2002	Green	Good Luck	Loving cup	$75.00 – 85.00

TABLE FAVORS

Year	Color	Shape	Value
1978	Ruby	Mug	$35.00 – 40.00
1979	Ice Blue	Mug	$35.00 – 40.00
1980	Green	Mug	$30.00 – 35.00
1981	Vaseline	Mug	$35.00 – 40.00
1982	Blue	Mug	$30.00 – 35.00
1983	Amber	Mug	$30.00 – 35.00
1984	Purple	Mug	$30.00 – 35.00
1985	Lt. Lavender	Mug	$30.00 – 35.00
1986	Ice Green Opal	Mug	$35.00 – 40.00
1987	White	Mug	$25.00 – 30.00
1988	Teal Blue	Mug	$35.00 – 40.00
1989	Shell Pink	Mug	$30.00 – 35.00
1990	Ruby	Mug	$35.00 – 40.00
1991	Rosalene	Mug	$40.00 – 45.00
1992	Lt. Teal Blue	Mug	$30.00 – 35.00
1993	Plum	Mug	$30.00 – 35.00
1994	Amber	Mug	$25.00 – 30.00
1995	Ice Blue	Mug	$30.00 – 35.00
1996	Aqua Opal	Votive	$20.00 – 22.00
1997	Plum Opal	Votive	$20.00 – 22.00
1998	White	Orange Tree glass	$22.00 – 25.00
1999	Violet	Orange Tree wine glass	$22.00 – 25.00

1979 Custard Good Luck loving cup, $75.00 – 95.00.

1980 Ice Green Good Luck hatpin holder, $100.00 – 125.00.

1983 Marigold over Milk Glass Good Luck loving cup, $75.00 – 95.00.

1985 Ruby Northwood Circle Scroll bell, $75.00 – 95.00.

1986 Green Opalescent Fenton Circle Scroll bell, $65.00 – 75.00.

1987 Cobalt Blue Millersburg Circle Scroll bell, $65.00 – 75.00.

1988 Marigold Imperial Circle Scroll bell, $65.00 – 75.00.

2002 Dark Green Good Luck hatpin holder, $75.00 – 85.00.

1989 Teal Dugan Circle Scroll bell, $65.00 – 75.00.

1988 Ice Blue Good Luck mug, $35.00 – 40.00.

1984 Amethyst Good Luck mug, $30.00 – 35.00.

1975 Ruby Good Luck decanter, $175.00 – 225.00.

1975 Ruby Good Luck shot glass, $15.00 – 18.00.

1979 Ruby Good Luck loving cup, $100.00 – 125.00.

INTERNATIONAL CARNIVAL GLASS ASSOCIATION

The International Carnival Glass Association was founded in Iowa in the early 1960s. The *Carnival Glass Pump*, its newsletter, is issued quarterly. In it you will find information on new glass being made, as well as new research into old glass. The group's convention is held in August of every year. I don't have as much information about this club as I would like, but I do know that if you collect carnival glass, it is a good idea to belong to all the national organizations.

Year	Pattern	Shape	Color	Value
1979	Ivy	Mini town pump	Purple	$50.00 – 65.00
1980	Ivy	Mini town pump	Marigold	$50.00 – 65.00
1981	Frolicking Bears	Cuspidor	Aqua Opalescent	$75.00 – 85.00
1982	Frolicking Bears	Cuspidor	Ruby Red	$75.00 – 85.00
1983	Frolicking Bears	Cuspidor	Vaseline Opal.*	$65.00 – 75.00
1983	Frolicking Bears	Cuspidor	Marigold Opal.*	$65.00 – 75.00
1984	Lions Plunger, Orange Tree	Rose bowl	Cobalt Blue	$65.00 – 75.00
1986	Poppy	Rose bowl	Emerald Green Opal.*	$50.00 – 55.00
1987	Hand Decorated	Miniature pitcher, 6"	Green, Enameled	$70.00 – 80.00
1988	Open-edge 2-row	Basket, applied handle	Topaz Opal.*	$70.00 – 80.00
1989	Thumbprint & Ovals	Hand-decorated vase	Cobalt Blue	$50.00 – 55.00
1990	Hand Decorated	Covered comport	Green	$65.00 – 75.00
1991	Beaded Melon Spiral	Hand-decorated pitcher	French Opal.*	$50.00 – 55.00
1992	Lions Plunger	Pedestal cake plate	Emerald Green	$75.00 – 85.00
1993	Frolicking Bears	King-size tumbler	Marigold	$75.00 – 85.00
1994	Diamond & Rib	JIP vase, 5½"	Ruby	$55.00 – 65.00
1995	Acanthus	Plate, 10"	Celeste Blue	$50.00 – 55.00
1996	Grape & Cable	Plate, 6"	Green	$50.00 – 55.00
1997	Frolicking Bears	Tumbler	Amethyst Opal.*	$65.00 – 70.00
1998	Frolicking Bears	Cuspidor	Green Opal.*	$65.00 – 70.00
1999	Santa Claus	Figurine	Green	$55.00 – 60.00

*Opal. = Opalescent.

1986 Green Opalescent Poppy rose bowl, $50.00 – 55.00. This photo is of a non-iridized vase, but the ICGA vase is iridized.

1971 Purple Carnival paperweight decorated with a town pump, $100.00 – 125.00, very rare.

PACIFIC NORTHWEST CARNIVAL GLASS ASSOCIATION

The Pacific Northwest Carnival Glass Association was the first club that Jerry and I joined when we began to collect carnival glass. We went to the convention every summer and learned how to recognize old carnival pieces as opposed to the new pieces. I still made mistakes, but not as many as I would have if I hadn't joined that club. I remember when we bought two Purple Carnival S Repeat punch cups. We looked in one price guide that had them listed for $2,500 each. Well, we thought we had died and gone to heaven. Every time I showed members of the club those cups, they said to me, "You need to call Don Moore." We thought they meant that he would be interested in buying them, so I called Don. Needless to say, he had to break it to me that the price guide we got our information from had dropped the line with the value of the punch bowl to the line for the punch cup. My cups were worth about $50, which was still more than we had paid. I still own one of them, to remind me that a person shouldn't take any price guide as a bible, because everyone makes mistakes — and yes, that includes me. Buy what you like for a price you are willing to pay. That way, you can't go wrong.

The thing I remember most about my conversation with Don was his willingness to share all his knowledge and the good humor he had about collecting. I learned from him that it is a mistake to take yourself too seriously. My favorite story about him is one he told frequently. Don's wife, Connie, always went directly to any carnival glass in a shop. Don told her that she should look around and not look at the carnival glass until she was ready to leave. The next shop they visited had a grouping of carnival glass in the window. Don walked all through the shop, talked about the glass in there, and, after he had spent a lot of time in the shop, asked the owner, "How much is that pretty glass in the window? I don't think I've seen it before." She answered, "It's carnival glass Mr. Moore. You know, it's that glass you write about in all the glass collector magazines." They both enjoyed a good laugh, and Connie had the biggest laugh of all. Don is gone, but his memory will live forever in the heart of every person who knew him.

I love all the memories we have of that club. It's a wonderful club with members who are willing to share knowledge and helping hands. When the club treasury was misappropriated, I saw a common carnival glass bowl, given to the club by a young member, sell at auction over and over with each buyer paying his or her bid but passing the bowl back to be auctioned again. After the club had made enough money to replenish the treasury, the final bidder gave the bowl back to the young girl. It was my first lesson in the fellowship of a club and is one I treasure.

1982 Peach Opalescent Fisherman mug, $75.00 – 85.00.

1983 Ice Blue Opalescent Fisherman mug, $75.00 – 85.00.

1984 Cobalt Blue Fisherman mug, $75.00 – 85.00.

1985 Ruby Fisherman mug, $85.00 – 95.00.

1986 French Opalescent Fisherman mug, $75.00 – 85.00.

1987 Emerald Green Fisherman mug, $75.00 – 85.00.

1988 Teal Fisherman mug, $75.00 – 85.00.

1989 Light Cobalt Blue Fisherman mug, $75.00 – 85.00.

1990 Light Green Opalescent Fisherman mug, $75.00 – 85.00.

1991 Petal Pink Fisherman mug, $65.00 – 75.00.

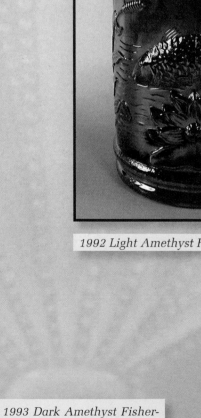

1992 Light Amethyst Fisherman mug, $65.00 – 75.00.

1993 Dark Amethyst Fisherman mug, $65.00 – 75.00.

WOODSLAND WORLD WIDE CARNIVAL GLASS ASSOCIATION

Woodsland World Wide Carnival Glass Association, created in 1996, has an entirely different concept from the earlier carnival glass clubs. It exists solely on the Internet, but like the others, holds a convention where collectors can gather and share their love of this beautiful glassware. It was the brainchild of Brian Pitman and Fred Stone, who were based in Topeka, Kansas. At the beginning it was a discussion group, but in 1999, when the group had grown phenomenally, the first convention was held in Las Vegas, and plans were made to formalize the group into a club with officers, members, and an online newsletter.

The growing membership list and the sale of tee shirts, baseball hats, etc., enabled the club to approach Fenton to make souvenirs for the members. Originally it was thought that the club could use the old Fenton Pine Cone pattern, but that didn't work out, and a new pine cone pattern was designed by Glen Thistlewood with some help from Fenton's designer, Jon Saffell. It bears some resemblance to Fenton's Pine Cone pattern, but

has a plumper fir cone. Imperial's Open Rose pattern was used for the exterior, and "Woodsland World Wide Carnival Glass Club" was written in script on the face of the plate. These pieces closely resemble the old advertising pieces made in the early 1900s that are shown in *Fenton, Glass Made for Other Companies, 1907 – 1980.*

While that first commemorative piece was beautiful and well received, the members decided that the Open Rose pattern on the exterior just wasn't what they wanted. Changing the exterior would require a new mould, so the club set out to raise the money to pay for it. Again, it was Glen Thistlewood who was asked to design a pattern that would represent the concept of this club. Her design, called Flowers of the World, includes a sunflower representing Kansas — the home of the club — and rosemary sprigs for remembrance of past members and friends.

As successful as this new club, one that embraces the Internet, has been, I expect that others will follow. You can find the WWWCGA website at www.carnivalglass.org.

This listing only covers the issued shapes. A great deal of whimseys were made each year. The values of those are much greater than the values of the shapes listed in this price guide. The only way to gauge the value of a whimsey is by your desire to own it. Pay the price you are comfortable paying.

Color	Shape	Year Issued	Edition	Value
Sea Mist Green	Plate, 6"	1999	300	$75.00 – 100.00
Cobalt Blue	Rose bowl	2000	250	$50.00 – 75.00
Ruby	JIP shape	2001	200	$75.00 – 100.00
Black	Plate, crimped edge	2002	200	$75.00 – 100.00
Favrene	Bowl	2003	250	$125.00 – 150.00
Ruby	Cuspidor	2004	103	$100.00 – 125.00
Deep Marigold	Bowl, ruffled 6"	2005	68	$50.00 – 75.00
Pastel Marigold	Bowl, ruffled 6"	2005	19	$75.00 – 95.00

Black Amethyst Woodsland
Pine plate.

Black Amethyst Woodsland Pine whimsey bowl.

Interior of the whimsey bowl.

Favrene Woodsland Pine bowl.

Interior of the Woodsland Pine bowl.

DUNCAN GLASS COLLECTORS CLUB

Fenton has made two donkey and cart sets for the Duncan Glass Collectors. They were made in Blue Opalescent and French Opalescent. They were sold over a four-year time period. The donkey was sold first, and the cart was sold the next year.

Shape	Color	Value
Cart	Blue Opalescent	$75.00 – 85.00
Cart	French Opalescent	$65.00 – 75.00
Donkey	Blue Opalescent	$75.00 – 85.00
Donkey	French Opalescent	$65.00 – 75.00

French Opalescent Donkey & Cart, $130.00 – 150.00 for set.

FENTON ART GLASS COLLECTORS OF AMERICA

The Fenton Art Glass Collectors of America, organized in 1976, was the creation of Otis and Ferill Jean Rice. A trip to the Fenton factory inspired Otis to convince his reluctant wife, Ferill, and Frank Fenton that it could work, but I doubt that any of the three envisioned the enormous club this organization has become. Ferill went to many meetings of other collector clubs searching for interested collectors. The first organizational meeting was held on New Years Day 1976. Ten collectors, Otis and Ferill Rice, Arvin and Betty Wolfgram, Don and

Nancy Moore, Lois and Marlon Rehmer, and Sylvia and Tom Landry, were at that meeting, and they became the first board of the newly incorporated FAGCA. This club has grown to great heights, becoming the largest of any glass collectors club. As of this writing, this club is in its 30th year, and we must congratulate the 10 original members for having the foresight to build this wonderful club.

This list, lengthy as it is, will probably miss a lot of items, but I will add those as I learn of them.

BANQUET FLAVORS

Year	Description	Value
1977	Colonial Green Hobnail Cat slipper signed by Otis Rice	$25.00 – 30.00
1978	Cameo Opalescent logo	$75.00 – 95.00
1979	Cameo Opalescent ring tree	$65.00 – 85.00
1980	Velva Rose Hobnail toothpick	$35.00 – 45.00
1981	Velva Blue Hobnail toothpick	$35.00 – 45.00
1982	Chocolate 1" Daisy & Button hat	$45.00 – 55.00
1983	Candleglow Yellow 1" Daisy & Button hat	$35.00 – 45.00
1984	Dusty Rose 1" Daisy & Button hat	$35.00 – 45.00
1985	Green Opalescent Daisy & Button Kitten slipper	$24.00 – 28.00
1986	Burmese small rose bowl w/Butterfly interior	$45.00 – 55.00
1987	Peaches and Cream small rose bowl w/Butterfly interior	$35.00 – 45.00
1988	Crystal Aztec toothpick	$18.00 – 20.00
1989	Ice Green Butterfly; some iridized, some not; some cut off, some not.	$25.00 – 35.00
1990	Ruby & Milk Glass shells, Hobnail or ribbed	$20.00 – 25.00 set of 4
1991	Rosalene Strawberry toothpick holder	$20.00 – 25.00
1992	Burmese Shiny Strawberry toothpick holder	$20.00 – 25.00
1993	Black Carnival or plain Sun Fish	$25.00 – 30.00
	Rosalene Sun Fish	$55.00 – 65.00
1994	Rosalene Satin Strawberry toothpick holder	$20.00 – 25.00
1995	Autumn Gold Sunfish	$20.00 – 25.00
1996	Plum Bell, marked "20th anniversary FAGCA 1976 – 1996"	$30.00 – 35.00
1997	Crystal Butterflies on stand, tinted in different colors	$25.00 – 30.00
1998	Crystal Butterflies on stand, tinted in different colors and satinized	$30.00 – 35.00
1999	Sea Mist Green Iridized Owl Ring Tree	$15.00 – 20.00
2000	Cobalt Blue Rock, "FAGCA" with the Butterfly emblem and "2000"	$30.00 – 35.00

Year	Description	Value
2001	6" sample spin plates in Custard, Shell Pink, and Sea Green, decorated with hand-painted violets	$20.00 – 25.00
2002	Black Bear decorated with White Butterfly	$25.00 – 30.00
2003	Ruby stretch Bunny painted with White Butterfly	$30.00 – 35.00
2004	Periwinkle Snail	$25.00 – 30.00
2005	Burmese Rock, "100 Anniversary FAGCA 2005"	$25.00 – 30.00

SPECIAL GLASS

Year	Description	Value
1978	Cranberry baskets, variety of spot moulds	$100.00 – 125.00
1979	Vasa Murrhina vases, Pink and White w/Green	$75.00 – 95.00
1980	Velva Rose Bubble Optic Melon vases	$75.00 – 95.00
1981	Amethyst w/Opal Hanging Hearts vase	$150.00 – 175.00
1982	Overlay baskets in pastel shades	$100.00 – 125.00
1983	Cranberry Opalescent 1-pc. fairy lamps	$175.00 – 200.00
	Variety of spot moulds	$275.00 – 350.00
1984	Blue Burmese vases w/Peloton treatment	$100.00 – 125.00
1985	Overlay vases in Dusty Rose w/Mica flecks	$75.00 – 85.00
1986	Ruby Iridized Art Glass vase	$100.00 – 125.00
1987	Dusty Rose Overlay vase with a Dark Blue Crest	$100.00 – 125.00
1988	Marble Teal and Milk Glass basket	$100.00 – 125.00
1989	Mulberry Opalescent Spot Optic basket	$150.00 – 175.00
1990	Jade Opaline Fern Optic basket	$100.00 – 125.00
1991	Rosalene Leaf Basket and Peacock & Dahlia basket	$75.00 – 85.00
1992	Blue-cased Opal Bubble Optic vase	$55.00 – 70.00
1993	Rosalene Satin Butterfly/Rose candy box	$65.00 – 75.00
1994	Rosalene Tulip vase, Opal Hanging Heart or optics	$125.00 – 150.00
1995	Celeste Blue Butterfly Net mug	$45.00 – 55.00
1996	Cobalt Blue Iridized Happy Cat	$65.00 – 85.00
1997	Topaz Opalescent Iridized Happy Cat	$65.00 – 85.00
1998	Sea Mist Green Iridized Satin Happy Cat	$65.00 – 85.00

Year	Description	Value
1999	Blue Burmese Satin or Shiny Butterfly Net basket	$100.00 – 125.00
2000	Empress Rose and Violet Priscilla baskets	$55.00 – 65.00
2001	Topaz Opalescent Satin 1-pc. fairy light	$125.00 – 150.00
2002	Blue Topaz Opalescent 1-pc. fairy light	$125.00 – 150.00
2003	Ruby Stretch Peacock vase, Star Crimp	$125.00 – 150.00
2004	Periwinkle Mandarin & Empress vases	(ea.) $50.00 – 65.00
2005	Chocolate Nymph in small bowl	$150.00 – 175.00

SOUVENIRS

Souvenirs are marked with a Butterfly outline, "FAGCA," and date.

Year	Description	Value
1978	Ruby Iridized Butterfly box	$75.00 – 95.00
1979	Pineapple footed comport in Ruby Iridized and Cameo Opalescent	$50.00 – 65.00 $30.00 – 35.00
1980	Velva Rose Butterfly on stand	$65.00 – 85.00
1981	Custard Shiny 2-handled bonbon w/Nutmeg stain	$50.00 – 65.00
1982	Burmese Hat, Butterfly decorated	$125.00 – 150.00
1983	Cobalt Blue bell, sandcarved Butterfly & Flowers, leaves	$50.00 – 65.00
1984	Plum Opalescent Strawberry cuspidor	$125.00 – 150.00
1985	Burmese satin Butterfly Net mug	$65.00 – 75.00
1986	Rosalene Butterfly Net mug	$65.00 – 75.00
1987	Ruby Slag Butterfly Net mug	$45.00 – 55.00
1988	Shell Pink Butterfly box	$65.00 – 85.00
1989	Ruby iridized Butterfly candleholder, 3-hole	$75.00 – 95.00
1990	Rosalene September Morn Nymph	$125.00 – 150.00
1991	Sea Foam Green Opalescent medallion bell, "Frank L. Fenton" and "John W. Fenton"	$50.00 – 65.00
1992	Rosalene #9280 Butterfly/Rose candy box	$50.00 – 65.00
1993	Cranberry Opalescent Jacqueline sugar & creamer	$100.00 – 125.00 set
1994	Cranberry Opalescent Jacqueline 48 oz. pitcher	$100.00 – 125.00
1995	Blue Burmese 1-pc. fairy light	$125.00 – 150.00
1996	Burmese ginger jar, hand-painted Butterfly & Flowers	$150.00 – 175.00

Year	Description	Value
1997	Topaz Opalescent blown egg, hand-painted Flowers & Butterfly	$100.00 – 120.00
1998	Royal Purple blown egg, hand-painted Flowers & Butterfly	$100.00 – 120.00
1999	Blue Burmese Satin 6½" vase	$75.00 – 95.00
2000	Lotus Mist Burmese Satin 9" hurricane lamp	$175.00 – 225.00
2001	Pink Chiffon Overlay Flame lamp with Crystal base	$75.00 – 85.00
2002	Burmese hurricane lamp, hand-painted Florals & Butterfly	$175.00 – 225.00
2003	Burmese #6504 Temple Jar, hand painted w/ Pink Hibiscus & Butterfly	$175.00 – 200.00
2004	Sea Mist Grn Pillar vase, hand-painted Lighthouse	$100.00 – 125.00
2005	Aquamarine 9" blown vase, White Flowers, Butterfly	$100.00 – 125.00

MISCELLANEOUS GLASS

Included in this list are gifts given to members who display their glass at convention and members who help with activities at convention

Year	Description	Value
1980	Topaz Opalescent oval logo, marked "FAGCA [Butterfly emblem] 1980"	$100.00 – 125.00
	Ice Green oval logo, "FAGCA," Butterfly emblem, and date	$100.00 – 125.00
	Velva Rose oval logo, FAGCA Butterfly emblem & date	$100.00 – 125.00
1981	Crystal and Crystal Velvet oval logos, FAGCA Butterfly emblem	(ea.) $35.00 – 40.00
1982	Chocolate Glass Butterfly On Stand, FAGCA Butterfly emblem	$65.00 – 75.00
	Chocolate Glass oval logo, FAGCA Butterfly emblem	$100.00 – 125.00
1984	Plum Opalescent Iridized Leaf/Butterfly bonbon	$85.00 – 100.00
1985	Green Opalescent 7" basket, Heart Spot mould	$100.00 – 125.00
	Green Opalescent Iridized Butterfly on Stand, FAGCA logo	$75.00 – 85.00
	Lt. Blue ornament, "Thanks FAGCA," worker's gift	$35.00 – 40.00
	Royal Blue 1924 hat, Heart Spot mould	$100.00 – 125.00
1986	Peaches 'n Cream hat, Heart Spot mould	$100.00 – 125.00
	Sapphire Blue Opalescent cruet, Heart Spot mould	$100.00 – 125.00

Year	Description	Value
	Burmese rectangle Fenton logo, display table award	$85.00 – 95.00
	Dusty Rose ornament, "Thanks FAGCA," worker's gift	$35.00 – 40.00
1988	Country Cranberry hats, Heart or Fern optics	(ea.) $75.00 – 85.00
	Country Cranberry hat baskets, Heart or Fern optics	$100.00 – 120.00
	Country Cranberry hat baskets, optics and decorated	$100.00 – 120.00
	Ruby & MG shells, Ribbed or Hobnail, sets of 4	(set) $25.00 – 30.00
1989	Black or Black Iridescent Butterfly mug, FAGCA emblem and date	$45.00 – 55.00
	Mulberry Vase with embossed Butterflies or Moths	$75.00 – 80.00
1990	Rosalene Butterfly on Stand, display table gift	$150.00 – 200.00
1991	Rosalene oval logo, FAGCA Butterfly emblem, worker gift	$100.00 – 125.00
	Favrene Butterfly on Stand, FAGCA Butterfly emblem & date	$85.00 – 95.00
	Favrene Butterfly is cut off stand	$85.00 – 95.00
	Favrene Mug, FAGCA Butterfly emblem & date	$65.00 – 75.00
1992	Rosalene Lovebird paperweight, worker's gift	$70.00 – 80.00
	Crystal Satin, painted or plain	$40.00 – 45.00
	Burmese Butterfly on Stand or cut off, not marked, Satin or Shiny	$75.00 – 85.00
	Cranberry Opalescent Heart Spot hat	$85.00 – 95.00
	Cranberry Opalescent Heart Spot hat basket	$100.00 – 125.00
1993	Favrene oval logo	$75.00 – 85.00
	Milk Glass Iridized or plain, oval logo	$65.00 – 75.00
	Rosalene small Butterfly is cut off the Butterfly/ Rose candy lid	$35.00 – 40.00
1994	Plum Opalescent Oval Logo, FAGCA Butterfly emblem	$125.00 – 150.00
	Black Iridized Happy Cat, display gift	$225.00 – 250.00
	Autumn Gold, plain or iridized Sun Fish	$20.00 – 25.00
	Steigel Green Happy Cat	$75.00 – 85.00
	Twilight Blue Iridized Happy Cat	$75.00 – 85.00
1995	Blue Burmese Happy Cat	$65.00 – 85.00
	Rosalene Shiny Butterfly/Rose candy box decorated, display gift	$65.00 – 75.00

Year	Description	Value
	Red Carnival oval logo with cylinder base, worker's gift	$65.00 – 70.00
1996	Blue Burmese 1-pc. fairy light, decorated, display gift	$150.00 – 175.00
	Blue Burmese top hat, decorated with violets	$125.00 – 150.00
	Mandarin Red Butterfly, cut off, metal stand	$45.00 – 55.00
	Burmese Satin Happy Cat, FAGCA Butterfly logo	$75.00 – 95.00
	Mandarin Red Happy Cat, FAGCA Butterfly logo	$65.00 – 85.00
	Mandarin Red Butterfly mug, FAGCA Butterfly logo	$45.00 – 55.00
	Plum oval logo on cylinder base, worker's gift	$75.00 – 85.00
	Twilight Blue Satin Happy Cat	$75.00 – 85.00
1997	Crystal Butterflies, tinted different colors (see photos)	$25.00 – 40.00
	Rosalene, Satin or Shiny, Happy Cat, FAGCA Butterfly logo	$65.00 – 85.00
	Cobalt Blue Satin Happy Cat	$60.00 – 70.00
	Favrene ginger jar, sand-carved Butterflies	$175.00 – 200.00
	Burmese Bulging Loop salt & pepper	(pr.) $45.00 – 55.00
	Burmese Embossed Roses salt & pepper, display gift	(pr.) $45.00 – 50.00
	Eggs on Stand, "F" on one side, "FAGCA Butterfly logo" on other	$20.00 – 24.00
	Gold Iridized oval logo, FAGCA Butterfly logo	$85.00 – 95.00
	Topaz Opalescent Duckling, worker's gift	$55.00 – 65.00
	Topaz Opalescent Rib blown egg, decorated	$100.00 – 125.00
1998	Royal Purple blown egg, decorated	$75.00 – 85.00
	Rosalene Hobnail cream & sugar	(set) $30.00 – 35.00
	Topaz Opalescent Solid Swan, worker's gift	$35.00 – 40.00
	Flat paperweights, 2½", with FAGCA Butterfly logo on top	$18.50 – 22.50
	Ruby Happy Cats with different treatments, display gift	(ea.) $65.00 – 85.00
	Ruby Butterfly Net mug, FAGCA Butterfly logo	$25.00 – 30.00
	Burmese Water Lily candleholders	(pr.) $65.00 – 75.00
	Burmese Hummingbird lamp, cloth shade	$200.00 – 250.00

Year	Description	Value
1999	Blue Burmese Shiny logo	$65.00 – 85.00
	Blue Burmese Satin hurricane lamp, hand-painted Blue Butterflies	$250.00 – 300.00
2000	Rocks in several different colors, "FAGCA Butterfly 2000," worker's gift	$25.00 – 30.00
	Blue Burmese Satin 9" hurricane lamp, hand-painted Hummingbirds	$175.00 – 200.00
	Shell Pink Iridized Happy Cat, FAGCA logo	$75.00 – 85.00
	Opal Happy Cat with Butterfly & Flower	$75.00 – 85.00
2001	Luv Bug, 25th anniversary issue, airbrushed with red heart	$15.00 – 18.00
	White Satin Happy Cat, Black tie, display gift	$75.00 – 95.00
	White Satin Happy Cat, tuxedo	$100.00 – 125.00
	6" flip vase, Willow Green HP with Violet Crest & Base, display gift	$100.00 – 125.00
2002	Country Cranberry vase, White Flowers & Butterflies, display gift	$75.00 – 95.00
	Sunset and Amethyst satinized Turtle, worker's gift	$25.00 – 30.00
	Black Koi plain or with Butterfly (see photos)	$25.00 – 40.00
	Blue Topaz Ribbed egg	$45.00 – 55.00
	Sunset Iridized Happy Cat	$75.00 – 85.00
	Patriotic White Satin Happy Cat	$100.00 – 125.00
	White Satin Happy Cat with Red, White & Blue flag-style hearts	$85.00 – 95.00
2003	Black Shiny Hobby Horse, decorated or plain	$25.00 – 30.00
	Black Shiny Sitting Stick Clown with White accents & rosebuds	$55.00 – 65.00
	Ruby Iridized Bunny with Heart or Yellow Daisy	$30.00 – 35.00
	Blue Topaz blown egg, decorated	$50.00 – 65.00
	Cobalt & Opal Slag, Shiny or Satin Butterfly	$40.00 – 45.00
	Burmese hurricane lamp, farm scene, display gift	$200.00 – 225.00
	Cobalt & Opal Slag, Shiny or Satin Happy Cat, FAGCA logo	$75.00 – 85.00
	Opal Happy Cat with Patriotic decoration	$100.00 – 125.00
2004	Purple Slag Happy Cat	$75.00 – 85.00
2005	Red Slag Happy Cat	$65.00 – 85.00

Azure Blue decorated Butterfly on Stand, $25.00 – 35.00.

Blue-Green Butterfly on Stand, $25.00 – 35.00.

Fuchsia Butterfly on Stand, $35.00 – 40.00.

Mandarin Red Butterfly on Stand, $35.00 – 40.00.

Pale Green Butterfly on Stand, $25.00 – 35.00.

Pale Pink Butterfly on Stand, $30.00 – 35.00.

Lime Satin Butterfly on Stand, $25.00 – 30.00.

Yellow-Green Butterfly on Stand, $25.00 – 30.00.

Black Satin Butterfly 3-hole candleholder, $35.00 – 50.00.

Black decorated Butterfly 3-hole candleholder, $45.00 – 55.00.

Blue Slag Satin Butterfly, $40.00 – 45.00.

Blue Slag Butterfly, $40.00 – 45.00.

Yellow Satin Butterfly on button, $18.00 – 20.00. Yellow Satin Butterflies, set of 3, $15.00 – 18.00.

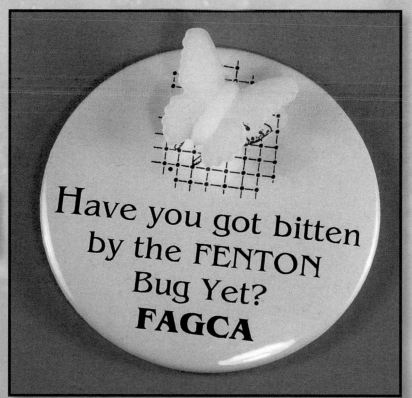

Have you got bitten by the FENTON Bug Yet? FAGCA

THE FENTON ART GLASS COLLECTORS OF AMERICA, INC.

presents its 1983 Souvenir

A beautiful Cobalt Blue Bell with a sandcarved butterfly surrounded with flowers and leaves. A deep rich color that combines with a light and sparkle unmatched by any other Cobalt Blue.

FAGCA provides the Fenton collector this *"one-time only"* opportunity to acquire this handmade bell. Each piece is marked: "FAGCA—1983".

Price is $25.00 each. (Postage and handling charge included.)

Quantity ordered by member *not* limited on this Souvenir but production *is limited* to 500 bells. Orders will be filled on a first come, first serve basis so don't delay placing your order at once.

Please use the order blank enclosed.

Cobalt Blue bell with a sand-carved butterfly, $50.00 – 65.00.

Celeste Blue Butterfly Net mug, $45.00 – 55.00.

Mandarin Red Butterfly Net mug, $45.00 – 55.00.

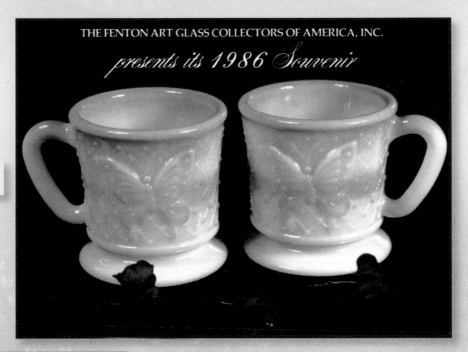

Rosalene Butterfly Net mug, $65.00 – 75.00.

Ruby Butterfly Net mug, $25.00 – 30.00.

Ruby Marble Butterfly Net mug, $45.00 – 65.00.

THE FENTON ART GLASS COLLECTORS OF AMERICA, INC.

presents its 1985 Souvenir

Burmese Butterfly Net mug, $65.00 – 75.00.

Azure Blue Butterfly & Berry footed bowl, $35.00 – 40.00.

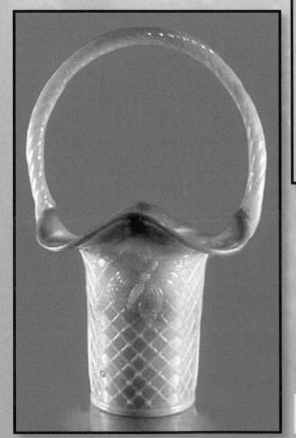

Blue Burmese Butterfly Net basket, $100.00 – 125.00.

THE FENTON ART GLASS COLLECTORS OF AMERICA, INC.

presents its 1981 Souvenir

Decorated Butterflies on Custard. A two-handled bonbon with embossed butterflies hand decorated in an antique finish. The color combination is similar to Fenton's old Custard with Nutmeg stain produced about 1915.

FAGCA provides the Fenton collector this *"one-time only"* opportunity to acquire this bonbon in the special Fenton finish. Each piece bears the FAGCA butterfly trademark and date.

Price is $20.00 each (postage and handling charge included)

Sales limited to two bonbons for each membership card.

Orders will not be accepted after July 1, 1981. Please use order blank enclosed.

Custard Butterfly bonbon, $50.00 – 65.00.

Favrene sand-carved Butterflies ginger jar, $175.00 – 200.00.

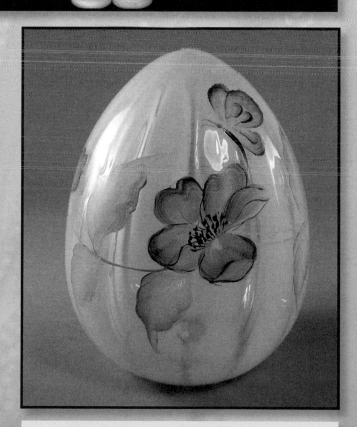

Blue Topaz Opalescent blown egg, decorated, $50.00 – 65.00.

Aquamarine vase, White Butterfly decoration, $75.00 – 95.00.

THE FENTON ART GLASS COLLECTORS OF AMERICA, INC.

PRESENTS THE 2002 SOUVENIR
"IN OUR BELOVED BURMESE".

*The decoration was designed by Kim Plauche'
who designed the blue burmese Hurricane Lamp last year.*

If you recall last year we had the #170 Hurricane Lamp in Blue Burmese, and the year before we had it in Lotus Mist (Green) Burmese. Now those of you who collect the yellow to rose Burmese can add this piece to your collections.

AND BEST OF ALL, THE CANDLE BASE IS ALSO IN BURMESE.

Again there will be a limited number of this souvenir so get your order in fast. The price is the same as for the Lotus Mist and the Blue Burmese Lamps. $135.00, Postage Paid.

Burmese hurricane lamp, decorated, $175.00 – 225.00.

Burmese temple jar, Butterfly decoration, $175.00 – 200.00.

THE FENTON ART GLASS COLLECTORS OF AMERICA, INC.

presents its 1982 Souvenir

Handpainted butterflies and blossoms on soft, translucent Burmese Glass. Fenton Glass Chemist Charles W. Goe worked many years until he found just the right formula to faithfully reproduce the delicate blushing loveliness of the original Burmese treatment.

FAGCA provides the Fenton collector this *"one-time only"* opportunity to acquire this 4" handpainted Burmese Hat. Each piece is signed by the artist and is marked FAGCA—1982.

Price is $35.00 each (postage and handling included)

Sales limited to one hat for each membership card.

Orders will not be accepted after July 1, 1982.

Please use order blank enclosed.

Burmese hat, Butterfly decoration, $125.00 – 150.00.

Black Koi, Butterfly decoration, $35.00 – 40.00.

Ruby Stretch Floppy Ear Rabbit, decorated, $30.00 – 35.00.

Sea Green Happy Cat, $75.00 – 85.00.

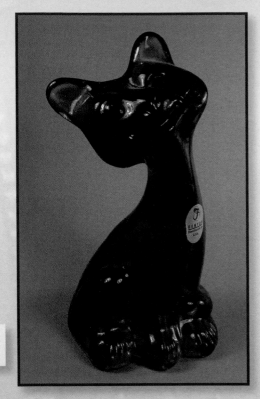

Ruby Happy Cat, $65.00 – 85.00.

Topaz Iridized Happy Cat, $65.00 – 85.00.

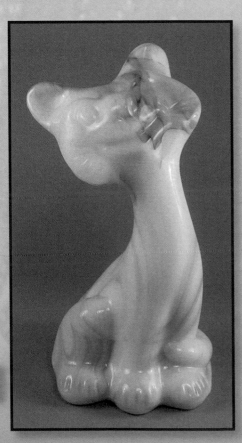

Red Slag Happy Cat, $65.00 – 85.00.

Periwinkle Blue Happy Cat, $40.00 – 50.00.

Cobalt Iridized Happy Cat, $65.00 – 85.00.

Blue Burmese Happy Cat, $65.00 – 85.00.

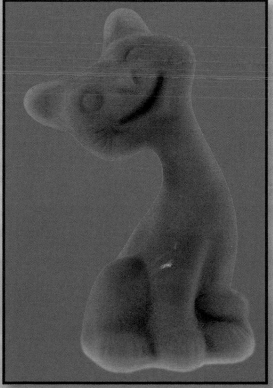

Opal Satin Happy Cat wearing a tuxedo (rare), $100.00 – 125.00.

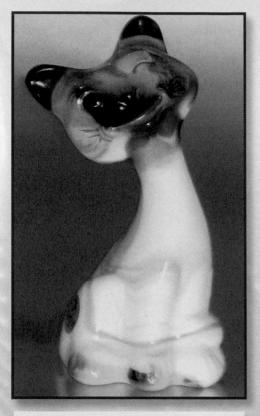

Purple Slag Happy Cat, $75.00 – 85.00.

Amber Sun Fish, $20.00 – 25.00.

Mandarin Red Happy Cat, $65.00 – 85.00.

Black Koi, $25.00 – 30.00.

Black Clown, decorated, $55.00 – 65.00.

FAGCA 25th Anniversary Love Bug, $15.00 – 18.00.

Black Rocking Horse, decorated, $55.00 – 65.00.

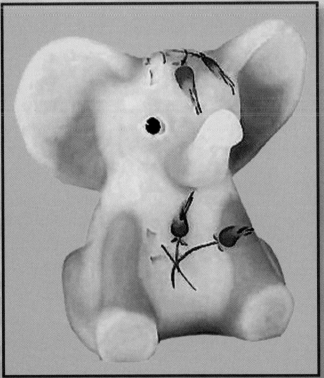

Burmese Elephant, Closed Rose, $40.00 – 50.00.

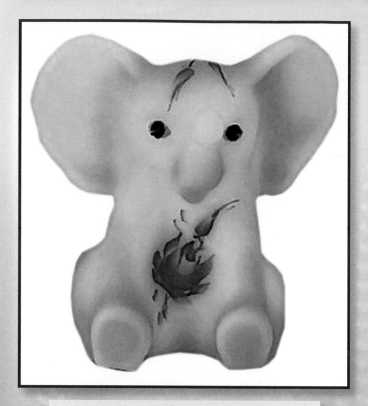

Burmese Elephant, Open Rose, $40.00 – 50.00.

Chocolate Snail, $25.00 – 35.00.

Ruby Stretch Floppy Ear Rabbit, decorated, $30.00 – 35.00.

Black Egg on Stand, scroll "F," $20.00 – 24.00.

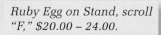

Ruby Egg on Stand, scroll "F," $20.00 – 24.00.

Blue Topaz Opalescent blown egg, decorated, $50.00 – 65.00.

Rosalene Nymph, Black block, $150.00 – 175.00.

Chocolate Nymph & bowl, $150.00 – 175.00.

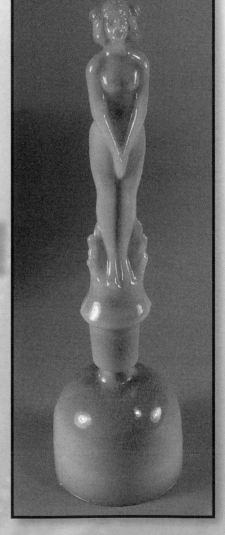

Peachalene Nymph on bust off, $150.00 – 175.00.

Blue Burmese oval logo, $65.00 – 85.00.

Blue Burmese decorated 1-pc. fairy light, $250.00 – 275.00. Only a few were decorated.

Blue Opalescent oval logo, $25.00 – 30.00.

Blue Burmese 1-pc. fairy light, $125.00 – 150.00.

Blue Topaz 1-pc. fairy light, $125.00 – 150.00.

CR Coin Dot 1-pc. fairy light, whimsey, $275.00 – 350.00.

CR Floral Lace 1-pc. fairy light, whimsey, $275.00 – 350.00.

Plum Opalescent Inverted Strawberry cuspidor, $125.00 – 150.00.

Dusty Rose Overlay w/Blue Crest vase, $100.00 – 125.00.

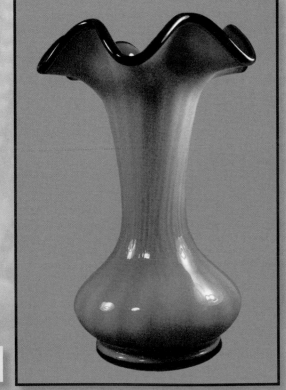

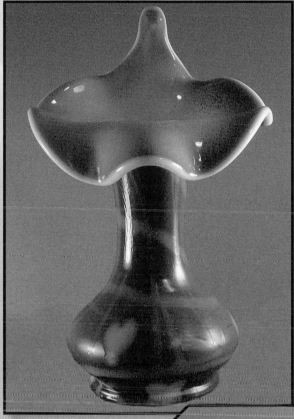

Rosalene w/Opal Hearts JIP vase, whimsey, $125.00 – 150.00.

Dusty Rose Overlay w/Blue crest JIP vase, whimsey, $120.00 – 140.00.

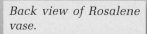

Back view of Rosalene vase.

Black w/Opal Hearts vase, Opal Crest, whimsey, $150.00 – 165.00.

the **FENTON ART GLASS COLLECTORS OF AMERICA, INC.**

Again Brings to the Collector the #170 Hurricane Lamp

This time in the well loved Blue Burmese

The Original design, was by Kim Plauche' and uses many of the same colors the Blue Burmese Hurricane Lamp with the blue Butterfly that was a 1999 gift to those who exhibited in the Display Room during that Convention, used. Thus, making a beautiful, though not matching, pair.

The price is the same as for the Lotus Mist Burmese, **"$135.00"**, Postage Paid. The Lotus Mist Burmese Hurricane Lamp sold out before Convention. These Blue Burmese ones are to be sold one each to regular members for the period of one month as there is only a limited number. If there are any left after that, the Associate members may purchase them. We will let you know in the next "NET"

Blue Burmese hurricane lamp, $175.00 – 225.00.

Lotus Mist Burmese decorated Pillar vase, $100.00 – 125.00.

Burmese Paisley covered box, $50.00 – 65.00.

Cameo Opalescent Owl ring tree, $65.00 – 85.00.

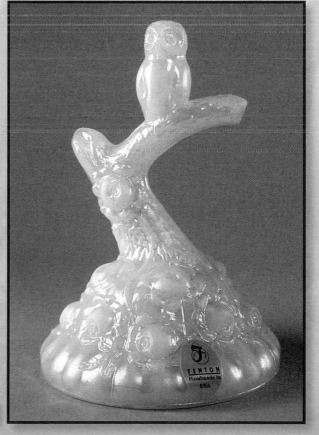

Sea Green Owl ring tree, $15.00 – 20.00.

FAGCO Ebony clock, celebrating 100 years of Fenton Art Glass, $65.00 – 75.00.

Pink Chiffon Flame lamp, $75.00 – 85.00.

Periwinkle Blue Satin Empress vase, $50.00 – 65.00.

Empress Rose Priscilla basket, $55.00 – 65.00.

Violet Priscilla basket, $55.00 – 65.00.

Ruby Stretch Peacock vase, $125.00 – 150.00.

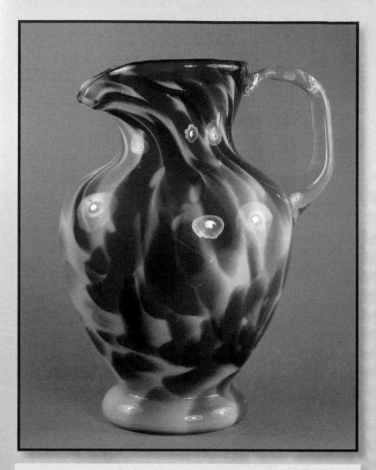

Pink, Purple & Opal Vasa Murrhina handled vase, whimsey, $75.00 – 95.00.

Pink, Purple & Opal Vasa Murrhina pitcher, whimsey, $75.00 – 95.00.

Rosalene Hobnail cream & sugar, $30.00 – 35.00.

Sapphire Blue Heart Optic cruet, $100.00 – 125.00.

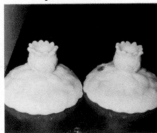

Burmese Assortment: Bulging Teardrop salt & pepper, Bulging Teardrop decorated salt & pepper, $45.00 – 55.00 pair. #2955 lamp, Hummingbird decoration, $200.00 – 250.00. Waterlily candlesticks, Shiny, $65.00 – 75.00 pair. Embossed Rose salt & pepper, $45.00 – 50.00 set.

FENTON FINDERS OF KANSAS CITY

The Fenton Art Glass Collectors of America is a national club whose smaller local branches call themselves Fenton Finders of (names chosen by the groups forming the clubs). The Kansas City club has been very active since its formation in the 1970s. Several of its members have held seats on the FAGCA board, and others have served on committees at convention. In 1999, the Kansas City club decided to hold its own convention, the "Gala." The Topaz Nymph set was made for that convention.

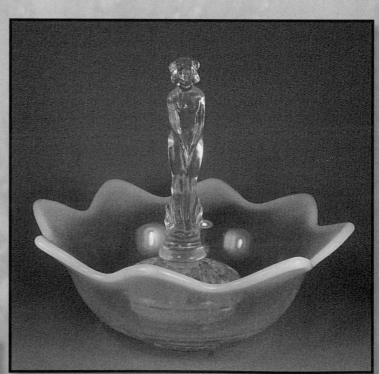

Topaz Opalescent Nymph & cupped petal bowl, $150.00 – 165.00.

Topaz Opalescent Nymph & flared petal bowl, $150.00 – 165.00.

NATIONAL FENTON GLASS SOCIETY

The National Fenton Glass Society was formed in 1990 and chartered by the state of Ohio in 1991. It works to promote the study of glassware made by the Fenton Art Glass Company as well as other handmade glass companies. Members receive the *Fenton Flyer*, its bimonthly newsletter, and meetings are held monthly in its club office, which is located at 156 Front Street in Marietta, Ohio. That building was purchased by the club in 1996. In the 16 years that the club has existed, it has grown substantially and continues to find new members. It holds a three-day convention every year, either in the last weekend of July or the first weekend of August. Attendees enjoy seminars, displayed glassware, a glass forum, a banquet, and, everyone's favorite, a dinner cruise on the sternwheeler based in Marietta, Ohio.

Mulberry Blue #7567 Miniature basket, $30.00 – 35.00.

Mandarin Red #7567 Miniature basket, $30.00 – 35.00.

Emerald Crest #7567 miniature basket, $35.00 – 40.00.

Emerald Snow Crest #7567 mini basket, $35.00 – 40.00.

Black Crest #7567 miniature basket, $35.00 – 40.00.

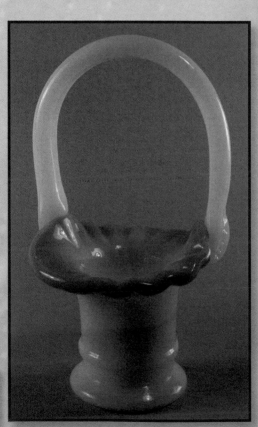

Burmese #7567 miniature basket, $30.00 – 35.00.

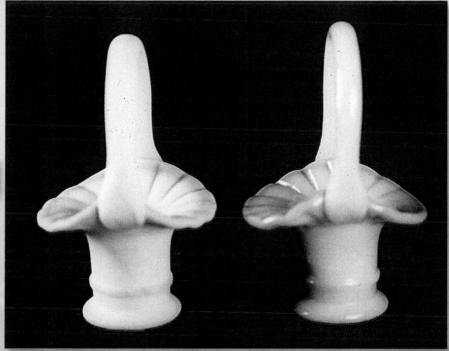

Blue Burmese #7567 minia-
ture basket, $30.00 – 35.00.

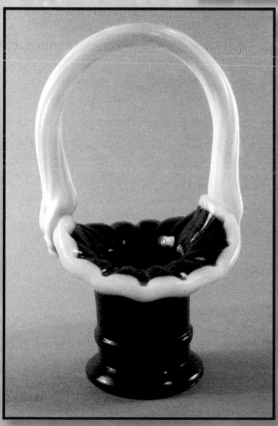

Opal Crest on Black miniature basket, $35.00
– 40.00.

Black Carnival miniature basket, $30.00
– 35.00.

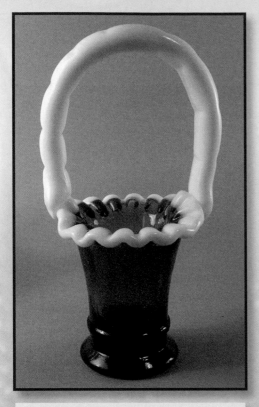

Amethyst Snow Crest miniature basket, $35.00 – 40.00.

Purple Crest miniature basket, $35.00 – 40.00.

Black glass vase, "Happy New Year 1999/2000," $25.00 – 30.00.

Black glass vase, flared top, signed base.

Blue Burmese decorated New World cruets, made for a fund-raiser, $125.00 – 150.00 each.

Rosalene miniature basket, $60.00 – 65.00.

Blue Burmese decorated New World cruet, made for a fund-raiser, $125.00 – 150.00.

Blue Burmese decorated New World cruets, made for a fundraiser, $125.00 – 150.00.

Plum Opalescent New World salt & pepper, $45.00 – 50.00.

Plum Opalescent New World cruet, $65.00 – 70.00.

Blue Burmese one-horn epergne, decorated Satin or Shiny, $75.00 – 85.00.

Blue Burmese one-horn epergne, Millennium decorated, $75.00 – 85.00.

Blue Burmese one-horn epergne, no decoration, $70.00 – 75.00.

Blue Burmese decorated child-size pitcher, tumblers & tray, $200.00 – 250.00.

Lotus Mist Burmese decorated child-size pitcher, tumblers & tray, $200.00 – 250.00.

Topaz Opalescent Rib Optic New World salt & pepper, $30.00 – 35.00 set.

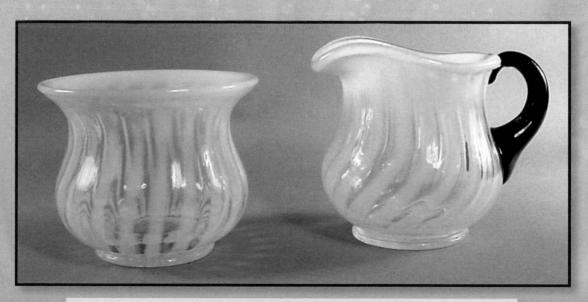

Topaz Opalescent Spiral or Rib New World cream & sugar, $45.00 – 50.00 set.

Cobalt Blue Mouse, $20.00 – 24.00.

Cobalt Blue Girl & Boy Mice, decorated, $25.00 – 30.00 each.

Mandarin Red top hat, $25.00 – 35.00.

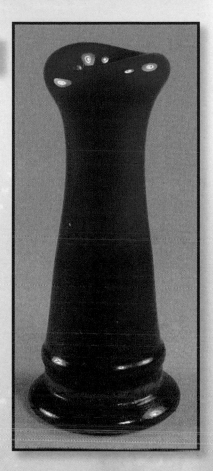

Mandarin Red swung vase, made from #7567 mini vase, $20.00 – 22.00.

Opaline dresser set & tray, $125.00 – 150.00.

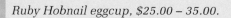

Ruby Hobnail eggcup, $25.00 – 35.00.

Ruby Overlay with Opal handles cream & sugar, $50.00 – 65.00 set.

Martha Stewart Green Peacock vase, $55.00 – 70.00.

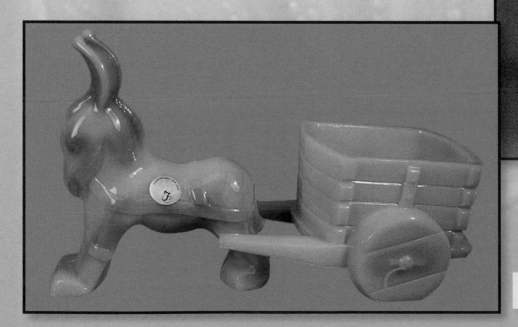

Lotus Mist Burmese Donkey & Cart, $75.00 – 95.00.

HEISEY COLLECTORS OF AMERICA

A.H. Heisey & Company closed its doors for Christmas vacation in 1957 and never reopened, disappointing its longtime customers. The Imperial Glass Corporation announced its purchase of Heisey moulds, etching plates, customer lists, production records, patents, copyrights, trademarks, and batch (color) formulas on April 30, 1958. For several years, Imperial made glass from the moulds, leaving the Heisey mark in them. When the company realized that its glassware was being sold as original Heisey, it made the decision to remove the mark from all the Heisey moulds, even though Imperial owned the right to use that mark.

In 1971, a group of Heisey collectors formed a collectors' club that would be dedicated to the study of Heisey glassware. There had been a group of collectors in California that had tried to form a national club, but that club dissolved shortly after it began. The new group would be based in Newark, Ohio, the home of the Heisey factory. In 1973, it was given the home of the prominent King family of Newark, but later it would have to be moved to a new site in the Sixth Street Museum Park, where it stands today. It is a magnificent museum with many lighted cabinets filled with old and often rare glassware. The club has reprinted many of Heisey's old catalogs, and souvenirs made from Heisey moulds are sold there.

Imperial made the first souvenirs for the Heisey Collectors of America in 1971 using the #1447 Rococo plate mould. In 1977, the club ordered copies of Heisey's plug horse, to be called "Oscar" by the group. In 1973, Imperial Glass Co. had become an extension of Lenox Inc., and the new mark added an *L* to the early Imperial mark, an *I* that was drawn through a *G*. In 1981, the factory was sold again, to Arthur Lorch, and an *A* was added to the mark. The company sold once more after Mr. Lorch wasn't able to make a profit. That sale was the final blow to this very old factory. Robert Stahl was the new owner,

and he did try to keep the doors open and the employees paid. It was not to be, and Imperial ran an ad notifying collectors and residents of the final sale, which was held December 21, 22, and 23, 1984.

The Heisey and Imperial moulds would be sold once again. This time, the Heisey Collectors of America club was able to buy all the Heisey animal moulds as well as a the child's Elephant handled mug and a few others. In 1987, those moulds were taken to Fenton so that the club's souvenirs could be made by FAGCO. Fenton made many beautiful pieces for the club, so in 1991 the club approached Frank Fenton to make a series of animals in Fenton's very desirable Rosalene color. That color would bring Fenton collectors to join the Heisey club so that they could also buy this set. The sets sold almost immediately, and the seconds that had been satinized also sold in short order. The problem with this arrangement was apparent very soon. Rosalene is a color that must be reheated in order to bring out the pink shading. In the case of some of the animals, such as the Giraffe, when they were reheated, the shapes changed. I was at the factory when a move of these was made, and I watched as the animals came through the lehr, where they were cooled to room temperature. A large quantity of Madonnas and Giraffes were bent almost in half. These had to be remade several times. To recover the costs of attempting to make these pieces look as they should, Fenton either had to charge the club for the bad pieces or be able to sell them in Fenton's gift shop. The problem couldn't be solved, so the Heisey Collectors took back the moulds so that they could be used by another glass factory.

A batch of Rosalene was being made when a power outage occurred. When work resumed, the Rosalene batch had become a peach color. Collectors dubbed it "Peachalene."

Year	Color	Shape	Edition	Value
1987	French Opalescent	Oscar	1500	$65.00 – 70.00
1988	Opal (translucent MG)	Oscar	1461	$50.00 – 60.00
1989	Teal	Oscar	1200	$60.00 – 65.00
1990	Rosalene	Oscar	1267	$75.00 – 100.00

Year	Color	Shape	Edition	Value
1990	Peachalene	Oscar	559	$100.00 – 125.00
1991	Sapphire Blue Opalescent, Glossy	Oscar	1154	$65.00 – 75.00
1991	Sapphire Blue Opalescent, Satin	Oscar	405	$75.00 – 95.00
1992	Burmese, Shiny	Oscar		$75.00 – 95.00
1992	Burmese, Satin	Oscar	150	$75.00 – 95.00
1992	Peachalene	Rooster		$125.00 – 150.00
1992	Rosealene	Rooster		$100.00 – 125.00
1987	French Opalescent	Madonna		$100.00 – 125.00
1989	Teal	Madonna		$75.00 – 100.00
1990	Rosalene	Madonna	17	$225.00 – 250.00
1987	Copper Blue	Sm. Elephant handled mug		$50.00 – 65.00
1987	Teal	Sm. Elephant handled mug		$50.00 – 65.00
1987	Ruby	Sm. Elephant handled mug		$65.00 – 75.00
1987	Light Blue	Sm. Elephant handled mug		$50.00 – 65.00
1987	French Opalescent	Small Elephant		$60.00 – 75.00
1992	Sea Mist Green	Small Elephant		$60.00 – 75.00
1987	French Opalescent	Medium Elephant		$75.00 – 95.00
1987	Off-color Blue Opalescent	Medium Elephant*		$75.00 – 95.00
1988	French Opalescent	Donkey		$75.00 – 95.00
1992	Sea Mist Green	Donkey		$60.00 – 75.00
1989	Teal, Shiny	Victorian Girl bell		$75.00 – 85.00
1989	Teal, Satin	Victorian Girl bell		$75.00 – 85.00
1989	Blue, Shiny	Horse Head		$50.00 – 60.00
1989	Blue, Satin	Horse Head		$50.00 – 60.00
1989	Ruby	Clover rope mug		$35.00 – 50.00
1992	Sea Mist Green, Shiny	Basket, #1415 (20th Century soda mould)		$40.00 – 50.00
1992	Sea Mist Green, Satin	Basket, #1415 (20th Century soda mould)		$40.00 – 50.00
1992	Sea Mist Green, Shiny	Roccoco basket		$40.00 – 55.00
1992	Sea Mist Green, Satin	Roccoco basket		$45.00 – 55.00

Year	Color	Shape	Edition	Value
1992	Dark Royal Blue, Shiny	Roccoco basket		$45.00 – 55.00
1992	Dark Royal Blue, Satin	Roccoco basket		$45.00 – 55.00
1992	Dusty Rose, Shiny	Sunflower basket		$50.00 – 60.00
1992	Dusty Rose, Satin	Sunflower basket		$50.00 – 60.00

*Three trademarks: Fenton's "F [in oval]," Imperial's "ALIG," and Heisey club's "HCA."

GOLD ANIMAL COLLECTORS SERIES – 450 SETS

The 450 sets are all Shiny Rosalene.
The satin animals are seconds.
All Rosalene items were made in 1992.

Item	Shiny	Satin
Head Forward Filly	$150.00 – 200.00	$120.00 – 150.00
Standing Duckling	$85.00 – 100.00	$75.00 – 85.00
Angelfish bookend	$150.00 – 175.00	$120.00 – 135.00
Rabbit paperweight	$100.00 – 125.00	$75.00 – 95.00
Gazelle	$150.00 – 200.00	$100.00 – 125.00
Cygnet	$85.00 – 100.00	$75.00 – 85.00
Airedale	$150.00 – 175.00	$120.00 – 150.00
Standing Colt	$100.00 – 125.00	$75.00 – 95.00
Giraffe	$150.00 – 200.00	$125.00 – 150.00
Tiger paperweight	$125.00 – 150.00	$100.00 – 125.00
Hen	$100.00 – 125.00	$75.00 – 100.00
Sow	$125.00 – 150.00	$100.00 – 125.00
Kicking Colt	$100.00 – 125.00	$75.00 – 95.00
Rearing (balking) Colt	$100.00 – 125.00	$75.00 – 95.00
Angelfish bookend in a Dark Plum Rosalene, 61 made	250.00 – 300.00	$225.00 – 275.00
Chicks, heads up, and chicks, heads down	(ea.) $25.00 – 35.00	(ea.) $20.00 – 24.00
Piglets	(ea.) $25.00 – 35.00	(ea.) $20.00 – 24.00

Rosalene Satin Airedale, $120.00 – 150.00.

Rosalene Angelfish, $150.00 – 175.00.

Rosalene Cygnet, $85.00 – 100.00.

Rosalene Filly, $150.00 – 200.00.

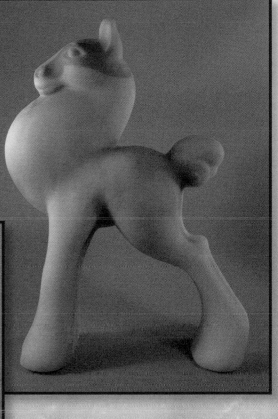

Rosalene Satin Filly, $120.00 – 150.00.

Rosalene Hen, $100.00 – 125.00. Rosalene Chicks, $25.00 – 35.00 each.

Rosalene Panther, $125.00 – 150.00.

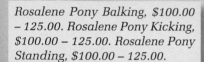

Rosalene Sow, $125.00 – 150.00. Rosalene Piglet, $25.00 – 35.00.

Rosalene Pony Balking, $100.00 – 125.00. Rosalene Pony Kicking, $100.00 – 125.00. Rosalene Pony Standing, $100.00 – 125.00.

Rosalene Satin Pony Balking, $75.00 – 95.00. Rosalene Satin Pony Kicking, $75.00 – 95.00. Rosalene Satin Pony Standing, $75.00 – 95.00.

Rosalene Rabbit, $100.00 – 125.00.

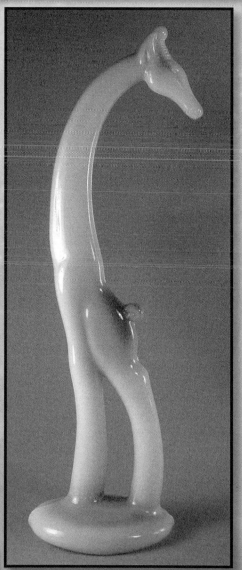

Rosalene Shiny Gazelle, $150.00 – 200.00. Rosalene Satin Gazelle, $100.00 – 125.00.

Rosalene Giraffe, $150.00 – 200.00.

Rosalene Plug Horse, $75.00 – 100.00.

Rosalene Rooster, $100.00 – 125.00.

Peachalene Plug Horse, $100.00 – 125.00.

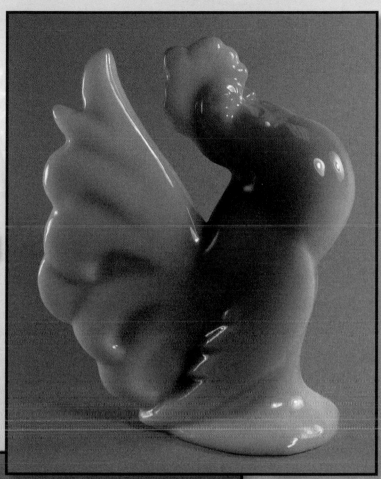

Peachalene Rooster, $125.00 – 150.00.

French Opalescent Medium Elephant, $75.00 – 95.00.

Cosmetics N Glass was a concept that had not been used since the forties, when Wrisley filled Fenton's French Opalescent Hobnail bottles with tinted cologne. The French Opalescent Hobnail Boxtel, limited to 800, was the first of two shapes made for Cosmetics N Glass. In 1982 and 1983, advertisements ran in the *Glass Review*, a magazine widely read by glass collectors. The contents read, "Cream Perfume and Body Powder will have the delicate fragrance of white gardenias." Of course, it didn't hurt that the Boxtle was one of the most desirable French Opalescent Hobnail pieces and was hard to find.

The second issue was a Cranberry Opalescent Hobnail #3761 tall decanter filled with foaming milk bath.

This was also a rare and desirable shape that Fenton collectors were anxious to own. It was limited to 600 pieces and sold quickly.

The concept was an interesting one, but the glass was the product desired, so many collectors just tossed the cosmetics away and put the glass on their shelves with the rest of their collection. Today, because so many new collectors have never heard of Cosmetics N Glass, these pieces have been mistaken as first issues. They were sold with labels on the bases, but it's possible that the signature will go unnoticed if a label is missing. Luckily, for those who mistake these two hobnail pieces as old, the values of the 1980s pieces are not much lower than those of the vintage Boxtel and decanter.

Two lovely limited items made by Fenton Art Glass in original molds exclusively for us.

TALL DECANTER – CRANBERRY OPALESCENT HOBNAIL
$60.00 plus $2.00 UPS – Limited to 600
comes filled with foaming milk bath
*
BOXTEL – FRENCH OPALESCENT HOBNAIL
$34.50 plus $2.00 UPS – Limited to 800
Perfume bottle and stopper attached to top of powder box,
comes filled with cream perfume and body powder
*
SEND CHECK OR MONEY ORDER TO:
COSMETICS N GLASS
P.O. Box 464G * Medina, OH 44258
TELEPHONE: (216) 725-0126
Ohio residents add 5⅝% sales tax

-- DEALER INQUIRIES INVITED --

Glass Review *advertisement for the decanter and Boxtle. Cranberry Opalescent decanter, $250.00 – 300.00.*

French Opalescent Boxtle, $150.00 – 175.00.

Coyne's Parade of Gifts

Coyne's & Company, operated by Ed Coyne, has been associated with the Fenton Art Glass Company for 50 years, beginning in 1955 as a sales representative for the upper Midwest. Over the years, its giftware lines have been greatly increased by the addition of imported giftware. In 1981, Parade of Gifts was developed, in catalog form, as a marketing and advertising tool to be used by retailers. By using that catalog as an advertising tool, smaller stores were able to compete with local or national chains. They also had the ability to sell exclusive products from many different giftware companies, including Fenton.

Because Fenton's records are not complete, I am only able to list some items made for Coyne's, but I will continue to try to find more information to be added to the next edition. If any of you have a *Parade of Gifts* catalog, please contact me so that those items offered in it can also be listed.

These items were sold in a 1984 Parade of Gifts *catalog.*

Pattern	Shape	Ruby	Peach Opalescent
Grape & Cable	Bowl, 10" ruffled		$100.00 – 125.00
Leaf Tiers	Bowl (all shapes), ftd.	$75.00 – 85.00	$85.00 – 100.00
Persian Medallion	Basket	$85.00 – 95.00	$120.00 – 150.00
Persian Medallion	Bowl	$45.00 – 65.00	$65.00 – 75.00

Peach Opalescent Grape & Cable 8 pt. bowl, $100.00 – 125.00.

Peach Opalescent Persian Medallion basket, $120.00 – 150.00.

Set a Festive Table

Ruby Leaf Tiers ftd. bowls, $75.00 – 85.00 each (all shapes).

Top: *Peach Opalescent Grape & Cable bowl, $100.00 – 125.00.*
Middle: *Ruby Persian Medallion basket, $85.00 – 95.00.*
Bottom: *Peach Opalescent Leaf Tiers ftd. bowl, $85.00 – 100.00.*

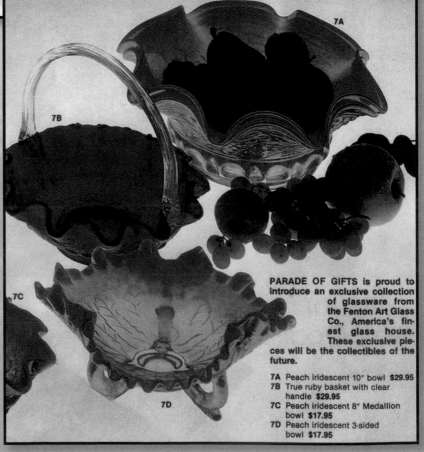

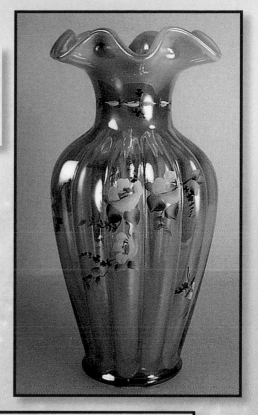

Sapphire Blue Opalescent 11" #7458LR vase decorated with White Florals and signed by Don Fenton, 1997. $125.00 – 150.00

French Opalescent (FO), Champagne Crest #3070 vase, $85.00 – 100.00.

Spruce Green #6585 basket, decorated, $100.00 – 125.00.

Sunset Satin #9144SX ring holder, $20.00 – 22.00. Sunset Satin #9157SX Fine Cut vase, $22.00 – 24.00.

Crystal Iridescent #9555 candleholder, $24.00 – 28.00.

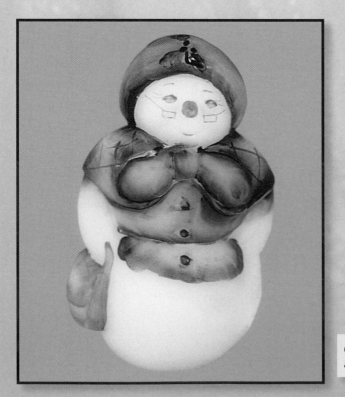

Opal Satin decorated #5369 Snowgirl, $65.00 – 75.00.

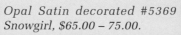

Opal Satin decorated #5266
Snowman, $65.00 – 75.00.

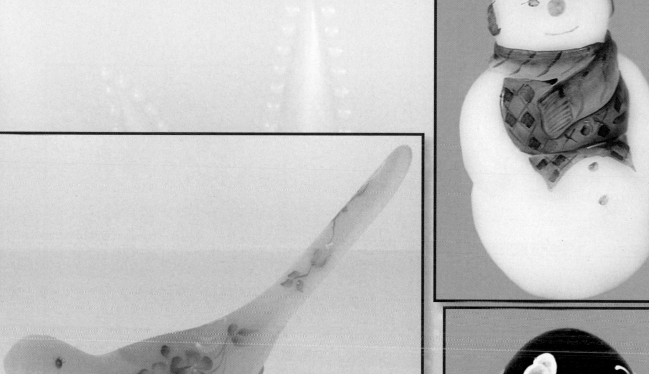

Rosalene Satin Happiness Bird, Floral decoration, $75.00 – 85.00.

Black decorated #5145 egg, $24.00 – 26.00.

Cobalt Blue decorated #5145 egg, $24.00 – 26.00.

Green Decorated #5145 egg, $24.00 – 26.00.

Ruby decorated #5145 egg, $24.00 – 26.00.

CRACKER BARREL

Cracker Barrel has been one of my favorite restaurants for years. Its brand of good Southern cooking is something I can't find on the West Coast, although Cracker Barrel is quickly moving this way, with locations as close to Seattle as Boise, Idaho. Not only does it make a great blackberry cobbler, it has a gift shop that is unique and fun, with items not found anywhere else.

The first Cracker Barrel Old Country Store was opened in 1969 in Lebanon, Tennessee. The food served today is the same as it was then. Corn bread is made from an old recipe using cornmeal, not a mix, and maple syrup, the authentic kind that comes from a tree. The country store is filled with items that are charming as well as usable. You can buy the "fixins" for many of the restaurant's menu items and, if you ask the cook, he or she will tell you what ingredients go into the restaurant's signature hash brown casserole.

Cracker Barrel has sold Fenton in its gift shop for over 25 years; most pieces have been regular line items, but not all. The store sold a lot of the Jack Daniels giftware made by Fenton in the early 1980s and has also purchased glass with special decorations, some of which is pictured in this chapter. The Coca-Cola items were featured in the Cracker Barrel gift shop and sold quickly. The values of those items are a little higher than expected, because they are collected by two completely different sets of collectors, Fenton collectors and Coca-Cola collectors.

The delicate shading of the blush of Rose on the Opal Satin is the perfect compliment to the Asters & Butterflies decoration that was designed by Robin Spindler. This beautiful collection was released in 1999. The Violet with Roses pattern, designed by Kim Plauché, was made in 2000 and sold out quickly. If you are lucky enough to find a piece of this, you should buy it while you can.

VIOLET IRIDESCENT WITH A LAYERED ROSE DECORATION
(Seen on page 117.)

Shape	Ware & Signature	Size	Value
Basket	#3535, Nancy Fenton	7"	$45.00 – 65.00
Bell	#4568, Don Fenton	6½"	$35.00 – 45.00
Bird	#5163, Shelley Fenton	4"	$30.00 – 35.00
Vase	#2557, Bill Fenton	5½"	$50.00 – 65.00

Experience Fenton . . . Handcrafted Glass Artistry since 1905.

ASTERS & BUTTERFLIES ON OPAL SATIN

Shape	Ware # & Signature	Size	Value
Basket	#2777, Bill Fenton	8"	$45.00 – 65.00
Bell	#6864, George Fenton	6"	$30.00 – 45.00
Cat	#5165, Don Fenton	3½"	$30.00 – 45.00
Doll	#5228, Shelley Fenton	7"	$45.00 – 65.00

Violet #1702 Coca-Cola bell, Hilda Clark design, 2002, $50.00 – 65.00.

Blue Topaz #1766 Coca-Cola bell, Juanita design, 2002, $50.00 – 65.00.

Pink Chiffon #1702 Coca-Cola bell, Duster Girl, 2002, $50.00 – 65.00.

Willow Green Coca-Cola bell, no opalescence, Hat Girl, 2002, $50.00 – 65.00.

Rose Magnolia Coca-Cola #2759 rose bowl, Duster Girl, $60.00 – 70.00.

French Opalescent Blossoms & Berries #2557 vase, $65.00 – 85.00.

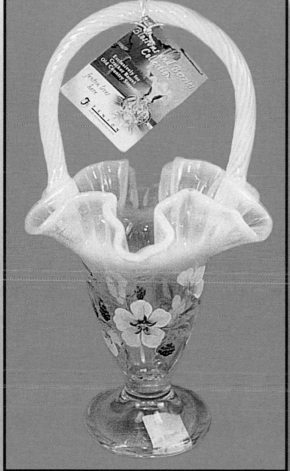

French Opalescent Blossoms & Berries #3535 basket, $65.00 – 85.00.

French Opalescent Blossoms & Berries #2759 candle bowl, $45.00 – 55.00.

French Opalescent Blossoms & Berries #5274 Frog, $50.00 – 65.00.

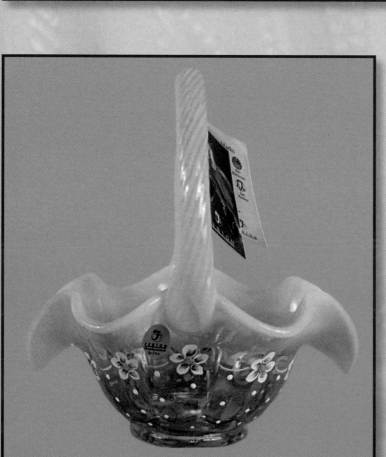

Rose Magnolia Dotted Swiss student lamp, 7" shade, $125.00 – 150.00.

Rose Magnolia Dotted Swiss #2777 basket, $75.00 – 85.00.

Rose Magnolia Dotted Swiss #7463 bell, $40.00 – 45.00.

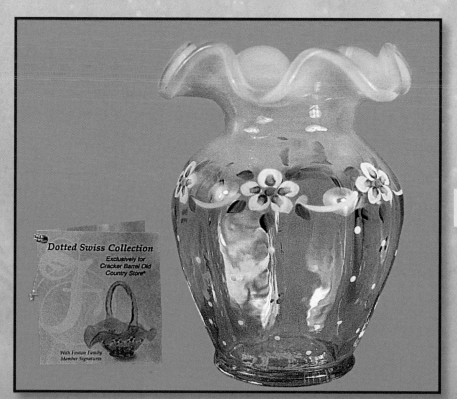

Rose Magnolia Dotted Swiss #3214 vase, $65.00 – 75.00.

Rose Magnolia Dotted Swiss
#5165 Cat, $45.00 – 55.00.

Country Cranberry Coin Dot #8958 pinch
vase, Pansy decoration, $65.00 – 85.00.

Opal flared-shade lamp with
Cracker Barrel decoration, only
one made, $350.00 – 450.00.

CRESCENT & SPRAGUE

The Crescent and Sprague Home Improvement store, who ordered this plate made for them by Fenton, is a part of the chain stores called Do It Best. The plate was probably made to be given to the employees of the store.

Amber #7418 plate with a farm scene, $35.00 – 40.00.

Over the years, Fenton has made glass sold by several companies dealing in limited editions, such as the Danbury Mint, but it is often the case that collectors do not recognize the pieces as Fenton products. The Blue Bird bell is easily recognized as Fenton, but the same is not true of the items with glass charms on the rings.

These little charms were used as handles for bells. A bell started life as an imported, blown goblet. The stem was removed, a clapper was put inside the bowl, and one of these charms was attached to the top as a handle. The bells were very popular, but not many Fenton collectors bought them.

Not Pictured: Burmese Diamond Optic #3242 10" basket, $90.00 – 110.00.

Crystal Wheel with attached charms. Not priced, because it would not be sold in this form.

Blue Topaz Opalescent Blue Bird bell, $70.00 – 85.00.

David Leo, husband of Diana Fenton, opened an antique mall in Williamstown several years ago. Diana is the granddaughter of Robert C. Fenton, who was the brother of Frank L. Fenton. The mall displayed some of the most beautiful glassware outside the museum. Many of the pieces were the Mosaic and Karnak Red style of glassware and had been owned originally by the Robert Fenton family.

Fenton made several special-order pieces for sale in the mall. The Blue Slag Reclining Bears were popular with mall customers, and bears that were not sold were decorated with the American flag and ribbon after September 11, 2001. A heart-shaped paperweight was also decorated with a patriotic theme. Mr. Leo's best-selling series was the Jillian Collection of bridesmaid dolls, named for his daughter. Most of the glass made for him was made from 2001 to 2004. The bridesmaid dolls are heavily collected and are not easy to find now.

JILLIAN COLLECTION — 5228 BRIDESMAID DOLLS

Year	Decoration	Color	Value
2001	Poinsettia	Ruby Iridized	$85.00 – 95.00
2001	Poinsettia	Opal Satin	$75.00 – 85.00
2002	Valentine	Ruby Iridized	$85.00 – 95.00
2002	Valentine	Opal Satin	$75.00 – 85.00
2002	July 4th	Opal Satin	$75.00 – 85.00
2002	July 4th	Cobalt Satin	$85.00 – 95.00
2002	September 11	Black Satin	$100.00 – 125.00
2002	September 11	White Satin	$100.00 – 125.00
2002	Jillian's Birthday	Topaz Satin	$100.00 – 125.00
2002	Autumn	Black Glossy	$85.00 – 95.00
2002	Christmas scene	Ruby Glossy	$100.00 – 125.00
2003	White Flowers	Celeste Blue	$85.00 – 95.00
2003	Lavender Flowers	Opal Satin	$75.00 – 85.00
2003	White Lilies	Ruby Glossy	$85.00 – 95.00
2003	Gold & Roses	Black Glossy	$85.00 – 95.00
2004	Florals	Violet	$75.00 – 85.00

MISCELLANEOUS

Description	Item #	Decoration	Color	Value
Basket, Chessie			Ruby Iridized	$100.00 – 125.00
Bear, 3½"	5251	Poinsettia	Opal Satin	$30.00 – 35.00
Bear, 3½"	5251	Poinsettia	Ruby Iridized	$35.00 – 40.00
Bear, 3½"	5251	Valentine	Opal Satin	$30.00 – 35.00
Bear. 3½"	5251	Valentine	Ruby Iridized	$35.00 – 40.00
Bear, 3½"	5251		Topaz Satin	$45.00 – 50.00
Bear, Reclining	5233		Blue Marble Satin	$50.00 – 65.00
Bear, Reclining	5233	Flag	Blue Marble Satin	$65.00 – 75.00
Bear, Reclining	5233	Ribbon	Blue Marble Satin	$65.00 – 75.00
Koi	5276		Ruby Iridized	$65.00 – 85.00

Black Heart paperweight, "Lest We Forget," $40.00 – 45.00.

Black doll #5228 decorated with Gold Leaves & Berries, $85.00 – 95.00.

Celeste Blue #5228 doll decorated with Spring Flowers, $85.00 – 95.00.

Opal Satin #5228 doll decorated with Poinsettias, $75.00 – 85.00.

Opal Satin #5228 doll decorated with Valentines, $75.00 – 85.00.

Ebony #5228 doll decorated with Roses, $85.00 – 95.00.

Cobalt Blue Satin #5228, 9/11 flag doll, $85.00 – 95.00.

Violet #5228 doll with White Flowers, $75.00 – 85.00.

Opal #5228 doll with Pink Floral decoration, $75.00 – 85.00.

Ruby #5228 doll with White Lilies, $85.00 – 95.00.

Ruby Iridized #5228 doll with Valentines, $85.00 – 95.00.

Ruby #5228 decorated Christmas doll, $100.00 – 125.00.

Ruby Iridized #5228 doll with Poinsettias, $85.00 – 95.00.

Blue Marble Satin #5233 Reclining Bear, Flag decorated, $65.00 – 75.00.

Blue Marble Satin #5233 Reclining Bear, Ribbon decorated, $65.00 – 75.00.

Ruby Iridized #5276 Koi, $65.00 – 85.00.

Doris Lechler is a well-known author of books covering children's glassware as well as many other articles made expressly for children. She began collecting toy glass in the 1970s and quickly realized that there was a need for a book that would help give direction to people who wanted to buy and collect antique toy glass. Collectors were in luck, because she decided to fill that void and write the book herself. She did a remarkable job. Her research is impeccable, something that isn't at all surprising when you know that she taught school in the Columbus, Ohio, school system for 30 years. She has written a total of eight books, six of which cover toy glass. Her writing has not been limited to books; she wrote articles for *Glass Review*, *Depression Glass DAZE*, and other publications for the antique collectors.

In 1980, Doris approached Fenton with her idea of reproducing some of her favorite glass sets. The company had no moulds for her to use, so she had moulds made for her and retained ownership of them. She limited the production of her sets to three colors per mould and five hundred sets per color per mould. All the sets sold out quickly and have increased in value so much that some sets are selling for $500 and up.

After all the years she put into teaching and writing, Doris and her husband now spend four months a year in France, where they buy antiques for the American market. It's almost impossible for a collector to really retire, but at least, they can indulge their hobby/work in a place as beautiful as Paris. I'm sure that collectors who have been educated by her book wish her a very happy retirement.

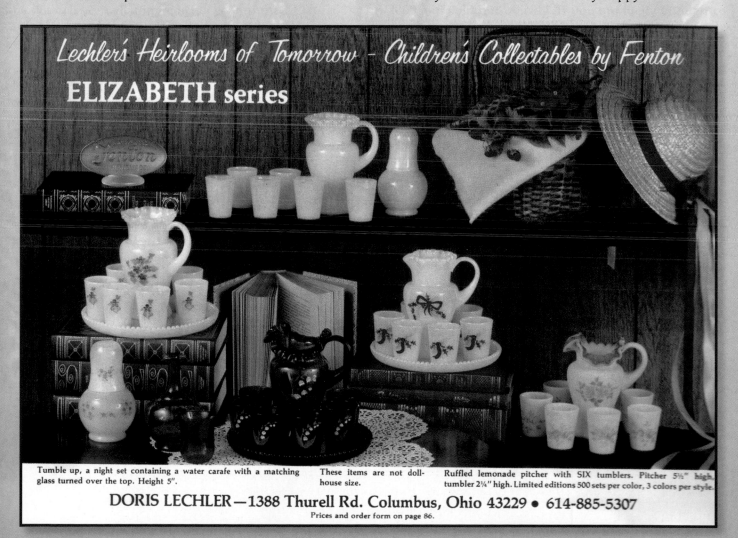

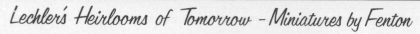

ELIZABETH SERIES

The Elizabeth Series water sets were sold as 5-piece or a 7-piece sets.
Prices are for 7-piece sets.

Shape	Color	Decoration	Price
Tray*	All colors	Plain	$50.00 – 75.00
Tumble up	Custard	None	$175.00 – 225.00
Tumble up	Custard	Violets	$225.00 – 275.00
Tumble up	Ruby Overlay	None	$300.00 – 350.00
Water set	Custard	Plain	$275.00 – 325.00
Water set	Custard	Violets	$325.00 – 400.00
Water set	Custard	Bow & Holly	$325.00 – 400.00
Water set	Burmese	Roses	$425.00 – 500.00
Water set	Amethyst	Plain	$275.00 – 325.00
Water set	Amethyst	Birds, Roses & Vine**	$400.00 – 450.00
Water set	Amethyst	Lily of the Valley	$325.00 – 400.00

*The tray was made in Cobalt Blue, Amethyst, Custard, and French Opalescent and was sold with all three series.

**Painted by Louise Piper.

GRACE & RUTH SERIES

Shape	Color	Pattern	Decoration	Value
Punch set	French Opalescent	Hobnail	Floral	$175.00 – 225.00
Punch set	Royal Blue	Hobnail	Floral	$200.00 – 250.00
Tumble up	Cased Blue Satin		Foral	$225.00 – 300.00
Tumble up	Cased Royal Blue*		Flower Bouquet	$225.00 – 300.00
Water set	Cranberry Opalescent	Hobnail		$450.00 – 500.00
Water set	French Opalescent	Hobnail		$350.00 – 400.00
Water set	Royal Blue Overlay	Hobnail	Flower Spray	$350.00 – 400.00

*The tumble up pitcher was also sold as a water set, with a tray and six tumblers. $450.00 – $500.00.

Lechler Heirlooms of Tomorrow by Fenton

Elizabeth's Victorian Motif

Louise Piper has created a special Victorian design for the last seventy-five (out of 500) ruffled toy lemonade sets. This is the last of the limited editions in the Elizabeth series.

The delicate 6" tall pitcher has gold trim to further enhance the bird, roses and vine design. The 2" tumblers are covered with the old fashion memory evoking motif and each one is graced with gold trim.

The special Louise Piper design created expressly for Doris Lechler is painted by Fenton artists and sells for $125. for the pitcher, six tumblers and the tray.

Send checks and orders to:

DORIS LECHLER—1388 Thurell Rd., Col., Oh. 43229, 614 885-9034 evenings.

Amethyst Elizabeth water set, no decoration, $275.00 – 325.00 full 6-pc. set.

Glass Review ad for the Elizabeth Amethyst water set decorated by Louise Piper with Birds, Roses & Vines, $400.00 – 450.00.

Burmese Elizabeth water set, Rose decoration, $425.00 – 500.00 full 6-pc. set.

Custard Elizabeth water set, Violets decoration, $325.00 – 400.00 full 6-pc. set.

Custard tumble up, Elizabeth series, $175.00 – 225.00.

CRANBERRY OPALESCENT HOBNAIL

Miniature Lemonade Set
one pitcher, 4 cups

$85 plus $2 UPS

*Made by Fenton Art Glass
expressly for Doris Lechler*

A French Opalescent tray will be available to
to hold this set for $18 plus $2 UPS

Glass Review *ad. Cranberry Hobnail water set,
$450.00 – 500.00 set.*

*Blue Overlay Grace series tumble up, Pink
Floral decoration, $225.00 – 300.00.*

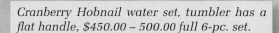

*Cranberry Hobnail water set, tumbler has a
flat handle, $450.00 – 500.00 full 6-pc. set.*

Lechler Heirlooms of Tomorrow

RUTH series

The new RUTH series opens with the first Lechler punch bowl set. The EIGHT piece assemblage consists of a French opalescent, hobnail punch bowl, six footed and pressed-handled cups and a matching tray large enough to hold all seven beautifully shaped pieces with maximum display power. A chain of baby pink roses and blue forget-me-nots hem the charming ruffled punch bowl's rim, while a single rose peeks from the bowl of each precious cup. The EIGHT pieces sell for $78.00 plus $2.25 UPS. (All Canada orders go by mail for $5.50 delivery).

This same set is available (without paint) in COBALT; a startling beauty selling for $70.00 for eight pieces plus the same UPS charge.

Remember the cranberry hobnail lemonade set? This set is now available in COBALT OVERLAY with the following features: SIX tumblers WITHOUT handles on a tray of cobalt, large enough to hold the seven pieces with ease. $80.00, plus $2.25 UPS.

Remember the blue satin (cased glass) tumble up with the tumbler fitting inside the neck of the tiny pitcher? It, too, is being made in cobalt overlay. Price and decorations to be decided.

RUTH series French opalescent (eight pieces) hobnail water
        set, $78.00, plus UPS

GRACE series COBALT overlay lemonade set (eight pieces)
        $80.00, plus UPS

NEW BOOK called CHILDREN'S GLASS DISHES CHINA and FURNITURE,
        $17.95, plus $2.00 UPS; $3.00 sending to Canada

Glass Review *ad. French Opalescent Ruth punch set, $175.00 – 225.00 set.*

Royal Blue Overlay Hobnail water set, $350.00 – 400.00 full 6-pc. set.

Royal Blue Overlay Grace series tumble up, White Floral, $225.00 – 300.00.

Royal Blue Hobnail, White Florals punch set, Ruth series, $200.00 – 250.00 8-pc. set.

Douglas Parks

Doug Parks is a longtime Fenton collector. Hobnail is his passion, and he approached Fenton to make a few pieces for him. The Topaz Opalescent Boxtle is a new shape for that color. All the pieces that were made for Mr. Parks are signed.

HOBNAIL

Shape	Ware #	Blue Opalescent	Topaz Opalescent
Bowl, 10" rolled edge		$65.00 – 75.00	$ 75.00 – 85.00
Boxtle	3896		$150.00 – 175.00
Comport	3728		$ 65.00 – 75.00
Plate, 12"		$65.00 – 75.00	$ 75.00 – 85.00
Vase, 12" swung ftd.	3753	$75.00 – 90.00	$ 75.00 – 85.00

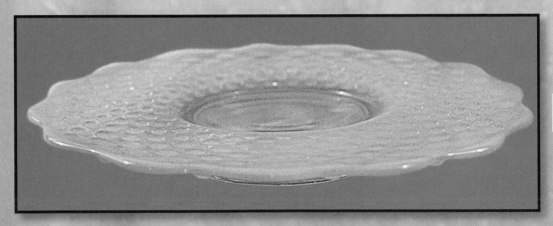

Blue Opalescent Hobnail 12" plate, $65.00 – 75.00.

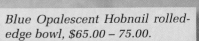

Blue Opalescent Hobnail rolled-edge bowl, $65.00 – 75.00.

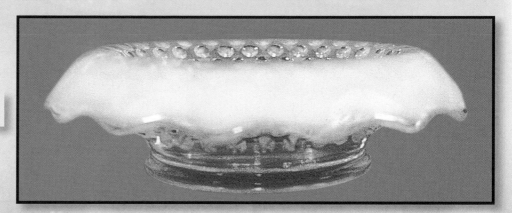

Topaz Opalescent Hobnail rolled-edge bowl, $75.00 – 85.00.

Topaz Opalescent Hobnail flared bowls, $75.00 – 85.00 each.

Topaz Opalescent Hobnail comport, $65.00 – 75.00.

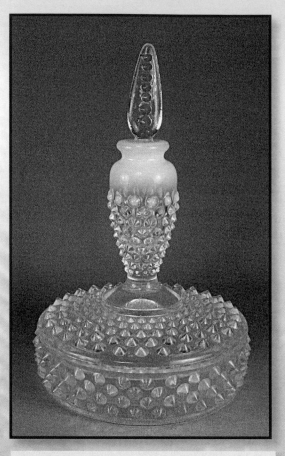

Topaz Opalescent Hobnail Boxtle, $150.00 – 175.00.

Topaz Opalescent Hobnail swung vases, $75.00 – 85.00 each.

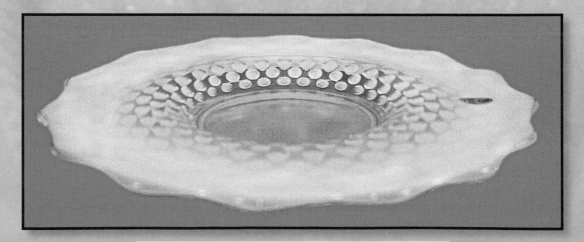

Topaz Opalescent Hobnail 12" plate, $75.00 – 85.00.

Dorothy Taylor began to love carnival glass when she, an active real estate agent, helped an elderly client with a garage sale. Dorothy purchased a large carnival glass vase from her client for $6 because she thought the woman needed the money. She was offered $40 for it later in the day, but turned the offer down because she didn't want to offend the client she was trying to help. The lady who offered the $40 did tell her that the vase was carnival glass. From that day forward, Dorothy was hooked on carnival glass. Dorothy and her husband, Bill, were part of a group of carnival glass collectors who formed the Heart of America Carnival Glass Association, one of the largest and most active clubs today. (You will find glass Fenton made for HOAGA on pages 39 – 44) Dorothy served as the group's first secretary and news editor.

As new carnival began to make an appearance, collectors of old carnival became certain that the new would decrease the value of the old. In order to protect her investment, Dorothy decided that she would learn everything she could about the new glass. To do that, she had to buy some of it. After purchasing several pieces, she found that she was buying more and more of the very pretty new carnival, and she wasn't alone. Many other collectors were finding the glass to be as beautiful as the old, and they were collecting new carnival glass as fast as it was being produced. Dorothy decided that a newsletter was necessary to document the new glass, so she created *Carnival Glass Encore*, a publication that covered the carnival glass being made by companies like Imperial, Westmoreland, and Fenton. Her ad stated, "Stop gambling! Know what you are buying, it could save you hundreds of dollars." The newsletter she produced was very successful, and collectors began asking for a book that could help them identify pieces of their new collections. In *Encore by Dorothy, Book 1*, Dorothy gave names to patterns that had only had numbers to identify them. She talked about the new colors and recommended that collectors buy new

glass when it was offered in stores and shops and not wait until it was discontinued and more expensive. She had a chart that identified marks being used for the new glassware. The first book was very successful, so a year later, *Book 2* was offered to collectors. Both books, long out of print, are highly sought after and bring much more than the low price of $6.95 each that I paid for my copies.

In 1978, due to high demand from collectors, the first Encore convention was held in Kansas. The attendance was 200, high for a first-time convention. Souvenirs for Taylor's conventions were made by both Mosser and Fenton. Fenton made a limited-edition Red Burmuda Carnival miniature seven-piece water set in the God and Home pattern for Encore's 1981 convention, and in 1983 made the Cobalt Carnival Vintage epergne for Taylor. She decided that a miniature basket in Fenton's Kitten pattern would be a perfect souvenir for Encore, so she asked Westmoreland, and later Imperial Glass, to make the basket for her. Neither of those companies were able to produce it, so the mould was taken to Fenton, where many baskets were made for her. A Ruby Carnival Kittens basket was made in 1982 to be used as a convention souvenir. It was marked "Encore, 1982, KC MO." The mould belonged to Dorothy, so the Fenton name doesn't appear on the base. The last souvenir was a Blue Carnival Kittens Umbrella, so unique that the value is much higher that you would expect.

The miniature Kittens basket was so successful that a series of baskets were made, using different plungers in order to add new designs to the interiors of the pieces. You will find a list of those patterns and the dates they were made in this chapter.

M.L.T. Glass Wholesale Division of Carnival Glass Encore was owned by Dorothy's son, Mike Taylor. The company was only advertised in 1981. Only three patterns were used — Atlantis, Hobnail, and a piece made from the bottom of the Beaded fairy lite.

ENCORE MINIATURES
(All colors are iridized.)

Pattern	Shape	Color	Year	Price
Dragon & Lotus	Basket	Peach Ice	1985	$65.00 – 75.00
Farmyard	Basket	Peach Opalescent	1984	$65.00 – 75.00
God & Home	Pitcher	Burmuda Red	1981	$55.00 – 65.00
God & Home	Tumbler	Burmuda Red	1981	$15.00 – 20.00
Kitten	Basket	Ruby	1982	$75.00 – 85.00
Kitten	Basket	Aqua Opalescent	1982	$75.00 – 85.00
Kitten	Basket	Rosalene	1990	$70.00 – 80.00
Kitten	Basket	Burmese*		$70.00 – 80.00
Kitten	Basket	Burmese		$70.00 – 80.00
Kitten	Umbrella	Blue		$75.00 – 85.00
Lion	Basket	Green Opalescent	1985	$65.00 – 75.00
Panther	Basket	Cobalt Blue	1983	$65.00 – 75.00
Parkersburg Elk	Basket	Meadow Green	1983	$70.00 – 80.00
Pony	Basket	Topaz Opalescent	1983	$75.00 – 85.00
Stag & Holly	Basket	Avon Blue	1984	$75.00 – 85.00
Vintage	Epergne	Cobalt Blue	1983	$85.00 – 95.00

*Not iridized.

A Limited Offering for the New Glass Collector of America

PEACH OPALESCENT CARNIVAL GLASS
ATLANTIS PATTERN
A Limited Edition Exclusively for M.L.T. Glass Wholesale Division of Carnival Glass Encore

This limited edition Peach Opalescent Carnival Glass was produced by skilled craftsmen in the Fenton tradition, each piece has the Fenton signature on the bottom. These pieces have gorgeous opalescence both inside and outside. The iridescence is outstanding. Two additional shapes not shown will be available soon. They are 5150 Pl D. Fan Vase 5150 Pl E. Rose bowl.

5150 Pl
Hi Bowl "A"

5150 Pl
Vase "B"

5150 Pl
Spittoon "C"

To order: mail to M.L.T. Glass
P.O. Box 11665
Kansas City, Missouri 64138   816 353 5722

Peach Opalescent Carnival Glass

A Limited Edition made Exclusively for M.L.T. Glass — Wholesale Division of Carnival Glass Encore

This limited edition of 687 pieces of Hobnail and 691 pieces of Beaded Fairy lite bottoms made in Peach Opalescent Carnival by Fenton Art Glass. Each piece marked Fenton. The iridescence & opalescence is outstanding both inside & outside.

The Green God & Home table sets are made by Wetzel Glass Co. also exclusively for MLT Glass.

Collectors contact your local dealers or Encore.

Hobnail
3628

A   B   C   D   E

3827   A   B   C   D

E

5150
CN

Dealers Mail to: MLT Glass
PO Box 11665
Kansas City, Mo. 64138
816-353-5722

MLT ASSORTMENTS

Pattern	Shape	Color	Price
Atlantis	High bowl	Peach Opalescent	$100.00 – 120.00
Atlantis	Fan vase	Peach Opalescent	$110.00 – 130.00
Atlantis	Rose bowl	Peach Opalescent	$100.00 – 120.00
Atlantis	Standard vase	Peach Opalescent	$100.00 – 120.00
Atlantis	Spittoon	Peach Opalescent	$120.00 – 135.00
Atlantis	Standard vase	French Opalescent*	$150.00 – 165.00
Hobnail	Double-crimped comport	Peach Opalescent	$45.00 – 55.00
Hobnail	Star-crimped comport	Peach Opalescent	$45.00 – 55.00
Hobnail	Footed rose bowl	Peach Opalescent	$45.00 – 55.00
Hobnail	Footed-crimped spittoon	Peach Opalescent	$60.00 – 75.00
Hobnail	Tri-top comport	Peach Opalescent	$45.00 – 55.00
Beaded	Flared bowl	Peach Opalescent	$25.00 – 35.00
Beaded	Double-crimped bowl	Peach Opalescent	$25.00 – 35.00
Beaded	Rose bowl	Peach Opalescent	$40.00 – 45.00
Beaded	Cake plate	Peach Opalescent	$40.00 – 45.00
Beaded	Banana stand	Peach Opalescent	$40.00 – 45.00
Beaded	Spittoon	Peach Opalescent	$55.00 – 70.00

*Not iridized.

Bermuda Red water set brochure, $125.00 – 150.00 7-pc. set.

Burmuda Red pitcher, $55.00 – 65.00; tumbler, $15.00 – 20.00.

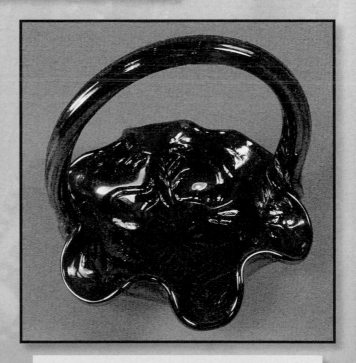

Cobalt Blue Panther mini basket, $65.00 – 75.00.

Meadow Green Parkersburg Elks mini basket, $70.00 – 80.00.

Avon Blue Stag & Holly mini basket, $75.00 – 85.00.

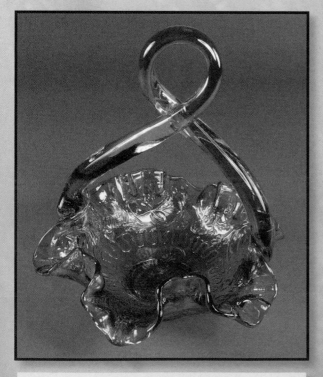

Peach Ice Dragon & Lotus mini basket, $65.00 – 75.00.

Green Opalescent Lion mini basket, $65.00 – 75.00.

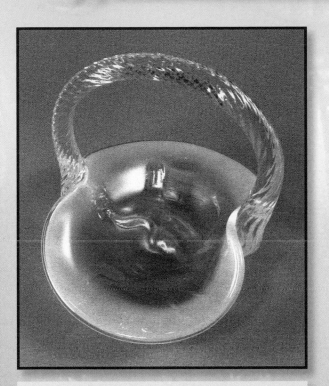

Peach Opalescent Farmyard mini basket, $65.00 – 75.00.

Ruby Carnival Kittens mini basket, $75.00 – 85.00.

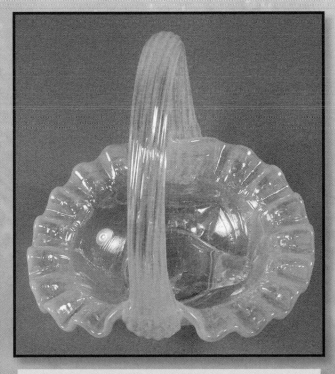

Topaz Opalescent Pony mini basket, $75.00 – 85.00.

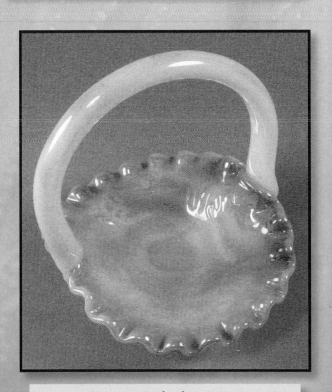

Burmese Kittens mini basket, $70.00 – 80.00.

Burmese Carnival Kittens mini basket, $70.00 – 80.00.

Rosalene Carnival Kittens mini basket, $70.00 – 80.00.

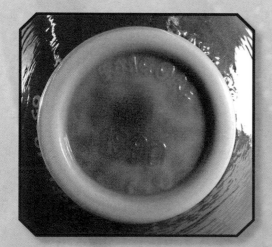

Base of the Rosalene Kittens basket.

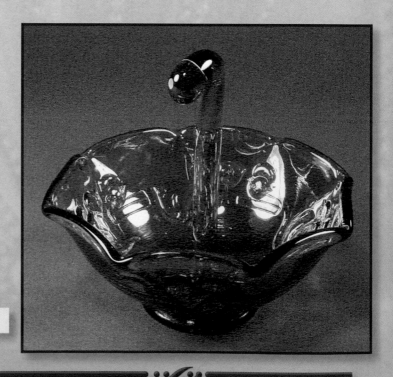

Aqua Blue Kittens Umbrella, $75.00 – 85.00.

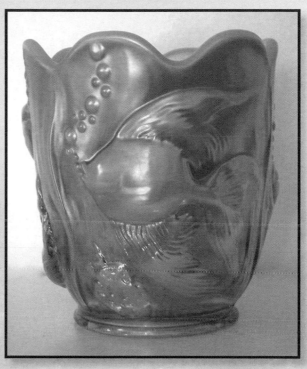

Peach Opalescent Atlantis standard vase, $100.00 – 120.00.

Royal Blue Vintage mini epergne, $85.00 – 95.00.

Peach Opalescent Atlantis rose bowl, $100.00 – 120.00.

Peach Opalescent Atlantis fan vase, $110.00 – 130.00.

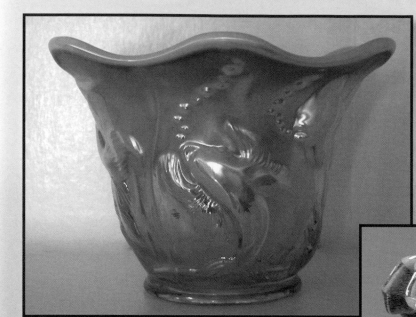

Peach Opalescent Atlantis high bowl, $100.00 – 120.00.

Peach Opalescent Hobnail double-crimped comport, $45.00 – 55.00.

Peach Opalescent Hobnail crimped comport, $45.00 – 55.00.

$\mathcal{E}$RIC $\mathcal{W}$EBER

Eric Weber started his mail order and Internet business in 2001. He has a love of Fenton glass, so it was only natural that he would approach FAGCO with an idea for a new decoration. Don Cunningham worked with him to perfect his decoration, which included violets, as a tribute to Louise Piper, and a bee, an idea he found on an antique plate. I think you will agree that it is a very attractive design.

The fox was made to sell at the 2002 FAGCA convention in Parkersburg, West Virginia. Mr. Weber will continue to buy special-order glass from Fenton, so we can look forward to seeing more beautiful glass from him. Each of his pieces is hand signed and comes with a certificate stating the number of pieces made.

Shape	Item #	Color	Edition	Value
Bell, star crimped	9662	Green Burmese	95	$65.00 – 85.00
Bell, double crimped	9662	Blue Burmese, Rosalene Crest	95	$65.00 – 85.00
Cat, stylized	5065	Green Burmese	100	$75.00 – 85.00
Epergne, single horn	7202	Green Burmese	60	$150.00 – 175.00
Fox (2002 convention)	5226	Opal Satin	95	$55.00 – 75.00

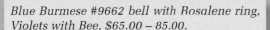

Blue Burmese #9662 bell with Rosalene ring. Violets with Bee, $65.00 – 85.00.

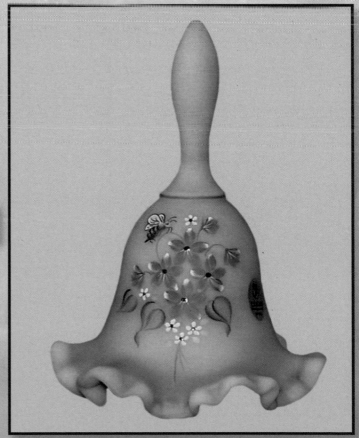

Lotus Mist Burmese #9662 bell, Violets with Bee, $65.00 – 85.00.

Lotus Mist Burmese #7202 one-horn epergne, Violets with Bee, $150.00 – 175.00.

Lotus Mist Burmese #5065 Elegant Cat, Violets with Bee, $75.00 – 85.00.

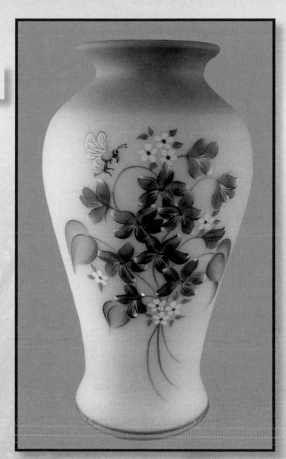

Lotus Mist vase, Violets with Bee, $125.00 – 150.00.

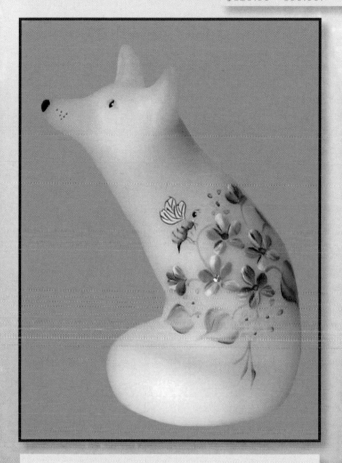

Opal #5226 Fox, Violets with Bee, $55.00 – 65.00.

Orchids in the Moonlight #7300 fairy light, $100.00 – 125.00.

The Ethan Allen Furniture company had its start in 1932, while this country was still suffering through the Great Depression. In 1936, it purchased a plant, in which it made the Colonial style furniture that made it famous. In 1943, it owned three saw mills and eleven manufacturing plants. In 1962, the company introduced an exciting new concept in merchandising, the gallery store. The Ethan Allen management has been the pioneer of the furniture industry, always changing with the changing times. It is that strategy that has kept the company at the forefront of the industry.

Every furniture store adds decorative glassware to its merchandise, because doing so gives its customers a chance to see and buy items that flatter the furniture they are buying. Fenton was a logical choice for Ethan Allen. In 1984, Ethan Allen purchased a grouping of Dusty Rose and Federal Blue items. Fenton's Pineapple pattern was revived and made in Federal Blue, a gunmetal gray-blue. The 9" handled tray is so rare than even this more recent piece is hard to find. The Dusty Rose Hex bowl, the Poppy lamp, and the Mandarin vase were made using moulds purchased from the Holophane Company, who had bought its moulds from the Verlys Company of France.

DUSTY ROSE SATIN (SO)
DUSTY ROSE OVERLAY (UD)

Description	Item #	Price
Bowl, hexagonal	8226 SO	$125.00 – 150.00
Bowl, rolled rim	4809 SO	$50.00 – 60.00
Candlesticks	7475 SO	(pr.) $50.00 – 60.00
Epergne, Diamond Lace	4809 SO	$150.00 – 200.00
Lamp, Dogwood	9650 UD	$125.00 – 150.00
Vase, Mandarin	8251 UD	$125.00 – 150.00

FEDERAL BLUE

Description	Item #	Price
Bowl, 12" square Pineapple	9622 FB	$75.00 – 85.00
Candlestick, double Pineapple	9672 FB	$65.00 – 75.00
Comport, 6" Pineapple	9628 FB	$40.00 – 50.00
Hen on Nest	5182 FB	$50.00 – 65.00
Tray, 9" oval Pineapple	9618 FB	$65.00 – 75.00

Dusty Rose Overlay #9650 lamp made from this vase, $145.00 – 165.00.

Dusty Rose Overlay #8251 Mandarin vase, $125.00 – 150.00.

Dusty Rose Satin #8226 hexagonal bowl, $125.00 – 150.00.

The Frederick Atkins Company is an international merchandising and marketing company that is based in New York. Many of the largest department stores in the United States are represented by it. It purchases large amounts of inventory at very reduced prices and distributes it to member stores. In 1995, Fenton made the glass shown in the photos to be sold in the stores.

Sea Mist Green #5053 rose bowl, $35.00 – 40.00.

Sea Mist Green #9537 Strawberry basket, $25.00 – 30.00.

Sea Mist Green #9531 Strawberry comport, $18.00 – 22.00.

Sea Mist Green #3265 Wide Rib pitcher, $25.00 – 28.00. This Pitcher was sold in Fenton's regular 1994 catalog, but it was decorated.

Gift Shop, FAGCO

The Fenton Art Glass Company Gift Shop may be attached to the glass factory, but it is a separate business that buys glass from Fenton and giftware from many other companies. The glass sold in the gift shop ranges from select seconds, gift shop exclusives, experimental and one-of-a-kind pieces, and first-quality Fenton at retail prices. It is the gift shop that sells the FAGCA special glass at the convention. After some consideration, I decided that it would be better to include the gift shop than to deny collectors important information.

BLACK CREST

In the 1960s, before Fenton signed its glassware, it made a large quantity of milk glass with a spun black edge. This treatment had been made for the Fred Meyer stores in the early 1950s, but those pieces were made with the more translucent Opal glass that was used for Aqua Crest. The 1960s pieces of Black Crest were displayed in the gift shop as a contrast to the Flame Crest that was sold in the Fenton catalog. No one knows why the beautiful Black Crest pieces were not added to the line. It couldn't have been because they weren't attractive, but of course, we are looking at it with the knowledge of the trends of the last 20 years, and we all know how colors come and go with the times. Maybe the company should try making it again now.

Shape	Ware #	Black Crest
Ashtray	7377	$45.00 – 50.00
Basket, 7"	7237	$125.00 – 150.00
Basket, 6½" crimped	7336	$150.00 – 175.00
Bowl, 12"	7321	$85.00 – 115.00
Comport, low foot	7228	$55.00 – 75.00
Comport, high foot	7429	$100.00 – 125.00
Plate, 6"	7219	$25.00 – 35.00
Plate, 8¼"	7217	$30.00 – 40.00
Plate 12"	7212	$50.00 – 65.00
Relish, heart shaped	7333	$125.00 – 150.00
Tidbit, 8½" bowl	7498	$65.00 – 75.00
Tidbit, 2-tier	7294	$65.00 – 75.00
Vase, 6¼" single-crimped fan	7357	$65.00 – 75.00
Vase, 6" melon	7451	$75.00 – 85.00

Black Crest #7294 2-tier tidbit, $65.00 – 75.00.

Black Crest #7377 ashtray, $45.00 – 50.00.

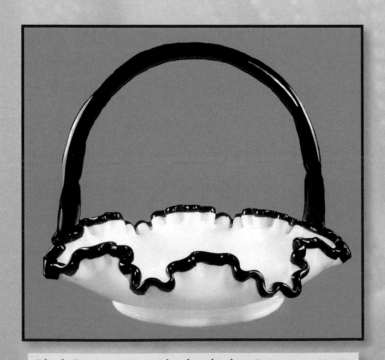

Black Crest #7236 6½" bonbon basket, $150.00 – 175.00.

Black Crest bonbon basket, top view.

Black Crest #7429 high ftd. comport, $100.00 – 125.00.

Black Crest #7357 fan vase, $65.00 – 75.00.

Black Crest #7228 low ftd. comport, $55.00 – 65.00.

Black Crest #7212 12" plate, $50.00 – 65.00.

Black Crest #1924 5" top hat, $45.00 – 55.00.

Black Crest #7333 heart-shaped relish, $125.00 – 150.00.

Black Crest #7421 melon vase, $75.00 – 85.00. Black Crest #7237 7" basket, $125.00 – 150.00.

LEADED GLASS WINDOW HANGINGS

In the 1980s, when business was slow, Fenton was trying a variety of new products. It added the Christine Victoria to its catalog and displayed it heavily in the gift shop. Another one of those products made in the name of diversity was the leaded glass window hanging, which had been made popular by decorating magazines. Several employees were sent to attend classes that were held to teach the finer points of making leaded glass. Fenton purchased the flat glass it needed from a wholesaler, and some very beautiful leaded glass pieces were created.

Once finished they were sent to the decorating department, where the final details were added. The decorators put their names on all the painted pieces, just as they do for any other products they decorate. If graded by the workmanship the experiment was a success, but in sales it was less successful, and the experiment ended. To identify Fenton pieces, look for an artist signature or a sand carving that is a Fenton design, such as the Sophisticated Ladies design on the piece shown here. All of these pieces can be considered rare and usually command high prices.

Iris Purple Slag & Purple Transparent leaded glass window hanging, $150.00 – 175.00.

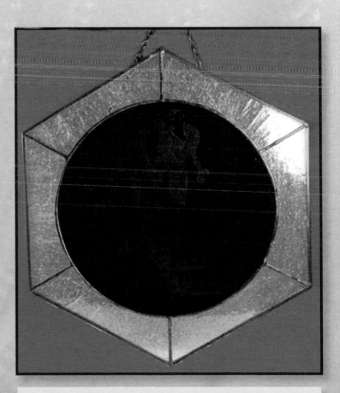

Sophisticated Ladies Ruby & Crystal window hanging, $175.00 – 195.00.

Strawberries on Opal with Green & Ruby frame, $125.00 – 150.00.

OFFHAND ART GLASS

Over the years, Fenton has experimented with making offhand glassware. The success of beautiful art glass almost never comes until several years after the production date. In 1926, Fenton hired a group of European glass workers who knew how to make this labor-intensive glassware. They worked for only one year, because Fenton simply couldn't sell the glass. It seemed too expensive to stores who bought the pressed or blown glass made by Fenton in its regular line of products. At the end of the experiment, Fenton offered the glassware that was still in its inventory to its employees at very reduced prices. Some items were sold for only a dollar or two, a fact that seems beyond our imaginations. Even small pieces of the 1926 art glass sell for several thousands of dollars today.

In the mid-1970s, Fenton hired Robert Barber to design a group of items that would be sold in very limited amounts. He was told make as much glass as he was able to, and the company would decide which pieces would be offered as part of the Barber Collection. This glass was intended to be sold in higher-priced furniture or gift shops, but once again, the plan simply didn't work. To make it desirable to accounts that were dubious that they could sell it, Fenton guaranteed the sales. It would take back any glass not sold in the time periods specified

by the stores who bought it. When the deadlines were up, Fenton found itself with a large inventory of returns. Again, the glass was sold at bargain prices in the gift shop. The gift shop also sold some of the glass Robert Barber made that didn't get added to the Barber Collection. A lot of those pieces were sold in a "cage sale" to Fenton's employees, but many pieces were sold in the FAGCA "Special Glass Room" event held at its convention. Once in a while, some of that glass can still be found in the Special Glass Room. Lucky are the collectors who recognize those pieces and add them to their own collections.

After the failure of the Barber Collection, Fenton decided to try a less difficult art glass that would still have the Hanging Heart design but would be made in a mould. After the glass came out of the mould, the hanging hearts and threading were added by the same process that was used for the more expensive offhand pieces designed by Robert Barber. The glass was still too expensive to make and was hard to sell. The design just didn't fit with the glassware most customers recognized as Fenton. Again, the gift shop bought the excess glass and sold it over several years' time.

All this has changed in the last 10 years. Now collectors are paying enormous prices for the 1926 art glass pieces and are also searching for the 1975 and 1976 Hanging Heart pieces. Fenton has had a lot of success with selling offhand glass made by Dave Fetty, a glass artist who had worked with Robert Barber. Dave retired only to find himself working almost full time to produce some of the most beautiful glass Fenton has ever sold. Originally, Dave came back to make his beautiful offhand glass for the FAGCA Special Glass Room. But the sale was such a success that the club asked him to do the same thing for the next year. His glass is in such demand that several pieces are sold in Fenton's catalogs of limited editions, and you can always find pieces in Fenton's gift shop.

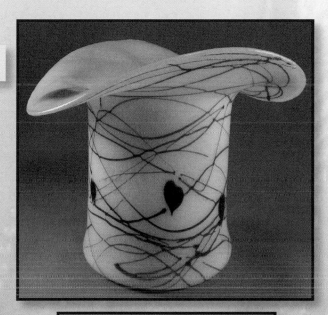

Custard & Black Hanging Heart #1920, 12" hat, $450.00 – 500.00.

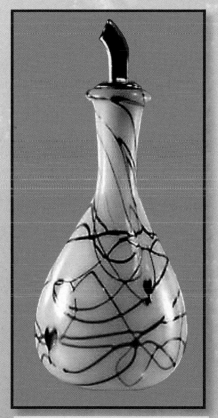

Custard & Black Hanging Heart offhand Barber bottle, ground pontil, $250.00 – 275.00.

Custard & Black Hanging Heart offhand large cruet, ground pontil, $225.00 – 250.00.

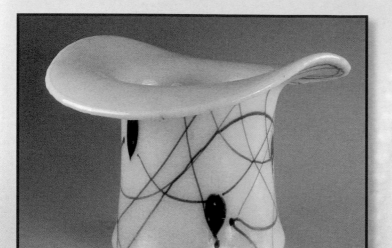

Turquoise & Black Hanging Heart #1923, 6" hat, $250.00 – 300.00.

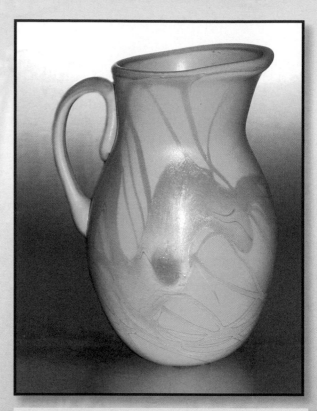

Turquoise & Gold-Threaded offhand pitcher, $175.00 – 225.00.

This tumbler was a color-test piece for Robert Barber. He was checking how colors would look when added to Crystal. $150.00 – 165.00.

Red & Opal Dave Fetty Bird, $125.00 – 145.00.

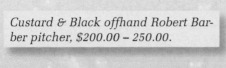
Custard & Black offhand Robert Barber pitcher, $200.00 – 250.00.

Most of the offhand pieces are easily recognized as Fenton, but the Controlled Bubble Barber bottle is a piece that has no resemblance to other Fenton products. This bottle was part of a grouping made by Delmar Stowasser, who had worked for Erickson Glass prior to coming to Fenton. Some, but not all, of Delmar's pieces have the acid-etched Fenton mark, but not all were signed. All were made in this color combination, with the exception of one that has been found in Ruby and Crystal. I have a partial list of shapes Delmar made in this style. There were several vases, wine and water glasses, horns of plenty, candlesticks, handled jugs, rose bowls and ashtrays. Prices range from $75 for the stemware and ashtrays to $200 to $275 for the larger or more collectible shapes like the candlesticks, jugs, etc. I've not seen many pieces made this way, so there is no way to set exact values. If you see a piece in this style, pay whatever price you are comfortable paying. Even if you overpay for one, it could reach that value soon after you buy it.

Controlled Bubble Barber bottle, Crystal & Jamestown Blue, $225.00 – 350.00.

February Sale

Every February, the Fenton Art Glass Gift Shop has a sale that includes colors and shapes that are not offered in the FAGCO catalog. The Almost Heaven Blue Slag pieces were made for the 1989 sale. I'm not sure of the dates for the Dusty Rose heart-shaped vase or the Sea Mist Green Marble, but they were also made for the February sale.

Almost Heaven #7236 6½" bonbon basket, February sale, $150.00 – 165.00.

Almost Heaven Hobnail bowl & pitcher set, $225.00 – 325.00.

Sea Mist Green Grape & Cable humidor, $150.00 – 175.00.

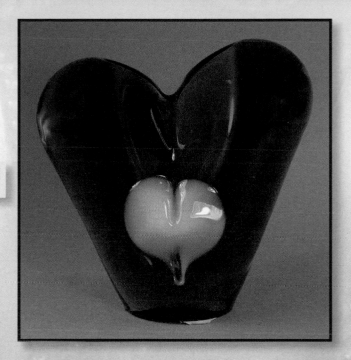

Dusty Rose heart-shaped vase with Opal heart on the front, $75.00 – 85.00.

SAMPLES AND FAGCA SPECIAL GLASS ROOM

Burmese sample of a Lion Head flowerpot, $100.00 – 120.00.

Colonial Green Butterfly 3-hole candleholder, $75.00 – 95.00.

Chocolate Glass doll, $45.00 – 50.00.

Experimental 1980s Blue & Green Ducklings. Blue, $50.00 – 65.00; Green, $50.00 – 65.00.

Experimental 1980s Iridized Purple Slag Duckling, $65.00 – 75.00, & Peach Satin Duckling, $50.00 – 65.00.

Both these Sunshine Yellow ducklings were experimental pieces, but the Sunshine Yellow Shiny Duckling was added to Fenton's catalog line later. Sunshine Yellow Satin, $50.00 – 65.00; Shiny, $35.00 – 45.00.

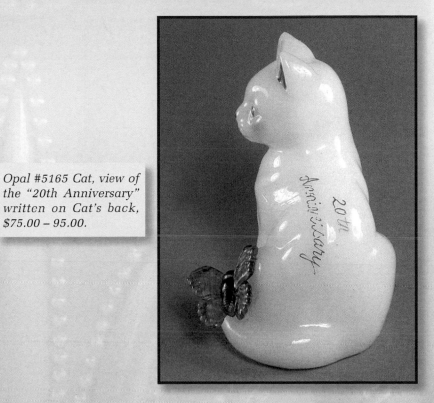

Opal #5165 Cat, view of the "20th Anniversary" written on Cat's back, $75.00 – 95.00.

Opal #5165 Cat with an attached Green Butterfly, blushed cheeks, $75.00 – 95.00.

Malachite Temple bell, experimental color, $100.00 – 125.00.

Malachite Grape & Cable tobacco jar, experimental color, $400.00 – 450.00.

Milk Glass Satin Praying Boy plaque (only one known), $225.00 – 250.00.

Milk Glass Satin Praying Girl plaque (only one known), $225.00 – 250.00.

Rosalene Knobby Bull's-eye covered candy, $200.00 – 225.00.

Rosalene Mother & Child open candy jar, $125.00 – 150.00.

Opaline with Rosalene Crest, Fern pattern, #4026 ewer, $150.00 – 175.00.

Rose Satin with a Crystal Crest, #1923 6" hat, $125.00 – 150.00. This hat looks very similar to the Rose Overlay hat with a Crystal Crest that was made for Weil Ceramics.

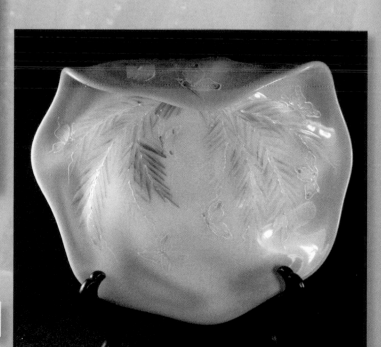

Rosalene Paisley plate, shaped with a turned-over edge, decorated, $125.00 – 150.00.

Favrene Alley Cat, made for FAGCA Special Glass Room, $700.00 – 750.00.

Purple Slag Alley Cat, made for FAGCA Special Glass Room, $450.00 – 500.00.

Green Marble #5151 Bear Cub, made for FAGCA Special Glass Room, $100.00 – 125.00.

Sea Mist Green 2" Bear, Violet #5251 Bear, and Twilight Blue 2" bear. The small 2" bears were only sold in the FAGCA Special Glass Room in Sea Mist Green, Sea Mist Green Iridized, Twilight Blue, and Twilight Blue Iridized. They all sell for $75.00 – 100.00. Violet Bear #5251 2½" is for size comparison only.

Opal Satin Santa Box made from an old Fostoria mould and sold in FAGCA Special Glass Room. The top and the base are irregular shaped and difficult to produce matching the lid to the base so will not be put into Fenton's catalog line in this shape, $200.00 – 225.00.

Rosalene powder, two perfumes, and tray sold in Special Glass Room. Optics on the perfume bottles and the powder jar seldom match. That doesn't devalue the set. $350.00 – 400.00.

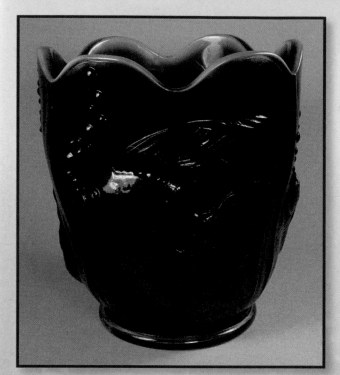

Plum Opalescent #5150 Atlantis vase, also made in Plum Opalescent Iridized, $150.00 – 175.00.

Pink Chiffon Iridized Mermaid vase (Holophane mould), $250.00 – 275.00.

Mermaid vase, Empress Rose mixed with another color, $250.00 – 275.00.

In 1985, as the business from Levay began to wind down, Fenton realized that it could do the same kind of business through the gift shop. The pieces included in a "Limited Offer to the Antique Trade" were marketed to the same group that had been Levay's customer base. None of the pieces appeared in a Fenton catalog or on a price list, which would make it much more difficult for future collectors to research. I don't have all the flyers for these pieces, but for those that are missing I will list the pieces I know were made.

This practice ended in 1992, about the same time that Fenton began its relationship with QVC. The Persian Pearl pieces were the last to be sold in this fashion.

SELECTED GREEN OPALESCENT BLOWN OPTICS

An assortment of blown optics in Green Opalescent handmade glassware. Each piece made in a different optic and blown with the quality and craftsmanship in the famous Fenton tradition. The opalescent portion shows a fiery quality when held to the light, a unique characteristic of fine opalescent glassware.

3138GO
7" Basket
Ribbed Spiral Optic
$49.00

1353GO
10" Tulip Vase
Fine Dot Optic
$40.00

1803GO
3 pc. Fairy Light
Fern Optic
Includes Candle
$85.00

2323GO
10" Double Crimped Bowl
Double Wedding Ring Optic
$55.00

1738GO
5½" Basket
Diamond Optic
$37.50

Handles on baskets are ribbed and struck creating a candy like appearance. Edges are crimped using our famous double crimp.

**Available at The Fenton Gift Shop
and Selected Antique Dealers**

The Fenton Art Glass Company *Fenton* Williamstown, WV 26187

Send $6.00 for our full color, 80-page catalog and supplement, Dept. GR4.

GREEN OPALESCENT SPECIAL OPTICS

Shape	Optic	Ware #	Value
Basket, 5½"	Diamond Optic	1738GO	$75.00 – 95.00
Basket, 7"	Ribbed Spiral	3138GO	$100.00 – 120.00
Bowl, 10" DC	Double Wedding Ring	2323GO	$75.00 – 95.00
Fairy light	Fern Optic	1803GO	$150.00 – 175.00
Pitcher, water	Twisted Drapery	2007GO	$225.00 – 250.00
Tumbler	Twisted Drapery	2007GO	$45.00 – 55.00
Vase, 10" JIP	Fine Dot	1353GO	$75.00 – 95.00

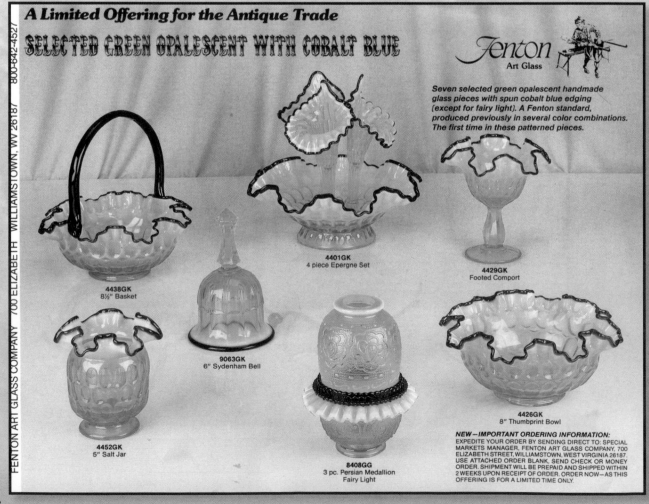

A Limited Offering for the Antique Trade

SELECTED GREEN OPALESCENT WITH COBALT BLUE

Fenton Art Glass

Seven selected green opalescent handmade glass pieces with spun cobalt blue edging (except for fairy light). A Fenton standard, produced previously in several color combinations. The first time in these patterned pieces.

FENTON ART GLASS COMPANY   700 ELIZABETH   WILLIAMSTOWN, WV 26187   800-642-4527

4438GK
8½" Basket

4401GK
4 piece Epergne Set

4429GK
Footed Comport

4452GK
5" Salt Jar

9063GK
6" Sydenham Bell

8408GG
3 pc. Persian Medallion
Fairy Light

4426GK
8" Thumbprint Bowl

NEW—IMPORTANT ORDERING INFORMATION: EXPEDITE YOUR ORDER BY SENDING DIRECT TO: SPECIAL MARKETS MANAGER, FENTON ART GLASS COMPANY, 700 ELIZABETH STREET, WILLIAMSTOWN, WEST VIRGINIA 26187. USE ATTACHED ORDER BLANK. SEND CHECK OR MONEY ORDER. SHIPMENT WILL BE PREPAID AND SHIPPED WITHIN 2 WEEKS UPON RECEIPT OF ORDER. ORDER NOW—AS THIS OFFERING IS FOR A LIMITED TIME ONLY.

GREEN OPALSCENT WITH COBALT BLUE EDGE

Shape	Pattern	Ware #	Value
Basket	Thumbprint	4438GK	$125.00 – 150.00
Bell	Sydenham	9063GK	$75.00 – 85.00
Bowl	Thumbprint	4426GK	$45.00 – 55.00
Comport	Thumbprint	4429GK	$35.00 – 40.00
Epergne	Thumbprint	4401GK	$275.00 – 350.00
Fairy light	Persian Medallion	8408GG	$125.00 – 150.00
Salt Jar, 5"	Thumbprint	4452GK	$75.00 – 85.00

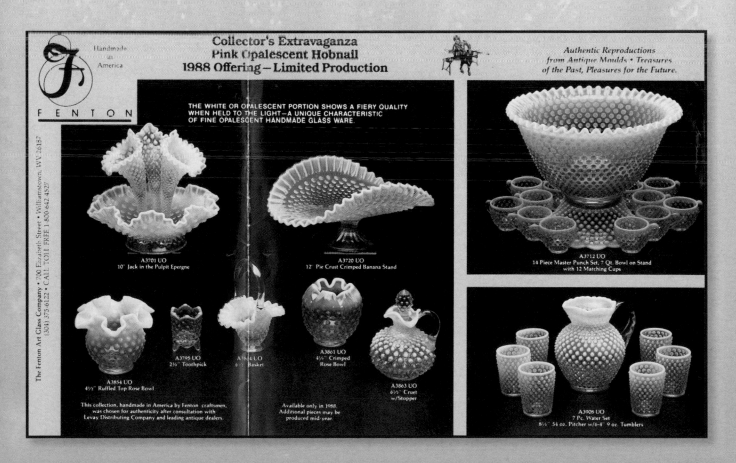

Collector's Extravaganza
Pink Opalescent Hobnail
1988 Offering – Limited Production

Handmade in America

FENTON

The Fenton Art Glass Company • 720 Elizabeth Street • Williamstown, WV 26187 • (304) 375-6122 • CALL TOLL FREE: 1-800-642-4527

THE WHITE OR OPALESCENT PORTION SHOWS A FIERY QUALITY WHEN HELD TO THE LIGHT—A UNIQUE CHARACTERISTIC OF FINE OPALESCENT HANDMADE GLASS WARE.

Authentic Reproductions from Antique Moulds • Treasures of the Past, Pleasures for the Future.

A3801 UO
Miniature Epergne Set

A3830 UO
10" Pie Crust Crimped Basket

A3000 UO
Pitcher and Bowl Set

A3335 UO
Looped Handle Basket

A3937 UO
7" Handled Bon Bon

A3362 UO
6½" Jack in the Pulpit Blown Vase

A3308 UO
25" Gone with the Wind Lamp

This collection, handmade in America by Fenton craftsmen, was chosen for authenticity after consultation with Levay Distributing Company and leading antique dealers.

PINK OPALSCENT HOBNAIL

Description	Ware #	Value
Banana stand	A3720UO	$150.00 – 165.00
Basket, 6½"	A3834UO	$65.00 – 75.00
Basket, loop handled	A3335UO	$100.00 – 120.00
Basket, 10"	A3830UO	$100.00 – 120.00
Bonbon, 7" handled	A3937UO	$45.00 – 55.00
Cruet, 6½"	A3863UO	$125.00 – 150.00
Epergne, miniature	A3801UO	$100.00 – 125.00
Epergne, 10" JIP	A3701UO	$200.00 – 250.00
Lamp, GWTW	A3308UO	$350.00 – 400.00
Pitcher & bowl set	A3000UO	$250.00 – 300.00
Punch bowl set, 14-pc.	A3712UO	$350.00 – 400.00

Description	Ware #	Value
Rose bowl, 4½" crimped	A3861UO	$65.00 – 75.00
Rose bowl, 4½" ruffled top	A3854UO	$65.00 – 75.00
Toothpick holder, 2½"	A3795UO	$25.00 – 35.00
Vase, 6½" JIP	A3362UO	$65.00 – 75.00
Water set, 7-pc.	A3908UO	$250.00 – 300.00

8234 XC
Persian Medallion
Double Crimped
Footed Comport

4801 XC
4 Pc. Diamond Lace
Epergne

9027 XC
Double Crimped Grape and Cable Bowl

8330 XC
7" Basketweave Open Edged Basket
with Looped Candy Striped Handle

9638 XC
3-toed Grape Basket
Double Crimped with
Candy Striped Handle

9580 XC
Button and Arch Covered Butter

8231 XC
Handled Multi-Fruit Comport
with 8-point Crimp

1803 XC
3 Pc. Fairy Light
Fern Optic

1865 XC
Fern Optic Cruet
with Candy Striped
Handle

2323 XC
10" Double Crimped Bowl
Double Wedding Ring Optic

1353 XC
10" Tulip Vase
(Jack in the Pulpit)
Fine Dot Optic

3138 XC
7" Ribbed Spiral Optic Basket
with Candy Striped Handle

1492 XC
Coin Dot Top Hat

1435 XC
5" Coin Dot Top Hat
Basket with Candy
Striped Handle

1461 XC
Coin Dot Creamer
with Struck
Ribbed Candy
Striped Handle

1830 XC
5½" Double Crimped Basket
Fern Optic with Candy
Striped Handle

Collector's Extravaganza
Persian Blue Opalescent
1989 Offering—Limited Production

Authentic Reproductions from Antique Moulds • Treasures of the Past, Pleasures for the Future.
This collection, handmade in America by Fenton craftsmen, was chosen for authenticity after consultation with Levay Distributing Company and leading antique dealers.

FENTON

The white or opalescent portion shows a fiery quality when held to the light.— A unique characteristic of the opalescent handmade glassware.

0640 AS
11 Pc. Persian Blue Opalescent Hobnail Assortment consisting of one water set and two each of the fairy light, cruet, bell, looped handle 7" basket and 4½" basket

3908 XC
7 Pc. Water Set
8¼" 54 oz. Pitcher w/6-4" 9 oz. Tumblers

3863 XC
6½" cruet w/stopper

3608 XC
Hobnail Fairy Light

3834 XC
4½" Basket with ribbed handle

3313 XC
21" Student Lamp with Prisms

3334 XC
7" Basket with ribbed looped handle

3645 XC
Hobnail Bell

3712 XC
14 Piece Master Punch Set, 7 Qt. Bowl on Stand with 12 Matching Cups

The Fenton Art Glass Co. • 700 Elizabeth St. • Williamstown, WV 26187 (304) 375-6122 Call Toll FREE to order 1-800-642-4527

FENTON

Persian Blue Opalescent

The opalescent that clings to the highlights of each pattern is created by special ingredients in the glass batch and the controlled and skillful firing by Fenton craftsmen. No two pieces are exactly alike.

0608AS
16 Pc. Persian Blue Opalescent Assortment

Includes one each of all items on this page except for the lamp and the water set.

33 hanging Crystal Prisms give this lamp a rare antique look.

1413 XC
22" Coin Dot Lamp

1404 XC
7 Pc. Coin Dot Water Set

PERSIAN BLUE OPALSCENT

Description	Pattern	Ware	Value
Basket, 4½"	Hobnail	3834XC	$55.00 – 65.00
Basket, 5" hat	Coin Dot	1435XC	$75.00 – 95.00
Basket, 5½" DC	Fern Optic	1830XC	$100.00 – 125.00
Basket, 7"	Basketweave Open Edge	8330XC	$75.00 – 85.00
Basket, 7"	Ribbed Spiral Optic	3138XC	$100.00 – 125.00
Basket, 7" loop handled	Hobnail	3334XC	$75.00 – 95.00
Basket, 3-toed	Fine Cut & Grape	9638XC	$100.00 – 120.00
Bell	Hobnail	3645XC	$25.00 – 35.00
Bowl, DC	Grape & Cable	9027XC	$65.00 – 80.00
Bowl, 10" DC	Double Wedding Ring Optic	2323XC	$80.00 – 100.00
Butter dish	Button Arches	9580XC	$80.00 – 100.00
Comport	Handled Multi-fruit	8231XC	$50.00 – 65.00
Comport, DC	Persian Medallion	8234XC	$75.00 – 85.00
Creamer	Coin Dot	1461XC	$45.00 – 55.00
Cruet, 6½"	Hobnail	3863XC	$65.00 – 75.00
Cruet	Fern Optic	1865XC	$150.00 – 175.00
Epergne, 4-pc.	Diamond Lace	4801XC	$200.00 – 225.00
Fairy light, 2-pc.	Hobnail	3608XC	$45.00 – 65.00
Fairy light, 3-pc.	Fern Optic	1803XC	$175.00 – 200.00
Hat	Coin Dot	1492XC	$45.00 – 55.00
Lamp, 22"	Coin Dot	1413XC	$250.00 – 300.00
Lamp, 21"	Hobnail	3908XC	$200.00 – 250.00
Punch set, 14-pc. master	Hobnail	3712XC	$350.00 – 400.00
Water set, 7-pc.	Hobnail	3908XC	$275.00 – 325.00
Water set, 7-pc.	Coin Dot	1404XC	$275.00 – 325.00

Light Amethyst Carnival
★ 1991 LIMITED EDITION OFFERING ★

Light Amethyst Carnival

Iridescent Glass was first developed in the mid 1800's in Europe. Fenton is known as the originator of Iridescent Glass (also known as carnival glass) in pressed patterned ware in the United States and made the first pieces in 1907. The original carnival was made in different shades of amethyst, from light to dark, as well as other colors. Fenton began to reissue Carnival Glass in 1970 in dark amethyst and other colors such as ruby and cobalt blue. This is the first time this beautiful light amethyst has been made since the early years of the company.

FENTON

4609 DT
5 pc. Water Set,
Fruit

4645 DT
Tumbler, Fruit

4646 DT
Basket w/
looped handle,
Innovation

4603 DT
Lamp, Innovation
15" h.

4680 DT
Butter w/Cover, Regency

5254 DT
Owl Figurine, 5½"

4643 DT
Cuspidor, 3-Toed, Innovation

4611 DT
Plate, Panelled Grape
Good Luck, 12"

4618 DT
Bowl, Oval, 10" l.

Collector's Extravaganza

Light Amethyst Carnival
★ 1991 LIMITED EDITION OFFERING ★

**0156 AS
12 Pc. Amethyst Carnival Assortment**
Includes one each of all pieces except the punch bowl set, water set and lamp.

FENTON

Handmade
in
America

4619 DT
Bowl,
Good Luck

4601 DT
14 pc. Punch Bowl
Set, Panelled Grape
(Punch Bowl—12" h. x
13¼" in.)

4642 DT
Punch Cup, Panelled
Grape

4679 DT
Covered Box, Eagle, 6½" w. x 6" h.

9065 DT
Bell, Sables Arch, 6"

9799 DT
Fenton Logo

4644 DT
Toothpick, Diamond and
Panel

4617 DT
Basket, 3-Toed,
Innovation,
7"

Collector's Extravaganza

The Fenton Art Glass Company • 700 Elizabeth Street • Williamstown, WV 26187 • (304) 375-6122 Call Toll Free Orders Only 1-800-933-6866 Customer Service Only 1-800-933-6766

LIGHT AMETHYST CARNIVAL

Description	Pattern	Ware #	Value
Basket, loop handled	Innovation	4646DT	$75.00 – 85.00
Basket, 7" 3-toed	Innovation	4617DT	$85.00 – 100.00
Bell, 6"	Sables Arch	9065DT	$50.00 – 65.00
Bowl	Good Luck	4619DT	$75.00 – 85.00
Bowl, 10" oval	Innovation	4618DT	$75.00 – 85.00
Butter w/cover	Regency	8680DT	$100.00 – 120.00
Covered box	Eagle	4679DT	$75.00 – 100.00
Cuspidor	Innovation	4643DT	$65.00 – 75.00
Figurine, 5½"	Owl	5254DT	$65.00 – 75.00
Lamp, 15"	Innovation	4603DT	$150.00 – 200.00
Logo	Fenton	9799DT	$45.00 – 55.00
Plate, 12"	Good Luck	4611DT	$65.00 – 85.00
Punch cup	Paneled Grape	4642DT	$20.00 – 22.00
Punch set, 14-pc.	Paneled Grape	4601DT	$275.00 – 325.00
Toothpick	Diamond & Panel	4644DT	$24.00 – 28.00
Tumbler	Innovation	4645DT	$20.00 – 25.00
Water set, 5-pc.	Innovation	4609DT	$150.00 – 200.00

STIEGEL BLUE OPALESCENT

Description	Pattern	Ware #	Value
Basket, single crimp, mini	Paneled Grape	4613BO	$65.00 – 75.00
Butter dish	Paneled Grape	4667BO	$75.00 – 95.00
Comport, covered	Saw Tooth	4612BO	$75.00 – 95.00
Creamer	Peacock	4673BO	$30.00 – 35.00
Sugar	Peacock	4673BO	$35.00 – 40.00
Water set, 5-pc. mini size	Paneled Grape	4614BO	$85.00 – 100.00
Water set, 5-pc. full size	Paneled Grape	4650BO	$150.00 – 175.00

FENTON

Historic Collection

Handmade in the age old manner in the USA

Persian Pearl
★ 1992 LIMITED EDITION OFFERING

Save 5%!
0058 AS
14 Pc. Persian Pearl Assortment
Includes 1 each of everything except the lamp, waterset and logo; and 2 each of the bell and mini basket.

3077 XV Basket, Spiral, 11"

4601 XV 14 Pc. Punch Bowl Set, Paneled Grape (1 bowl, 1 base, 12 cups)

4642 XV Punch Cup, Paneled Grape

3701 XV 4 Pc. Epergne, Hobnail

3183 XV Vase, Tulip, 6½"

3567 XV Bell, Spanish Lace, 6"

2056 XV Vase, Curtain, 5"

3938 XV Bowl, Hobnail, 12"

2726 XV Creamer, Button & Arch

2727 XV Miniature Tumbler

2725 XV Basket, Button & Arch, 7"

2728 XV Basket, Button & Arch, 4"

1876 XV Tumbler, Fern

1870 XV 5 Pc. Water Set, Fern

1875 XV Pitcher, Fern, 8½"

2730 XV 5 Pc. Miniature Water Set

3674 Candle Hob 6"

The Fenton Art Glass Company • 700 Elizabeth Street • Williamstown, WV 26187 • (304) 375-6122 • Call Toll Free Orders Only 1-800-933-6866 • Customer Service Only 1-800-933-6766

PERSIAN PEARL

Description	Pattern	Ware #	Value
Basket, 4"	Button & Arch	2728XV	$50.00 – 65.00
Basket, 7"	Button & Arch	2725XV	$65.00 – 85.00
Basket, 11"	Spiral Optic	3077XV	$125.00 – 150.00
Bell, 6"	Spanish Lace	3567XV	$45.00 – 55.00
Bowl, 12"	Hobnail	3938XV	$65.00 – 75.00
Candlestick	Hobnail	3674SV	(ea.) $45.00 – 55.00
Candy box, ftd. covered	Hobnail	3784XV	$75.00 – 95.00
Creamer	Button Arches	2726XV	$40.00 – 45.00
Epergne, 4-pc.	Hobnail	3701XV	$125.00 – 150.00
Lamp, 21"	Fern Optic	1801XV	$325.00 – 350.00

Description	Pattern	Ware #	Value
Pitcher	Fern Optic	1875XV	$150.00 – 175.00
Punch set, 14-pc.	Paneled Grape	4601XV	$300.00 – 350.00
Punch cup	Paneled Grape	4642XV	$20.00 – 22.00
Tumbler, miniature	Button Arches	2727XV	$10.00 – 12.00
Tumbler	Fern Optic	1876XV	$20.00 – 24.00
Vase, 6½" tulip	Fern Optic	3183XV	$45.00 – 55.00
Vase, beaded melon	Curtain Optic	2056XV	$65.00 – 85.00
Water set, 5-pc. mini	Button & Arches	2730XV	$75.00 – 85.00
Water set, full size	Fern Optic	1870XV	$250.00 – 275.00

Glass Press — Glass Collector's Digest

The Glass Press is a publishing company located in Marietta, Ohio. David Richardson is the owner of the company, but he was previously in business with his father under the names Richardson Printing Corporation and the better-known Antique Publications. It was that company that published all of Bill Heacock's books, as well as books written by Jim Measell, Lorraine Kovar, and several other authors.

The first *Glass Collector's Digest* was printed in 1987, and the magazine itself was published until 2001. It offered an opportunity for researchers and collectors to write articles that would provide information to collectors. It contained articles on new and old glass and was well received by the collecting public, but it took time to gain subscribers. In order to speed the process, an advertisement was placed in the back cover of the magazine offering a heart-shaped Peaches and Cream candy or nut dish. If you sent in the names and addresses of five of "your loving friends," the digest would send each of them a colored brochure about the magazine. If two of those people subscribed, the magazine would send you the candy dish free. That candy dish and the bells were also sold in the Fenton catalog, and were only used by *Glass Collector's Digest* as incentives. The promotions must have worked well for the magazine, because it was only a few years later that Fenton made special-order glass for it that was sold in the magazine.

CHRISTMAS COMPORT
(All of these pieces are iridized.)

Date	Color	Value
1997	Aqua	$175.00 – 200.00
1997	Green	$150.00 – 175.00
1997	Ruby	$200.00 – 225.00
Unknown	Cobalt Blue	$175.00 – 200.00
1998	Green Opalescent	$185.00 – 220.00
2000	Plum Opalescent	$200.00 – 225.00

Date	Description	Shape	Color	Value
1988	Candy/nut dish*	Heart	Peaches & Cream	$25.00 – 35.00
1991	Bell, hand decorated*		Assorted	$15.00 – 25.00

*These items were not exclusive to Glass Press.

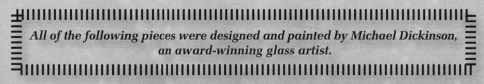

All of the following pieces were designed and painted by Michael Dickinson, an award-winning glass artist.

Date	Description	Decoration	Color	Value
1993	Lamp, 10" shade	Appalachian Woodland**	Opal Satin	$550.00 – 600.00
1997	Fairy lamp, 4"	Cabin in the Woods	Opal Satin	$85.00 – 95.00
1997	Fairy lamp, 4"	Church in the Snow	Opal Satin	$85.00 – 95.00
1997	Fairy lamp, 4"	Gazebo on the Lake	Opal Satin	$85.00 – 95.00
1997	Lamp, 22"	Cabin in the Woods	Opal Satin	$350.00 – 400.00
1997	Lamp, 22"	Church in the Snow	Opal Satin	$350.00 – 400.00
1997	Lamp, 22"	Gazebo on the Lake	Opal Satin	$350.00 – 400.00
1997	Plate, 8"	Cabin in the Woods	Opal Satin	$85.00 – 95.00
1997	Plate, 8"	Church in the Snow	Opal Satin	$85.00 – 95.00
1997	Plate, 8"	Gazebo on the Lake	Opal Satin	$85.00 – 95.00

**Signed, numbered, and sold with a certificate of authenticity.

Deep Aqua Iridized Christmas Comport made from an old Dugan mould, $175.00 – 200.00.

Glass Collector's Digest *advertisement. Peaches & Cream Heart dish. This was not limited and was part of Fenton's catalog line.* $25.00 – 30.00.

Cobalt Blue Iridized Christmas Comport, $175.00 – 200.00.

Cobalt Blue Iridized Christmas Comport, inside shot, $175.00 – 200.00.

Green Iridized Christmas Comport with straight sides, $150.00 – 175.00

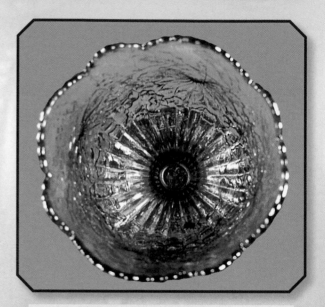

Green Iridized Christmas Comport, inside shot, $150.00 – 175.00.

Green Opalescent Iridized Christmas Comport, $185.00 – 220.00.

Plum Opalescent Iridized Christmas Comport, $200.00 – 225.00.

Cameo Opalescent Poinsettia #3137 vase, $75.00 – 95.00.

Cameo Opalescent Swirled Loop 7" basket, $100.00 – 120.00.

Ruby Carnival Christmas Comport, $200.00 – 225.00.

Gracious Touch was a party plan, similar to Tiara, that was started by Fenton in 1986 but was contracted out to Clevenger & Associates in Missouri. Like Tiara, Gracious Touch worked by signing associates who would book parties with hostesses who could earn glass according to the dollar amounts sold at their parties. Historically, this type business plan has been very successful. You only have to look at Tupperware, Princess House, and Tiara to see the potential of the party plan.

Fenton produced attractive catalogs, made beautiful pieces of special-order glassware, and held several conventions for Gracious Touch sales associates. Advertisements were placed in the *Glass Review*, a magazine aimed at the new or experienced glass collector. Initially sales were good, but not as good as Fenton needed in order to call the program a success. Gracious Touch had not been able to

recruit as many sales associates as it needed, and the costs of printing the sales kits were more than the ratio of costs to sales warranted. In 1990, Fenton discontinued the program and Gracious Touch became Fenton history.

You will probably recognize that some of the glass in this section was made using moulds that Fenton bought from other companies. There is a Cambridge Caprice vase that was made into a basket and Ram's Head candlesticks that were made using a Cambridge mould. Several McKee moulds were used. The Crystal pieces as well as a few pieces in other colors were made using McKee Plytec moulds. The Vulcan Pillar moulds as well as the Two Flowers moulds belonged to McKee. The Barred Oval pattern was an original Duncan pattern. When Fenton makes glass using other companies' moulds, each piece is signed with a scroll "F."

Sapphire Blue Opalescent Dinnerware

Sapphire Blue Opalescent
 rich and elegant that you and
 ur guests will be thrilled. Enter-
 in with a flourish. You'll be "the
 ostess with the mostess!" Hobnail
 cessories that look good enough
 eat.

Q3635 BX
7" 3 Toed Bowl
$14.50

Q3606 BX
Cream &
Sugar Set
$19.75 set

Ice Cream
Dish
Q3630 BX
$8.75

Q3002 BX Set
of 4 Dishes
$30.00

Q3949 BX
9 oz. Tumbler
$11.75

8" Hobnail
Pie Crimp Plate

Q3005 BX Set of
4-8" Plates
$44.75

(8" Plates
sold only in sets
of 4)

Q3003 BX Set of
4 Iced Teas $49.75

Q3842 BX $12.75
Hobnail Footed Iced Tea

Q3806 BX
Salt & Pepper
$18.75 Set

Q3007 BX Set of
4 Tumblers
$39.75

Q3312 BX $15.25
9¾" Dinner Plate

Q3006 BX Set of 4-9¾" Plates
Introductory Offer $49.75

HOBNAIL DINNERWARE

Shape	Ware #	Peaches 'n Cream	Sapphire Blue Opalescent
Bonbon, handled	3937	$20.00 – 22.00	$22.00 – 24.00
Bowl, 3-toed	3635	$20.00 – 24.00	$24.00 – 26.00
Bowl, ruffled ice cream	3635	$15.00 – 18.00	$18.00 – 22.00
Cream & sugar w/lid	3606	$25.00 – 30.00	$28.00 – 32.00
Pitcher, ice lip	3664	$100.00 – 125.00	$125.00 – 150.00
Plate, 8" crimped edge	3005	$20.00 – 22.00	$22.00 – 24.00
Plate, 9½" crimped edge	3312	$22.00 – 24.00	$24.00 – 26.00
Salt & pepper shakers	3806	(pair) $30.00 – 35.00	$35.00 – 38.00
Tumbler, flat	3007	$14.00 – 18.00	$16.00 – 22.00
Tumbler, footed ice tea	3842	$24.00 – 28.00	$25.00 – 32.00

Sapphire Blue Opalescent #2851 Wild Rose & Bowknot vase, $85.00 – 100.00. Country Cranberry #5838 7½" basket, $75.00 – 100.00.

Antiques of the Future

Last summer, during the Fenton Art Glass Collectors of America convention in Marietta, Ohio, a local businessman was overheard saying, "Every other business makes products that wear out and become less valuable each year. Fenton Glass makes products that increase in value every year. That's a very unique position to be in." You know what? He was absolutely right.

Each Fenton item in this catalog is designed to appreciate in its worth. It's quite probable that you can buy these pieces, use them for a period of years, and then sell them for more than the original price. Two of the pieces that are designed with this in mind are:

Q2851 IA — Vase in Wild Rose & Bowknot pattern. Made in Sapphire Blue Opalescent and iridized with a special mother of pearl finish. A carnival glass collector's dream. $25.00.

Q5838CC — Country Cranberry Basket. Pure gold ruby glass is encased in an outer layer of sparkling crystal before the twisted crystal handle is skillfully applied. $45.00.

Q2851 IA
Carnival Vase
8"

Q5838 CC
Country Cranberry
7½" Basket

Sapphire Blue Opalescent #2851 Wild Rose & Bowknot vase, $85.00 – 100.00.

Shell Pink Iridescent #2851 Wild Rose & Bowknot vase, $85.00 – 100.00.

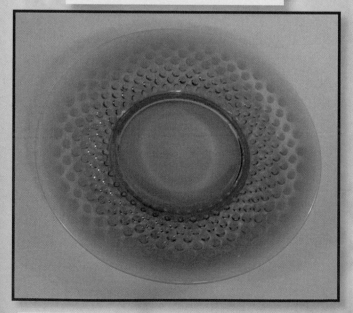

Sapphire Blue Opalescent 9¾" crimped plate, $24.00 – 26.00.

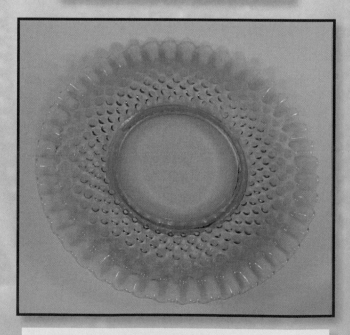

Sapphire Blue Opalescent 8" plate, smooth edge, $22.00 – 24.00.

Sapphire Blue Opalescent ice cream #3005 plate & #3635 bowl, $40.00 – 45.00 set.

For distinctive entertaining

Peaches & Cream Opalescent

Q3664 UO
Ice Lip Pitcher, $49.50

Q3004 UO
Dinnerware Service, pitcher and four iced teas, $89.50

Q3002 UO
Set of 4 dishes, $30.00

Q3630 UO
Ice Cream Dish $8.50

Q3003 UO
Set of 4 iced teas $49.50

Q3001 UO
8" Plate, set of 4, $35.00

Q3842 UO
Footed Iced Tea, $12.50

Peaches & Cream Opalescent . . . Extraordinary glass from the extraordinary glass artists at Fenton. One look and you'll be captivated. Add to your service as you are able. So compatible with so many dinnerware patterns of today.

More Sapphire Blue accents because you asked for them. See pages 12 & 13 for additional Sapphire Blue items.

Q8261 BX
Hearts and Flowers Basket, 10" $39.50

Q1990 KK
Daisy and Button Boot, $7.50

Q1990 OC
Daisy and Button Boot, $7.50

Q5165 BX
Cat, $15.00

Q8229 BX
Hearts and Flowers Bowl, 10" $27.50

Peaches & Cream #3664 ice-lip pitcher, $100.00 – 125.00; ice cream set, $35.00 – 40.00 set; footed ice tea tumblers, $24.00 – 28.00 each; Sapphire Blue Opalescent #8261 Heart & Flowers 10" basket, $100.00 – 125.00; #8229 Hearts & Flowers 10" bowl, $55.00 – 65.00; #1990 Daisy & Button boot, $15.00 – 18.00 Teal, $16.00 – 20.00 Cobalt Blue; #5165BX Cat, $65.00 – 75.00.

Special Gifts and Buys

BONUS BUYS

Any guest purchasing $50 or more may order either of these items at 50% off.

Absolutely beautiful pink iridized fairy light.

Sparkling Sapphire Blue Strawberry patterned basket

Q8405 UI Fairy Light
Regular Price $23.50
Special Price $11.50

Q9433 BX 7" Strawberry Basket
Regular Price $23.00
Special Price $11.50

Dinnerware Gifts

Q3937 BX

Q3937 UO

Buy $75.00 or more of dinnerware and get one bonbon free

7" bonbons
$13.50 value

25

Pink Iridized #8405 fairy light, $65.00 – 85.00; #9433BX Strawberry basket, $45.00 – 60.00; #3937BX handled Hobnail bonbon, $22.00 – 24.00; #3937UO handled Hobnail bonbon, $20.00 – 22.00.

Cobalt Blue Opalescent #1274 cruet, $100.00 – 125.00.

Gemstone Quality

Sapphire Blue Opalescent— A gemlike reproduction of the romantic and lovely blue sapphire. A touch of glass-making genius. A source of pride to those who give and those who receive it. Accented by the opalescence which clings to each small, white, bell shaped flower. You can almost smell the lovely fragrance. And it's handmade in America!

Q8437 BX—6" handled basket in lily of the valley pattern. Each little flower is touched and transformed by the glassmaker's flame. $23.50.

Q8489 BX — A covered candy box in lily of the valley. To grace your home . . . unforgettably. $25.00.

Q8265 BX—Lily of the valley bell 6" tall. A must for every bell collector. $15.00.

Q8450 BX—Handkerchief vase. Unique arrangements in this lily of the valley creation. $15.00.

Q8489 BX
Covered Candy Box

Q8450 BX
Handkerchief
Vase

Q8437 BX
6" Handled Basket

Q8265 BX
6" Bell

13

Sapphire Blue Opalescent Lily of The Valley items: #8437 6" basket, $75.00 – 95.00; #8489 covered candy, $65.00 – 85.00; #8265 6" bell, $45.00 – 55.00; #8450 handkerchief vase, $45.00 – 55.00.

Cobalt Blue Opalescent #2472KF cruet, $100.00 – 125.00.

Sapphire Blue Opalescent Diamond Lace one-horn epergne, $100.00 – 125.00.

Cobalt Blue Opalescent #3172KF cruet, $100.00 – 125.00.

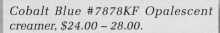

Cobalt Blue #7878KF Opalescent creamer, $24.00 – 28.00.

Sapphire Blue Opalescent

Q8453 BX—Lily of the valley rose bowl. A dramatic accent for any room. $13.50.
Q8458 BX—10" bud vase handformed by skilled craftsmen. $15.00.
Q9030 BX—Lacy edge shell inexpensive and versatile. $7.50.

Q5163 BX—Blue bird of happiness. A gift with a thoughtful wish. $15.00.
Q9299 BX—Owl ringtree. Buy several. So easy to give. So easy to use. $7.50.

Q8453 BX
Rose Bowl

Q8458 BX
Bud Vase

Q5163 BX
Blue Bird of Happiness

Q9299 BX
Owl Ring Tree

Q9030 BX
Lacy Edge Soap Holder

Sapphire Blue Opalescent assortment: #5163 Blue Bird of Happiness, $45.00 – 50.00; Lily of the Valley #8453 rose bowl, $65.00 – 75.00; #8458 bud vase, $45.00 – 50.00; #9299 Owl ring tree, $35.00 – 40.00; #903 Lacy Edge soap holder, $22.00 – 24.00.

Sapphire Blue #5228 doll, $75.00 – 85.00.

Teal with Milk Glass Crest #3501 Spanish Lace
Console Set: *Bowl, $65.00 – 75.00, candlesticks, $40.00 – 45.00 pair.*
Other Pieces: *#3195FF Floral vase, $60.00 – 70.00; #1628VJ decorated Opal Satin comport; #0207AS Cobalt Blue Opalescent cruet & creamer set, $125.00 – 150.00; #0208AS Teal Opalescent cruet & creamer set, $105.00 – $120.00; #1765ZY Amber 6" bell, $18.00 – 20.00; #5151 Teal Iridescent Bear Cub, $55.00 – 65.00.*
Ruby Pieces: *#8361RU 6" Barred-oval bell, $20.00 – 24.00; #3628RU Hobnail 6" comport, $24.00 – 26.00; #3608RU Hobnail fairy light, $25.00 – 35.00.*

Gracious Touch SPECIAL

A Dream For Collectors and Glass Lovers

Effective June 1, 1989

Q3501TX Console Set
Bowl & 2 Candleholders
Teal with Milk Crest
$66.50
Collector's Special

Q3195FF 7" Floral Vase
Regular $65.00
Sale $43.50

Q0207AS Cruet & Creamer Set
Royal Blue
$41.00
Collector's Special

Q1628VJ 6" Comport
Hand Decorated
Regular $25.00
Sale $18.50

Q0208AS
Cruet & Creamer Set
Teal Opalescent
$41.00
Collector's Special

Q1765ZY 6" Bell
Hand Decorated
Regular $15.00
Sale $9.75

Q51510I Sitting Bear Cub
Teal Iridescent
Regular $15.00 Sale $11.50

Tell a Friend about the Gracious Touch Opportunity. It could be the nicest thing you have ever done. Ask your Associate for more information on becoming a part of Gracious Touch. It's fun, educational, and rewarding.

Please accept our invitation to call the National Sales Office 1-800-527-8208 at 1003 Oldtime Drive, Excelsior Springs, Missouri 64024.

Collector's Special

Handmade iridescent glass with skillfully spun opal edges, artistically handpainted vases and bells. Cruets and pitchers with optics embedded in the glass. Your guarantee of quality and craftsmanship and collectibility is the Fenton trademark on each piece.

OUR SPECIAL GIFT FOR THE HOSTESS: Hold a Gift Show of $150 WITH one Booking and receive your choice of one of the following:
Ruby Fairy Light   Reg. $16.50
Ruby Comport   Reg. $19.50
Ruby Bell   Reg. $16.50

Q8361RU
6" Bell
Barred-Oval
Value $16.50

Q3628RU
6" Comport
Hobnail
Value $19.50

Q3608RU
Fairy Light
Hobnail
Value $16.50

Dusty Rose Velvet

Dusty Rose Velvet—Today's top selling decorator color. So at home and yet so luxurious in our secret "velvet" treatment. The unusual clarity of pattern and elegant soft look of handcrafted glass. "Lily of the Valley" is handmade in the United States and brings each possessor a very special pride of ownership.

Q9299 DK—Owl ring tree in clear dusty rose. For bathroom or dresser or over the kitchen sink. $7.50.

Q8489 VO—Lily of the valley covered candy box. It can be used for candies, soaps or jewelry. $27.50.

Q8265 VO—Lily of the valley bell. An accent collectible. $16.50.

Q8450 VO—Lily of the valley handkerchief vase for special bouquets. Finished "off hand" so that no two are exactly the same size or shape. $16.50.

Q8489 VO
Covered Candy Box

Q9299 DK
Owl Ring Tree

Q8265 VO
6" Bell

Q8450 VO
Handkerchief Vase

Dusty Rose Velvet assortment: Lily of the Valley #8489VO covered candy jar, $65.00 – 85.00; #8265VO bell, $45.00 – 55.00; #8450VO Handkerchief vase, $45.00 – 55.00; #9299DK Owl ring tree, 35.00 – 40.00.

Handmade in the age old manner

Q8437 VO—6" Lily of the valley basket. A rare creation of the glassmaker's skill. $26.50.

Q8458 VO—10" bud vase. White hot glass is hand-swung in baton-like fashion at the end of a metal rod until desired length and shape is achieved. No two vases are ever the exact same height or shape. $16.50.

Q9030 DK—Lacy edge shell. For soap or candles or pins. $7.50.

Q8453 VO—Rose Bowl—For flowers or plants or just to sit there and look pretty. $15.00.

Q7607 JG—Garden bridge student lamp. A special icing technique. Handpainted artistry and beauty. Each lamp is proudly signed by the artist. 16" h. $195.00.

Q8458 VO
Bud Vase

Q8437 VO
6" Basket

Q9030 DK
Lacy Edge Shell

Q8453 VO
Rose Bowl

9

Dusty Rose Velvet assortment: *Lily of the Valley, #8437VO 6" basket, $75.00 – 95.00; #8458 bud vase, $45.00 – 50.00; #8453VO rose bowl, $65.00 – 75.00; #9030DK Lacy Edge Shell soap holder, $22.00 – 24.00; #7607JG Garden Bridge 16" student lamp, $275.00 – 325.00.*

Dusty Rose with Opal Crest #7333DM heart-shaped relish, $75.00 – 95.00.

Dusty Rose items: #8261DK Hearts & Flowers 10" basket, $100.00 – 125.00; #8229DK 10" Hearts & Flowers bowl, $55.00 – 65.00; #6603FQ Floral candle light, $75.00 – 85.00; #9372DK Ram's Head candlesticks, $55.00 – 65.00 pair.; #5238ID Iridized Dusty Rose Bird on a Log, $65.00 – 75.00.

Inset items: Blue Royale #4453KK Thumbprint swung vase, $25.00 – 30.00; #1990KK Daisy & Button boot, $20.00 – 22.00; decorated Opal #3567SD Spanish Lace bell, $28.00 – 30.00; #3522SD Spanish Lace comport, $26.00 – 30.00.

Dusty Rose and Blue Royale

Blue Royale in Thumbprint and Daisy & Button. Spun crystal edges on lustrous Milk Glass and then hand-painted. For the collector or the person who appreciates the finer things in life.

Q4453 KK Thumbprint Swing Vase $24.75

Q3522 SD Comport $27.75

Q3567 SD Bell $24.75

Q1990 KK Daisy & Button Boot $7.75

Q8261 DK Hearts & Flowers 10" Basket $41.75

Q8229 DK Hearts & Flowers 10" Bowl $29.75

Q6603 FQ Floral Candlelight $23.00

Q5238 ID Bird on Log $19.75

Q9372 DK Ramshead Candleholder $19.75 per pair

Dusty Rose—Sparkling Accent

Special Gifts and Buys

GUEST CLUB GIFTS

Any hostess having 10, 15 and 20 guests at her showing will receive the following gifts in appreciation for her efforts.

10 buying guests — hand-painted mini chick (1)
15 buying guests — sparkling crystal votive w/rib optic (2)
20 buying guests — hand-painted bud vase (3)

The special items on pgs. 21 & 22 can only be acquired by meeting the requirements stated for each item. These special handmade works of art are no longer available to the public which adds to their *collectibility.*

(1)   (2)   (3)

BONUS BUYS

Any guest purchasing $50 or more may order either of these items at 50% off.

Q8405 DK—Dusty Rose Beaded Fairy Light. Regular price $18.50. *Special price $9.25.
(2) **Q8638 BX**—Sapphire Blue Opalescent Basket Regular price $18.50. *Special price $9.25.

(1)   (2)   21

Yellow #5213NY miniature 2½" Chick (Natural Animal Series), $16.00 – 18.00; #7275 French Opalescent ftd. Rib Optic votive, $18.00 – 22.00; Rose on Custard #9056 bud vase, $18.00 – 22.00; Dusty Rose #8405DK Beaded fairy light, $75.00 – 85.00; #8638BX Provincial Blue Opalescent basket, $65.00 – 75.00.

Rose and Blue Accents

Q1765 FI
Crystal "50th
Anniversary"
Bell,
$16.50

Q1765 HI
Crystal
"Happy
Anniversary"
Bell,
$16.50

Q1765 TI
Crystal "25th Anniversary"
Bell, $16.50

Happy Anniversary . . . the perfect gift for that happy occasion. Banded by hand in silver or gold. The silver is actually 20K white gold and the gold is 22K yellow gold. Decorated in exceptional detail.

Q0937
Square Basket
w/eyelet
$9.00

Q2802 BX
16½" Student Lamp Wild Rose and Bowknot $99.00

Sapphire Blue Opalescent and Solid Brass . . . To last through the ages.

Q8229 DK
Hearts and Flowers Bowl, 10"
$27.50

Q0939
Standing Porcelain Goose,
$19.75

Q0938
Swan w/potpourri,
$17.50

Q6603 FQ
Floral Candle light,
$19.50

Gracious Touch also sold Fenton's Christine Victoria assortment, mixing it with the glass. #1765 Crystal bells, $18.00 – 20.00 each; Dusty Rose #8229 Hearts & Flowers 10" bowl, $55.00 – 65.00; #6603FQ Floral candle light, $75.00 – 85.00.

Away in the Manger assortment: #1714N5 tree ornament, $22.00 – 25.00; #9460N5 6½" bell, $50.00 – 60.00; #7300N5 fairy light, $65.00 – 85.00; #9506MI hurricane lamp with a Milk Glass base, $40.00 – 45.00.

1988

"Away in the Manger"

The true beginning of Christmas is warmly expressed in these unusual art pieces. Each is completely handpainted on opal satin glass. Then a hand application of small particles of glass (icing) gives the design texture and a three dimensional effect. Each piece proudly signed by the artist.

Milk Glass Hurricane Candlelight. Beautiful for holiday or year round decorating. Comes with a 2" by 4" white pillar candle.

D. Q9506 MI – 8" Milk Glass Hurricane Candlelight. (with white pillar candle) $18.50

E. Q9948 – Set of 2 white pillar candles. $8.00

A. Q1714 N5 – "Away in the Manger" tree ornament. $12.50

B. Q9460 N5 – "Away in the Manger" 6½" Bell. $28.50

C. Q7300 N5 – "Away in the Manger" 2 pc. fairy light with candle. $28.50

Ruby Carnival #8233RN bowl, $65.00 – 85.00; decorated and Iridized Milk Glass #7580UD Dolphin candy box, $75.00 – 85.00.

Collector's Delight

Red Carnival—one of the most sought after antique colors that commands the highest prices. Fenton's Orange Tree and Cherry Chain bowl could well be the premier creation in this year's collection. An investment to be on every BUY LIST.

Dolphin Candy Box—made originally by Fenton in 1926, this unique and decorative item is bound to excite even the most conservative collector. Pearlized and handpainted—each piece is proudly signed by the artist.

Q8233 RN
Orange Tree & Cherry Bowl
$35.50

Q7580 UD
Dolphin Candy Box
$45.50

Handpainted Rose Bouquet

Peach Roses—handpainted on handcrafted opal satin glass and each piece proudly signed by the artist. HANDMADE IN AMERICA by the famous glassmakers at Fenton. The perfect accents for today's homes with the added value of being "a collectible".

Q8600 RP—Alarm clock w/quartz movement. Battery operated for freedom of placement, lovely wherever it is. $49.50.

Q5160 RP—Gentle fawn figurine to bring warmth and beauty to each home it graces. $19.50.

Q7663 RP—Large oval bell collectible. $22.50.

Q8600 RP
Alarm clock w/quartz movement

Q5160 RP
Fawn

Q7663 RP
Large Oval Bell
6½"

6

Peach Roses on Opal Satin assortment: #8600RP alarm clock with quartz movement, $100.00 – 120.00; #5160RP Fawn, $40.00 – 45.00; #7663RP large Oval bell, $50.00 – 65.00.

Historic Covered Bridge

Rustic Covered Bridge on custard satin glass. Handpainted and proudly signed by the artist. Collectibles that are so early American you can almost hear the British coming!

Q8600 JV
Alarm clock w/
battery operated
quartz movement
$59.50

Q7668 JV
Bell
$35.00

Q7204 JV
16" Hammered Colonial Lamp
$195.00

18

Historic Covered Bridge assortment:
#8600JV alarm clock with quartz movement, $100.00 – 120.00; #7668JV bell, $50.00 – 65.00; #7204JV 16" hammered Colonial lamp, $250.00 – 325.00.

Handpainted "Pretty Pansies"

Pretty pansies on custard satin glass. The glass gets its color from uranium. After satin finishing, it then receives its added beauty from the skillful brush of the artist. Then a hand application of small particles of glass give it Fenton's unique petal "icing". Each piece is proudly signed by the artist.

Q9238 PP
Crimped Basket
$32.50

Q7252 PP
7" Vase
$32.50

Q7275 PP Votive w/candle
$16.50

Q5161 PP Swan
$19.50

Q7463 PP Bell
$22.50

Pretty Pansies on Custard assortment:
#7252PP 7" vase, $65.00 – 75.00; #7255PP votive, $24.00 – 26.00; #9238PP basket, $50.00 – 65.00; #5161 Swan, $25.00 – 30.00; #7463PP bell, $40.00 – 45.00.

Always right for any room setting

Legency Crystal—Start your table service here. Elegance from the past that's "at home" in the future.

Q8680 CY—Regency covered butter & cheese. Base also makes a great arranger for a pillar candle and flower ring. $27.50.

Q8602 CY—Regency sugar & cream set. Either piece can also be used as a planter or floral container. $22.50.
Q8606 CY—Regency salt & pepper set. Sturdy, yet so attractive. $16.50.
Q5117 CY—Spoonholder. Hang on the wall as a decoration. Use with a pillar candle. Or, as intended, as a spoon rest. $7.50.

Q8680 CY
Covered Butter & Cheese

Q8602 CY
Sugar & Cream Set

Q8606 CY
Salt & Pepper Set

Q5117 CY
Spoonholder

Crystal assortment (McKee Plytec moulds): #8680CY covered butter or cheese, $50.00 – 60.00; #8606CY salt & pepper, $20.00 – 25.00; #8602CY cream & open sugar, $45.00 – 50.00; #5117CY Sunflower spoon holder, $18.00 – 22.00.

"Sparkling Crystal"

Sparkling Crystal—So versatile! So right! So beautiful! Add brilliance to your decorating scheme with those reproductions from the past. Call it country, call it Victorian, but call it American. Handmade from the original moulds. An ancient art, still unchanged.

Q8642 CY — Oval relish, candy or nut dish. Float a flower for an unusual touch on your coffee table. $9.50.
Q8638 CY — Regency crimped basket for candies or flowers. $18.50.
Q8650 CY—Lucille bud vase to luxuriously hold that beautiful rose. $15.00.

Q8625 CY
Compote

Q8650 CY
Bud Vase

Q8642 CY
Oval Relish or Nut Dish

Q8638 CY
Basket

Q8625 CY — Puritan compote. A jelly, candy or nut dish. A truly handsome heirloom from yesteryear. $17.50.

Crystal assortment: #8642CY oval relish or nut dish, $20.00 – 22.00; #8625CY Two Flowers comport (McKee mould), $30.00 – 35.00; #8638CY basket, $40.00 – 45.00; #8650CY bud vase, $18.00 – 24.00.

The Rose . . . world's most popular flower

Cherished gifts in hand-painted peach roses.
Q9056 RP—Bud vase, no two are exactly alike because of the unique manufacturing process. $22.50.
Q5151 RP—Bear cub. Start your collection here. The ideal accent for any room. $19.50.

Q8637 RP—Oval basket. Really different. Handle dexterously applied by the skilled glassworker. Great for nuts or flowers. $34.50.
Q7664 RP — Petite oval bell. An accent collectible. $15.00.
Q9308 RP — Student lamp. An exquisite focal point for any home. Styling and craftsmanship make this an outstandingly lovely accessory. $175.00.

Q9056 RP Bud Vase

Q9308 RP Student 20" Lamp

Q8637 RP Oval Basket 7½"

Q5151 RP Bear Cub

Q7664 RP Petite Oval Bell

7

Peach Roses on Opal Satin assortment: #9056RP bud vase, $65.00 – 70.00; #5151RP Bear Cub, $45.00 – 50.00; #8637RP oval basket, $75.00 – 85.00; #7664RP petite oval bell, $35.00 – 45.00; #9308RP 20" student lamp, $200.00 – $250.00.

Victorian Christmas and Ruby

Decorate your tree and home with these nostalgic Victorian ornaments and bears from Christine Victoria. Burgundy covered with lace and ecru covered with lace . . . so romantic.

A. Q0928—12 pc. Victorian ornament assortment (burgundy). $39.00
B. Q0929—12 pc. Victorian ornament assortment (ecru). $39.00
C. Q0930—Bear with hat (burgundy). $8.50
D. Q0931—Bear with hat (ecru). $8.50
E. Q9506 RU—8" Ruby Hurricane Candlelight (with 2" by 4" white pillar candle) $20.00

Fenton Ruby . . . Rich, warm and beautiful. An elegant accent in holiday decorating.

#9506RU Ruby hurricane lamp, $45.00 – 55.00.

Gracious Touch SPECIAL

To our party guests: Items A, B and C may be purchased with any other purchase of $15.00 or more.

All Handmade in the U.S.A.

A. Q7333 DM Heart Relish or Candy. A ribbon of pure milk glass is skillfully spun around the edge of the dusty rose bowl. After crimping and shaping, a handle is dertly applied. A sweetheart of an item. Limited, numbered and exclusive. $25.00

D. Q8651 RU Crimped Triangle Vase . . . A unique collectible from the famous glassmakers at Fenton. Just right for a small bouquet. Value $12.50.

B. Q5151 RU Unusual and Cuddly Bear. Shades from ruby to ruby amberina. Not exclusive forever, but only from Gracious Touch for 1987. $15.00

C. Q8638 RU Ruby Handled Basket. Color so near to the precious gemstone. A very special buy at $19.50.

E. Q8642 RU Ruby Amberina Oval Relish or Nut Dish. Made especially to reward our Associates and Hostesses. Value $11.50.

A special gift to Associates and Hostesses: Your choice of items D and E for every $250.00 party . . . while they last!

Dusty Rose items: *#7333DM Dusty Rose with Opal Crest heart-shaped relish/candy, $75.00 – 95.00.*
Ruby items: *#8651RU Triangle-crimped vase, $45.00 – 50.00; #8642RU Ruby/Amberina oval relish, $20.00 – 24.00; #8638RY basket, $40.00 – 45.00; #5151RU Bear Cub, $35.00 – 40.00.*

1989 Limited Edition Preferred Hostess Gift

This beautiful "Gracious Lady" Doll is your exclusive gift for hosting four gift shows or $900.00 in sales within a calendar *year*. Be sure to be a winner and receive the "Gracious Lady" made in pearlized shell pink. (Q5228 PE).

#5228PE Pearlized Shell Pink Gracious Lady, $75.00 – 85.00.

Gracious Touch SPECIAL

A Dream For Collectors and Glass Lovers

Tell a Friend about the Gracious Touch Opportunity. It could be the nicest thing you have ever done. Ask your Associate for more information on becoming a part of Gracious Touch. It's fun, educational, and rewarding.

Please accept our invitation to call the National Sales Office 1-800-527-8208 at 1003 Oldtime Drive, Excelsior Springs, Missouri 64024.

Q3830 MI 10" Basket Reg. $27.00 Sale $17.50

Q3991 MI 3" Hat Reg. $7.50 Sale $5.00

Q8376 RU 11" Hurricane Candle Reg. $27.50 Sale $18.00

Q9519 RU 5¾" Heart Candy Reg. $15.00 Sale $10.00

Q8361 RU 6" Barred Oval Bell Reg. $16.50 Sale $11.00

Q8321 RU 6½" Barred Oval Bowl Reg. $17.50 Sale $6.75

Q8335 OI 7¼" Basket Weave Open-Edge Basket Reg. $25.00 Sale $16.50

Q9732 OC 8½" Basket Reg. $25.00 Sale $16.50

OUR SPECIAL GIFT FOR THE HOSTESS: Hold a Gift Show of $150 WITH one Booking and receive this elegant Crystal Velvet Basket free.

Q9737 VE Think elegance with the Satin handcrafted Crystal Velvet Basket $35.00 Value

Effective Oct.-Dec. 1989

Milk Glass items: #3830MI 10" Hobnail basket, $50.00 – 65.00; #3991MI 3" hat, $12.00 – 15.00.
Ruby items: #8376RU 11" hurricane lamp, $75.00 – 85.00; #9519RU 5¾" heart dish, $18.00 – 22.00; #8321RU Barred-oval 6½" bowl, $20.00 – 24.00; #8361RU Barred-oval 6" bell, $24.00 – 26.00.
Teal items: #8335OI Iridized Open-Edge Basket Weave 7¼" basket, $45.00 – 50.00; #9732OC (Caprice) basket, $65.00 – 75.00; #9737VE basket, $30.00 – 35.00.

Left side: #5251QN Natural Squirrel, $50.00 – 65.00; #8651BX Provincial Blue Opalescent (Plytec) tritop vase, $40.00 – 45.00; #8642BX oval relish, $25.00 – 30.00.
Top box, French Opalescent Country Garden: #9571JF ftd. candleholder (Vulcan mould), $25.00 – 30.00; #9667JF Aurora 6" bell, $30.00 – 35.00; #9576JF 2½" votive, $18.00 – 20.00; #9555JF 4" votive/vase, $24.00 – 26.00: #9519JF Heart candy, $16.00 – 18.00.
Lower box: #7646JF Country Garden bud vase, $18.00 – 20.00; #3067NK Cobalt Blue Iridized Wave Hobnail bell, $25.00 – 30.00; both of these pieces were sold in Fenton's catalog line. Federal Blue Overlay #2034OF basket, $65.00 – 75.00; #9658OF Dogwood vase, $75.00 – 85.00.

Gracious Touch SPECIAL

For Collectors and Glass Lovers

Q5215 QN Squirrel, Red Reg. $17.50 Now Only $10.50

F E N T O N
Country Garden

Delicate little handpainted pink flowers with a subtle beauty all their own combine with the rich opalescence of the glass to create simplicity, style and the unusual.

Q9571 JF Candleholder/ Nut Dish Reg. $16.50 Now Only $11.00

Q9667 JF Bell, Aurora, 6" Reg. $18.50 Now Only $12.50

Q9576 JF Votive, w/Candle, 2½" Reg. $10.50 Only $6.50

Q9555 JF Votive/Vase, w/ Candle & Cup, 4" Reg. $16.50 Only $10.00

Q9519 JF Heart Candy Reg. $17.50 Now Only $11.00

Q8651 BX Crimped Triangle Vase ...A unique collectible from the famous glassmakers at Fenton. Just right for a small bouquet. Value $12.50 Now Only $7.75

OUR SPECIAL GIFT for the Hostess Book and hold a Gift Show and select a Gift of your choice. Select either the Country Garden Bud Vase or Carnival Hobnail Bell for a Minimum Gift Show of $150.00 and one booking. For two bookings you may select the Federal Blue Overlay Basket or Vase.

Q8642 BX Blue Opalescent Oval Relish or Nut Dish Regular $11.50 Now $6.75 Also available in Ruby Amberina Q8642 RU Now $6.75

Q7646 JF The Country Garden Bud Vase, 7½" $19.50 Value

Q3067 NK Bell Wave Hobnail $18.50 Value

Q2034 OF $32.50 Value

Q9658 OF $29.50 Value

6/15/88

#6602UO Peaches 'n Cream 9" electric lamp with a solid brass base, $75.00 – 85.00; #2057CC Country Cranberry Curtain Optic 7" vase, $50.00 – 65.00; #8321RU Ruby 6½" Barred-oval bowl, $20.00 – 24.00; #7438ZQ Teal Overlay with hand-painted Roses 6½" top hat basket, $65.00 – 75.00; #5158RC Roses on Custard Elephant, $40.00 – 45.00; #5158DC White Daisy on Custard Elephant, $40.00 – 45.00; #2534CC Country Cranberry 7" basket with an optic pattern, $65.00 – 75.00.

Gracious Touch SPECIAL

Effective Oct.-Dec. 1988

Stock up on these at this Special Price for all this year's Special Remembrances.

Tell a Friend about the Gracious Touch Opportunity. It could be the nicest thing you have ever done. Ask your Associate for more information on becoming a part of Gracious Touch. It's fun, educational and rewarding. Please accept our invitation to call the National Sales Office 1-800-527-8208.

G. OUR SPECIAL GIFT FOR THE HOSTESS. Book and hold a $200 party and receive this beautiful "gold ruby" basket shown below. (not for sale)

Q6602UO
Electric lamp, 9"
with solid brass base.
Regular price—$35.00
Special price—$22.00

Q2057CC
Cranberry Curtain Vase, 7"
Delightful, with the
curtain optic.
Regular price—$25.00
Special price—$22.00

Q8321RU
Ruby bowl, 6½"
a beautiful red color.
Regular price—$17.50
Special price—$6.75

Q5158DC
Elephant, white daisies on
custard glass.
Regular price—$17.50
Special price—$10.50

Q7438ZQ
Top hat basket, 6½"
Teal and milk overlay,
hand decorated with white roses.
Special value—$30.00

Q5158RC
Elephant, red roses on
custard glass.
Limited quantity of 48
only available.
Regular price—$17.50
Special price—$10.50

Q2534CC
Basket, 7"
cranberry glass with an
optic pattern.
(not for sale—see above)
Value—$39.50

★ Handmade in America ★

Gracious Touch SPECIAL

Think: Valentine's Day, Mother's Day, Birthdays, Anniversaries and Buy Now at These Special Prices.

JANUARY AND FEBRUARY SPECIALS

What a delightful pair. Everyone loves Scotties. It's a perfect gift for children. Start them out a serious collection.

Q5214 WH
Scottie, White
Reg. $15.00
Now Only $8.50

Q5214 NH
Scottie, Gray
Reg. $17.50
Now Only $10.50

Dusty Rose . . . today's top selling decorator color. The elegant Swan candleholders will be the perfect accent to any decor. Think Weddings or Anniversaries.

Q5172 DK
Candleholders, Swan
Regular $22.50
Now Only $13.50 a pair.

Q7660 VC
Vase, 7½"
Reg. $32.50
Only $18.00

Q7254 VC
Vase, 4½"
Reg. $19.50
Only $11.00

Pretty "Pastel Violets" on custard Satin Glass. Each piece is proudly signed by the artist. Perfect accent pieces for any room. Gift for any occasion.

Q5151 VC
Bear Cub
Reg. $18.50
Now Only $10.50

Stock up on these at this Special Price for all this year's Special Remembrances.

Tell a Friend about the Gracious Touch Opportunity. It could be the nicest thing you have ever done. Ask your Associate for more information on becoming a part of Gracious Touch. It's fun, educational and rewarding. Please accept our invitation to call the National Sales Office 1-800-527-8208.

OUR SPECIAL GIFT for the Hostess. Book and hold a Gift Show during the months of January or February and receive this beautiful Ruby Basket as an added gift.

Q9237 R2
Rich Ruby Rose
embossed Basket
edged with 23K gold
paint and accented
with a gold rose
on the handle.

$35.00 Value

Top left and right: #5214WH White Scottie, $45.00 – 50.00; #5214NH Gray Scottie, $45.00 – 50.00; #5172DK Dusty Rose Swan candlesticks, $65.00 – 75.00 pair.
Middle, Pastel Violets on Custard assortment: #7254VC 4½" vase, $35.00 – 40.00; #7660VC 7½" vase, $65.00 – 75.00; #5151VC Bear Cub, $45.00 – 50.00.
Bottom right: #9237RZ Ruby 23K gold–trimmed Rose pattern basket, $60.00 – 65.00.

Gracious Touch SPECIAL

A Dream For Collectors and Glass Lovers

Minted Cream,
soft teal opalescent
Trinket Box, hexagonal
QB9687 EO
Reg. $15.00
Now $8.75

Victorian Pitcher
and Cruet. The look
of a century ago.
Cobalt Bubble Optic Cruet
and French Opalescent
Optic Pitcher
A collector's delight.

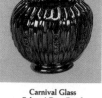

Carnival Glass
Fabergé Rose Bowl
Q9653 NK
Reg. $17.50
Now only $10.50

Pitcher
Q1277 FO
Reg. $30.00
Now only $17.50

Cruet
Q2472 KF
Reg. $50.00
Now only $28.75

Special Moment Bells for Mother's Day and every
other day. Start a collection of Petite Pastel
Bells. Love Bell is perfect for Weddings
and Anniversaries.

Q7662 LK   Q1777 WF
    Q1777 GR   Q7662 WE

Q7662 LK Love
Q1777 GR Grandmother
Q1777 WF Mother
Q7662 WE Mother
Reg. $10.50
Now only $6.75

Stock up on these at this Special Price for all
this year's Special Remembrances.

Tell a Friend about the Gracious Touch
Opportunity. It could be the nicest thing you
have ever done. Ask your Associate for more
information on becoming a part of Gracious
Touch. It's fun, educational and rewarding.
Please accept our invitation to call the
National Sales Office 1-800-527-8208.

OUR SPECIAL GIFT for the Hostess. Hold a Gift Show
of $150 with one booking and receive this elegant Crystal
Velvet Basket free, or choose $25 in merchandise from
the catalog.

Q9737 VE
Think elegance
with the Satin
handcrafted Crystal
Velvet Basket
$35.00 Value

Top: #QB9687EO Minted Creme Teal Opalescent hexagonal trinket box, $40.00 – 45.00; #9653NK Cobalt Carnival Fabergé rose bowl, $35.00 – 40.00.
Bells: #7762LK Love, #1777GR Grandmother, #1777WF Mother, #7662WE Mother's Day, $22.50 – 25.00 each.
Other items: #1277FO creamer, $18.00 – 20.00; #2472KF Royal Blue cruet, $100.00 – 125.00; #9737VE Think Elegance basket, $30.00 – 35.00.

Hallmark stores are in almost every city in the United States. Although Hallmark's specialty is the wonderful greeting cards it sells, it also has some unique gift lines in its stores. Fenton is a product line that has been sold by Hallmark for years. While most of the Fenton it sells is bought out of the regular catalog line, occasionally special glass is made for Hallmark. I don't have a complete list of its special-order glass, but I can show you some of the pieces made for the company.

#7653GY Willow Green Opalescent Daffodil vase, $65.00 – 75.00.

Description	Pattern	Ware #	Petal Pink
Basket	Sheffield	6634PN	$50.00 – 65.00
Bell	Sheffield	6665PN	$35.00 – 40.00
Bowl, console	Sheffield	6624PN	$45.00 – 50.00
Bowl, crimped	Sheffield	6626PN	$30.00 – 35.00
Candlesticks	Sheffield	6672PN	(ea.) $25.00 – 30.00
Rose bowl	Sheffield	6658PN	$25.00 – 30.00
Vase, small	Sheffield	6650PN	$35.00 – 45.00
Vase, large	Sheffield	6654PN	$50.00 – 55.00

Description	Decoration	Ware #	Opal Satin
Basket	Primrose	7631KX	$65.00 – 70.00
Bear	Primrose	5151KX	$45.00 – 50.00
Bell	Primrose	9667KX	$40.00 – 45.00
Bird	Primrose	5163KX	$40.00 – 45.00
Cat	Primrose	5165KX	$40.00 – 45.00
Comport	Primrose	1628KX	$35.00 – 40.00
Lamp, student	Primrose	9308KX	$150.00 – 175.00

★ Four items in the Thumbprint pattern in
two top selling colors - Sea Mist Green & Petal Pink.

★ We've combined the 4 exclusive pieces into an
assortment (for each color) with other best selling items
from the Fenton line.

★ Each assortment gives you a 5% DISCOUNT...and with
an order totaling to the different Hallmark Plus
discount levels, receive an additional 5%, 8% or 10% !

Description	Ware #	Petal Pink PN	Sea Mist Green LE
Basket, 5½"	9243	$35.00 – 40.00	$35.00 – 40.00
Basket, 8" Vulcan	9544	$40.00 – 45.00	$40.00 – 45.00
Bear, 3½" sitting	5151	$22.00 – 25.00	$22.00 – 25.00
Bell, 7" Paisley	6761	$20.00 – 25.00	$20.00 – 25.00
Bird, 6½" open	5240	$35.00 – 40.00	$35.00 – 40.00
Bonbon	4435	$22.00 – 24.00	$22.00 – 24.00
Candleholder, 3½"	4470	(ea.) $12.00 – 15.00	(ea.) $12.00 – 15.00
Candleholder, 4¼"	9596	(ea.) $10.00 – 12.00	(ea.) $10.00 – 12.00
Candy box, oval	4486	$35.00 – 40.00	$35.00 – 40.00
Cat, 3¾"	5165	$22.00 – 25.00	$22.00 – 25.00
Comport, ftd	4429	$20.00 – 22.50	$20.00 – 22.50
Slipper, 6" Rose	9295	$18.00 – 22.00	$18.00 – 22.00
Vase, daffodil	4655	$45.00 – 50.00	$45.00 – 50.00

The Rodefer Gleason Glass Company of Bellaire, Ohio, was the last company to produce lightning balls. When it closed its doors in the 1980s, it could have been the end of the line for these beautiful ornamental glass balls that adorned lightning rods. But in 1993, Harger joined with Fenton to reproduce several styles in the following colors: Vaseline, Ruby, Cobalt Blue, and White Milk Glass. The following colors were added soon after the first introduction: Clear Gray-Green, Ruby Carnival, and Rosalene. Only 140 Rosalene pieces were made, and they sold out almost immediately. In 1994, a purple slag (Plum), Clear Plum, Iridized Plum, and Plum with a silver nitrate coating and Cranberry were introduced. I have also seen an opaque Yellow example and I know there are others, but I haven't been able to find a list of those. For the most part, the plain colors sell for between $50 and $75. Special colors that are opaque or iridized sell between $75 and $100.

W.C. Shinn Gray-Green lightning ball, $65.00 – 75.00.

Harger Rosalene lightning ball, $150.00 – 175.00.

Ruby Diamond pattern lightning ball, $50.00 – 60.00.

Ruby Ribbed pattern lightning ball, $50.00 – 60.00.

Heartlights

Heartlights is a lighting company. From 1989 until 2002, it ordered reproduction Swan kerosene lamps from Fenton. Each of these is signed and dated, so there is very little chance that one will be mistaken for an antique. When the company acquired a mould for the Thespian Masks, it took it to Fenton and had the Ruby and Topaz example made. That it acquired this mould would imply there is an old one, but if there is, I've never seen or heard of one. The lamps are beautiful, but I would just call the masks unique.

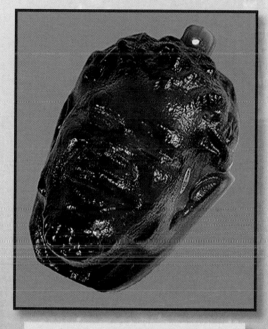

Ruby Thespian Mask, $75.00 – 95.00.

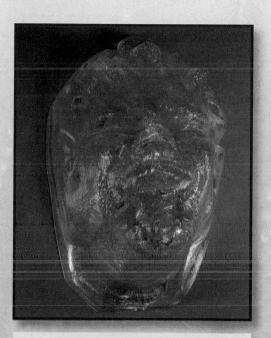

Topaz Thespian Mask, $75.00 – 95.00

Swan bases: *Cobalt Blue, Crystal, Black, Dusty Rose, Green. Complete lamps, $125.00 – 150.00 each.*

Swan lamp, Amber Iridized. Complete lamp, $125.00 – 150.00.

Purple Slag Swan lamp, $145.00 – 165.00.

Topaz lamp. Complete, $150.00 – 165.00.

Topaz lamp, $150.00 – 165.00; Amber Iridized, complete, $125.00 – 150.00; Opal lamp, complete, $125.00 – 150.00.

Swan lamp base with the Heartlights insignia.

Swan lamp with a cased center, $150.00 – 165.00.

In 1991, the Heinz company asked Fenton to make it a copy of an old store jar, usually used for candy but occasionally used for other food items like pickles, etc. These jars were never put on the market, but were instead given as gifts or awards to Heinz employees. That fact would make them almost impossible to find, but Fenton also sold them, without the label, in its gift shop.

They are not marked with the Fenton trademark but there are ways to distinguish the old from the new. The old container is 11¾" tall, and the Fenton one is 11½".

The bottom of the lid and the neck of the jar on the old container is sandblasted. The Fenton jar has no sandblasting. The base of the lid (which fits inside the jar) is 2¾" on the old jar. On the Fenton jar, it is 3", making it impossible to interchange lids.

Ferill Rice wrote an article in the December 2001 *Butterfly Net* that made it possible for me to have this information. The *Butterfly Net* is an important resource for learning about the glass made by Fenton and sold by its dealers, as well as information about special-order glass.

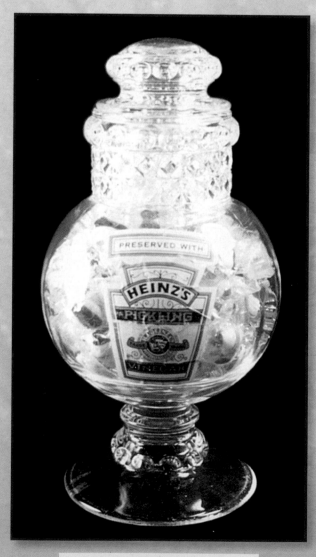

Crystal candy jar, $75.00 – 85.00.

The Hershey's chocolate factory and gift shop is located in Hershey, Pennsylvania. In about 1988, Fenton made a group of samples decorated by Louise Piper for Hershey's gift shop. While they may have been only samples, there is a possibility some designs were made in quantities to be sold by it. I will list those pieces with as much information as I have, but it is incomplete. I don't have mould numbers of those pieces but they will be signed on the base, "Hand Painted Especially for Hershey's World."

Fenton did make a series of animals decorated with a Chocolate Rose on Custard from 1978 until 1985. Fenton did make a Chocolate Rose group of animals for its line, but those pieces were on Cameo Satin, a color that is more brown than the yellow-toned custard made for Hershey. I am including a catalog picture of the Chocolate Rose on Cameo Bird. The picture in the catalog was smaller than I would have liked, but I think you can see the difference in the two colors. Hershey's World animals can also be identified by the inscriptions on the bottoms, which read, "Hand Painted Especially for Hershey's World," and by the artists' signatures.

CHOCOLATE ROSES ON CUSTARD ANIMALS

Description	Item #	Value
Bear	5151	$55.00 – 65.00
Bird	5163	$50.00 – 55.00
Bunny	5162	$50.00 – 55.00
Cat	5165	$55.00 – 65.00
Elephant	5158	$55.00 – 65.00
Fawn	5160	$60.00 – 65.00
Happiness Bird	5197	$60.00 – 65.00
Kitten	5119	$40.00 – 45.00
Whale	5152	$55.00 – 65.00

SAMPLE ITEMS – CHOCOLATE ROSES ON CUSTARD

The prices are estimates not meant to set the values of items this rare.

Description	Item #	Value
Basket , 7"	7237HR	$125.00 – 150.00
Bud vase	9056HR	$75.00 – 95.00
Vase, 4½"	7254HR	$100.00 – 125.00
Bell	8267HR	$75.00 – 95.00

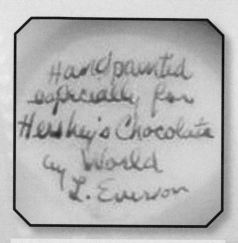

Inscription on the base of the rabbit.

#5162 Rabbit, Chocolate Rose on Custard, $75.00 – 85.00.

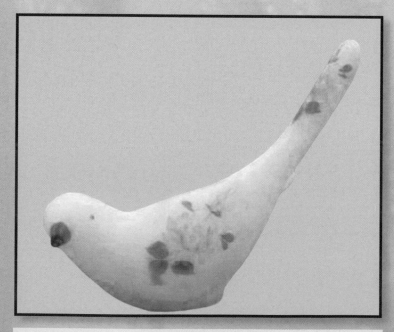

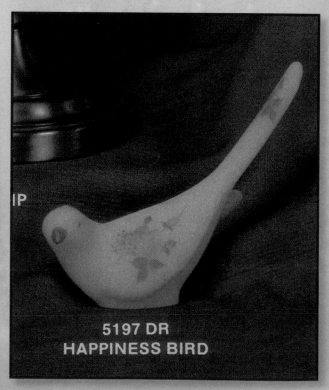

5197 DR
HAPPINESS BIRD

#5197 Happiness Bird, Chocolate Rose on Custard, $75.00 – 85.00.

Catalog photo of the Chocolate Rose on Cameo Happiness Bird sold in the catalog.

HOLOPHANE — VERLYS OF AMERICA

The Societe Holophane Francais, a French subsidiary of the Holophane Company of USA, was making headlights in the early 1920s. In 1925, the newly created department called Verlys made bowls and vases that were smooth on the outside and decorated on the inside. It was 1930 before it made the sculptured designs that made the Verlys name famous. The soft satin finish, opalescent, colored, and clear glass made by Verlys composed the majority of the glass made in France. The French production was signed with a moulded signature, either "Verlys" or "Verlys, made in France." In the 1930s, France was embroiled in a war that involved all of Europe. Art glass like that of Verlys was decreased in order to produce glass devoted to military needs.

In 1935, Verlys of America was created as a subsidiary of Holophane Lighting Company of America. The French moulds were purchased by Verlys of America, where they were used from 1935 to 1951. The American production was signed in script with a diamond pencil. The signatures differ because they were signed by many different employees. Colors made by Verlys of France and Verlys of America were Crystal Etched, Opalescent Crystal, Amber, Smoky Topaz, Directoire Blue, and Dusty Rose.

In 1954, the Verlys moulds were leased to the A. H. Heisey Glass company. Three years later, in 1957, Heisey returned the moulds to Holophane. Heisey made a very limited amount of glass in those moulds in Crystal and Limelight, a pale shade of aqua.

After several years of negotiations, in 1966 Fenton was able to purchase all of the moulds from Holophane, but it did not purchase the rights to the Verlys name. It felt that Fenton was a more recognizable name. As a condition of the purchase, there was a stipulation that Fenton would produce glass from the moulds to be given to Holophane's employees. Those pieces are listed here.

GLASS MADE FOR HOLOPHANE EMPLOYEES

Year	Color	Mould	Value
1984	Crystal Satin	Rose bowl	$45.00 – 55.00
1985	Crystal Satin	Thistle bowl	$45.00 – 55.00
1986	Crystal Satin	Pine Cone bowl	$45.00 – 55.00
1987	Crystal Satin	Hex bowl	$65.00 – 85.00
1988	Crystal Satin	Chinois bowl	$50.00 – 65.00
1989	Crystal Satin	Swallows cigarette box	$65.00 – 85.00
1990	French Opalescent Satin	Fish bowl	$85.00 – 120.00
1991	Crystal Satin	Empress vase	$85.00 – 115.00
1992	Crystal Satin	Love Bird vase	$75.00 – 95.00
1993	Dusty Rose Satin	Rose bowl	$65.00 – 85.00
1994	Sea Mist Green Satin	Pine Cone bowl	$75.00 – 85.00
1995	Amber Satin	Thistle bowl	$75.00 – 85.00
1996	Plum	Love Bird vase	$125.00 – 150.00
1999	Misty Blue Opalescent	Rose bowl	$65.00 – 80.00
2000	Spruce Green	Hex bowl	$125.00 – 150.00

Year	Color	Mould	Value
2001	Blue Topaz	Butterfly box	$150.00 – 175.00
2003	Violet Satin	Pine Cone bowl	$65.00 – 75.00
2004	Rose Milk	Rose dish	$65.00 – 75.00
2005	Cobalt	Pine Cone bowl	$65.00 – 75.00

Some of the pictures in this chapter are of glass made in Holophane moulds that were sold through the gift shop or may have been made for unknown customers. Those will be priced in the photo captions.

If you look at the Colonial Green Mermaid vase, it will look different from the other Mermaid pieces. This is the design of the original Verlys Mermaid vase made in France. It was made with a flared, cupped, or straight top. The straight-top vase was used by Verlys as a lamp base. Fenton preferred an allover pattern, so the top section was removed.

1984 Crystal Satin Roses bowl, $45.00 – 55.00.

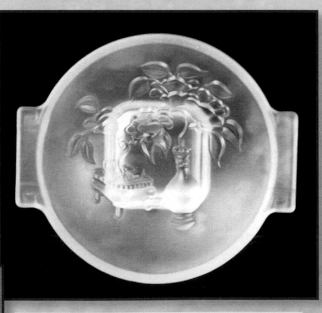

1988 Crystal Satin Chinois bowl, $50.00 – 65.00.

1990 French Opalescent Satin Fish bowl (not iridized), $95.00 – 120.00. Iridized bowl sold in gift shop, $75.00 – 100.00.

1995 Amber Satin Thistle bowl, $75.00 – 85.00.

1996 Plum Love Bird vase, $125.00 – 150.00.

1999 Misty Blue Opalescent rose bowl, $65.00 – 80.00.

2000 Spruce Green Satin hexagonal bowl was sold in the gift shop, $125.00 – 150.00.

2000 Spruce Green hexagonal bowl, $125.00 – 150.00.

2001 Blue Topaz Butterfly box, $150.00 – 175.00.

2003 Violet Satin Pine Cone bowl , $65.00 – 75.00.

Violet Empress vase, $125.00 – 150.00.

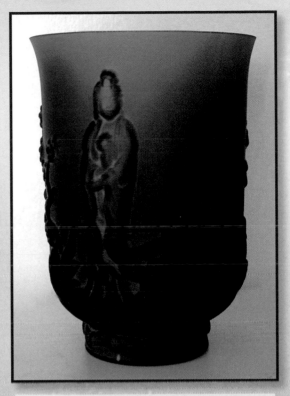

Violet Satin Empress vase, $125.00 – 150.00.

Spruce Green Satin Empress vase, $125.00 – 150.00.

Crystal Satin Butterfly box, $85.00 – 100.00.

Amethyst Carnival Fish bowl, $85.00 – 95.00.

Malachite hexagonal planter, $250.00 – 275.00.

Malachite Vessel of Gems vase, $225.00 – 250.00.

Malachite Roses bowl, $125.00 – 150.00.

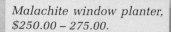

Malachite window planter, $250.00 – 275.00.

Colonial Green Mermaid vase made in Holophane's original shape, $125.00 – 150.00.

Sapphire Blue Empress vase, $125.00 – 150.00.

Thistle Crystal Satin lamp shade made from the vase, $75.00 – 85.00.

Crystal Shell oval ftd. plate with Satinized Shells (not opalescent).

HOUSE WARMINGS

House Warmings is another trade name used by Fenton for items that were sold to smaller stores who were looking for giftware lines that fit into their price structures. It was a new approach to Old Virginia Glass, 1980 style. The Christine Victoria line was combined with a group of low-price items in the appealing colors of the time. Dusty Rose, Crystal Iridized, and Shell Pink were the only colors that were being made and sold in Fenton's regular line. A slightly lighter color of Dusty Rose, called Dusty Pink, and

a vibrant shade of blue that fits its name, Beautiful Blue, completed the color line for House Warmings.

Several moulds are new to most Fenton collectors, and I'm sure that collectors would like to see some of them made in the future. The 9217 nut dish, 9253 5" cornucopia, and the 9241 basket are very attractive. As far as I could find, these were only made for House Warmings and were never introduced into Fenton's regular line.

The crystal pieces were decorated but not made by Fenton. Values would be between $15.00 and $22.50.
Dusty Pink, row 1: *#9217HK fan nut dish, $20.00 – 22.00; #6691HK covered trinket box, $22.50 -25.00; #9233HK ftd. basket, $20.00 – 22.50; #1760LJ decorated petite bell, $16.00 – 18.00.*
Row 2: *#9253HK 5" cornucopia vase, $25.00 – 30.00; #9268HK Bow & Drape bell, $18.00 – 20.00; #9241HK 7" basket, $35.00 – 40.00; #5228HK 7" doll figurine, $60.00 – 75.00; #9150HK 7" bud vase, $22.50 – 24.00.*

Beautiful Blue, row 1: *#9217BB fan nut dish, $22.00 – 24.00; #9233BB ftd. basket, $22.50 – 24.00; #1760MJ decorated petite bell, $18.00 – 20.00; #6691 covered trinket box, $18.00 – 22.00.*
Row 2: *#9253BB 5" cornucopia vase, $30.00 – 35.00; #5228BB doll figurine, $65.00 – 75.00; #9268BB 7" Bow & Drape bell, $22.00 – 24.00; #9241BB 7" basket, $40.00 – 45.00; #9150BB 7" bud vase, $24.00 – 26.00.*

Victorian French Blue
Blue Victorian offers the same full look in a traditional home decorating color.

Beautiful Blue
A spirited color which captures attention. These fine quality glass items create impulse purchases. Especially effective when paired with Victorian Blue House Warmings.

Shell Pink, row 1: *#9766PE Butterfly & Berry 6½" basket, $40.00 – 45.00; #9129PE 6½" Pineapple comport, $30.00 – 35.00.*
Row 2: *#8687PE covered trinket box, $45.00 – 50.00; #9465PE 6" Strawberry bell; #8654PC 7½" bud vase, $24.00 – 26.00.*
Crystal Satin Iridized, row 3: *#5160IJ Fawn, $45.00 – 55.00; #5163IJ 4" Bird, $35.00 – 40.00; #5243IJ 3½" Cat, $35.00 – 40.00.*
Dusty Rose, row 1: *#9241DK 7" basket, $35.00 – 40.00; #9129DK 6½" Pineapple comport, $30.00 – 35.00.*
Row 2: *#9465DK 6" Strawberry bell, $35.00 – 38.00; #6691DK 4" covered trinket box, $22.50 – 25.00; #9150DK 7" bud vase, $24.00 – 26.00; #9233DK 5½" ftd. basket, $20.00 – 22.50.*

This "Local and Long Distance Telephone" shade is a copy of an old example brought to Fenton and used to create a new mould. The new is very slightly larger than the original, but I wasn't able to measure them together, so I have no details. One of the easiest methods to determine whether a shade is old or new is to look inside it. The color of the Opal used for the old shade is very gray toned. The underside of the Fenton shade is white. On the old shade, the lettering is more narrow than it is on the Fenton example. Again, that is hard to see if you don't have an old shade to use for comparison. All of the Fenton shades are marked either in the necks or on the lower edges of the bells. It may be difficult to see, but under close inspection of a Fenton shade, you should be able to see an oval or a scroll "F." That mark was used because the mould was not owned by Fenton.

Even though this shade is modern, it is very rare because not many were produced for the buyer.

Blue over Milk Glass lamp shade, replica of an old shade, $250.00 – 300.00.

Kaleidoscope contracted with Fenton to press a series of Nursery Rhyme cup plates for it beginning in January of 1982. These were sold as parts of a set, with a new cup plate released every two months. Each would have a nursery rhyme character and each would be a different color. A ruby 13th cup plate was to be given to the subscriber as a gift or bonus. All seconds would be destroyed, and the price was guaranteed for each piece. The subscriber would pay $11.95 in advance of the release of the next cup plate. Although they were very cute, these cup plates did not sell as well as was expected. That the pieces had to be purchased as a set may have caused the slow sales. I think there may have been a second problem with the acceptance of this set. Fenton collectors seem to collect by categories, and the cup plates really didn't fall into any of Fenton's most popular classifications, like Hobnail or Crests. If Kaleidoscope had seen a desire on the part of Fenton collectors to buy more cup plates, another series may have been introduced, but due to low sales, this was the first and last series by the company. Because of the low sales, these are hard to find, but the prices have not followed the general rule of rarities, which would have driven them higher. The cup plates sell for only a little more than they did when released.

Kaleidoscope advertisement for the set of cup plates.

#1, Jack Be Nimble, $14.00 – 18.00.

#2 Little Bo Peep, $14.00 – 18.00.

#3 Humpty Dumpty, $14.00 – 18.00.

#4 Three Little Kittens, $14.00 – 18.00.

#5 Jack & Jill, $14.00 – 18.00.

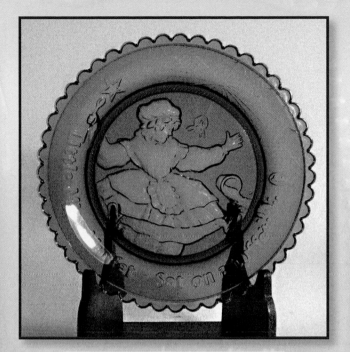

#6 Little Miss Muffet, $14.00 – 18.00.

#7 Hey Diddle Diddle, $14.00 – 18.00.

#8 The Lion & the Unicorn, $14.00 – 18.00.

#9 This Little Pig, $14.00 – 18.00.

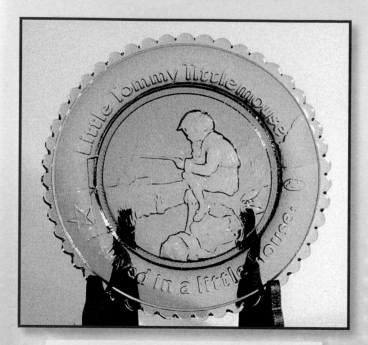

#10 Little Tommy Tiddlemouse, $14.00 – 18.00.

#11 Ole King Cole, $16.00 – 20.00.

#12 Little Robin Redbreast, $14.00 – 18.00.

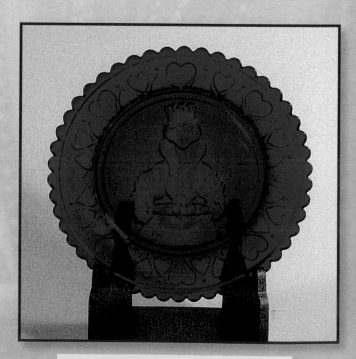

Bonus Queen of Hearts, $16.00 – 20.00.

Fenton has been making lamps almost since the discovery of electricity. I was lucky enough to find a copy of the lamp shade catalog pages Fenton used to show lamp companies what moulds were available. In these pages, there are some very rare colors and designs. Although there is no date, I am certain the catalog was issued in the mid-1960s and was used into the 1970s. While we can't identify all the lamp companies who bought shades for this catalog, at least we know what shapes and colors were sold.

On the first page there is a color, Honeydew, that has never been documented by any author, although many years ago these pages were printed in the FAGCA *Butterfly Net*. At that time, this color went unnoticed by everyone. Honeydew is Fenton's Colonial Green glass cased with a French Opalescent layer. The Colonial Green color is so light that Honeydew is hard to distinguish from French Opalescent glass. I found a shade for Frank Fenton several years ago. He had forgotten how pretty the color was.

The fifth page shown also has several interesting shades. The top row pictures a Thumbprint shade in a color called Burgundy. It appears to be a very deep shade of ruby overlay that almost looks plum. If you look at the Coin Dot shades on row two and three, the color is called Rose Opalescent, not Cranberry Opalescent. Rose Opalescent may be the Burgundy color cased with French Opalescent glass. On the other pages, the usual name for this color, Cranberry Opalescent, is used. On the bottom row, there are two lamp shades in Amber with an Opal Crest. These are also very rare.

With the Ruby Lamp Company catalog shown in *Fenton, Glass Made for Other Companies, 1907 – 1980* and the lamp parts shown in this book, most of the shades made by Fenton can be identified. There are no sizes listed in these pages, but when I know the size I will list it. I would rather not guess.

Row 1: S-9071AR Amber Poppy fount, $35.00 – 10.00; S-9021CG Colonial Green Poppy shade, $45.00 – 50.00; T-9052CG Colonial Green round fount, $30.00 – 35.00; G-1450HS Honeysuckle fount, $35.00 – 45.00; P-1421HS Honeysuckle shade, $45.00 – 65.00; G-1425HS Honeysuckle fluted shade, $45.00 – 65.00.

Row 2: G-1473HS Honeysuckle Coin Dot Temple Jar fount; S-1424CG Colonial Green Thumbprint student shade, $35.00 – 45.00; P-1454CG Colonial Green Thumbprint fount, $15.00 – 16.00; S-1455HD Honeydew Coin Dot fount, $65.00 – 75.00; N-1424HD Honeydew Coin Dot 10" student shade, $75.00 – 95.00.

Row 3: T-1429HS Honeysuckle Coin Dot hurricane shade, $75.00 – 95.00; N-1424CG Colonial Green Thumbprint 10" student shade, $65.00 – 75.00; S-1455CG Colonial Green Thumbprint fount, $20.00 – 22.00; S-1429HS Honeysuckle Coin Dot Tear Drop shade, $75.00 – 95.00.

Row 4: G-1422HS Honeysuckle Coin Dot wide Tear Drop, $85.00 – 100.00; P-1457HS Honeysuckle Coin Dot fount, $25.00 – 35.00; N-1424AR Amber Thumbprint 10" student shade, $65.00 – 75.00; S-1455AR Amber Thumbprint fount, $20.00 – 22.00; G-2722AR Amber Honeycomb lg. Tear Drop, $65.00 – 75.00.

Fine Handblown Glass — LAMP PARTS — MANUFACTURED BY *The Fenton Art Glass Company* WILLIAMSTOWN, WEST VIRGINIA

COLOR CODE
AR—Amber HD—Honeydew
CG—Colonial Green HS—Honeysuckle

Row 1: 3832HA Honey Amber Hobnail 10" shade, $50.00 – 60.00; P-1425FO large ball-shaped shade, $75.00 – 95.00; G-1428FO small ball-shaped shade, $60.00 – 75.00.

Row 2: 3831HA 7" Honey Amber Hobnail 7" shade, $40.00 – 50.00; N-1424FO Coin Dot 10" shade, $100.00 – 125.00; S-1424FO Coin Dot 7" shade, 75.00 – 85.00.

Row 3: T-3853HA Honey Amber Hobnail lg. fount, $30.00 – 35.00; T-3753HA Honey Amber Hobnail sm. fount, $25.00 – 30.00; T-3720HA Honey Amber Hobnail shade, $35.00 – 45.00; P-1454FO Small Coin Dot fount, $35.00 – 45.00.

Row 4: T-3870HA Honey Amber Hobnail fount, $40.00 – 45.00; S-1455FO, $45.00 – 55.00.

Row 5: T-3867CR Hobnail handled decanter-type fount, $125.00 – 150.00; J-3866CR ftd. handled Hobnail fount, $65.00 – 75.00; T-3866AR Amber Hobnail ftd. handled fount, $45.00 – 50.00; S-1471FO French Opalescent Coin Dot lg. vase-style fount, $100.00 – 120.00.

Row 1: S-3827CR Hobnail hurricane shade, $70.00 – 80.00; S-3827AR Hobnail hurricane shade, $35.00 – 45.00; T-3853CR Hobnail fount, $50.00 – 65.00; T-3853AR Hobnail fount, $30.00 – 35.00; T-3753CR Hobnail fount, $45.00 – 50.00; T-3753AR Hobnail fount, $25.00 – 30.00.

Row 2: S-3826AR Hobnail 5" shade, $35.00 – 40.00; S-3826CR Hobnail 5" student shade, $65.00 – 75.00; 3831AR Hobnail 7" student shade, $40.00 – 50.00; 3831CR 7" Hobnail student shade, $100.00 – 120.00.

Row 3: S-2820MI Wild Rose & Bowknot 7" shade, $65.00 – 75.00, and S-2850MI fount, $35.00 – 45.00; S-2820HA Wild Rose & Bowknot 7" shade, $45.00 – 50.00, and S-2850HA fount, $30.00 – 35.00; S-2820CP Colonial Pink Wild Rose & Bowknot 7" shade, $65.00 – 75.00, and S-2850CP fount, $35.00 – 45.00.

Row 4: T-3720CR Hobnail shade, $65.00 – 75.00; T-3720AR Hobnail shade, $35.00 – 40.00; 3832CR 10" hobnail student shade, $150.00 – 175.00; 3832AR 10" hobnail student shade, $50.00 – 60.00.

Row 1: *3831CB Colonial Blue Hobnail 7" student shade, $50.00 – 65.00; T-3753CB Hobnail fount, $30.00 – 45.00; T-3720CB Hobnail shade, $45.00 – 60.00.*
Diamond Optic shades, row 2: *T-1723AR flared shade, $65.00 – 75.00; T-1723CB flared shade, $75.00 – 85.00; T-1723RO flared shade, $100.00 – 120.00.*
Poppy 7" shades, row 3: *S-9021AR Amber, $45.00 – 50.00; S-9021CB Colonial Blue, $65.00 – 75.00; S-9021CP Colonial Pink, $65.00 – 75.00.*
Poppy shades & founts, row 4: *T-9052AR fount, $30.00 – 35.00; T-9022 round shade, $65.00 – 75.00; T-9052CB fount, $35.00   15.00; T-9022 round shade, $90.00 – 100.00; T-9052CP fount, $35.00 – 45.00; T-9022CP round shade, $90.00 – 100.00.*

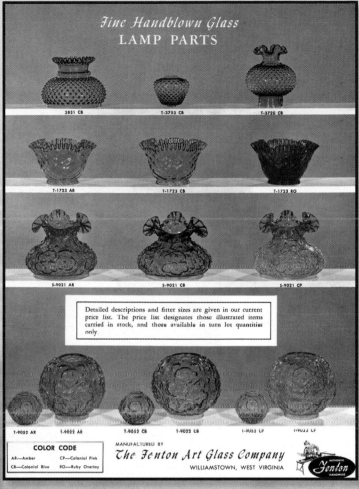

Row 1: *Burgundy Thumbprint G-1450BY fount, $40.00 – 45.00; S-1424BY 7" student shade, $150.00 – 175.00; S-1455BY fount, $45.00 – 50.00.*
Row 2: *Coin Dot P-1425RL Rose Opalescent lg. round shade, $150.00 – 175.00; S-1455RL fount, $75.00 – 85.00; P-1425FO lg. round shade, $75.00 – 95.00.*
Row 3: *Coin Dot S-1426RL small ball shade $125.00 – 150.00; S-1455HS fount, $45.00 – 55.00; S-1426HS small ball shade, $60.00 – 75.00.*
Row 4: *Coin Dot N-1424HS 10" student shade, $100.00 – 125.00; S-1412HS 7" student shade, $75.00 – 85.00; P-1454HS, $20.00 – 25.00; S1431FO hurricane shade, $50.00 – 60.00.*
Row 5: *Wild Rose & Bowknot T-2822AL Amber with Opal Crest 7" student shade, $75.00 – 100.00; S-2850AR fount, $30.00 – 35.00; S-2831AL hurricane shade, $85.00 – 95.00; Poppy S-9025AR flared shade, $75.00 – 100.00; S-9022AR lg. ball shade, ruffled top, $70.00 – 80.00.*

Fine Handblown Glass
LAMP PARTS

T-2652 CR   T-2652 FO   T-2650 FO   T-2650 CR   T-2658 CR   T-2358 RO

T-2656 CR   T-2656 FO   T-2657 CR   T-2357 RO

T-2620 CR   T-2620 FO   T-2621 CR   T-2621 FO

S-2628 CR   T-2328 RO   S-2627 FO   S-2627 CR

COLOR CODE

CR—Cranberry
FO—French Opalescent
RO—Ruby Overlay

MANUFACTURED BY

The Fenton Art Glass Company

WILLIAMSTOWN, WEST VIRGINIA

Row 1: Spiral T-2652CR, $45.00 – 55.00; T-2652FO, $30.00 – 35.00; T-2650FO $30.00 – 35.00; T-2650CR, $45.00 – 55.00; T-2658CR, $45.00 – 50.00; Double Wedding Ring T-2358 RO fount, $35.00 – 40.00.

Row 2: Spiral T-2656CR fount, $50.00 – 60.00; T-2656FO, $40.00 – 45.00; T-2657CR fount, $45.00 – 50.00; Double Wedding Ring T-2357RO, $35.00 – 40.00.

Row 3: Spiral T-2620CR 7" student shade, $100.00 – 125.00; T2620FO, $65.00 – 85.00; T-2621CR shade, $85.00 – 95.00; T-2621FO, $65.00 – 75.00.

Row 4: Spiral S-2628CR lg. ball shade, $125.00 – 150.00; Double Wedding Ring T-2328RO, $100.00 – 125.00; Spiral S-2627 FO lg. ball shade, crimped top, $125.00 – 150.00; S-2627CR, $150.00 – 175.00.

Lenox Catalog Sales

For many years, the Lenox Company was only known for its beautifully crafted porcelain dinnerware and giftware. Then it purchased the Imperial Glass Company and glass became an important addition to the Lenox product line. For several years, the Imperial Glass Company added to its bottom line, but in the 1980s, sales dropped enough to induce Lenox to sell the glass division, a move that would spell the end for Imperial Glass. Lenox's experience with Imperial made it aware of the many customers looking for glass that would decorate their homes or compliment their china.

In the late 1990s, Lenox added Fenton to its product line, but only purchased special-order pieces. It's not been possible for me to find a list of items made for Lenox, but I am adding everything that I become aware of to the list I have now. I will update this in the next edition. Lenox continues to buy special-order glass from Fenton and lists it on its website and in its catalogs. If you collect Fenton's menagerie of animals, you may want to acquire the Lenox catalog.

FENTON'S ANIMAL FIGURINES

Description	Item #	Color	Decoration	Value
Baby Dolphin	5087	Celeste Blue	Shells	$55.00 – 60.00
Bird	5163	Violet	Floral	$35.00 – 40.00
Bunny*	5162	Rose Milk	Floral	$50.00 – 55.00
Cat, grooming	5074	Celeste Blue Satin	Honeysuckles	$65.00 – 75.00
Cat, grooming	5074	Black	Hydrangeas	$50.00 – 65.00
Cat, Scaredy	5291	Black	Spiderwebs	$40.00 – 45.00
Cat, stylized	5065	French Opalescent Iridized	"Thinking of You Makes Me Smile"	$45.00 – 55.00
Elephant	5158	Rose	White Bellflowers	$45.00 – 55.00
Fawn	5160	Autumn Gold Irid.	Bittersweet Buds	$40.00 – 45.00
Fox	5226	Autumn Gold	Bittersweet Buds	$45.00 – 55.00
Frog	5274	Willow Green Satin	Daffodils	$45.00 – 50.00
Owl	5258	Black	Halloween Spiderwebs	$55.00 – 60.00
Piglet	5021	Rose	Floral Necklace	$45.00 – 55.00
Puppy	5085	Opal Satin	Holly & Red Scarf	$45.00 – 55.00
Rooster, 3½"	5084	Amber	Sunflowers	$35.00 – 40.00
Sleeping Kitten	5064	Rose Satin	Roses	$45.00 – 50.00
Turtle	5266	Rose Iridescent	Floral	$45.00 – 55.00

*Swarovski crystal.

Black with Spiderwebs #5291 Scaredy Cat, $40.00 – 45.00.

Black with Jack O' Lanterns #7379 basket, $75.00 – 85.00.

Black with Spiderwebs #5258 Owl figurine, $55.00 – 60.00.

French Opalescent Booo Ghost figurine, $45.00 – 50.00.

Celeste Blue Satin bud vase, Hummingbird & Floral decoration, $35.00 – 45.00.

Celeste Blue Satin #3050 vase. Hummingbird & Floral decoration, $65.00 – 85.00.

Celeste Blue Satin #5074 Honeysuckle-decorated Grooming Cat, $55.00 – 65.00.

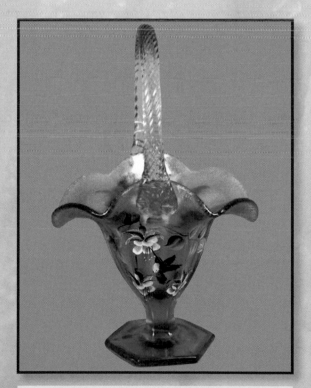

Celeste Blue stretch glass #5937 basket, Hummingbird & Floral decoration, $85.00 – 95.00.

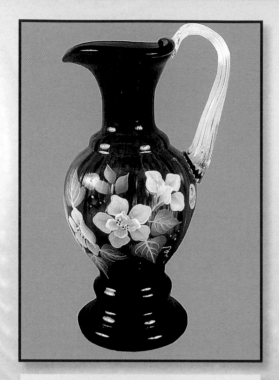

Cobalt Blue #2973 pitcher vase, White Flowers, $85.00 – 95.00.

Cobalt Blue #3249 vase, White Flowers, $65.00 – 75.00.

Cobalt Blue #5931 basket, White Flowers, $85.00 – 95.00.

Cobalt Blue #3249 vase, Winter decoration, $65.00 – 75.00.

Emerald Green #3071 vase, Poinsettia decoration, $75.00 – 85.00.

Emerald Green #7379 basket, Poinsettia decoration, $85.00 – 95.00.

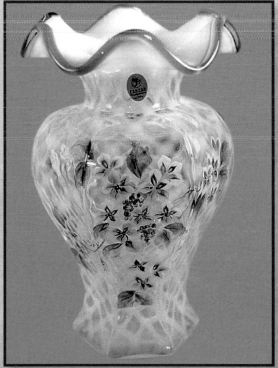

CR Opalescent Heart Spot #1537 vase, $120.00 – 135.00.

FO Diamond Optic #1554 vase, Violet Crest, decorated with Purple Flowers, $85.00 – 95.00.

"Kiss Me Good Morning" #2759 Rose Milk rose bowl & candle, $40.00 – 50.00.

"My Sister, My Friend" #2759 Violet rose bowl & candle, $40.00 – 50.00.

Violet #9598 jewel box, Purple Florals, $50.00 – 65.00.

Ruby #6833 basket, White Floral decoration, $85.00 – 100.00.

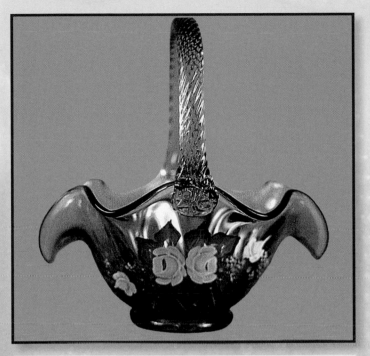

Violet #2777 basket, White Roses decoration, $85.00 – 100.00.

Violet #5163 Fat Bird, White Roses decoration, $35.00 – 40.00.

Violet #1689 vase, White Roses decoration, $85.00 – 95.00.

LENOX

Gifts That Celebrate Life

A slow-moving sweetheart in Fenton art glass

CREATED EXCLUSIVELY FOR LENOX

Rose Iridescent #5266 Turtle, Floral decoration, $45.00 – 55.00.

Rose #5158 Elephant with Bellflower decoration,
$45.00 – 55.00

Rose Milk Satin #5162 Bunny, Swarovski crystal, $50.00
– 55.00.

Rose Milk Satin #4780 basket, Floral decoration, $85.00 – 100.00.

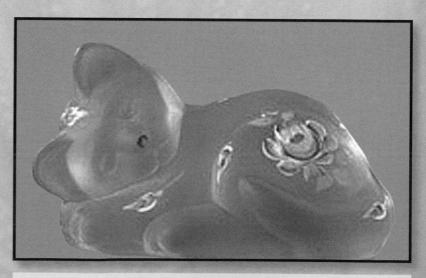

Rose Satin #5064 Sleeping Kitten, Pink Rose decoration, $45.00
– 50.00.

Sunset over Milk Glass #1009 vase, Floral decoration, $85.00 – 95.00.

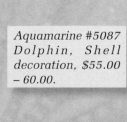

Sunset Satin #4200 lamp, $125.00 – 150.00.

Black #5074 Grooming Cat, Blue Hydrangeas decoration, $50.00 – 65.00.

Aquamarine #5087 Dolphin, Shell decoration, $55.00 – 60.00.

Ice Blue Iridescent #5535 Tree, $60.00 – 70.00.

Amber #5084 Rooster, Sunflower decoration, $35.00 – 40.00.

Willow the Frog, #5274, non-striking Willow Green, $45.00 – 50.00.

Levay Glass — Gary and Dodie Levay

Gary Levay, of Edwardsville, Illinois, decided very early in life that he would like to be in the merchandising business. Even though he had no glass factory and owned no moulds, he was able to make a name for himself in a trade that had been perfected by Si Wright, owner of the L.G. Wright Company. Levay did have an ability to choose colors and treatments for glass made in antique moulds for patterns like Grape and Cable, Cactus, and Cherry Chain. Levay, named for his grandfather, Michael John Levay, maintained a retail storefront but primarily ran a mail order business. Most of the glass made for the Levays was sold to antique stores and dealers who sold to the general public. All the glass made for them by Fenton is signed and was well advertised as Fenton, a fact that Fenton collectors would come to appreciate in just a few years. The first exclusives made for the Levays by Fenton were Turtle ring trees in Colonial Blue and Colonial Amber. That first order was in 1973, but there were no large orders placed by them until 1977, when they bought Fenton's Burmese glass decorated with painted Violets. Five types of pieces, baskets, rose bowls, cruets, fairy lights, and vases, were ordered, and each type was limited to 1,000 pieces. That amount may sound like a large quantity, but the collectors who have searched for these pieces for years would say that 1,000 pieces were not enough.

Aqua Opalescent Carnival, Purple Slag, Chocolate Glass, Ruby Carnival, Vaseline and Blue Opalescent were the colors that Fenton made for the Levay Company in the early years of the 1980s. The 1980s were difficult years for FAGCO, and the orders placed by Gary and Dodie were very welcome. Some of the colors made for them were experimental and very innovative.

Wistblueria was advertised this way: "Is it Ice Blue Carnival? No. Is it Wisteria Carnival? No. It is 'Wistblueria Carnival.' The combination of both pastel blue and lavender are the dominant colors in this unique experimental glass with brilliant pink iridescent highlights." I wish I could show you a picture of this unusual color, but like most of you, I have never seen a piece that fits this description. Only 200 pieces of each style were made. The selling price was $25 each. Don't you wish we could go back and buy all of them? When I saw the color Deep Cranberry Opalescent Carnival advertised, I thought it must be a mistake, because you can't press Cranberry without it turning purple. Well, that is exactly what happened. Today, these pieces are listed as Plum Opalescent Carnival, but that name is incorrect for the Drapery and Grape & Cable pieces sold in the early 1980s.

I have listed everything that I know was made for Levay, but that doesn't mean that I haven't missed something. I found that the company bought small orders of items that may have been samples made in very small quantities. Many of those were sold without being put on an order blank or invoice. In some cases, like the Plum Opalescent Hobnail, iridescence was added to a small quantity but it's impossible to discover and list all of these kinds of pieces. Add 10% to the price for the iridized items.

Aqua Opalescent Cactus covered sugar/candy, $75.00 – 95.00.

AQUA OPALESCENT CARNIVAL

Pattern	Shape	Edition	Ware #	Value
Butterfly & Berry	Basket, 7½" loop handled		8240/2	$75.00 – 85.00
Butterfly & Berry	Basket, 7½" piecrust oval	95	8240/5	$65.00 – 75.00
Butterfly & Berry	Handkerchief vase, 5½"		8240/7	$60.00 – 70.00
Butterfly & Berry	Spittoon, 4"		8240/4	$85.00 – 100.00
Butterfly & Berry	Vase, 3¾" DC		8240/1	$50.00 – 55.00
Butterfly & Berry	Vase, 3¾" piecrust crimped		8240/6	$50.00 – 55.00
Butterfly & Berry	Vase, 9" beaded top swung		8240/3	$65.00 – 70.00
Cactus	Basket, 7"		3437IO	$125.00 – 150.00
Cactus	Bowl, 7" crimped		3423IO	$50.00 – 60.00
Cactus	Bowl, 10" DC berry		3420IO	$55.00 – 65.00
Cactus	Comport, DC		3423IO	$40.00 – 45.00
Cactus	Cream pitcher		3468IO	$50.00 – 65.00
Cactus	Cruet		3463IO	$150.00 – 165.00
Cactus	Goblet, ftd.			(ea.) $25.00 – 30.00
Cactus	Pitcher		3407IO	$300.00 – 350.00
Cactus	Rose bowl		3453IO	$75.00 – 85.00
Cactus	Sugar or candy, covered		3488IO	$75.00 – 95.00
Cactus	Toothpick, crimped		3495IO	$35.00 – 40.00
Cactus	Vase, 7"		3457IO	$65.00 – 85.00
Cherry Chain/Orange Tree	Banana bowl, candy ribbon edge	500	1281IO-J	$125.00 – 150.00
Cherry Chain/Orange Tree	Basket, 9" candy ribbon edge	500	1281IO-D	$150.00 – 175.00
Cherry Chain/Orange Tree	Basket, 9" DC loop handled	500	1281IO-E	$250.00 – 300.00
Cherry Chain/Orange Tree	Basket, loop handled banana shape	500	1281IO-F	$250.00 – 300.00
Cherry Chain/Orange Tree	Bowl, 8" 12 pt. crimped	500	1281IO-H	$85.00 – 95.00
Cherry Chain/Orange Tree	Bowl, 9" DC	500	1281IO-I	$85.00 – 95.00
Cherry Chain/Orange Tree	Bowl, 9" candy ribbon edge	500	1281IO-K	$85.00 – 95.00

Pattern	Shape	Edition	Ware #	Value
Cherry Chain/Orange Tree	Chop plate, 11"	500	1281IO-G	$85.00 – 100.00
Drapery	Basket, 8½" ribbon candy edge	200	9435IO	$145.00 – 165.00
Drapery	Basket, loop-handled rose bowl	200	9436IO	$175.00 – 200.00
Drapery	Bowl, 8" ribbon candy edge	200	9425IO	$75.00 – 95.00
Drapery	Rose bowl, 5"	200	8454IO	$85.00 – 100.00
Drapery	Swung vase, 12"	200	9456IO	$100.00 – 125.00
Grape & Cable	Basket, 10½"	500	1281IO	$200.00 – 250.00
Grape & Cable	Bowl, 10" berry	50	200IO	$75.00 – 95.00
Grape & Cable	Spittoon, 7½"	50	300IO	$125.00 – 150.00
Grape & Cable	Swung vase, 15"	50	100IO	$100.00 – 120.00
Hobnail	Basket, 6½"		3834IO	$65.00 – 85.00
Hobnail	Banana stand, 12" piecrust edge		3720IO	$125.00 – 150.00
Hobnail	Bell		3645IO	$65.00 – 85.00
Hobnail	Champagne punch set, 10-pc.		3611IO	$375.00 – 425.00
Hobnail	Cruet & stopper, 6½"		3863IO	$125.00 – 150.00
Hobnail	Cruet & stopper, 4½"		3869IO	$75.00 – 85.00
Hobnail	Epergne, 10" triple JIP		3701IO	$250.00 – 325.00
Hobnail	Toothpick		3795IO	$40.00 – 50.00
Hobnail	Water set, 7-pc.		3908IO	$300.00 – 350.00
Inverted Strawberry	Basket, 7" DC	200	400A	$125.00 – 175.00
Inverted Strawberry	Basket, 7" loop-handled	200	400B	$175.00 – 200.00
Inverted Strawberry	Basket, 7" oval	200	400C	$125.00 – 150.00
Inverted Strawberry	Jack in Pulpit, 8" stemmed	100	500	$120.00 – 145.00
Inverted Strawberry	Rose bowl, 6½" stemmed	100	600	$120.00 – 145.00
Inverted Strawberry	Spittoon, 6" stemmed	100	700	$175.00 – 200.00
Orange Tree	Basket, 6" rose bowl	500	1281IO	$150.00 – 165.00
Orange Tree	Basket, 6" crimped rose bowl	500	1281IO	$145.00 – 160.00
Wild Rose & Bowknot	Student lamp		2805IO	$250.00 – 275.00

Aqua Opalescent Cactus goblet, $25.00 – 30.00.

Aqua Opalescent Cactus rose bowl, $75.00 – 85.00.

Aqua Opalescent Cactus toothpick, $35.00 – 40.00.

Aqua Opalescent Cactus vase, $65.00 – 85.00.

Cherry Chain with Orange Tree Exterior
Aqua Opal Carnival Glass
Rarest, most sought-after color of old Carnival Glass — prized above all others by the connoisseur.
EACH A LIMITED EDITION OF 500

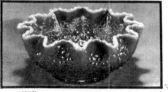

1281 H
TWELVE POINT CRIMPED BOWL
3½" DEEP   8" IN DIAMETER

by FENTON

1281 I
DELUXE MULTI-CRIMPED BOWL
3½" DEEP   9" IN DIAMETER

1281 J
CANDY RIBBON BANANA BOWL
4" TALL   11" ACROSS

1281 K
CANDY RIBBON BOWL
2½" DEEP   9" IN DIAMETER

Cherry Chain with Orange Tree Exterior
Aqua Opal Carnival Glass
Rarest, most sought-after color of old Carnival Glass —
prized above all others by the connoisseur.
EACH A LIMITED EDITION OF 500

1281 D
CANDY RIBBON EDGE BASKET
APPLIED HANDLE
9" TALL   9" IN DIAMETER

1281 E
DELUXE MULTI-CRIMPED BASKET
APPLIED LOOPED HANDLE
9" TALL   9" IN DIAMETER

by FENTON

1281 F
CANDY RIBBON BANANA BASKET
APPLIED LOOPED HANDLE
9" TALL   11" WIDE

1281 G
CHOP PLATE
11" IN DIAMETER

Aqua Opalescent Cherry Chain basket, loop handle, $250.00 – 300.00.

Top view of Cherry Chain basket.

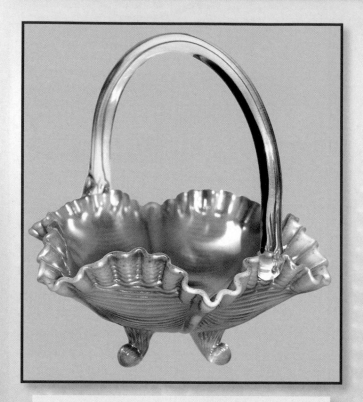

Aqua Opalescent Drapery basket, $145.00 – 165.00.

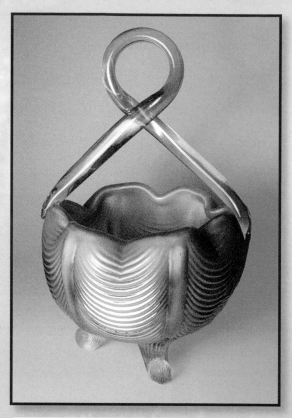

Aqua Opalescent Drapery rose bowl loop-handled basket, $175.00 – 200.00.

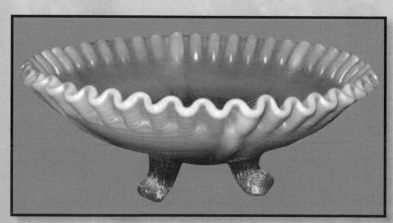

Aqua Opalescent Drapery ftd. bowl, $75.00 – 95.00.

Aqua Opalescent Grape & Cable basket, $200.00 – 250.00.

Aqua Opalescent Grape & Cable spittoon, $125.00 – 150.00.

Aqua Opalescent Orange Tree basket, $150.00 – 165.00.

INVERTED STRAWBERRY

Limited Edition

Aqua Opal Carnival Glass

Rarest, most sought-after color of old Carnival Glass —
prized above all others by the connoisseur.

400B Basket
Limited to only 200 pieces

400A Basket
Limited to only 200 pieces

700 – 6" Spittoon
Limited to only 100 pieces

600 – 6½" Rosebowl
Limited to only 100 pieces

400C Basket
Limited to only 200 pieces

500 8" Jack in the Pulpit
Limited to only 100 pieces

by Fenton

*Aqua Opalescent Inverted Strawberry basket,
$125.00 – 175.00.*

Aqua Opalescent Hobnail basket, $65.00 – 75.00.

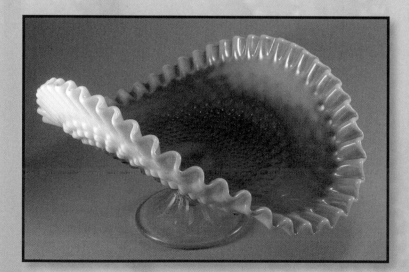

Aqua Opalescent Hobnail banana bowl, $125.00 – 150.00.

Aqua Opalescent Hobnail cruet w/stopper, $125.00 – 150.00.

Aqua Opalescent Hobnail epergne, $250.00 – 325.00.

Aqua Opalescent Hobnail tumbler, $40.00 – 45.00.

BLUE OPALESCENT

Pattern	Shape	Ware #	Edition	Value
Diamond Optic	Pitcher & tumbler set, 7-pc.	1764BO	5000	$200.00 – 250.00
Diamond Optic	Rose bowl, 3¼"	1724BO	5000	$50.00 – 65.00
Cactus	Basket, 7"	3437BO		$125.00 – 150.00
Cactus	Bowl, 7" crimped	3423BO		$45.00 – 55.00
Cactus	Bowl, 10" DC berry	3420BO		$50.00 – 65.00
Cactus	Comport, DC	3429BO		$40.00 – 50.00
Cactus	Cream pitcher	3469BO		$40.00 – 50.00
Cactus	Cruet	3463BO		$125.00 – 150.00
Cactus	Rose bowl	3453BO		$65.00 – 75.00
Cactus	Sugar or candy, covered	3488BO		$75.00 – 85.00
Cactus	Toothpick, crimped	3495BO		$25.00 – 30.00
Cactus	Vase, 7"	3457BO		$65.00 – 75.00
Hobnail	Banana stand, 12" piecrust edge	3720BO		$100.00 – 125.00

Pattern	Shape	Wate #	Edition	Value
Hobnail	Basket, 6½"	3834BO		$65.00 – 75.00
Hobnail	Bell	3645BO		$45.00 – 50.00
Hobnail	Butter, 8½" rd. covered	3677BO		$100.00 – 125.00
Hobnail	Champagne punch set, 10-pc.	3611BO		$375.00 – 425.00
Hobnail	Cruet & stopper, 6½"	3863BO		$150.00 – 165.00
Hobnail	Cruet & stopper, 4½"	3869BO		$65.00 – 85.00
Hobnail	Epergne, 10" triple JIP	3701BO		$225.00 – 275.00
Hobnail	Punch set, master 14-pc.	3712BO		$375.00 – 425.00
Hobnail	Toothpick, 2¾"	3795BO		$20.00 – 30.00
Hobnail	Water set, 7-pc.	3908BO		$275.00 – 325.00
Hobnail	Wash bowl & pitcher set*		400 sets	$350.00 – 400.00

* Mother-of-pearl iridization.

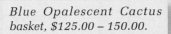

Blue Opalescent Cactus basket, $125.00 – 150.00.

Blue Opalescent Cactus goblet, $40.00 – 45.00.

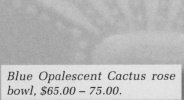

Blue Opalescent Cactus rose bowl, $65.00 – 75.00.

the Antique Trade
BLUE OPALESCENT

Fenton Art Glass

THE WHITE OR OPALESCENT PORTION SHOWS A FIERY QUALITY WHEN HELD TO THE LIGHT—
A UNIQUE CHARACTERISTIC OF FINE OPALESCENT HANDMADE GLASSWARE.

3701 BO
10" Jack in the Pulpit Epergne

3908 BO
7 pc. Water Set
8¼" 54 oz. Pitcher—w/6 - 4" 9 oz. Tumblers

3720 BO
12" Pie Crust Crimped Banana Stand

3611 BO
Champagne Punch Set
12½" diameter bowl—w/8 - 3½" matching champagnes

3712 BO
14 Pc. Master Punch Set, 7 Qt. Bowl on Stand
with 12 matching cups

3869 BO
Mini-Cruet
w/Stopper

3834 BO
6½" Basket

3645 BO
5½" Bell

3677 BO
8¼" diameter Covered Butter

3795 BO
2¾" Toothpick

3863 BO
6½" Cruet
w/Stopper

FASCINATING
Fenton Art Glass

BLUE OPALESCENT HOBNAIL

14 piece Master Punch Set, 14 inch, seven quart Pie Crust Crimped Bowl on stand with 12 matching cups. The white, or opalescent portion, shows a fiery quality when held to the light . . . a unique characteristic of the finest opalescent **handmade** glassware!

3712 BO
14 pc. Punch Set

Blue Opalescent Hobnail butter dish, $100.00 – 125.00.

Iridized Blue Opalescent pitcher, $175.00 – 200.00; tumbler, $40.00 – 45.00.

BURMESE, GLOSSY & SATIN FINISH
(All pieces made in both finishes.)

Pattern	Shape	Ware #	Value
Square shape, plain	Basket, 7" satin	7535BR	$125.00 – 150.00
Ribbed pink handle	Basket, 7" glossy DC	2834BE	$125.00 – 150.00
Ribbed pink handle	Basket, 7" satin DC	2834BR	$125.00 – 150.00
No pattern	Bowl, 7" satin DC	7227BR	$65.00 – 85.00
No pattern	Vase, 7" JIP glossy	7552	$75.00 – 85.00
No pattern	Vase, 7" JIP satin	7552	$75.00 – 85.00
Wild Rose & Bowknot	Basket, 7"	2834BE – 2834BR	$150.00 – 165.00
Wild Rose & Bowknot	Rose bowl, 5"	2824BE – 2834BR	$85.00 – 100.00
Wild Rose & Bowknot	Vase, 7½" DC	2857BE – 2857BR	$85.00 – 100.00
Wild Rose & Bowknot	Vase, 9" JIP	2854BE – 2854BR	$100.00 – 125.00

BURMESE, PAINTED VIOLETS

Shape	Edition	Ware #	Value
Basket, 8"	1,000	7437	$350.00 – 400.00
Cruet, 7"	1,000	7468	$325.00 – 375.00
Fairy light, 5"	1,000	7492	$275.00 – 325.00
Rose bowl, 3½"	1,000	7424	$150.00 – 175.00
Vase, 7"	1,000	7252	$175.00 – 200.00

Burmese Glass

Burmese Glossy Wild Rose vase, $85.00 – 100.00.

Glossy Burmese Wild Rose basket, handle is placed correctly, $150.00 – 165.00.

Glossy Burmese Wild Rose basket, handle is on sideways, $150.00 – 165.00.

Glossy Burmese Wild Rose Jack-in-Pulpit vase, $100.00 – 125.00.

Glossy Burmese Wild Rose rose bowl, $85.00 – 100.00.

CHOCOLATE GLASS

Pattern	Shape	Ware #	Value
Butterfly & Berry	Bowl, 9" crimped	8248CK	$100.00 – 125.00
Butterfly & Berry	Plate, 10" ftd.	1252CK	$125.00 – 150.00
Button & Arch	Butter, covered	9580CK	$125.00 – 150.00
Cactus	Cracker jar, covered	3480CK	$200.00 – 225.00
Cactus	Cruet	3463CK	$150.00 – 175.00
Cherries	Cream & sugar	8402CK	(set) $125.00 – 150.00
Craftsman	Stein	9640CK	$65.00 – 85.00
Daisy & Button	#2 hat	1992CK	$40.00 – 45.00
Hobnail	Kitten slipper, 6"	3995CK	$25.00 – 30.00
Lincoln Inn	Water set, 7-pc.	9003CK	$300.00 – 350.00
Orange Tree & Leaf	Rose bowl, 5½"	8223CK	$125.00 – 145.00
Pinwheel	Comport	8427CK	$75.00 – 85.00
Strawberry	Toothpick	8295CK	$35.00 – 40.00

THE LEVAY DISTRIBUTING COMPANY • 209 East Vandalia Street • Edwardsville, Illinois 62025 • Telephone (618)656-6268

Fine handmade art glass for the Antique Trade

CHOCOLATE GLASS

Also known as Carmel Slag. The man who invented this unique form of colored glass was Jacob Rosenthal. He developed the formula for Chocolate Glass as a chemist for the Indiana Tumbler and Goblet Company at Greentown, Indiana. Mr. Rosenthal later became Fenton's first glassmaker and introduced the Chocolate Glass in 1907.

3480 CK
Cactus Covered Cracker Jar

9003 CK
7 pc. Lincoln Inn Water Set
4½" Tumblers, 7½" Pitcher

9640 CK
Craftsman Stein

8402 CK
Cherries Cream
and Sugar

8427 CK
Oval Pinwheel
Comport

3995 CK
6" Kitten Slipper

9580 CK
Button and Arch Covered Butter

8295 CK
Strawberry Toothpick Holder

Chocolate Butterfly & Berry ftd. plate, $125.00 – 150.00.

Chocolate Butterfly & Berry bowl, $100.00 – 125.00.

Butterfly & Berry pattern shot.

Chocolate Button & Arches butter dish, $125.00 – 150.00.

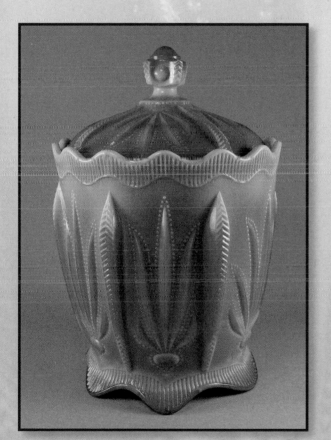

Chocolate Cactus cracker jar, $200.00 – 225.00.

Chocolate Cactus cruet, $150.00 – 175.00.

Chocolate Daisy & Button #2 hat, $40.00 – 45.00.

Chocolate Hobnail 3" vase, $50.00 – 65.00.

Chocolate Lincoln Inn pitcher, $200.00 – 225.00.

Chocolate Pinwheel comport, $75.00 – 85.00.

Chocolate Strawberry toothpick, $35.00 – 40.00.

Chocolate Cherry creamer, $65.00 – 80.00.

Chocolate Cherry sugar bowl, $60.00 – 70.00.

DEEP CRANBERRY OPALESCENT CARNIVAL
(Plum Opalescent)

Pattern	Shape	Edition	Ware #	Value
Drapery	Basket, 8½" ribbon candy	200	9435DCO	$200.00 – 225.00
Drapery	Basket, 8½" loop-handled rose bowl	200	9436DCO	$225.00 – 250.00
Drapery	Bowl, ribbon candy edge	200	9425DCO	$125.00 – 150.00
Drapery	Rose bowl, 5"	200	8454DCO	$175.00 – 200.00
Grape & Cable	Bowl, 10½" DC	40		$250.00 – 275.00
Grape & Cable	Bowl, 11½" crimped	40		$250.00 – 275.00
Grape & Cable	Spittoon, 7½"	40		$300.00 – 325.00

Deep Cranberry Opalescent Carnival Drapery ftd. bowl, $125.00 – 150.00.

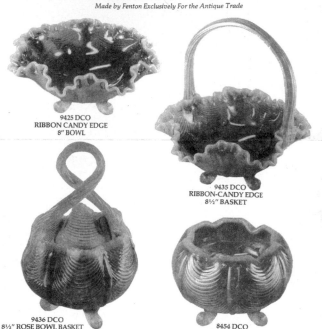

LIMITED EDITION "DRAPERY" COLLECTION
DEEP CRANBERRY OPALESCENT CARNIVAL

THE GOLD IN THIS GLASS PRODUCES A RICH PLUM COLOR OF CRANBERRY, UNIQUE IN CARNIVAL GLASS.
FOUR PIECE DRAPERY COLLECTION LIMITED TO 200 SETS.

Made by Fenton Exclusively For the Antique Trade

9425 DCO
RIBBON CANDY EDGE
8" BOWL

9435 DCO
RIBBON-CANDY EDGE
8½" BASKET

9436 DCO
8½" ROSE BOWL BASKET

8454 DCO
5" ROSE BOWL

THE LEVAY DISTRIBUTING COMPANY   209 East Vandalia Street   Edwardsville, Illinois 62025

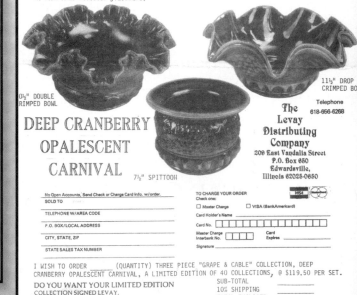

GRAPE and CABLE
LIMITED EDITION COLLECTION

Dear Levay Dealer:

I am pleased to present to you the three-piece collection in faithful reproduction of the "GRAPE AND CABLE" pattern, in deep cranberry opalescent carnival. This shimmering iridescence of deep cranberry, made with gold, presents a rich plum color. Created exclusively for the ANTIQUE TRADE, by The Fenton Art Glass Company, it sells for $119.50 wholesale and is sold only as a collection. Limited to 40 Collections only.

The artistic flair of the deep cranberry opal carnival collection is a reflection of the fine example of American handmade glass. Using the imagination of the glass craftsman, all items in this collection were created from the same mold and is another fine example of The Fenton Art Glass Company's excellent craftsmanship.

Variation of color will appear, this being part of the unique quality in the tradition of American handmade glassware.

10½" DOUBLE CRIMPED BOWL

11½" DROP CRIMPED BOWL

DEEP CRANBERRY OPALESCENT CARNIVAL

7½" SPITTOON

The Levay Distributing Company
Telephone 618-656-6268
209 East Vandalia Street
P.O. Box 650
Edwardsville,
Illinois 62025-0650

No Open Accounts, Send Check or Charge Card Info. w/ order.
Check one:

SOLD TO

TELEPHONE W/AREA CODE

P.O. BOX/LOCAL ADDRESS

CITY, STATE, ZIP

STATE SALES TAX NUMBER

TO CHARGE YOUR ORDER
Check one:
☐ Master Charge   ☐ VISA (BankAmericard)
Card Holder's Name
Card No.
Master Charge Interbank No.   Card Expires
Signature

I WISH TO ORDER _____ (QUANTITY) THREE PIECE "GRAPE & CABLE" COLLECTION, DEEP CRANBERRY OPALESCENT CARNIVAL, A LIMITED EDITION OF 40 COLLECTIONS, @ $119.50 PER SET.

DO YOU WANT YOUR LIMITED EDITION COLLECTION SIGNED LEVAY, DATED & NUMBERED? YES___NO___

SUB-TOTAL _____
10% SHIPPING _____
TOTAL ENCLOSED _____

BUTTERSCOTCH
(Green with a Marigold spray.)

Pattern	Shape	Ware#	Edition	Value
Drapery	Basket, 8½" ribbon candy edge	9435	200	$175.00 – 195.00
Drapery	Basket, 8½" rose bowl, loop-handled	9436	200	$200.00 – 225.00
Drapery	Bowl, 8" ribbon candy edge	9425	200	$100.00 – 125.00
Drapery	Rose bowl, 5"	8454	200	$85.00 – 100.00
Drapery	Vase, ftd. swung	9456	200	$125.00 – 145.00
Inverted Strawberry	Ladies cuspidor, stemmed	9540		$150.00 – 175.00
Inverted Strawberry	Rose bowl, 6½" ftd.	9546		$125.00 – 150.00
Inverted Strawberry	Vase, 8" ftd. JIP	9542		$145.00 – 165.00

Butterscotch Drapery loop-handled rose bowl basket, $200.00 – 225.00.

Butterscotch Drapery basket, $175.00   195.00.

ELECTRIC BLUE CARNIVAL

Pattern	Shape	Edition	Ware #	Value
Alley Cat	Doorstop, 10"		5177BN	$225.00 – 250.00
Butterfly & Berry	Basket		9134BN	$125.00 – 150.00
Butterfly & Berry	Bowl		8428BN	$65.00 – 75.00
Butterfly & Berry	Hat vase		9495BN	$65.00 – 75.00
Butterfly	On stand	limited		$75.00 – 85.00
Diamond Lattice	Cruet		1768BN	$125.00 – 150.00
Diamond Lattice	Tall creamer			$65.00 – 75.00
Diamond Lattice	Water set, 7-pc.	300	1707BN	$250.00 – 300.00
Fantail	Chop plate, 3-ftd.		8419BN	$125.00 – 150.00
Leaf & Orange Tree	Rose bowl, 3-ftd.		8223BN	$125.00 – 150.00
Owl	Blown, hollow		5178BN	$175.00 – 225.00
Persian Medallion	Basket, 7"		9135BN	$65.00 – 85.00

Pattern	Shape	Edition	Ware #	Price
Persian Medallion	Rose bowl, 3-sided		9123BN	$50.00 – 65.00
Poppy	Lamp, GWTW	500	9101BN	$225.00 – 275.00
Rabbit	Blown, hollow		5178BN	$175.00 – 225.00
Strawberry	Basket, mini		9133BN	$65.00 – 85.00
Strawberry	Toothpick, spittoon shaped		8295BN	$50.00 – 65.00

Electric Blue Carnival Art Glass by Fenton

Made exclusively for the Antique Trade. A new color and iridescent treatment for Carnival Glass collectors.

22 PC. STARTER ASSORTMENT (quantities of each item in assortment are shown in parentheses after ware number)— After purchasing 1 starter assortment you may then order any quantity of any item (8295 Toothpick is packed 2 per carton) and also qualify to purchase the lamp and 7 piece water set.

8419 BN (1)
Fantail –3 Footed Chop Plate

5178 BN (1)
6½" Owl

8223 BN (2)
Leaf & Orange Tree Rose Bowl

5177 BN (1)
10" Alley Cat (Door Stop)

1768 BN (2)
Diamond Lattice Cruet

5174 BN (1)
Rabbit

9135 BN (1)
Persian Medallion Basket

9123 BN (2)
Pers. Medallion 3-Sided Rose Bowl

9134 BN (2)
Butterfly & Berry Basket

9495 BN (2)
Butterfly & Berry Hat

8428 BN (1)
Fantail (Butterfly & Berry) Bowl

8295 BN* (4)
Strawberry Toothpick

9133 BN (2)
Mini Strawberry Basket

*Toothpick not flared as shown

AVAILABLE THROUGH
MAY 31, 1980

For Information Contact:
LEVAY DISTRIBUTING COMPANY
209 East Vandalia Street
Edwardsville, Illinois 62025
Phone: 618-656-6268

9101 BN

Limited To
500

ABOVE: Poppy Gone With The Wind Lamp electrified with three way switch and night light in base. 24" tall.

These two items are sold individually and not included in basic assortment.

BELOW: Truly one of *the* collector's items in antiques of the future.

Diamond Lattice 7 Piece Water Set
10½" Tankard Pitcher—4¾" Tumbler

Limited To
300 Sets

1707 BN

Electric Blue Persian Medallion 3-sided rose bowl, $50.00 – 60.00.

Electric Blue Butterfly & Berry flared vase, $65.00 – 75.00.

Electric Blue Strawberry basket, $65.00 – 85.00.

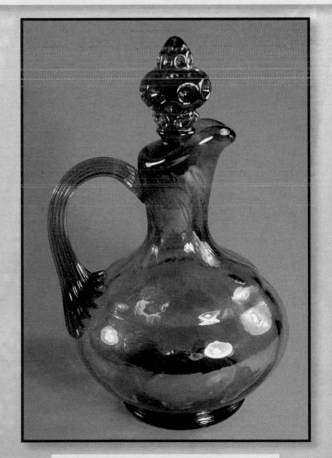

Electric Blue cruet, $125.00 – 150.00.

Electric Blue blown Owl, $175.00 – 225.00.

Electric Blue blown Rabbit, $175.00 – 225.00. Both the Owl and the Rabbit were made from old U.S. Glass moulds.

Electric Blue Butterfly & Berry ruffled vase, $65.00 – 75.00.

Electric Blue tall creamer, $65.00 – 75.00.

SPRINGTIME GREEN CARNIVAL
(Signed "Levay," numbered, and dated "1977.")

Pattern	Shape	Edition	Ware #	Value
Alley Cat	Doorstop	181	5177	$350.00 – 400.00
Cactus	Cracker jar, 8"	1000	3481	$225.00 – 275.00
Cactus	Cruet	3463		$150.00 – 175.00
Craftsman	Bell, star crimped			$65.00 – 75.00
Faberge	Bell, star crimped			$65.00 – 75.00
Grape & Cable	Humidor			$225.00 – 275.00
Orange Tree & Leaf	Rose bowl			$125.00 – 175.00
Owl	Hollow, 6½"	276	5178	$200.00 – 250.00
Rabbit	Hollow, 5½"	252	5174	$200.00 – 250.00
Sunflower	Pin tray	448	4444	$50.00 – 65.00

Springtime Green Alley Cat (U.S. Glass mould), $350.00 – 400.00.

Springtime Green blown Owl, $200.00 – 250.00.

Springtime Green blown Rabbit, $200.00 – 250.00.

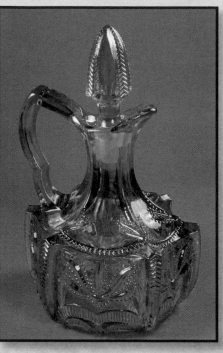

Springtime Green Cactus cruet, $150.00 – 175.00.

Springtime Green Grape & Cable humidor, $225.00 – 275.00.

CELESTIAL BLUE SATIN

Pattern	Shape	Item #	Price
Wild Rose & Bowknot	Basket, loop-handled	2836ES	$150.00 – 175.00
Wild Rose & Bowknot	Basket, 7" deep double crimped	2834ES	$150.00 – 175.00
Wild Rose & Bowknot	Bowl, 7" JIP	2853ES	$65.00 – 75.00
Wild Rose & Bowknot	Bowl, 9" double crimped	2823ES	$65.00 – 75.00
Wild Rose & Bowknot	Pitcher, ruffled top	2864ES	$100.00 – 125.00
Wild Rose & Bowknot	Rose bowl, 5"	2824ES	$75.00 – 85.00
Wild Rose & Bowknot	Vase, 9" JIP	2854ES	$85.00 – 95.00
Wild Rose & Bowknot	Vase, 7½" DC	2857ES	$75.00 – 85.00

CELESTIAL BLUE SATIN

2836ES
Pie Crust Crimped Basket
with Looped Handle

Glass of Silk

Wild Rose and Bowknot

2857ES
7½" Double
Crimped Vase

2864ES
Ruffled Top Pitcher

2854ES
9" Ruffled Jack
in the Pulpit Vase

2823ES
9" Double
Crimped Bowl

2834ES
7" Double
Crimped Basket

2824ES
5" Crimped Rose Bowl ⟷ Jack in the Pulpit Bowl

2853ES

THE GENTLE INTERLACING OF PURE WHITE AND AZURE HAS THE LOOK OF A SUMMER SKY. THE SATIN FINISH GIVES EACH PIECE THE FEEL OF LUXURIOUS SILK.

RED SUNSET CARNIVAL

Pattern	Shape	Ware #	Value
Cactus	Basket, 7½" loop-handled double crimped	3436RN	$200.00 – 225.00
Cactus	Basket, loop-handled banana single crimped	3432RN	$250.00 – 275.00
Cactus	Basket, 10" double crimped cracker	3431RN	$200.00 – 250.00
Cactus	Basket, 10" double crimped	3433RN	$175.00 – 200.00
Cactus	Basket vase, 10"	3434RN	$150.00 – 175.00
Cactus	Comport, double crimped	3429RN	$75.00 – 85.00
Cactus	Cracker jar & cover	3480RN	$225.00 – 300.00
Cactus	Cream & covered sugar	3408RN	$125.00 – 150.00
Cactus	Cruet & stopper	3463RN	$125.00 – 150.00
Cactus	Gentleman's spittoon	3427RN	$200.00 – 225.00
Cactus	Goblet, 10 oz. ftd.		$45.00 – 55.00
Cactus	Lady's cuspidor	3426RN	$150.00 – 175.00
Cactus	Pitcher		$225.00 – 275.00
Cactus	Toothpick holder	3495RN	$45.00 – 55.00
Cactus	Vase, Jack in Pulpit double crimped	3441RN	$125.00 – 150.00
Cactus	Vase, 9" swung	3463RN	$150.00 – 165.00
Cactus	Water set, 7-pc.	3407RN	$350.00 – 400.00
Fine Cut & Grape	Basket, 8½", loop-handled DC	9037RN	$200.00 – 225.00
Fine Cut & Grape	Bowl, 5½" double crimped	9046RN	$125.00 – 150.00
Fine Cut & Grape	Bowl, 6½" JIP	9053RN	$125.00 – 150.00
Fine Cut & Grape	Rose bowl, 4"	9044RN	$135.00 – 155.00
Fine Cut & Grape	Spittoon, 4"	9043RN	$150.00 – 175.00
Fine Cut & Grape	Vase, 6" handkerchief	9060RN	$125.00 – 150.00
Hobnail	Wine set, 77 made		$275.00 – 325.00
Hobnail	Decanter, 120 made		$200.00 – 225.00

Red Sunset Cactus basket, $175.00 – 200.00.

ntique Trade

...val pieces made with ruby glass and given a
... Ribbed handled pieces are done by skilled
...nest Fenton tradition.

3463 RN Cruet
3495 RN Toothpick
3436 RN 7½" Double Crimped Basket with ribbed looped handle
3433 RN 10" Double Crimped Basket
7 pc. Water Set 6-10 oz. Goblets
48 oz. Pitcher
3407 RN
3406 RN Covered Sugar/Creamer Set
3480 RN Covered Cracker Jar

A Limited Offering for the

RED SUNSET CARNIVAL CACTUS

Handcrafted ...
scarlet iridesc...
craftsmen in t...

3429 RN Footed Double Crimped Compote
3432 RN Single Crimped Pie Crust Banana Basket with ribbed looped handle.
3431 RN 10" Double Crimped Cracker Basket
3434 RN 10" Basket Vase
3426 RN Ladies' Cuspidor
3427 RN Gentlemen's Spittoon
3483 RN 9" Swung Vase
3441 RN Double Crimped Jack in Pulpit Vase

Red Sunset Cactus 10" cracker basket, $200.00 – 250.00.

Red Sunset Cactus banana basket, loop-handled, $250.00 – 275.00.

Red Sunset Cactus pitcher, $225.00 – 275.00.

Red Sunset Cactus goblet, $45.00 – 55.00.

THE LEVAY DISTRIBUTING COMPANY • 209 East Vandalia Street • Edwardsville, Illinois 60625 • Telephone (618)

RED SUNSET CARNIVAL
(scarlet iridescence)

Fenton Art Glass

"FINE CUT AND GRAPES"
Limited Edition 1000 Mini-collections

9060RN
Handkerchief Vase
Height 6"

9037RN
Looped Handled Double
Crimped Basket
Height 8½"

9046RN
Double Crimped
Bowl 5½" Diameter

9043RN
Spittoon
Height 4"

9053RN
Jack in the Pulpit
6½" Diameter

9044RN
Rose Bowl Cupped
Height 4"

THE ARTISTIC FLAIR OF EACH "FINE CUT AND GRAPES" LIMITED EDITION IS A REFLECTION OF EXCELLENT AMERICAN HANDCRAFTED GLASSWARE. USING THE IMAGINATION OF THE GLASS CRAFTSMAN, ALL OF THESE LIMITED EDITIONS WERE CREATED FROM THE SAME MOULD.

PEACH OPALESCENT CARNIVAL, DARK SHADE

Pattern	Shape	Edition	Ware #	Value
Grape & Cable	Spittoon,* 7½"	200	100MO	$275.00 – 325.00
Grape & Cable	Bowl, 10" double crimped		200MO	$200.00 – 220.00
Grape & Cable	Bowl,* 9½" pleated 8-pt.		201MO	$200.00 – 220.00

*Also made for Coyne's Parade of Gifts.

PEACH (APRICOT) OPALESCENT CARNIVAL, PASTEL SHADE

Pattern	Shape	Edition	Ware #	Value
Grape & Cable	Spittoon, 7½"	200	100AO	$225.00 – 250.00

Peach Opalescent Grape & Cable 8 pt. bowl, also sold by Coyne's Parade of Gifts, $100.00 – 135.00.

WISTBLUERIA

Pattern	*Shape*	*Edition*	*Value*
Grape & Cable	Bowl, 10" berry	200	$400.00 – 450.00
Grape & Cable	Spittoon, 7½" crimped	200	$450.00 – 500.00

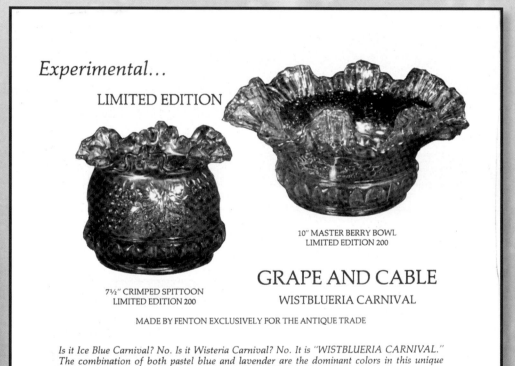

Experimental...

LIMITED EDITION

10" MASTER BERRY BOWL
LIMITED EDITION 200

7½" CRIMPED SPITTOON
LIMITED EDITION 200

GRAPE AND CABLE

WISTBLUERIA CARNIVAL

MADE BY FENTON EXCLUSIVELY FOR THE ANTIQUE TRADE

Is it Ice Blue Carnival? No. Is it Wisteria Carnival? No. It is "WISTBLUERIA CARNIVAL." The combination of both pastel blue and lavender are the dominant colors in this unique experimental glass with brilliant pink iridescent highlights.

Wistblueria brochure. Grape & Cable spittoon, $450.00 – 500.00; Grape & Cable bowl, $400.00 – 450.00.

VASELINE OPALESCENT GLOSSY FINISH

Pattern	*Shape*	*Ware #*	*Value*
Coinspot	Basket, 7"	2437VO	$125.00 – 150.00
Coinspot	Cruet, 6½"	2473TO	$145.00 – 165.00
Coinspot	Rose bowl, 4"	2424TO	$100.00 – 120.00

Pattern	Shape	Ware #	Value
Hobnail	Banana stand, 12" piecrust	3720TO	$225.00 – 250.00
Hobnail	Basket, 6" tall	3834VO	$150.00 – 165.00
Hobnail	Basket, small	3335TO	$125.00 – 145.00
Hobnail	Basket, small	3837TO	$125.00 – 145.00
Hobnail	Basket, 7" double crimped	3337TO	$145.00 – 165.00
Hobnail	Basket, 10"	3830TO	$175.00 – 200.00
Hobnail	Bell, 5½" flared	3667VO	$45.00 – 65.00
Hobnail	Bell, fluted	3667VO	$45.00 – 65.00
Hobnail	Butter, 8¼" covered	3677TO	$225.00 – 250.00
Hobnail	Bowl, 9" single crimped	3324TO	$100.00 – 125.00
Hobnail	Bowl, 9" double crimped	3924TO	$100.00 – 125.00
Hobnail	Bowl, 11" ftd. double crimped	3325TO	$100.00 – 125.00
Hobnail	Candleholder, 4"	3974TO	(ea.) $65.00 – 70.00
Hobnail	Candlestick, cornucopia	3874 TO	(ea.) $100.00 – 120.00
Hobnail	Cream & open sugar	3901TO	$65.00 – 85.00
Hobnail	Cream & covered sugar	3606TO	$100.00 – 125.00
Hobnail	Cruet	3869TO	$60.00 – 75.00
Hobnail	Cruet, 6"	3863VO	$150.00 – 165.00
Hobnail	Epergne, 4-pc.	3801TO	$175.00 – 200.00
Hobnail	Epergne, 10" triple JIP	3701TO	$250.00 – 275.00
Hobnail	Kitten slipper	3995TO	$35.00 – 45.00
Hobnail	Pitcher, 54 oz.	3908TO	$225.00 – 250.00
Hobnail	Punch set, 14" master size	3712TO	$375.00 – 450.00
Hobnail	Rose bowl, 4½" cupped	3323TO	$75.00 – 85.00
Hobnail	Rose bowl, 4½" ruffled top	3854TO	$75.00 – 85.00
Hobnail	Rose bowl, 4¼" crimped	3861TO	$75.00 – 85.00
Hobnail	Salt & pepper, ftd.	3609TO	(pr.) $75.00 – 95.00
Hobnail	Toothpick holder	3392TO	$35.00 – 40.00
Hobnail	Toothpick holder	3795TO	$35.00 – 40.00
Hobnail	Tumbler, 3½"	3945VO	$45.00 – 55.00
Hobnail	Tumbler, 9 oz.	3908TO	$55.00 – 65.00
Hobnail	Vase, 4" ruffled	3952VO	$65.00 – 75.00

Pattern	Shape	Ware #	Value
Hobnail	Vase, 4" crimped-edge fan	3953VO	$65.00 – 75.00
Hobnail	Water set, 7-pc.	3306TO	$325.00 – 375.00
Orange Tree	Bowl, 6" 3-ftd.	8223VO	$100.00 – 120.00
Orange Tree	Rose bowl, 6" dia. 3-ftd.	8223VO	$125.00 – 150.00
Persian Medallion	Chalice, 6½"	8244VO	$100.00 – 125.00
Persian Medallion	Rose bowl, 3½"	8247VO	$125.00 – 145.00
Persian Medallion	Rose bowl, 6½" stemmed	8244VO	$125.00 – 145.00
Three Fruits	Comport, 6" oval	8242VO	$75.00 – 100.00
Three Fruits	Comport, 8" fluted	8242VO	$75.00 – 100.00
Three Fruits	Comport, 6" square	8242VO	$75.00 – 100.00

VASELINE OPALESCENT SATIN

Pattern	Shape	Ware #	Value
Hobnail	Basket, 6"	3834	$125.00 – 150.00
Hobnail	Bell, 5½" flared	3667	$65.00 – 85.00
Hobnail	Cruet, 6"	3865	$145.00 – 165.00
Hobnail	Juice pitcher	3965	$150.00 – 175.00
Hobnail	Juice tumbler	3945	$35.00 – 40.00
Hobnail	Vase, 4" ftd. double crimped	3952	$50.00 – 65.00
Hobnail	Vase, 4" single crimped	3953	$50.00 – 65.00
Orange Tree	Rose bowl, 5½"	8223	$100.00 – 125.00
Persian Medallion	Chalice	8244	$100.00 – 125.00
Persian Medallion	Rose bowl, 5½"	8247	$100.00 – 125.00
Persian Medallion	Rose bowl, stemmed	8244	$100.00 – 125.00
Three Fruits	Comport, 8" oval	8242	$75.00 – 100.00
Three Fruits	Comport, 8" square	8242	$75.00 – 100.00

VASELINE OPALESCENT CARNIVAL

Pattern	Shape	Edition	Ware #	Value
Hobnail	Basket, 6"	525	3834	$135.00 – 150.00
Hobnail	Bell, 5½" flared	325	3667	$75.00 – 85.00

Pattern	Shape	Edition	Ware #	Value
Hobnail	Bell, 5½" ruffled	325	3667	$75.00 – 85.00
Hobnail	Juice pitcher	110	3965	$150.00 – 175.00
Hobnail	Juice tumbler	880	3945	$40.00 – 44.00
Hobnail	Vase, 4" ftd. double crimped	400	3952	$65.00 – 70.00
Hobnail	Vase, 4" single crimped	400	3953	$65.00 – 70.00
Orange Tree	Rose bowl, 6"	500	8223	$120.00 – 140.00
Persian Medallion	Chalice	100	8244	$145.00 – 165.00
Persian Medallion	Rose bowl, 3½"	450	8247	$145.00 – 165.00
Persian Medallion	Rose bowl, stemmed	300	8244	$145.00 – 165.00
Three Fruits	Comport, 8" oval	300	8242	$85.00 – 115.00
Three Fruits	Comport, 6" square	300	8242	$85.00 – 115.00

Page Two

LEVAY GLASS COMPANY

A-3863 Hobnail Cruet

B-3965 Hobnail Juice Set

C-3952 Hobnail Crimped Vase

D-8223 Orange Tree Rose Bowl

E-3953 Hobnail Fan Vase

F-3834 Hobnail Basket

G-8247 Persian Medallion Rosebowl

H-8223 Orange Tree Bowl

K-8242 Three Fruits Oval Compote

J-8242 Three Fruits Compote Top View

I-8242 Three Fruits Square Compote

L-8244 Persian Medallion Stemmed Rose Bowl

M-8244 Persian Medallion Chalice

N-3667 Hobnail Bell

0-3667 Hobnail Crimped Bell

Fenton Art Glass

3801 TO
4 pc. Epergne Set

3335 TO
Double Crimped Basket

3874 TO
Cornucopia Candleholder
(each)

3325 TO
11" Footed Double Crimped Bowl

3874 TO
Cornucopia Candleholder
(each)

3324 TO
9" Single Crimped Bowl

3323 TO
4½" Cupped Rose Bowl

3337 TO
7" Double Crimped Basket

3392 TO
Toothpick Holder

3901 TO
Cream & Sugar Set

3609 TO
Salt & Pepper Set

Fine handmade art glass for the Antique Trade

VASELINE OPALESCENT HOBNAIL

3306 TO
7 pc. Water Set

7 PIECE WATER SET CONSISTS OF AN 11 INCH BLOWN GLASS PITCHER WITH PLAIN TOPAZ HANDLE, CAPACITY 46 OZ. AND 6 PRESSED GLASS TUMBLERS MEASURING 4½ INCHES AND HOLDING 9 OZ. EACH.

THE WHITE OR OPALESCENT PORTION SHOWS A FIERY QUALITY WHEN HELD TO THE LIGHT—A UNIQUE CHARACTERISTIC OF FINE OPALESCENT HANDMADE GLASSWARE. ALL PIECES IN THIS COLLECTION ARE DONE BY SKILLED CRAFTSMEN IN THE FINEST FENTON TRADITION.

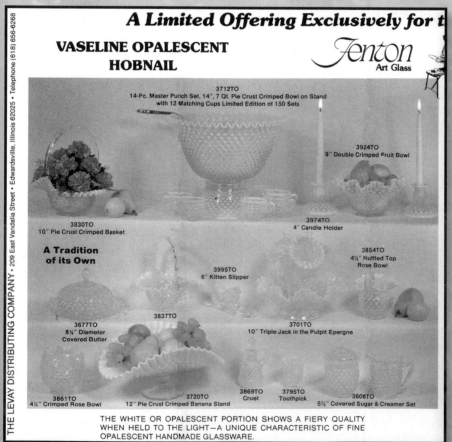

A Limited Offering Exclusively for t

VASELINE OPALESCENT HOBNAIL

Fenton Art Glass

3712TO
14-Pc. Master Punch Set, 14", 7 Qt. Pie Crust Crimped Bowl on Stand with 12 Matching Cups Limited Edition of 150 Sets

3924TO
9" Double Crimped Fruit Bowl

3830TO
10" Pie Crust Crimped Basket

3974TO
4" Candle Holder

A Tradition of its Own

3995TO
6" Kitten Slipper

3854TO
4½" Ruffled Top Rose Bowl

3677TO
8¾" Diameter Covered Butter

3837TO

3701TO
10" Triple Jack in the Pulpit Epergne

3861TO
4¼" Crimped Rose Bowl

3720TO
12" Pie Crust Crimped Banana Stand

3869TO
Cruet

3795TO
Toothpick

3606TO
5½" Covered Sugar & Creamer Set

THE WHITE OR OPALESCENT PORTION SHOWS A FIERY QUALITY WHEN HELD TO THE LIGHT—A UNIQUE CHARACTERISTIC OF FINE OPALESCENT HANDMADE GLASSWARE.

Topaz Opalescent Hobnail butter dish, $225.00 – 250.00.

Topaz Opalescent Hobnail punch bowl set, $375.00 – 450.00 complete.

Topaz Opalescent Hobnail banana stand, $225.00 – 250.00.

Levay Glass
209 E. Vandalia Street
Edwardsville, Illinois
62025
Telephone 618-656-6096

OPALESCENT VASELINE

VOP = Vaseline Opalescent (NOT IRIDESCENT) unlimited
VOI = Vaseline Opalescent Carnival (IRIDESCENT) *Limited Edition!

Number	Discription	VOP	VOI	*Edition
3667	Bell, hobnail flared 5⅜" tall	$15.00	$20.00	*325
3667	Bell, hobnail fluted 5⅜" tall	$17.00	$24.00	*325
3834	Basket, hobnail fluted applied handle 6" tall	$18.00	$25.00	*525
3863	Cruet, hobnail handblown, applied handle 6" tall	$35.00	$50.00	*200
3945	Tumbler, hobnail, 3½" tall	$10.00	$15.00	*1100
3952	Vase, miniture hobnail 4" tall fluted	$ 9.00	$14.00	*400
3953	Vase, miniture hobnail 4" tall, Fan	$ 9.00	$14.00	*400
3965	Pitcher, handblown applied handle 5⅜" X 6"		$50.00	*110
8223	Bowl orange tree, 3 footed 6" diam	$20.00		
8223	Rosebowl, orange tree, 3 footed 5½" tall		$30.00	*500
8242	Compote, handled, three fruit, flaired 8"	$20.00	$30.00	*300
8242	Compote, handled, three fruit, fluted 8"	$20.00	$30.00	*300
8244	Chalice, Persian Medallion, 6½" tall	$20.00	$25.00	*100
8244	Rosebow, Stemed, Persian Medalliaon 6½" tall	$20.00	$25.00	*300
8247	Rosebow, persian medallion 3½" tall	$15.00	$22.00	*450

Address Correction Requested

VELVA ROSE CARNIVAL

Pattern	Shape	Edition	Ware #	Value
Alley Cat	doorstop, 10"	200	5177	$350.00 – 400.00

ALLEY CAT
DOOR STOP

10" Tall

Rose Pink Carnival

Made by Fenton
for Levay — $55.00

Limited
Edition
of 200

THE LEVAY DISTRIBUTING
COMPANY, 209 E. Vandalia,
Box 650, Edwardsville, IL
62025. (618) 656-6268.

Rose Pink (Velva Rose) Alley Cat,
$350.00 – 400.00.

PURPLE STRETCH GLASS

Pattern	Shape	Edition	Ware #	Value
Diamond & Thread	Basket, 9" piecrust edge		8435VY	$150.00 – 175.00
Diamond & Thread	Vase, 7" double crimped		8455VY	$75.00 – 95.00
No pattern	Basket, 4" miniature		7567VY	$75.00 – 95.00
No pattern	Bell, 6½" star crimped		7563VY	$65.00 – 85.00
No pattern	Epergne, 5-pc. JIP		7505VY	$325.00 – 350.00
No pattern	Hand vase, 4" miniature		5153VY	$65.00 – 85.00
No pattern	Toothpick holder, 2"		7590VY	$40.00 – 45.00
No pattern	Water set, 7-pc. tankard	500	7509VY	$350.00 – 400.00
Dolphin	Fan vase, 6"		7551VY	$125.00 – 145.00
Dolphin	Loving cup, 5½"		7581VY	$125.00 – 145.00

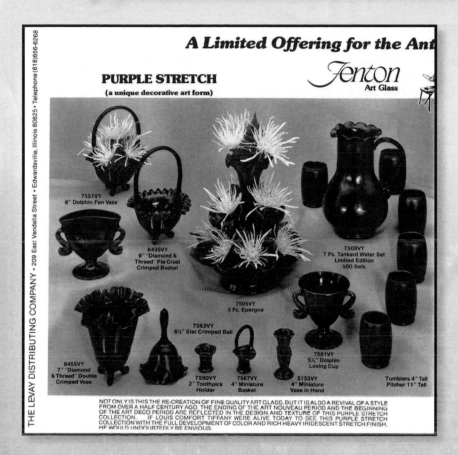

A Limited Offering for the Ant[ue] Trade

PURPLE STRETCH
(a unique decorative art form)

Fenton
Art Glass

7551VY
6" Dolphin Fan Vase

8435VY
9" "Diamond & Thread" Pie Crust Crimped Basket

7509VY
7 Pc. Tankard Water Set
Limited Edition
500 Sets

7505VY
5 Pc. Epergne

7563VY
6½" Star Crimped Bell

8455VY
7" "Diamond & Thread" Double Crimped Vase

7590VY
2" Toothpick Holder

7567VY
4" Miniature Basket

S153VY
4" Miniature Vase in Hand

7581VY
5½" Dolphin Loving Cup

Tumblers 4" Tall
Pitcher 11" Tall

NOT ONLY IS THIS THE RE-CREATION OF FINE QUALITY ART GLASS, BUT IT IS ALSO A REVIVAL OF A STYLE FROM OVER A HALF CENTURY AGO. THE ENDING OF THE ART NOUVEAU PERIOD AND THE BEGINNING OF THE ART DECO PERIOD ARE REFLECTED IN THE DESIGN AND TEXTURE OF THIS PURPLE STRETCH COLLECTION. IF LOUIS COMFORT TIFFANY WERE ALIVE TODAY TO SEE THIS PURPLE STRETCH COLLECTION WITH THE FULL DEVELOPMENT OF COLOR AND RICH HEAVY IRIDESCENT STRETCH FINISH, HE WOULD UNDOUBTEDLY BE ENVIOUS.

STAR CRIMPED EPERGNE
(limited edition of 1000)

7505 VY
5 Piece Star Crimped Epergne

THIS UNUSUAL STRETCH GLASS EPERGNE IN PURPLE STRETCH IS, IN ITSELF, A UNIQUE DECORATIVE ART FORM. THIS EDITION IN THIS COLOR TREATMENT WILL BE *STRICTLY LIMITED TO 1,000 SETS*. EACH SET IS HANDCRAFTED BY SKILLED ARTISANS IN THE FENTON TRADITION. ACTUAL SIZE IS THIRTEEN INCHES IN HEIGHT.

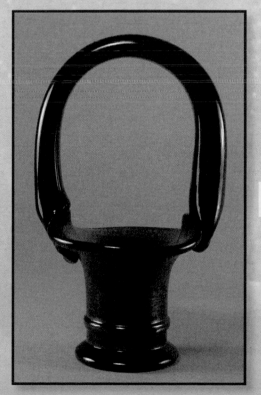

Purple Stretch miniature basket, $75.00 – 95.00.

PURPLE CARNIVAL

Fenton made several pieces of Grape & Cable in Purple Carnival, but not the humidor. That piece was made for Rose Presznick only. Fenton assured her that the humidor, which was Fenton's first piece of new carnival, would not be made for anyone else. These pieces are signed "Levay," numbered, and dated "1977."

Pattern	Shape	Edition	Ware #	Value
Diamond Optic	Pitcher, 10½" 44 oz.	50	1764	$200.00 – 225.00
Diamond Optic	Tumbler, 4½" 10 oz.	300	1740	$35.00 – 40.00
Diamond & Hobnail	Epergne, 10½" tall	300	4821	$325.00 – 400.00
Grape & Cable	Basket, 10" DC	500		$250.00 – 275.00
Grape & Cable	Bowl, 10" berry	500		$175.00 – 200.00
Grape & Cable	Spittoon, 7½"	500		$250.00 – 275.00
Grape & Cable	Vase, 13" swung	500		$200.00 – 225.00
Hobnail	Cruet, 6"	267	3863	$125.00 – 150.00
Hobnail	Decanter, 13½" handled	350	3761	$200.00 – 250.00
Hobnail	Goblet, 5½"	510	3845	$35.00 – 40.00
Hobnail	Pitcher, 10½"	164	3845	$200.00 – 225.00
Hobnail	Hand vase, 6¼"	155	389	$150.00 – 175.00
Hobnail	Tumbler, 4½"	600		$35.00 – 40.00
Hobnail	Water set	100 sets	1764	$400.00 – 450.00
Hobnail	Water pitcher, 10½"	164	3845	$250.00 – 275.00
Hobnail	Wine set	100 sets	3761	$250.00 – 275.00
Hobnail	Wine, ftd.	2100	3843	$35.00 – 40.00
Poppy	Lamp, 18" kerosene style	250	9105	$250.00 – 295.00
Poppy	Lamp, 19" student		9100	$250.00 – 295.00

Purple Carnival Hobnail cruet,
$125.00 – 150.00.

NEW! 3761 Hobnail Decanter 13½"
tall Purple Carnival by Fenton
for Levay Glass Blown with an
applied handle Limited to apx.
350 pcs.............$35.00 net

3843 Hobnail Wine Purple Carnival
Limited 900 pcs. $7.50 each net

Purple Carnival Hobnail wine, $35.00 –
40.00, and decanter, $200.00 – 250.00.

9100

Purple Carnival Poppy student
lamp, $250.00 – 295.00.

Purple Carnival Poppy kerosene-
style lamp, $250.00 – 295.00.

Purple Carnival Diamond
Optic with Flowers tum-
bler, $35.00 – 40.00, and
pitcher, $200.00 – 225.00.

#1764 Diamond Optic Purple Carn-
ival 7 piece Water Set Decorated
with a bouquet of tiny white violets, blown with applied handle
by Fenton for Levay Glass Limited
to only 50 Sets Artist Signed
.........................$100.00 net

Pattern	Shape	Ware #	Value
Lincoln Inn	Tumbler, 4½"	9003XB	$50.00 – 65.00
Lincoln Inn	Water pitcher, 7½"	9003XB	$250.00 – 325.00

RAVEN (BLACK) CARNIVAL

RAVEN CARNIVAL
(purple iridescence)

"LINCOLN INN"
Water Set Limited Edition of 500

9003XB

Tumblers 4½" Tall   Water Pitcher 7½" Tall

THE "LINCOLN INN" WATER SET HANDMADE FROM THE ORIGINAL 1928 MOULDS IN RAVEN CARNIVAL LOADED WITH RAINBOW IRIDESCENCE, IS SURE TO PLEASE ALL CARNIVAL AND FENTON COLLECTORS ACROSS OUR GREAT LAND. LIMITED EDITION SET CONSISTS OF A PITCHER AND SIX TUMBLERS.

Raven Carnival Lincoln Inn tumbler, $50.00 – 65.00, and pitcher, $250.00 – 325.00.

Raven Carnival Lincoln Inn tumblers, $50.00 – 65.00, and pitcher, $250.00 – 325.00.

Raven Carnival Decorated Lincoln Inn pitcher, $350.00 – 425.00, and tumbler, $85.00 – 95.00.

PLUM OPALESCENT HOBNAIL

Pattern	Shape	Ware #	Value
Hobnail	Banana stand, 12" piecrust edge	3720PO	$225.00 – 250.00
Hobnail	Basket, 5½"	3735PO	$75.00 – 95.00
Hobnail	Basket, 8½"	3638PO	$150.00 – 175.00
Hobnail	Basket, 12" DC	3734PO	$200.00 – 250.00
Hobnail	Bell, crimped	3645PO	$65.00 – 85.00
Hobnail	Bowl, 12" DC	3938PO	$75.00 – 85.00
Hobnail	Epergne, triple JIP	3701PO	$300.00 – 325.00
Hobnail	Fairy light, 3-pc. ftd. round	3804PO	$175.00 – 200.00
Hobnail	Relish, heart-shaped	3733PO	$150.00 – 175.00
Hobnail	Pitcher, round	3664PO	$225.00 – 250.00
Hobnail	Pitcher, vase shaped	3306PO	$250.00 – 300.00
Hobnail	Pitcher & bowl set	3303PO	$300.00 – 325.00
Hobnail	Tumbler, 8 oz.	Sold w/3306	$45.00 – 50.00
Hobnail	Vase/rose bowl, crimped	3323PO	$75.00 – 95.00
Hobnail	Water set, 7-pc.	3306PO	$350.00 – 400.00

A Limited Offering for the Antique Trade

DEEP PLUM OPALESCENT HOBNAIL

Handcrafted deep plum opalescent hobnail . . . the rarity in value is like the pure gold" contained within the art glass. Fenton has not produced this color since 1961. The 1984 treatment is formulated to create a *deep* plum color with an opalescence that is a light opaque plum. The shading of plum will vary as the nature of the glass dictates. None of the items shown has been produced before. Begin and complete your collection while this offer lasts.

Fenton Art Glass

3303 PO
Pitcher and Bowl Set

3754 PO
12" Double Crimped Basket

3733 PO
Heart Relish

3308 PO
7 pc. Water Set

3845 PO
Crimped Bell

3323 PO
4½" Crimped Vase

*The gold used in each pot of glass increases the cost of the raw glass approximately seven times over other glasses currently being produced.

(See reverse side)

RPC–99958

Plum Opalescent Hobnail pitcher, $225.00 – 250.00.

Plum Opalescent Hobnail small basket, $75.00 – 95.00.

Plum Opalescent Hobnail ftd. fairy light, $175.00 – 200.00.

Plum Opalescent Hobnail ftd. banana stand, $225.00 –
250.00.

Plum Opalescent Hobnail rose bowl, $75.00 – 95.00.

Iridized Plum Opalescent Hobnail 4" mini
vase, $65.00 – 75.00.

Iridized Plum Opalescent Hobnail rose bowl, $85.00
– 110.00.

PURPLE SLAG

Pattern	Shape	Ware #	Value
Alley Cat	Doorstop	5177PS	$400.00 – 450.00
Butterfly	Bonbon, handled	8230PS	$45.00 – 65.00
Grape & Cable	Tobacco jar	9188PS	$175.00 – 225.00
Happiness Bird	Figurine, 7"	5197PS	$40.00 – 55.00
Heart & Vine	Bowl	8237PS	$75.00 – 95.00
Hobnail	Bell, 5½"	3667OS	$50.00 – 65.00
Kitten	Slipper	3995PS	$35.00 – 40.00
Leaf & Orange Tree	Rose bowl	8223PS	$100.00 – 125.00
Multi-fruit	Comport	8231PS	$75.00 – 85.00
Orange Tree & Cherry	Basket, 10"	9136PS	$200.00 – 225.00
Orange Tree & Cherry	Bowl, 10"	8233PS	$75.00 – 95.00
Peacock	Vase, 8"	8257PS	$125.00 – 150.00
Rabbit	Figurine, 3"	5162PS	$65.00 – 75.00
Strawberry	Mini basket, 6½"	9133PS	$65.00 – 75.00
Strawberry	Toothpick holder	8295PS	$35.00 – 40.00
Turkey, covered*	Lg. Wright mould		$150.00 – 175.00

*This appears on a price sheet as having been made by Fenton in 1980.

Purple Slag Bunny, $65.00 – 75.00.

PURPLE SLAG

A Limited Offering for the A...

The spellbinding beauty of Fenton's timeless "Purple Slag" collection is sure to ple... American made glassware. Through the years, beginning with the first production of variega... 1850 "Slag Glass" has had, and will always have, a magical appeal. The luscious shading a... colors has had several names over the years, including Marble Glass and End of Day G... manufacturer. No two pieces of Slag Glass are alike, each reflecting the individuality of the... inherent individuality of the glass itself. From the kitten slipper to the grape and cable... artistry is recreated for the collectors of generations to come.

8231PS
Multi-fruit Compote

3667PS
5½" Hobnail Bell

5177PS
10" Alley Cat Doorstop

5162PS
3" Rabbit

5197PS
7" Happiness Bird

9133PS
6½" Strawberry Mini-basket

8233PS
Orange Tree & Cherry Bowl

9188PS
Grape & Cable
Tobacco Jar

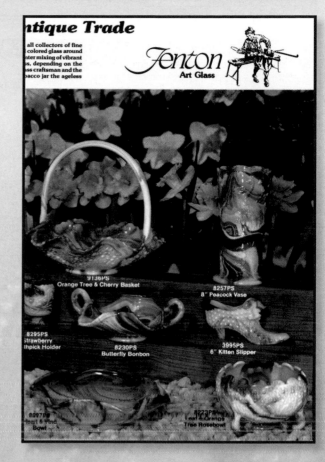

...ntique Trade

...all collectors of fine
...colored glass around
...ter mixing of vibrant
...ss, depending on the
...ass craftsman and the
...bacco jar the ageless

9136PS
Orange Tree & Cherry Basket

8257PS
8" Peacock Vase

8295PS
Strawberry
Toothpick Holder

8230PS
Butterfly Bonbon

3995PS
6" Kitten Slipper

8007PS
...eaf & Vine
Bowl

8223PS
Leaf & Orange
Tree Rosebowl

*Purple Slag Alley Cat,
$400.00 – 450.00.*

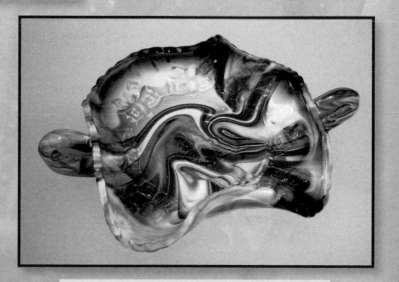

Purple Slag Butterfly bonbon, $45.00 – 65.00.

Purple Slag Cherry Chain handled comport, $75.00 – 85.00.

Purple Slag Grape & Cable humidor, $175.00 – 225.00.

Purple Slag Heart & Vine bowl, $75.00 – 95.00.

Purple Slag Hobnail bell, $50.00 – 65.00.

Purple Slag Orange Tree rose bowl, $100.00 – 125.00.

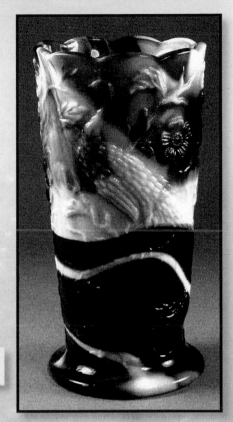

Purple Slag Peacock vase, $125.00 – 150.00.

Purple Slag Strawberry miniature basket, $65.00 – 75.00.

Purple Slag Strawberry toothpick, $35.00 – 40.00.

RUBY MARBLE

Pattern	Shape	Ware #	Value
Alley Cat	Doorstop, 10"	5177RX	$450.00 – 500.00
Miniature	Basket, loop-handled		$75.00 – 85.00
Miniature	Basket		$65.00 – 75.00
Bear Cup	Figurine	5151RX	$75.00 – 85.00
Bunny	Figurine	5162RX	$75.00 – 85.00
Butterfly on Stand	Figurine	5171RX	$75.00 – 85.00
Fawn	Figurine	5160RX	$75.00 – 85.00
Grape & Cable	Bowl, DC	9027RX	$125.00 – 150.00
Grape & Cable	Cuspidor	9058RX	$200.00 – 225.00
Grape & Cable	Tobacco jar, 7½"	9188RX	$200.00 – 225.00
Hen on Nest	Candy, small	5186RX	$120.00 – 140.00
Mouse	Figurine		$60.00 – 75.00
Regency	Basket, 6½"	8634RX	$140.00 – 165.00
Regency	Basket, 10"	8635RX	$200.00 – 225.00
Regency	Butter dish, rd.	8680RX	$150.00 – 165.00
Regency	Rose bowl, 6"	8623RX	$125.00 – 150.00
Thumbprint	Epergne, triple JIP	4401RX	$350.00 – 425.00

Ruby Marble Bear Cub, $75.00 – 85.00.

Ruby Marble Alley Cat, $450.00 – 500.00.

Ruby Marble Bear Cub on Stand, $100.00 – 120.00.

Ruby Marble Regency butter dish (McKee Plytec mould), $150.00 – 165.00.

Ruby Marble Fawn, $75.00 – 85.00.

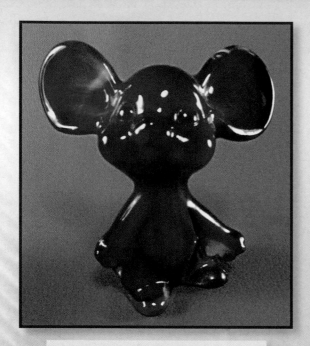

Ruby Marble Mouse, $60.00 – 75.00.

Ruby Marble Bunny, $75.00 – 85.00.

Ruby Marble Bunny on Stand, $100.00 – 120.00.

Ruby Marble Regency rose bowl, $125.00 – 150.00.

Ruby Marble miniature basket, loop-handled, $75.00 - 85.00.

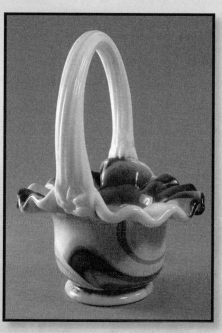

Ruby Marble miniature basket, Milk Glass handle, $65.00 – 75.00.

Ruby Marble Grape & Cable humidor, $200.00 – 225.00.

CRANBERRY OPALESCENT

Pattern	Shape	Edition	Ware #	Value
Coin Dot	Basket, small		1439CR	$75.00 – 85.00
Coin Dot	Basket, 7"		1446CR	$125.00 – 150.00
Coin Dot	Bottle vase		1483CR	$100.00 – 125.00
Coin Dot	Ewer		1493CR	$100.00 – 125.00
Coin Dot	Fairy light, 3-pc.		1403CR	$200.00 – 225.00
Coin Dot	Rose bowl, 4½" DC		1436CR	$85.00 – 100.00
Coin Dot	Vase, DC		1479CR	$85.00 – 100.00
Coin Dot	Vase, 7" JIP		1489CR	$100.00 – 125.00
Fern	Basket, 8"	102	1479CR	$175.00 – 200.00
Hobnail	Banquet lamp, 36"		9201CR	$200.00 – 250.00
Hobnail	Basket, 8"		3333CR	$80.00 – 100.00
Hobnail	Basket, 8" loop-handled		3347CR	$125.00 – 150.00
Hobnail	Basket, 10"		3830CR	$125.00 – 150.00

Pattern	Shape	Edition	Ware #	Value
Hobnail	Cruet & stopper		3863CR	$100.00 – 125.00
Hobnail	Pitcher, 11"			$200.00 – 225.00
Hobnail	Tumbler, 4½"			$45.00 – 50.00
Hobnail	Vase, 6½" JIP		3362CR	$75.00 – 85.00

Fine handmade art glass for the Antique Trade

CRANBERRY OPALESCENT HOBNAIL

Handcrafted cranberry opalescent hobnail... the rarity in value is like the pure gold contained within this art glass. Baskets and Water Pitcher have applied candy stripe handles. All pieces in this collection are done by skilled craftsmen in the finest Fenton tradition.

11" Pitcher with ribbed opalescent handle.

3347 CR
8" Looped handled Basket

3362 CR
6½" Jack in Pulpit Vase

4½" Tumblers

3909 CR
7 pc. Water Set

3863 CR
Cruet with opalescent ribbed handle and opalescent stopper.

3333 CR
8" Basket

3830 CR
10" Basket—Single Pie Crust Crimp with ribbed opalescent handle.

Banquet Lamp measures 36 inches in height

9201 CR

Fine handmade art glass for the Antique Trade
CRANBERRY OPALESCENT COIN DOT

Fenton

Handcrafted cranberry opalescent . . . the rarity in value is like the pure gold contained within this art glass. Baskets and Ewer have applied candy stripe handles. All pieces in this collection are done by skilled craftsmen in the finest Fenton tradition.

1493 CR
Ewer with
candy stripe handle

1489 CR
7" Jack in Pulpit
Vase

1483 CR
Bottle Vase

1479 CR
Double Crimped Vase

1446 CR
7" Basket with
candy stripe
handle

1439 CR
Small Basket
with candy stripe handle

1436 CR
4½" Double Crimped
Rose Bowl

1403 CR
3 pc. Fairy Light

THE LEVAY DISTRIBUTING COMPANY • 209 East Vandalia Street • Edwardsville, Illinois 62025 • Telephone (618)656-6268

RED SATIN

Pattern	Shape	Ware #	Value
Hobnail	Basket, 7"	3837RA	$75.00 – 95.00
Hobnail	Bell	3667RA	$50.00 – 65.00
Hobnail	Bowl, 9"	3924RA	$50.00 – 65.00
Hobnail	Candleholder	3974RA	(ea.) $40.00 – 50.00
Hobnail	Comport	3628RA	$50.00 – 65.00
Hobnail	Fairy light	3608RA	$150.00 – 165.00
Poppy	GWTW lamp	9109RA	$300.00 – 350.00

A Limited Offering for the Antique Trade

RED SATIN GLASS

Luxurious Red Satin, a favorite among art glass collectors. Velvet to the touch, regal to the eye. **"Poppy"** Gone With The Wind Lamp 24" tall, Lights top and bottom.

9101 RA
24" "Poppy"
Gone With The Wind Lamp

3924RA
9" Bowl

3608RA
Fairy Light

3628RA
Footed Comport

3667 RA
Bell

3974RA
Pr. of Candleholders

3837 RA
7" Basket

THE LEVAY DISTRIBUTING COMPANY • 209 East Vandalia Street • Edwardsville, Illinois 60625 • Telephone (618) 656-6268

MARIGOLD CARNIVAL
(Signed "Levay," numbered, and dated "1977.")

Pattern	Shape	Edition	Ware #	Value
Diamond & Rib	Vase, 12" – 13" swung	175	0178	$100.00 – 120.00
Diamond & Rib	Vase, 5" – 6" JIP star crimped	95	0181	$125.00 – 150.00
Diamond & Rib	Vase, 5" – 6" JIP piecrust edge	100	0182	$125.00 – 150.00

WISTERIA CARNIVAL

Pattern	Shape	Edition	Ware #	Value
Persian Medallion	Bowl, 8"	300	8224	$75.00 – 85.00
Persian Medallion	Plate, 9½"	500	8219	$85.00 – 95.00

MISCELLANEOUS PATTERNS
(Pale Blue, probably Federal Blue.)

Pattern	Shape	Edition	Ware #	Value
Inverted Strawberry	Basket			$75.00 – 85.00

L.G. Wright Company

The death of Si Wright in 1969 could have spelled the end of the L.G. Wright Company, but Si Wright's wife, Verna Mae (Toots) Wright, stepped up to the challenge and continued to sell well-made, beautiful glassware for the next 20 years. She knew what her husband had planned for the company and she set about doing it. Si had been planning to add Custard glass to his product line, so she did that with the help of the Fentons. More items were decorated by Wright artists. She added a new line that was made in the overlay colors of Dark Blue, Light Blue, Amber, and Amethyst. A beautiful logo plate, which depicted the old building on the Wright family farm that had served as Wright's first warehouse, was made in Crystal without a date, Crystal Satin and dated "1971," Amber Satin and dated "1972," and a beautiful shade of Aqua Satin and dated "1973." The Crystal plate that has no date may have been the first one made.

Cobalt Blue was added to the line in 1970. The very dark blue was a beautiful addition and it was used for both pressed and blown patterns. During the 1970s, Fenton made less glass for Wright. Frank Fenton, who was deeply involved with the carnival glass clubs and a collector himself, made a decision to not make the iridized glassware for Wright. Because Wright was determined to offer carnival glass in its line, it went to Westmoreland and Imperial, who were willing to supply it. Frank's decision was based on the reluctance of Toots Wright to sign the glassware with a mark that would distinguish it from the old. In fact, Wright was using the Northwood mark, an *N*, on both Custard and carnival glass. Frank Fenton insisted that the mark be removed from the moulds it was using to make the Custard glass

pieces, so a line was added to the *N* that turned it into a strange-looking *W*. At the same time, the American Carnival Glass Association was registering the trademark so that it could never be used to make glass that would fool the collectors. Wright used the Northwood mark for just one year, 1975. There is another way to detect the age of a carnival glass pitcher. The handles on old carnival were never iridized, unlike those of the new pieces.

Although Fenton didn't make carnival glass for Wright, it did continue to produce the beautiful opalescent glassware that made Wright famous. In the 1980s, Fenton made Dark Cobalt Blue and its Cranberry Opalescent color for a pattern called Eye Dot and Daisy that is now called Christmas Snowflake. Wright's artist painted the Mary Gregory decoration on the same dark blue opalescent glass. In about 1983, I went to our Seattle Gift Mart building to see Scott Williams, the Fenton representative, who was a friend of mine. I had a chance that day to also tour the L.G. Wright showroom. The glass displayed was so very beautiful that I wanted to buy out the showroom. Of course, I could never afford to do that, but my memory of it is a pleasant one.

In 1990 Toots Wright died, leaving the Wright company in the hands of cousin Dorothy Stephan and Dorothy's daughter, Phillis Stephan Beuttner. With the help of loyal employees, some of whom had worked there for 30 or 40 years, Dorothy and Phillis were able to continue business for the next 10 years, but the company sold less of its famous glassware. In 1999, a final auction emptied the warehouse of products and moulds, ending forever the legacy built by Si Wright.

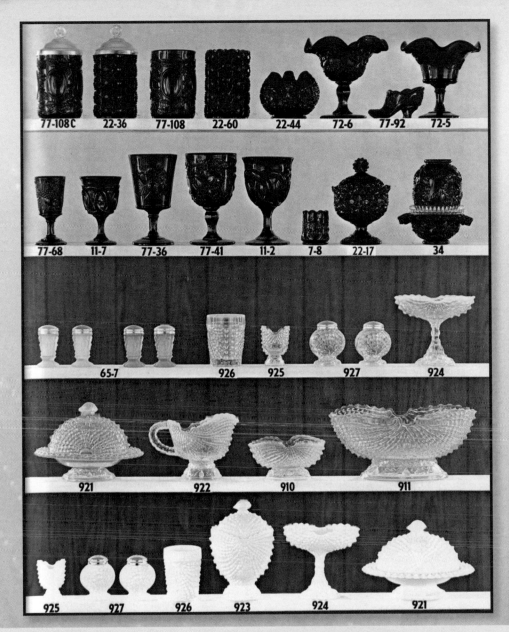

Cobalt items, row 1: *Mirror Rose pickle jar,* $175.00 – 200.00; *Daisy & Button pickle jar,* $175.00 – 200.00; *Mirror Rose spooner,* $75.00 – 95.00; *Daisy & Button spooner,* $75.00 – 95.00; *Daisy & Button rose bowl,* $55.00 – 65.00; *Wild Rose 6" open comport,* $55.00 – 65.00; *Queen Anne slipper,* $40.00 – 50.00; *Strawberry & Currant 6" comport,* $55.00 – 65.00.
Row 2: *Strawberry & Currant wine,* $20.00 – 25.00; *Double Wedding Ring wine,* $20.00 – 25.00; *Strawberry & Currant goblet,* $25.00 – 30.00; *Wild Rose goblet,* $25.00 – 30.00; *Double Wedding Ring goblet,* $25.00 – 30.00; *Cherry toothpick,* $15.00 – 18.00; *Daisy & Button 4" covered compote,* $65.00 – 85.00; *Embossed Rose fairy lamp,* $100.00 – 115.00.
Satin, row 3: *Blue Satin Three Face salt & pepper,* $35.00 – 45.00 pair; *Amber Satin salt & pepper,* $25.00 – 35.00 pair.
Blue Opalescent Argonaut assortment, row 3: *Tumbler,* $35.00 – 45.00; *toothpick,* $15.00 – 18.00; *salt & pepper,* $50.00 – 65.00 pair; *stemmed jelly,* $65.00 – 75.00.
Row 4: *Butter & cover,* $150.00 – 175.00; *lg. creamer,* $65.00 – 75.00; *5" Shell bowl,* $35.00 – 45.00; *11" Shell bowl,* $75.00 – 95.00 (not shown, sugar & cover, $85.00 – 95.00).
Custard Argonaut assortment, row 5: *Toothpick,* $15.00 – 18.00; *salt & pepper,* $45.00 – 50.00 pair; *tumbler,* $24.00 – 28.00; *sugar & cover,* $65.00 – 75.00 (not shown, lg. creamer, $55.00 – 65.00); *stemmed jelly,* $50.00 – 65.00; *butter & cover,* $125.00 – 150.00.

Topaz Opalescent items, row 1: Daisy & Button 5" 4-toed candleholder, $50.00 – 55.00 each; Daisy & Button 5" 4-toed bowl, $35.00 – 45.00; Beaded DC candleholder, $50.00 – 65.00 ea.; large DC ftd, comport, $100.00 – 125.00.

Row 2: Daisy & Fern Barber bottle, $145.00 – 165.00; 7" Hen on Nest, $75.00 – 95.00; Cherry sugar, $45.00 – 50.00; Cherry creamer, $50.00 – 60.00; Daisy & Fern round cruet, $200.00 – 225.00; Daisy & Fern oval cruet, $200.00 – 225.00.

Row 3: Daisy & Button 4" sq. sauce, $20.00 – 22.00; Daisy & Button with Panel, $35.00 – 40.00; Daisy & Button with Panel wine, $25.00 – 30.00; Daisy & Button sugar bowl, $25.00 – 30.00; Daisy & Button creamer, $30.00 – 35.00; Daisy & Button 4" fan toothpick, $25.00 – 30.00; Daisy & Button ftd. toothpick, $25.00 – 30.00.

Row 4: Paneled Grape 8 oz. goblet, $35.00 – 40.00; Moon & Star 9 oz. goblet, $35.00 – 40.00; Wildflower 8 oz. goblet, $30.00 – 35.00; Wildflower 2 oz. wine, $30.00 – 35.00; Strawberry & Currant 6½" crimped comport, $45.00 – 50.00; Beaded small crimped comport, $45.00 – 50.00.

Row 5: Beaded large flared ftd. comport, $125.00 – 150.00; Daisy & Button 10" plate (not Opalescent), $25.00 – 30.00; Daisy & Fern tumbler, $40.00 – 45.00; Daisy & Fern 2½ qt. water pitcher, $300.00 – 325.00.

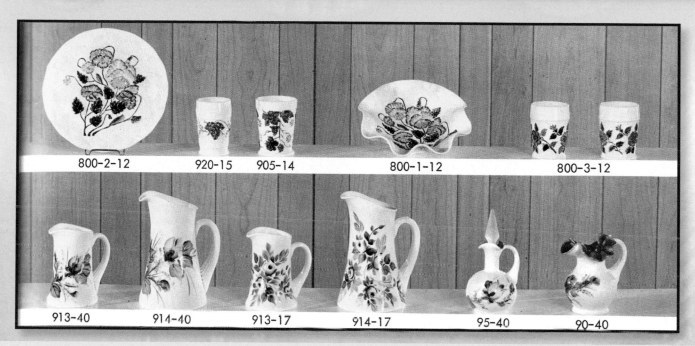

Decorated Custard assortment, row 1: *Cosmos 9" plate, $65.00 – 75.00; Grape 6 oz. tumbler, $25.00 – 30.00; Grape & Daisy 7 oz. tumbler, $25.00 – 30.00; Cosmos crimped 7" bowl, $50.00 – 65.00; Cosmos 7 oz. tumblers, $25.00 – 30.00 each.*
Row 2: *Moss Rose tankard cream pitcher, $75.00 – 85.00; Moss Rose tankard milk pitcher, $100.00-125.00; Rose Vine tankard cream pitcher, $75.00 – 85.00; Rose Vine tankard milk pitcher, $100.00 – 125.00.*
Peach Blow, row 2: *Moss Rose round cruet, $125.00 – 145.00; Moss Rose tall creamer, $65.00 – 75.00.*

Made by L. E. Smith:

This page represents glass made for Levay by L. E. Smith. On the bottom half of the page, you will see that Smith made several pieces of Moon & Star items in Blue and Green Opalescent. Several of those pieces — the bell, the bud vase, and the ftd. fairy light — were put into my Fenton, Glass Made for Other Companies, 1907 – 1980. I didn't know that L. E. Smith had made any Opalescent Moon & Star until I received this flyer along with all the other Levay information sent to me by Singleton Bailey. Rather than just describe the pieces made by Smith, I decided that you would get more information from seeing the pieces made by that company. The prices would be in the same range as those of L.G. Wright.

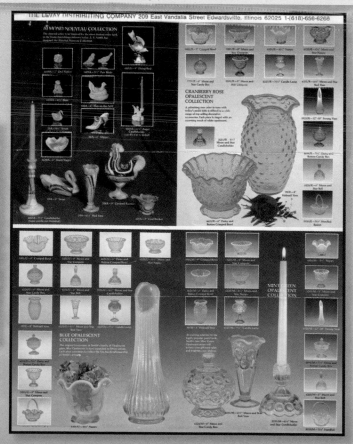

MOON & STAR

Description	Amber	Green, Blue, Amethyst	Ruby, Topaz	Opalescent Colors*
Ashtray, 5"	$10.00 – 12.00	$15.00 – 18.00	$16.00 – 20.00	$18.00 – 22.00
Ashtray, 8½"	$17.00 – 20.00	$20.00 – 22.00	$24.00 – 26.00	$24.00 – 28.00
Bowl, 12"	$40.00 – 45.00	$50.00 – 55.00	$55.00 – 65.00	$65.00 – 75.00
Bowl, 11" console	$40.00 – 45.00	$50. 00 – 55.00	$55.00 – 60.00	$65.00 – 75.00
Bowl, 8" console	$30.00 – 35.00	$40.00 – 45.00	$45.00 – 50.00	$55.00 – 65.00
Bowl, Flower & Block	$45.00 – 55.00	$50.00 – 60.00	$60.00 – 70.00	$65.00 – 75.00
Butter & cover	$35.00 – 40.00	$40.00 – 50.00	$55.00 – 70.00	$75.00 – 85.00
Cake plate, 12"	$65.00 – 85.00	$75.00 – 95.00	$120.00 – 150.00	$150.00 – 195.00
Candleholder, 9"	(ea.) $23.00 – 25.00	(ea.) $25.00 – 27.00	(ea.) $35.00 – 40.00	(ea.) $40.00 – 45.00
Candleholder, 6"	(ea.) $18.00 – 20.00	(ea.) $24.00 – 26.00	(ea.) $32.00 – 38.00	(ea.) $35.00 – 40.00
Champagne	$18.00 – 20.00	$20.00 – 24.00	$24.00 – 28.00	$28.00 – 32.00
Comport, 4" covered	$26.00 – 30.00	$45.00 – 50.00	$70.00 – 85.00	$85.00 – 100.00
Comport, lid, 6" x 7½" low ftd.	$35.00 – 40.00	$50.00 – 65.00	$70.00 – 85.00	$85.00 – 100.00
Comport, 6" x 10" h. tall covered	$50.00 – 60.00	$65.00 – 75.00	$80.00 – 100.00	$100.00 – 120.00
Comport, 7" open stemmed flared	$30.00 – 35.00	$40.00 – 45.00	$65.00 – 75.00	$75.00 – 95.00
Comport, 5" open stemmed flared	$25.00 – 30.00	$30.00 – 45.00	$55.00 – 60.00	$65.00 – 75.00
Comport, 4" x 8" covered	$45.00 – 50.00	$50.00 – 65.00	$65.00 – 85.00	$85.00 – 100.00
Comport, 8" x 12" covered	$65.00 – 70.00	$85.00 – 100.00	$100.00 – 125.00	$125.00 – 150.00
Comport, 6½" open	$30.00 – 35.00	$35.00 – 45.00	$45.00 – 55.00	$65.00 – 75.00
Comport, 8" open	$35.00 – 40.00	$45.00 – 55.00	$60.00 – 75.00	$75.00 – 85.00
Comport, open 10"	$50.00 – 60.00	$65.00 – 75.00	$75.00 – 95.00	$100.00 – 125.00
Creamer, large	$20.00 – 25.00	$35.00 – 45.00	$45.00 – 55.00	$65.00 – 75.00
Cruet	$55.00 – 65.00	$75.00 – 85.00	$85.00 – 100.00	$125.00 – 150.00
Decanter	$75.00 – 85.00	$85.00 – 100.00	$150.00 – 170.00	$200.00 – 250.00
Epergne, small	$65.00 – 85.00	$85.00 – 120.00	$125.00 – 150.00	$150.00 – 175.00
Epergne, medium	$100.00 – 120.00	$120.00 – 150.00	$150.00 – 175.00	$200.00 – 225.00

Description	Amber	Green, Blue, Amethyst	Ruby, Topaz	Opalescent Colors*
Fairy lamp	$65.00 – 75.00	$75.00 – 95.00	$75.00 – 115.00	$100.00 – 125.00
Finger bowl	$20.00 – 25.00	$25.00 – 30.00	$30.00 – 33.00	$34.00 – 36.00
Goblet	$18.00 – 24.00	$25.00 – 27.00	$30.00 – 35.00	$35.00 – 40.00
Ice tea	$18.00 – 22.00	$26.00 – 30.00	$35.00 – 40.00	$40.00 – 45.00
Jelly, 4½" covered high ftd.	$35.00 – 40.00	$55.00 – 60.00	$75.00 – 85.00	$100.00 – 125.00
Juice, ftd.	$10.00 – 14.00	$18.00 – 22.00	$22.00 – 25.00	$25.00 – 28.00
Lamp, 10" shade, font & base	$150.00 – 185.00	$200.00 – 250.00	$250.00 – 300.00	$350.00 – 400.00
Lamp, 14" shade**	$125.00 – 175.00	$175.00 – 225.00	$250.00 – 325.00	$300.00 – 350.00
Lamp, miniature	$150.00 – 175.00	$175.00 – 200.00	$175.00 – 200.00	$225.00 – 250.00
Nappy, 6"	$16.00 – 18.00	$20.00 – 25.00	$25.00 – 30.00	$35.00 – 40.00
Pitcher, water	$100.00 – 150.00	$175.00 – 200.00	$200.00 – 225.00	$225.00 – 250.00
Plate, 8" scalloped edge	$10.00 – 12.00	$12.00 – 15.00	$15.00 – 18.00	$20.00 – 24.00
Plate, 13½"	$25.00 – 35.00	$35.00 – 50.00	$45.00 – 65.00	$55.00 – 70.00
Relish, oval	$15.00 – 20.00	$20.00 – 25.00	$25.00 – 30.00	$30.00 – 35.00
Relish, 8" handled	$35.00 – 40.00	$40.00 – 50.00	$50.00 – 65.00	$65.00 75.00
Relish, 8" rectangular	$35.00 – 45.00	$45.00 – 60.00	$55.00 – 70.00	$75.00 – 80.00
Relish, 13" pickle or celery (canoe)	$55.00 – 65.00	$65.00 – 85.00	$75.00 – 100.00	$100.00 – 125.00
Rose bowl	$35.00 – 45.00	$45.00 – 55.00	$55.00 – 65.00	$65.00 – 75.00
Salt dip	$ 8.00 – 10.00	$10.00 – 12.00	$12.00 – 15.00	$15.00 – 18.00
Shakers	$20.00 – 25.00	$25.00 – 30.00	$30.00 – 40.00	$35.00 – 45.00
Salver, 12" lg.	$50.00 – 60.00	$60.00 – 75.00	$85.00 – 95.00	$100.00 – 125.00
Salver, 10" med.	$40.00 – 50.00	$55.00 – 65.00	$75.00 – 85.00	$85.00 – 95.00
Salver, 8" small	$35.00 – 45.00	$45.00 – 55.00	$65.00 – 75.00	$75.00 – 85.00
Sauce, ftd.	$12.00 – 14.00	$15.00 – 18.00	$18.00 – 22.00	$22.00 – 25.00
Sherbet, high ftd.	$18.00 – 20.00	$22.00 – 24.00	$30.00 – 35.00	$35.00 – 40.00
Soap dish	$25.00 – 30.00	$30.00 – 40.00	$40.00 – 45.00	$45.00 – 50.00
Spoonholder	$28.00 – 30.00	$35.00 – 45.00	$45.00 – 50.00	$50.00 – 60.00
Sugar, covered lg.	$35.00 – 40.00	$40.00 – 50.00	$50.00 – 65.00	$65.00 – 70.00
Sugar, low covered	$20.00 – 25.00	$25.00 – 30.00	$45.00 – 50.00	$50.00 – 60.00
Sugar shaker	$45.00 – 55.00	$75.00 – 85.00	$85.00 – 100.00	$100.00 – 125.00

Description	Amber	Green, Blue, Amethyst	Ruby, Topaz	Opalescent Colors*
Tumbler, ftd.	$18.00 – 20.00	$24.00 – 28.00	$30.00 – 35.00	$40.00 – 50.00
Vase, celery	$30.00 – 35.00	$38.00 – 45.00	$50.00 – 55.00	$70.00 – 80.00
Wine	$18.00 – 20.00	$22.00 – 25.00	$30.00 – 35.00	$35.00 – 40.00

*Some items may not exist in opalescent colors.
**Opalescent, $275.00 – 325.00.

Row 1, 8" Moon & Star comports & covers: BO, $85.00 – 100.00; Pink* or Green, $50.00 – 65.00; Amber, $45.00 – 50.00; Ruby, $65.00 – 85.00.

Row 2, high ftd. covered jellies: Green, $55.00 – 60.00; Ruby, $75.00 – 85.00; Amber, $35.00 – 40.00.

Row 2, 8" large sugars & covers: Ruby, $50.00 – 65.00; Blue Opalescent, $65.00 – 75.00; Amber, $35.00 – 40.00.

Row 3, 6" x 10" tall covered comports: Amber, $50.00 – 55.00; Blue Opalescent, $100.00 – 120.00; Ruby, $80.00 – 95.00; Green or Pink*, $65.00 – 75.00.

Row 4, 6" x 7½" low covered comports: Blue Opalescent, $85.00 – 100.00; Green, $50.00 – 65.00; Amber, $35.00 – 40.00; Ruby, $70.00 – 85.00.

Row 5, 8" x 12" lg. covered comports: Amber, $65.00 – 70.00; Ruby, $100.00 – 125.00; Green or Pink,* $85.00 – 100.00; Blue Opalescent, $125.00 – 150.00.

* Most, but not all, of the Pink made for L.G. Wright came from the Fostoria Glass Company.

Row 1, 4½" Moon & Star wines: *Ruby, $30.00 – 35.00; Green, $22.00 – 25.00; Amber, $18.00 – 22.00; Blue Opalescent, $35.00 – 40.00.* **Decanters & stoppers:** *Amber, $75.00 – 85.00; Green, $85.00 – 100.00; Blue Opalescent, $200.00 – 250.00; Ruby, $150.00 – 170.00.*

Row 2, 4" x 5¼" low sugars & covers: *Blue Opalescent, $50.00 – 60.00; Ruby, $45.00 – 50.00; Amber, $20.00 – 25.00.* **3" x 5¾" creamers:** *Blue Opalescent, $65.00 – 75.00; Ruby, $45.00 – 55.00; Amber, $20.00 – 25.00.*

Row 3, salt & pepper shakers: *Green, $25.00 – 30.00; Ruby, $30.00 – 40.00; Amber, $20.00 – 25.00; Blue Opalescent, $35.00 – 45.00.* **Sugar shakers:** *Ruby, $85.00 – 100.00; Green, $75.00 – 85.00; Blue Opalescent, $100.00 – 125.00; Amber, $50.00 – 55.00.* **Rectangular relishes:** *Blue Opalescent, $75.00 – 80.00; Green, $45.00 – 60.00.*

Row 4, 6" crimped nappies: *Ruby, $25.00 – 30.00; Amber, $16.00 – 18.00; Blue Opalescent, $35.00 – 40.00; Green, $20.00 – 25.00.* **5 oz. juice glasses:** *Amber, $10.00 – 14.00; Green, $18.00 – 22.00; Blue Opalescent, $25.00 – 28.00; Ruby, $22.00 – 25.00.*

Row 5, 7 oz. tumblers: *Blue Opalescent, $40.00 – 50.00; Green, $24.00 – 28.00; Ruby, $30.00 – 35.00.* **5¾" x 6" Spooners:** *Blue Opalescent, $50.00 – 60.00; Ruby, $45.00 – 50.00; Amber, 28.00 – 30.00.*

Row 6, 5¾" x 6" round butters & covers: *Amber, $40.00 – 50.00; Blue Opalescent, $75.00 – 85.00; Ruby, $55.00 – 70.00.* **6" candleholders:** *Amber, $18.00 – 20.00 each.* **Ftd. console bowls:** *Amber, $30.00 – 35.00; *Pink was made in limited amounts by Fenton but most pieces in this color were made by Fostoria.*

Row 7, 8" x 2" handled relishes: *Green, $40.00 – 50.00; Amber, $35.00 – 40.00; Blue Opalescent, $65.00 – 75.00.* **8" oval relishes:** *Amber, $15.00 – 20.00; Blue Opalescent, $30.00 – 35.00; Green, $20.00 – 25.00.*

Row 1, 6½" x 5" open comports: Green, $35.00 – 45.00; Blue Opalescent, $65.00 – 75.00; Amber, $30.00 – 35.00; Ruby, $45.00 – 55.00.

Row 2, 8" x 5½" medium open comports: Amber, $35.00 – 40.00; Green, $45.00 – 55.00; Ruby, $60.00 – 75.00; Blue Opalescent, $75.00 – 85.00.

Row 3, 1 qt. 7½" water pitchers: Ruby, $200.00 – 225.00; Blue Opalescent, $225.00 – 250.00; Green, $175.00 – 200.00; Amber, $100.00 – 150.00.

Row 4, 10" x 7" large open comports: Amber, $50.00 – 60.00; Pink, $65.00 – 75.00; Blue Opalescent, $100.00 – 125.00; Ruby, $75.00 – 95.00. Row 5: Green, $65.00 – 75.00.

Row 5, 12" x 5" cake plates/salvers: Blue Opalescent, $125.00 – 195.00; Ruby, $120.00 – 150.00.

Row 6, 12" x 5" cake plates/salvers: Green, $95.00 – 120.00; Pink, $95.00 – 120.00; Amber, $65.00 – 95.00.

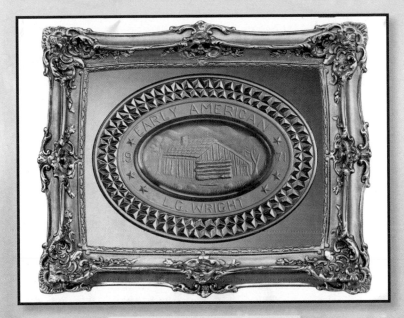

Blue logo plate, $50.00 – 65.00.

Ruby Paneled Grape covered comport, $75.00 – 85.00.

Green Priscilla covered comport, $75.00 – 85.00.

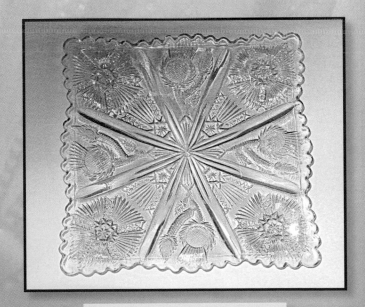

Green 7½" plate, $45.00 – 50.00.

Crystal Thistle 7½" round plate, $20.00 - 25.00.

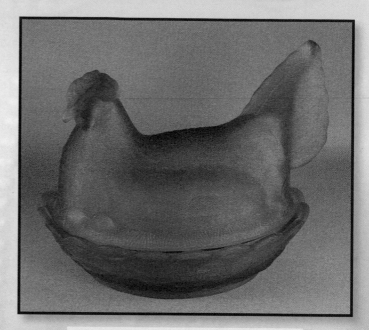

Blue Satin Hen on Nest, $50.00 - 65.00.

Purple Slag Hen on Nest, $65.00 - 85.00.

Amber Daisy & Button 11½" Canoe, $50.00 - 65.00.

Amber Daisy & Button Bell candy, $75.00 – 95.00.

Ruby Daisy & Button Bell candy, $120.00 – 145.00.

OVERLAY ASSORTMENT
Add 10% for decorated items.

Shape	Amber	Blue, Amethyst	Dark Blue, Rose
Barber bottle, fluted	$85.00 – 100.00	$145.00 – 165.00	$165.00 – 195.00
Barber bottle, round	$85.00 – 100.00	$145.00 – 165.00	$165.00 – 195.00
Candy box*	$100.00 – 125.00	$120.00 – 145.00	$145.00 – 160.00
Creamer, tall	$45.00 – 55.00	$65.00 – 75.00	$65.00 – 85.00
Cruet, fluted	$55.00 – 65.00	$65.00 – 75.00	$75.00 – 95.00
Cruet, oval/round	$45.00 – 50.00	$60.00 – 70.00	$75.00 – 95.00
Cruet, paneled Sprig	$55.00 – 65.00	$65.00 – 75.00	$85.00 – 100.00
Fairy light	$85.00 – 95.00	$125.00 – 150.00	$155.00 – 180.00
Milk pitcher	$50.00 – 65.00	$65.00 – 75.00	$75.00 – 85.00
Pickle castor	$75.00 – 100.00	$125.00 -150.00	$200.00 – 250.00

Shape	Amber	Blue, Amethyst	Dark Blue, Rose
Rose bowl, lg.	$55.00 – 65.00	$75.00 – 85.00	$80.00 – 95.00
Rose bowl, sm.	$45.00 – 55.00	$65.00 – 75.00	$75.00 – 85.00
Salt & pepper	$40.00 – 50.00	$50.00 – 60.00	$65.00 – 75.00
Spooner	$40.00 – 45.00	$50.00 – 55.00	$60.00 – 75.00
Sugar shaker	$65.00 – 75.00	$75.00 – 85.00	$95.00 – 125.00

*Shaped like a round canister.

Satin Amber Overlay decorated round cruet, $65.00 – 75.00.

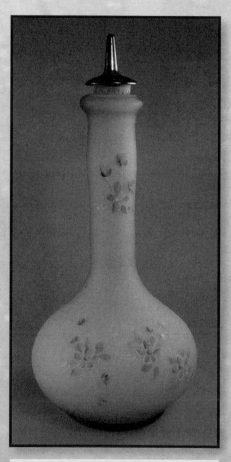

Satin Amber Overlay decorated round Barber bottle, $100.00 – 120.00.

Satin Amber Overlay decorated paneled Sprig cruet, $100.00 – 120.00.

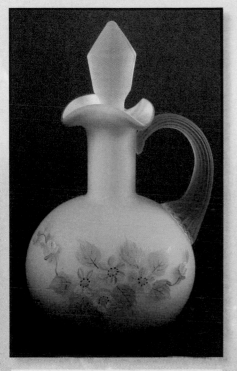

Satin Dark Blue Overlay decorated round cruet, $125.00 – 150.00.

Satin Dark Blue Overlay decorated paneled sugar shaker, $100.00 – 120.00.

Satin Dark Blue Overlay decorated fluted cruet, $125.00 – 150.00.

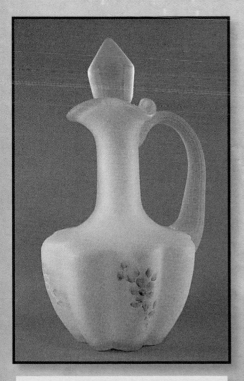

Satin Light Blue Overlay decorated fluted cruet, $125.00 – 150.00.

Satin Light Blue Overlay decorated round cruet, $125.00 – 150.00.

Light Blue Overlay round cruet, $85.00 – 100.00.

Lt Blue Overlay decorated round Barber bottle, $145.00 – 165.00.

Amethyst Overlay decorated tall creamer, $75.00 – 85.00.

Amethyst Overlay decorated round Sprig cruet, $75.00 – 85.00.

Gold & Amethyst Overlay paneled Sprig cruets, $85.00 – 100.00 each.

Wild Rose Overlay decorated round Barber bottle, $145.00 – 165.00.

Light Blue Overlay decorated pickle castor, $165.00 – 195.00.

Pink Overlay Maise pickle castor, $200.00 – 250.00.

Blue Overlay 13" bowl & frame, $65.00 – 75.00; Pink Overlay decorated 13" bowl & frame, $125.00 – 145.00; Milk Glass decorated 13" bowl, $50.00 – 65.00.

Wild Rose Overlay decorated oval cruet, $145.00 – 165.00.

Blue Overlay 13" bowl, $65.00 – 75.00.

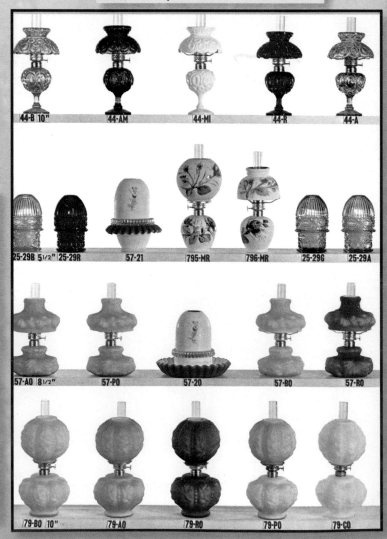

Row 1, Moon & Star miniature lamps: *Blue, $175.00 – 200.00; Amethyst, $200.00 – 225.00; Milk Glass, $175.00 – 200.00; Ruby, $200.00 – 225.00; Amber, $150.00 – 175.00. (Not shown, Blue Opalescent, $225.00 – 250.00.)*

Row 2, miniature lamps & fairy lights. Eye Winker fairy lights: *Blue, $55.00 – 65.00; Ruby, $65.00 – 75.00; Green, $55.00 – 65.00; Amber, $45.00 – 55.00.* **Rose Spray fairy lights:** *Peach Blow, $150.00 – 175.00; Moss Rose Peach Blow rd. shade, oval base, $200.00 – 225.00; Moss Rose Peach Blow half shade, oval base, $165.00 – 185.00.*

Row 3, Plume miniature lamps & Rose Spray fairy light. Plume lamps: *Amber Satin Overlay, $165.00 – 185.00; Pink Overlay, $250.00 – 275.00; Lt. Blue Overlay, $225.00 – 245.00; Wild Rose Overlay, $250.00 – 275.00;* **Rose Spray fairy light:** *Peach Blow large base, $200.00 – 225.00.*

Row 4, Beaded Curtain miniature lamps: *Lt. Blue Overlay, $250.00 – 275.00; Amber Overlay, $225.00 – 250.00; Wild Rose Overlay, $300.00 – 350.00; Pink Overlay, $250.00 – 275.00; Crystal Over MG, $225.00 – 250.00.*

Ruby Satin Plume lamp, $175.00 – 200.00.

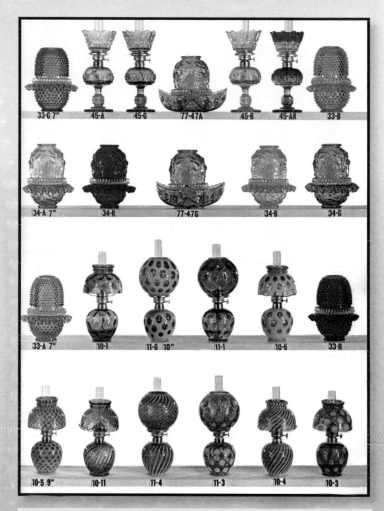

Rose Satin Rosette double-shade lamp, $375.00 – 450.00.

Row 1, Hobnail fairy lights: *Green, $75.00 – 85.00; Blue, $75.00 – 85.00.* **Embossed Rose triangle-base fairy light:** *Amber, $85.00 – 95.00.* **Daisy & Cube miniature lamps:** *Amber, $100.00 – 125.00; Green, $150.00 – 175.00; Blue, $150.00 – 175.00; Amberina, $175.00 – 195.00.*

Row 2, Embossed Rose fairy lights: *Amber, $65.00 – 75.00; Ruby, $85.00 – 100.00; Green with triangle base, $100.00 – 115.00; Blue, $75.00 – 85.00; Green, $75.00 – 85.00.*

Row 3, Hobnail fairy lights: *Amber, $65.00 – 75.00; Ruby, $85.00 – 100.00.* **Miniature lamps:** *Cranberry Thumbprint half shade, oval base, $150.00 – 175.00; CR* Coin Dot round shade, oval base, $275.00 – 300.00; Cranberry Thumbprint round shade, oval base, $175.00 – 225.00; CR Coin Dot half shade, oval base, $250.00 – 275.00.*

Row 4, Miniature lamps: *CR Eye Dot half shade, oval base, $250.00 – 275.00; Cranberry Spiral half shade, oval base, $150.00 – 175.00; CR Spiral round shade, oval base, $275.00 – 300.00; CR Opalescent Dot round shade, oval base, $275.00 – 300.00; CR Spiral half shade, oval base, $250.00 – 275.00; CR Opalescent Dot half shade, oval base, $250.00 – 275.00.*

*CR = Cranberry Opalescent.

Ruby Satin Embossed Rose GWTW lamp, $350.00 – 400.00.

85-RS

Ruby Satin Iris lamp, $400.00 – 450.00.

Ruby Overlay (Cranberry) double lamp with lg. double crimped hurricane shades, $350.00 – 400.00.

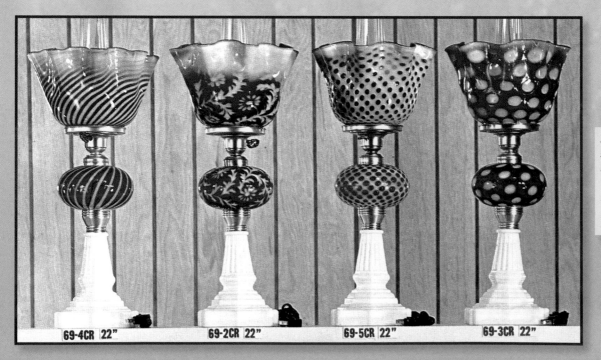

69-4CR 22"   69-2CR 22"   69-5CR 22"   69-3CR 22"

Lamps, Gothic bases, round founts, fluted shades: CR Spiral, CR Daisy & Fern, CR Honeycomb, CR Opalescent Dot, $350.00 – 400.00 each.

MARY GREGORY

Shape	Royal Blue
Barber bottle	$100.00 – 125.00
Basket, lg. with loop handle	$250.00 – 275.00
Cruet	$125.00 – 150.00
Lamp	$200.00 – 250.00
Pitcher, water	$225.00 – 275.00
Tumbler, water	$50.00 – 65.00

Royal Blue loop-handled basket, $250.00 – 275.00.

Royal Blue Oval cruet, $125.00 – 150.00.

Royal Blue lamp, $200.00 – 250.00. A pair of lamps would have facing figures.

Royal Blue Opalescent Christmas Snowflake lamp made from syrup jug, $225.00 – 250.00.

Blue Opalescent Daisy & Fern lamp made from syrup jug, $200.00 – 225.00.

Topaz Opalescent Daisy & Fern lamp made from syrup jug, $225.00 – 250.00.

Topaz Opalescent Daisy & Fern hurricane lamp, $350.00 – 375.00.

CR Daisy & Fern large straight-side canister, $375.00 – 425.00.

CR Daisy & Fern medium straight-side canister, $325.00 – 375.00.

CR Daisy & Fern small straight-side canister, $300.00 – 350.00.

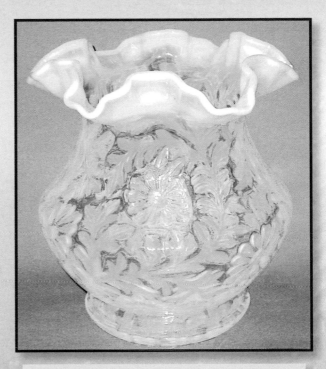

Topaz Opalescent #183 vase, $175.00 – 200.00.

CHRISTMAS SNOWFLAKE

Christmas Snowflake was introduced in the 1980 catalog supplement.

Shape	Cobalt Opalescent/ Cranberry Opalescent
Barber bottle	$275.00 – 325.00
Basket, 7"	$250.00 – 275.00
Bowl, 11"	$150.00 – 175.00
Creamer, tall	$150.00 – 175.00
Cruet, oval	$225.00 – 250.00
Lamp, 17"	$450.00 – 500.00
Lamp, 21" hurricane	$425.00 – 475.00
Pitcher, milk	$175.00 – 200.00
Pitcher, water	$325.00 – 375.00
Rose bowl, small	$165.00 – 195.00
Rose bowl, large	$200.00 – 250.00
Spooner	$85.00 – 95.00
Sugar shaker	$225.00 – 275.00

Shape	Cobalt Opalescent/ Cranberry Opalescent
Syrup pitcher	$300.00 – 325.00
Tumbler	$100.00 – 125.00

Cranberry Opalescent Daisy & Fern Luster, $400.00 – 450.00.

Ruby Overlay bulbous small canister, $75.00 – 95.00.

Ruby Overlay straight-sided small canister, $75.00 – 95.00.

Ruby Overlay bulbous large canister, $150.00 – 175.00.

Lois Radcliff was a longtime Fenton collector, but she also had a mail-order business, advertising in the *Glass Review* and the *Daze*, two periodicals written for glass collectors. She had a particular love for Jack-in-the-Pulpit vases, sometimes called tulip vases, and she loved the shading of Fenton's beautiful Burmese glassware. The Wave Crest–style vases were not being made for Fenton's catalog line, so Lois asked Frank to make those for her in Burmese. They sold very well for her and are now in great demand. Some were iridized and some were decorated with roses.

She also had art glass apples made in Rosalene, Burmese, and Ruby Carnival. When Fenton decided to make a new version of Blue Ridge for its 80th anniversary, Lois added the Blue Ridge JIP vase to her offerings. The blue carnival Butterfly may have been the first piece of Fenton glass to be made for Elemar. All of these pieces were made in the 1980s.

Blue Ridge Tulip (Jack-in-Pulpit) vase, $125.00 – 150.00.

Burmese Iridized Wave Crest vase, DC top, $150.00 – 175.00.

Burmese Iridized Wave Crest tulip vase, $175.00 – 200.00.

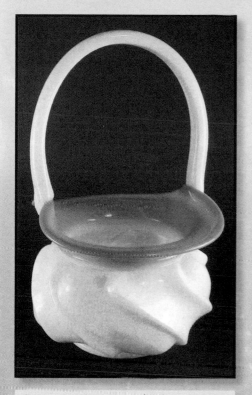

Burmese Wave Crest basket, $200.00 – 250.00.

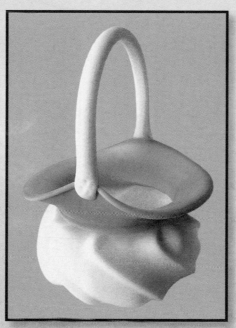

Burmese Satin Wave Crest basket, $200.00 – 250.00.

Burmese Satin, Roses decorated basket, $250.00 – 300.00.

Burmese Satin Wave Crest double-crimped vase, $150.00 – 175.00.

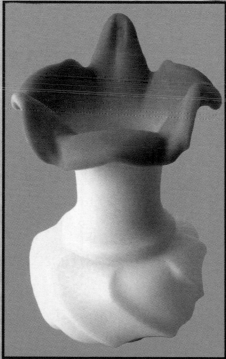

Burmese Satin Wave Crest tulip vase, $175.00 – 200.00.

Burmese Satin, Roses decorated double-crimped vase, $200.00 – 225.00.

Colonial Blue Carnival Butterfly on Stand, $65.00 – 85.00.

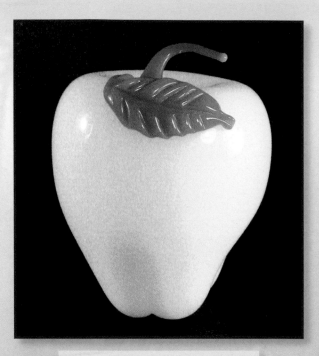

Burmese Apple, $125.00 – 150.00.

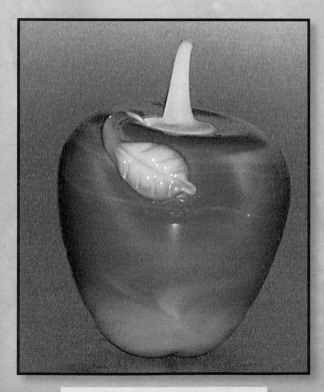

Rosalene Apple, $125.00 – 150.00.

Ruby Carnival Apple, $125.00 – 150.00.

Longaberger Baskets

The Longaberger family has been making baskets for almost a century, but it was 1972 before its name became synonymous with baskets. In 1972, the company only had a few dozen employees, but it now has 5,400 working in Ohio and another 70,000 working as independent home consultants.

Fenton has made several pieces for Longaberger, each featuring a basket of flowers. Not all of the pieces pictured here were chosen to be sold in its gift shop, but I was unable to determine which were just samples.

Iridized Opal with Green Crest Snowman with Basket decoration, #7254 vase, $65.00 – 85.00.

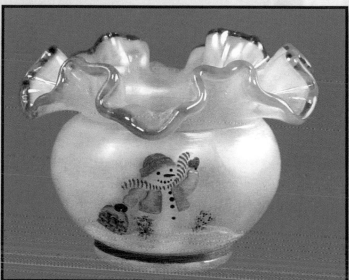

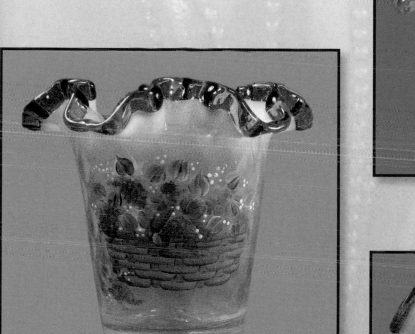

French Opalescent with Violet Crest flip vase with basket of flowers decoration, $75.00 – 85.00.

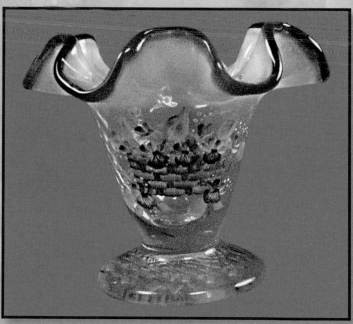

French Opalescent with Violet Crest #7354 vase, decorated with basket of flowers, $55.00 – 60.00.

French Opalescent with Pink Crest #3429 vases, decorated with baskets of flowers, $75.00 – 85.00 each.

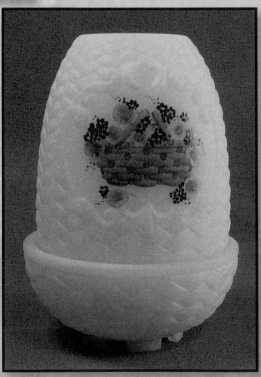

Opal Satin fairy light with basket of flowers decoration, $100.00 – 120.00.

Opal Satin Doll figurine carrying basket of flowers, $75.00 – 85.00; Opal Angel, $75.00 – 85.00.

*Opal Satin Dolls with slightly different baskets of flowers,
$75.00 – 85.00 each.*

*Opal Satin Angels, each with different baskets of flowers,
$75.00 – 85.00 each.*

Madonna Inn of San Luis Obispo, CA

The Madonna Inn of San Luis Obispo, California, is one of the most famous inns on the West Coast, situated on the Pacific coastline halfway between Los Angeles and San Francisco. It's a full-line resort with something for everyone and some of the best restaurants in the state. It can also claim to have the most unique and famous urinals in any state. Women have been known to sneak into one of the men's rooms just for a peek at these very famous urinals. One of these is a trough and wheel similar to an old mining waterwheel in the Wild, Wild West. An electronic eye beam activates the waterwheel to splash water into the trough. If you are a gentleman who is a little shy, you might want to find another bathroom, to avoid those women bearing cameras.

The embossed rose goblets were designed by Alex Madonna to match the pink floral-patterned carpet in Alex Madonna's Gold Rush Steak House. Fenton has been making these beautiful embossed rose goblets for the Madonna Inn for many years. When you order lunch or dinner, your beverage is served in one of these. You can also buy them from the gift shop or online. The original goblets were taller, with "Madonna Inn" in raised letters on an otherwise plain rim. Those are very hard to find and are more expensive. Because they are still sold in the gift shop and online, the value of the newer glasses is the present retail value.

*Goblet, $14.50; goblets with lettering, $30.00 – 35.00.
Wines, $11.75; wines with lettering, $25.00 – 30.00.*

Cobalt Blue wine, $11.75.

Colonial Blue goblet, $14.50.

Lt. Amethyst goblet, $14.50.

Jamestown Blue goblet with lettering, $30.00 – 35.00.

Photo of the lettering.

Lt Aqua wine, $11.75.

Lt. Aqua goblet, $14.50.

Pink goblet, $14.50.

Rare Pink Opalescent goblet, $20.00 – 25.00; Rare Topaz wine, $18.00 – 22.00.

Ruby goblet, $14.50.

Ruby wine, $11.75.

Yellow wine, lettered, $25.00 – 30.00.

MARSHALL FIELDS, FREDERICK & NELSON

Frederick and Nelson Department Store was a Seattle, Washington, based division of Marshall Fields. Probably the most famous of the products sold in Frederick's was its Frango candy, a tasty chocolate that melts in your mouth and is often flavored with rum, raspberry, mint, and other flavors. They are still so popular that there was a court battle to see who would have the rights to sell them when Fredericks closed in the 1990s. In the 1970s, Fenton made a butterfly-decorated box that was sold filled with Frangos. The base is marked with both "Fenton" and "Frango." These boxes have only been found in Satin Milk Glass and a shiny Lime Sherbet.

Six pieces of Burmese painted with butterflies were made for Frederick and Nelson. They are a 7" vase, a large tulip vase, a 5" vase, a rose bowl, a basket, and a 21" lamp.

BURMESE, FLORAL & BUTTERFLIES
by Louise Piper

Description	Ware #	Value
Basket	7437	$250.00 – 275.00
Lamp, 21"	7412	$400.00 – 450.00
Rose bowl	7424	$125.00 – 175.00
Vase, 5"	7457	$150.00 – 195.00
Vase, 7"	7252	$195.00 – 250.00
Vase, JIP	7255	$200.00 – 275.00

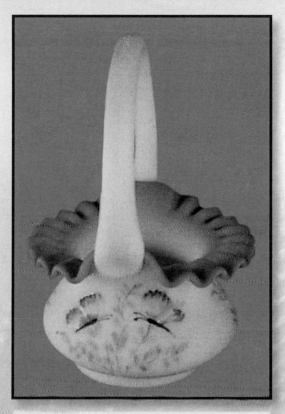

Burmese butterfly-decorated #7437 basket, $250.00 – 275.00.

Burmese butterfly-decorated #7255 Tulip vase, $200.00 – 275.00.

Burmese butterfly-decorated #7424 rose bowl, $150.00 – 175.00.

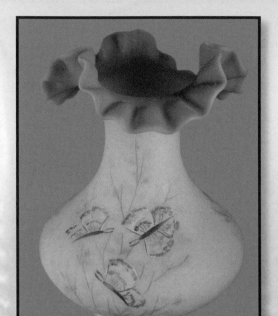

Burmese butterfly-decorated #7252, 7"
vase, $195.00 – 250.00.

Burmese butterfly-decorated #7412
lamp, $400.00 – 450.00; with match-
ing fount, $450.00 – 500.00.

FRANGO BOXES

Description	Value
White satin	$75.00 – 95.00
Lime Sherbet (glossy)	$75.00 – 95.00

Milk Glass Satin Frango box, $75.00 – 95.00.

Shiny Lime Sherbet Frango
box, $75.00 – 95.00.

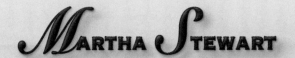

Martha Stewart, daytime diva of the kitchen, single-handedly brought jade-colored glassware back into the kitchens of people who would have never thought of themselves as collectors. Behind her, in every show, were white cabinets filled with beautiful jade-colored glassware. For the most part, her cabinets were filled with Fire King Jadite kitchenware and dinnerware, but suddenly, everyone discovered the beauty of all types of jade-colored glass. Glass dealers sold the beautiful toned glassware so fast that the prices had to rise just so they could keep some of it in stock. Gene Florence, author of *Kitchen Glassware of the Depression Years* and *Anchor Hocking's Fire King and More*, told me that when he took boxes of Jadite into his space in the antique mall, it was gone before he could leave. It was a craze that would eventually become a memory, probably because most of the people buying it were not collectors. They were people who were happy when they had enough to brighten their kitchens.

Martha discovered that she could take advantage of the craze she had created by having jade glass made to be sold in her catalog, *Martha by Mail*. Fenton was the first company to produce her glassware. Because of the success of jade, she thought she could do the same thing for milk glass and a beautiful, translucent color of pink. Those two colors never found the extreme popularity of jade, but they did sell well for her. Fenton made all three colors, some of it in its moulds, but new shapes were also made for her. Glass made from old moulds took on a new use in kitchens, offices, and bathrooms. The bottom to a footed candy became a spoon, toothbrush, or pen and pencil holder. Covered leftover dishes became soap or ring holders. Martha gave old glass new life by using it less traditionally.

Eventually, Fenton was not able to keep up with the demand being created by Martha Stewart. Fenton had to pass the business along to L.E. Smith, who made glass for her for a few years. Most of the pieces made by it were from its moulds. For example, the Smith turkey-shaped candy with a lid was a popular piece sold in *Martha by Mail*.

This is an accurate list of every piece Fenton made for Martha Stewart.

Description	Jade (SU)	Milk Glass (MI)	Shell Pink (SL)
Bowl, cereal/ice cream	$18.00 – 22.00		$18.00 – 22.00
Bowl, deep	$23.00 – 27.00		$23.00 – 27.00
Bowl set			
Bowl, shallow soup	$30.00 – 35.00		$30.00 – 35.00
Bowl, spout	$25.00 – 30.00		$25.00 – 30.00
Bowl, spout w/handle	$35.00 – 45.00		$35.00 – 45.00
Bowl, shallow soup	$24.00 – 28.00		$24.00 – 28.00
Butterfly pins	(ea.) $15.00 – 18.00	(ea.) $15.00 – 18.00	
Candy box, covered	$65.00 – 85.00		
Candy dish, no lid		$35.00 – 55.00	
Chick on Nest	$65.00 – 75.00		$65.00 – 75.00
Eggcup	$15.00 – 18.00		$15.00 – 18.00
Egg holder, Rabbit	$20.00 – 22.00		$20.00 – 22.00
Flowerpot, small	$18.00 – 20.00	$12.00 – 15.00	$18.00 – 20.00

Description	Jade (SU)	Milk Glass (MI)	Shell Pink (SL)
Flowerpot, large	$24.00 – 26.00	$22.00 – 24.00	$24.00 – 26.00
Hen on Nest	$65.00 – 85.00		$65.00 – 85.00
Hen egg server	$125.00 -150.00		$150.00 – 175.00
Picture hanger (flower)	$15.00 – 18.00	$15.00 – 18.00	$15.00 – 18.00
Rabbit on Nest	$75.00 – 85.00		$75.00 – 85.00
Plate, lg. Leaf	$30.00 – 35.00		$30.00 – 35.00
Plate, lunch	$20.00 – 22.00		$20.00 – 22.00
Plate, sm. Leaf	$24.00 – 26.00		$24.00 – 26.00
Platter	$35.00 – 40.00		$35.00 – 40.00
Rolling pin	$85.00 – 100.00	$65.00 – 75.00	$85.00 – 100.00
Salt dish, open	$12.00 – 15.00		$12.00 – 15.00
Soap box (leftover), lg.	$45.00 – 55.00		
Soap box (leftover), sm.	$40.00 – 50.00		
Tumbler	$18.00 – 22.00	$15.00 – 18.00	$18.00 – 22.00

Jade deep bowl, $25.00 – 28.00; Shell Pink, $25.00 – 28.00.

Jade & Shell Pink Rabbit egg holders, $20.00 – 22.00 each; Milk Glass and Jade Butterfly thumbtacks, $15.00 – 18.00 each.

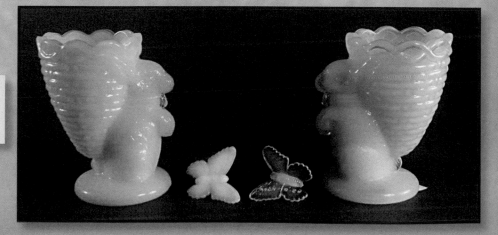

Jade & Shell Pink tumblers, $18.00 – 22.00 each.

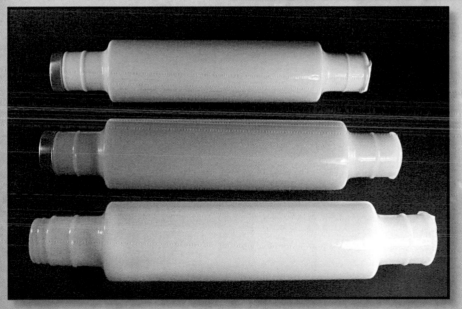

Jade & Shell Pink rolling pins, $85.00 – 100.00 each; Milk Glass, $65.00 – 75.00.

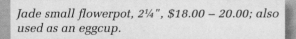

Jade small flowerpot, 2¼", $18.00 – 20.00; also used as an eggcup.

Jade spouted bowl, $25.00 – 30.00; deep bowl, $23.00 – 27.00; Crystal muddler, $8.00 – 10.00; Jade muddler, $12.00 – 14.00.

Jade Chick on Nest, $65.00 – 75.00.

Jade medium flowerpot, 3", $20.00 – 22.00.

Jade Hobnail eggcup, $30.00 – 35.00.

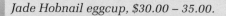

Jade 11" Leaf plate, $30.00 – 35.00.

Jade 8" low bowl, $24.00 – 28.00.

Top view of 8" low bowl.

Jade spouted & handled bowl, $35.00 – 45.00; spouted bowl, $25.00 – 30.00.

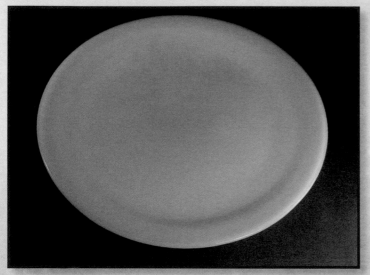

Jade 13" platter, $35.00 – 40.00.

Jade Rabbit & Nest, $75.00 – 85.00.

Jade small soap box, $40.00 – 50.00; lg. soap box, $45.00 – 55.00.

Jade rolling pin, $85.00 – 100.00.

Jade square candy, side view, $65.00 – 85.00.

Jade dinner plate, 9¾", $28.00 – 32.00.

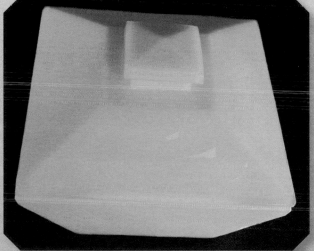

Jade square candy box & lid, top view.

Picture hangers. Milk Glass, $15.00 – 18.00; Shell Pink, $15.00 – 18.00.

Milk Glass picture hanger, $15.00 – 18.00.

Milk Glass soap dish, $14.00 – 16.00.

Milk Glass medium flowerpot, $18.00 – 20.00; small flowerpot, $12.00 – 15.00.

Milk Glass rolling pin, $65.00 – 75.00.

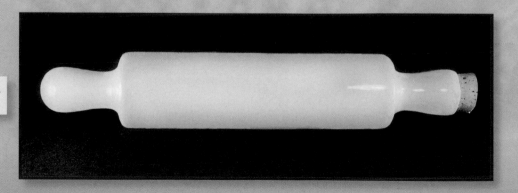

Milk Glass large flowerpot, $22.00 – 24.00.

Milk Glass flip vase, $25.00 – 28.00.

Shell Pink Fish covered dish, $25.00 – 30.00; small Fish tray, $22.00 – 24.00; lg. Rabbit covered dish, $75.00 – 85.00; small Rabbit covered dish, $28.00 – 30.00.

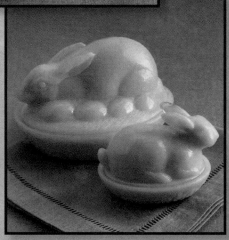

Milk Glass Rabbit on Nest, $75.00 – 85.00.

*Shell Pink Chick on Nest,
$65.00 – 75.00.*

*Shell Pink and Jade Rabbit on Nest,
dishes $75.00 – 85.00 each.*

*Shell Pink deep bowl, $23.00
– 27.00; ice cream or cereal
bowl, $18.00 – 22.00.*

*Shell Pink cereal bowl,
$18.00 – 22.00.*

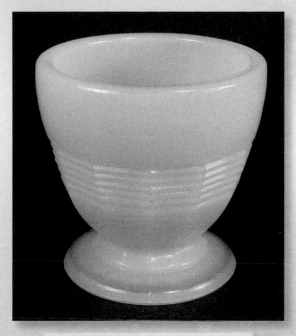

Shell Pink eggcup, $18.00 – 24.00.

Shell Pink picture hanger, $15.00 – 18.00.

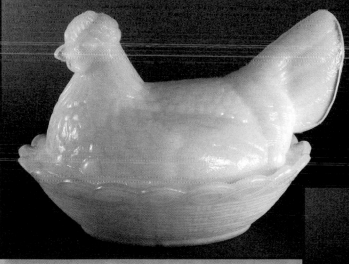

Shell Pink Hen on Nest, $65.00 – 85.00.

Shell Pink Hen egg server, $150.00 – 175.00.

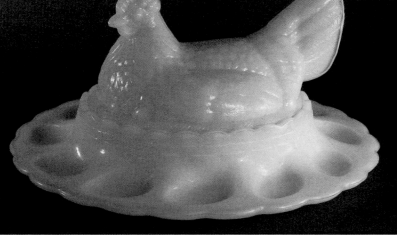

Shell Pink lg. 11" Leaf plate, $30.00 – 35.00.

Shell Pink 13" platter, $35.00 – 40.00.

Shell Pink spouted handled bowl, $35.00 – 45.00; spouted bowl, $25.00 – 30.00.

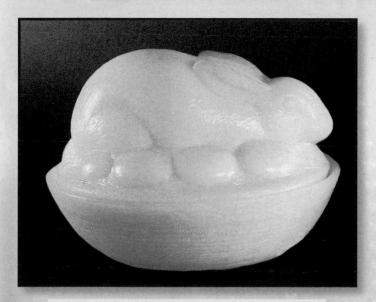

Shell Pink Rabbit covered dish, $75.00 – 85.00.

Shell Pink Rabbit egg holder, $20.00 – 22.00.

Mary Walrath & Daughters

Mary Walrath is a name recognized by any serious Burmese collector. She married her husband, Arthur Walrath, on March 15, 1981, and in 1982, introduced one of Fenton's most beautiful collections of Burmese glass decorated in one of her own designs, Love Bouquet. That collection included six pieces: a 6½" Jack-in-the-Pulpit vase, a 10" Jack-in-the-Pulpit vase, a hat basket with a crimped edge, a cupped rose bowl, a crimped rose bowl, and a 6" bud vase. This grouping of beautifully done glass sold for the low price of $224 ($229 including shipping). That price, which seems cheap now, met a lot of resistence, and the pieces didn't sell as well as expected. Today, the Love Bouquet pieces bring four or five times the prices of the original issues. If only foresight was as good as hindsight!

The Love Bouquet collection didn't sell as quickly as one might have expected, but this didn't deter Mary from continuing to offer special glass. She began asking Bill Fenton to produce a miniature collection in Burmese. Of course, his answer was, "Mary, you can't press Burmese glass." Not the kind of person to be discouraged, Mary would call Bill occasionally to ask him if Fenton had figured out a way to press Burmese. It was four and a half years later that Mary heard the words, "We can do it." The first samples of pressed Burmese left a lot to be desired, but finally, the color was acceptable and the Miniature Burmese Collection was made. Again, this collection, which was offered at $185.00 for the entire set, met with a great deal of price resistance.

The year of 1986 was a terrible year for Mary. Not only was she having trouble selling her miniature collection, but her husband died of cancer. It would be 1993 before she even thought about ordering a new collection made. It was when she saw the new 8" doll figurine Fenton was producing that she decided to get back into the mail-order business. She loved the look of the 8" doll figurine (#5141) with the flowing hair and the beautiful lines of the dress. She ordered that figurine transformed into a bell and called the items her Southern Belle collection. This was meant to be a six-piece collection, but upon learning that a run of Holiday Green had been made for her, she had 200 painted in memory of her sister, Peg, as a special edition. Each piece in the bell collection is signed with Mary's name, the edition number, the doll's name, and the number of the bell itself. There is a certificate of authenticity that documents the date of production and the number produced. This collection represented several firsts for a collection. It was the first time the figurine was converted into a bell, the first time it was iridized, and the first time it was hand painted with a decoration as well the edition number, name of the bell, and its individual number. The certificate of authenticity included a signature and a photo of Bill Fenton. To top it all, only 300 of each bell were made.

In 1996, at the age of 80, Mary had Fenton make a three-piece Farewell Burmese collection that was to be the end of her mail-order career. That collection consisted of a basket, a pitcher, and a cat, with a limit of 150 matching numbered sets. The pieces are fully painted on both sides. This Mary C. Walrath Burmese Exclusive production has 16 Burmese items and a poem, "My Love Bouquet," written by Mary.

On February 2, 2002, Mary became Mrs. Stanley Jachim. On her first anniversary, she ordered three more pieces from Fenton, which were called My Faith Bouquet. The design, painted by Diane Gessel, has a white rose center with two rosebuds, three sprays of blue forget-me-nots, and three sprays of pink lilies of the valley. All three of the pieces are sandblasted, and each has a special inscription on the base. The frog and the cat are limited to 222 pieces, to honor her anniversary, 2/2/02. All the pieces are signed by Diane Gessel and Mary Jachim. On the cat is an inscription that reads, "Faith in Christ's Purr-fect Love." On the frog an inscription says, "Leap with Faith," and the vase is inscribed, "Faith Sees the Unseen." This last group is as beautiful as all the glass made for Mary Walrath.

LOVE BOUQUET			
Date	*Shape*	*Item #*	*Value*
1982	Basket, 5"	7235WQ	$175.00 – 200.00
1982	Bud vase, 6"	7558WQ	$125.00 – 150.00
1982	Crimped vase, 4½"	7546WQ	$125.00 – 150.00
1982	Cupped rose bowl, 4½"	7424WQ	$150.00 – 175.00
1982	Jack-in-pulpit vase, 6½"	7255WQ	$150.00 – 175.00
1986	Basket, 5½"	9230WQ	$150.00 – 175.00
1986	Bell, 4½" petite	7662WQ	$100.00 – 125.00
1986	Boot, 2¾"	9590WQ	$100.00 – 125.00
1986	Rose bowl, 3¼"	9558WQ	$125.00 – 150.00
1986	Slipper, 5¼"	9591WQ	$100.00 – 125.00

Date	Shape	Item #	Value
1986	Toothpick/votive, 2¾"	9592WQ	$125.00 – 150.00
1996	Basket	7437WQ	$175.00 – 200.00
1996	Cat	5165WQ	$75.00 – 100.00
1996	Pitcher		$200.00 – 225.00

Burmese Love Bouquet assortment: *4½" rose bowl, $150.00 – 175.00; 6" bud vase, $125.00 – 150.00; 10" JIP vase, $175.00 – 200.00; 6½" JIP vase, $150.00 – 175.00; 4½" vase, $125.00 – 150.00; 5" basket $175.00 – 200.00*

A Limited Offering for the Antique Trade *from Fenton*

The name Burmese is attributed to Queen Victoria who is said to have exclaimed that the rich tones of blushing pink reminded her of a Burmese sunset. Pure gold, uranium and another precious metal are used to achieve this exotic glass color.

PRODUCED EXCLUSIVELY FOR CHERISHED EDITIONS
211 Pike Street
Brownville, N.Y. 13615
315-782-0879

HISTORIC BURMESE

Inspired by Mary Walrath, this handpainted "LOVE BOUQUET" series is limited to not more than 500 complete collections. Complete collections will be signed and numbered. This arrangement of lilies of the valley, forget-me-nots, one rose and rosebud is breathtakingly beautiful. Pieces may also be purchased singly.

SHIPPING $5.00 per collection $2.00 per piece N.Y. res. please add sales tax. Allow 2 weeks for delivery.

7424 WQ 4½" Rose Bowl $23.50
7558 WQ 6" Bud Vase $32.50
7255 WQ 10" Jack-in-Pulpit Vase $47.50
7552 WQ 6½" Jack-in-Pulpit Vase $32.50
7546 WQ 4½" Vase $29.50
7235 WQ 5" Basket $42.50

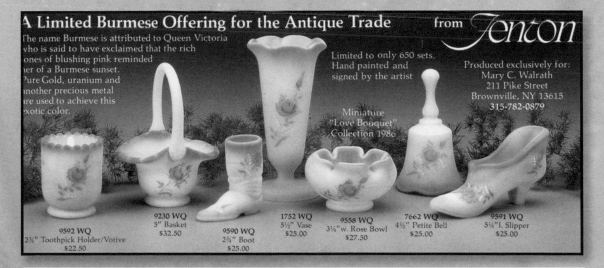

A Limited Burmese Offering for the Antique Trade *from Fenton*

The name Burmese is attributed to Queen Victoria who is said to have exclaimed that the rich tones of blushing pink reminded her of a Burmese sunset. Pure Gold, uranium and another precious metal are used to achieve this exotic color.

Limited to only 650 sets. Hand painted and signed by the artist

Miniature "Love Bouquet" Collection 1986

Produced exclusively for:
Mary C. Walrath
211 Pike Street
Brownville, NY 13615
315-782-0879

9592 WQ 2¾" Toothpick Holder/Votive $22.50
9230 WQ 5" Basket $32.50
9590 WQ 2¾" Boot $25.00
1752 WQ 5½" Vase $25.00
9558 WQ 3¼"w. Rose Bowl $27.50
7662 WQ 4½" Petite Bell $25.00
9591 WQ 5¼"l. Slipper $25.00

Burmese Love Bouquet pressed assortment: *2¾" toothpick, $125.00 – 150.00; 5" basket, $150.00 – 175.00; 2¾" boot, $100.00 – 125.00; 5½" vase, $125.00 – 150.00; 3¼" rose bowl, $125.00 – 150.00; 4½" petite bell, $100.00 – 125.00; 5¼" slipper, $100.00 – 125.00.*

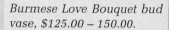
Burmese Love Bouquet petite bell, $100.00 – 125.00.

Burmese Love Bouquet bud vase, $125.00 – 150.00.

Burmese Love Bouquet toothpick, $125.00 – 150.00; crimped rose bowl, $125.00 – 150.00.

Burmese Love Bouquet slipper, $125.00 – 150.00.

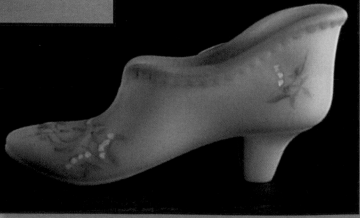

Burmese Love Bouquet crimped rose bowl,
$125.00 – 150.00.

Burmese Farewell Collection of Love Bouquet; basket, $175.00 – 200.00; Cat, $85.00 – 100.00; pitcher, $200.00 – 225.00.

Pink Carnival Fish paperweight, $75.00 – 95.00.

Ruby Fish paperweight, $75.00 – 100.00.

Ruby Carnival Fish paperweight, $75.00 – 100.00.

SOUTHERN BELLE COLLECTION

Date	Name	Color	Decoration	Edition	Value
5/94	Anna	Light Gold	Yellow/White Daisies	254	$150.00 – 175.00
6/94	Carol	Petal Pink	Pinks	299	$150.00 – 175.00
7/94	Marianne	Persian Blue Opalescent	Impatiens	286	$150.00 – 175.00
8/94	Susan	Crystal Lustre	Red Roses	274	$150.00 – 175.00
10/94	Stephanie	Rose Magnolia	Magnolias	252	$150.00 – 175.00
11/94	Michelle	Sea Mist Green	White Poinsettias	281	$150.00 – 175.00
1995	Peg	Holiday Green	Assorted	200	$150.00 – 175.00

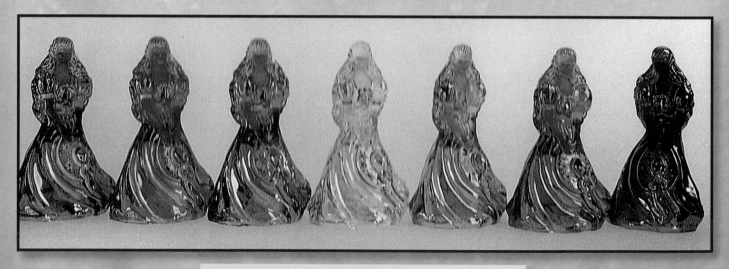

Set of seven Southern Belle bells, $150.00 – 175.00 each.

"Susan" Crystal Luster bell, $150.00 – 175.00.

"Anna" Lt. Gold Carnival bell, $150.00 – 175.00.

"Carol" Petal Pink Carnival bell, $150.00 – 175.00.

"Marianne" Persian Blue Carnival bell, $150.00 – 175.00.

"Michelle" Sea Mist Green Carnival bell, $150.00 – 175.00.

"Stephanie" Rose Magnolia Carnival bell, $150.00 – 175.00.

"Peg" Holiday Green Carnival bell, $150.00 – 175.00.

MARY JACHIM

MY FAITH BOUQUET 2002 – 2003 Jachim Collection The only collection signed as Mary Jachim.			
Shape	*Color*	*Edition*	*Value*
Sitting Cat	Willow Green Satin	222	$75.00 – 100.00
Frog	Burmese Satin	222	$75.00 – 100.00
Feather vase, 11"	Rosalene Satin	55	$250.00 – 275.00

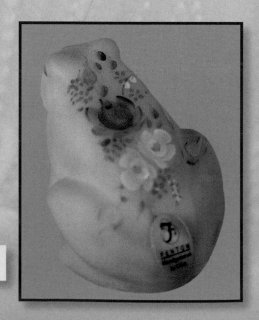

Burmese Satin My Faith Frog, $75.00 – 100.00.

Rosalene Satin Feather vase, My Faith, $250.00 – 275.00.

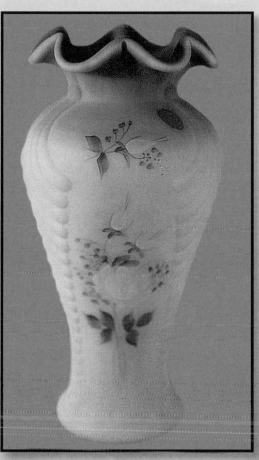

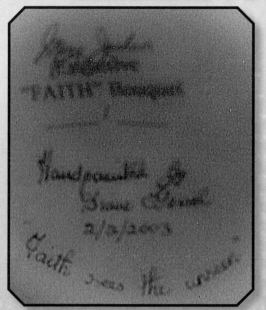

Inscription on the base of the Rosalene vase.

Willow Green My Faith Sitting Cat, $75.00 – 100.00.

Inscription on the base of the cat.

JOYCE COLELLA & MARY JACHIM

Mary meant the Farewell Collection to be her final journey into the mail-order world, but her daughter, Joyce Colella, was reluctant to see her mother's rich history of special-order Burmese go by the wayside. The Love Bouquet pieces were too important to her. Joyce, a avid glass collector, is Mary's youngest daughter. She had been thinking of a way to keep that design alive. By adding a dove holding white streamers that connected the Love Bouquet design with one designed by Judy, a grouping of Pink and White roses with Lavender forget-me-nots, her mother's legacy would continue. The pieces with the Circle of Love are signed by both Joyce Colella and Mary Walrath and are numbered by Joyce. The bottom reads, "Produced exclusively for Judy Colella," with the year of production. Many collectors have purchased two of each piece because the front and the back of each piece is so different and each is too beautiful to not be displayed.

Mary Walrath-Jachim died on December, 1, 2004, but her legacy is intact and will not be forgotten.

CIRCLE OF LOVE
By Joyce Colella

Number	Item	Color	Item #	Edition	Value
I	Pitcher	Burmese		53	$200.00 – 225.00
II	Rose bowl, cupped	Burmese		80	$100.00 – 125.00
III	Rose bowl, crimped	Burmese		163	$85.00 – 100.00
IV	Rose bowl & Nymph	Burmese, Rosalene		205	(set) $175.00 – 250.00
V	Cruet	Topaz, Blue Crest		155	$175.00 – 200.00
VI	Lamp, 10"	Burmese		60	$400.00 – 450.00
VII	Cat	French Opalescent	5165	125	$65.00 – 85.00
VIII	Vase, crimped tulip	Burmese, Blk. Crest		69	$165.00 – 185.00
IX	Vase, smooth tulip	Burmese, Blk. Crest		120	$165.00 – 185.00
X	Cat, sitting	Burmese Satin	5165	53	$100.00 – 115.00
XI	Cat, sitting	Burmese Glossy	5165	35	$100.00 – 115.00
XII	Bear	Burmese Satin	5151	140	$85.00 – 100.00
XIII	Bear	Burmese Glossy	5151	50	$85.00 – 100.00
XIV	Perfume bottle	Burmese Satin		60	$120.00 – 140.00
XV	Rose bowl, crimped	Royal Purple		80	$95.00 – 125.00
XVI	Temple jar	Blue Burmese Glossy		50	$200.00 – 225.00
XVII	Temple jar	Blue Burmese Satin		130	$200.00 – 225.00
XVIII	Stylized cat	Burmese Glossy	5065	69	$85.00 – 100.00

Number	Item	Color	Item #	Edition	Value
XX	Bell, crimped	Blue Burmese, Rosalene		98	$100.00 – 125.00
XXI	DO* tumble up	Green Burmese Satin		128	$189.00 – 225.00
XXII	DO tumble up	Green Burmese Glossy		14	$189.00 – 225.00
XXIII	DO tumble up	Burmese Satin		116	$189.00 – 225.00
XXIV	DO tumble up	Burmese Glossy		51	$189.00 – 225.00
XXV	Bridesmaid doll**	Topaz		100	$85.00 – 115.00
XXVI	Student lamp, 18"	Cranberry		52	$450.00 – 500.00

*DO = Diamond Optic.
**Named Elisa Joy.

CIRCLE OF LOVE BOUQUET

Number	Item	Color	Item #	Edition	Value
1-A	Sitting Cat	Burmese Glossy	5165	68	$85.00 – 100.00
1-B	Sitting Cat	Burmese Satin	5165	132	$85.00 – 100.00
2	Bear	Rosalene Satin	5151	175	$85.00 – 100.00
3	Frog	Burmese Satin		75	$85.00 – 100.00
4	Vase, 9½"	Burmese	1218		$165.00 – 195.00

Black Satin Circle of Love stylized Cat, $100.00 – 125.00.

Blue Burmese Forget-Me-Not temple jar, $135.00 – 150.00.

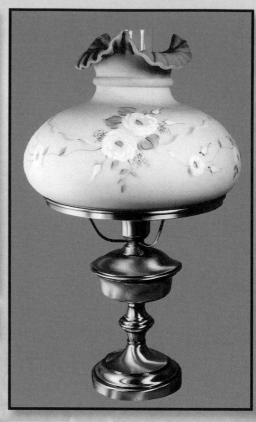

Burmese Circle of Love Cat, $85.00 – 100.00.

Burmese Circle of Love Sitting Bear, $85.00 – 100.00.

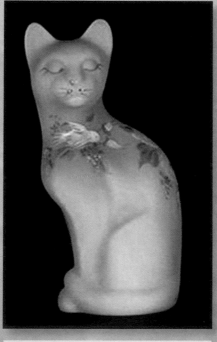

Burmese Circle of Love lamp, side 1, $400.00 – 450.00.

Burmese Satin Stylized Cat, $85.00 – 100.00.

Burmese lamp, side 2.

Burmese Circle of Love Stylized Cat, $85.00 – 100.00.

Burmese Diamond Optic Circle of Love Twin Rib guest set, $189.00 – 225.00.

French Opalescent Circle of Love Sitting Cat, $65.00 – 85.00.

Lotus Mist Circle of Love Bell with Opal Crest, $100.00 – 125.00.

Lotus Mist Green Circle of Love Stylized Cat, $100.00 – 125.00.

Royal Purple Circle of Love rose bowl, $95.00 – 125.00.

Lotus Mist Diamond Optic Circle of Love Twin Rib guest set, $189.00 – 225.00.

Topaz Opalescent Drapery Circle of Love cruet with Cobalt Blue Crest, $175.00 – 200.00.

Burmese Circle of Love JIP vase with Black Crest, $165.00 – 185.00.

Topaz Iridized Circle of Love doll figurine, $85.00 – 115.00.

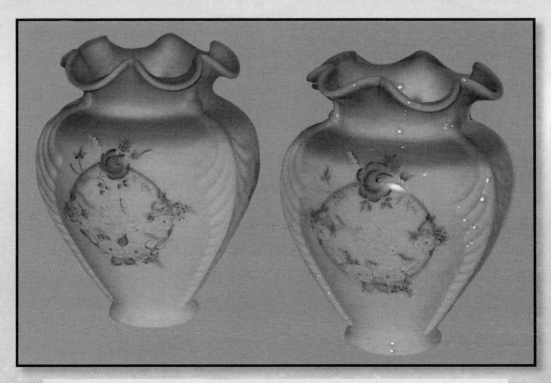

Burmese Satin and Shiny Circle of Love Feather vases, $275.00 – 325.00 each.

FORGET-ME-NOTS

In 2005, Joyce added a new design, Forget-Me-Nots, to her list of items made for her. This design consists of Lavender forget-me-nots with pansies. This is a smaller design that works well on the smaller pieces offered in the collection. As with the Circle of Love items, Judy personally signs her pieces.

Number	Item	Color	Item #	Edition	Value
A	Butterfly	Lotus Mist		66	$75.00 – 100.00
B	Doll	Topaz Glossy Carnival	5228	100	$85.00 – 115.00
C	Sitting Cat	Burmese Satin	5165	122	$65.00 – 100.00
D	Elegant Cat	Lotus Mist Burmese	5065	88	$100.00 – 125.00
E	Sitting Bear	Rosalene Glossy	5151	56	$100.00 – 115.00
F	Sitting Bear	Rosalene Satin	5151	275	$100.00 – 115.00
G	Frog	Burmese Satin		75	$75.00 – 100.00
H	Vase, 9½"	Burmese	1218		$275.00 – 325.00

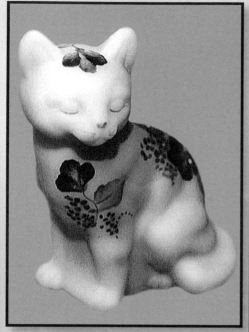

Burmese Forget-Me-Nots Sitting Cat, $85.00 – 100.00.

Lotus Mist Green Forget-Me-Nots Stylized Cat, $100.00 – 125.00.

Lotus Mist Green Forget-Me-Nots Butterfly, $100.00 – 125.00.

Topaz Carnival Forget-Me-Nots Doll figurine, $85.00 – 115.00.

Burmese Satin and Shiny Forget-Me-Nots Feather vases, $275.00 – 325.00 each.

JOYCE COLELLA

In the last months of 2005, Judy decided to add one more design, one to honor her mother. It is called In Loving Memory of My Mother. This is similar to Circle of Love, but instead of a circle, there is a heart shape.

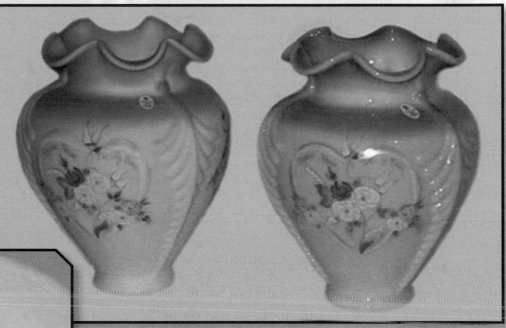

Burmese Satin and Shiny Feather vases, $275.00 – 325.00.

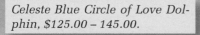

Inscription on base of vases.

Celeste Blue Circle of Love Dolphin, $125.00 – 145.00.

CAROL'S ANTIQUES AND ART

In 1987, Carol Wood, owner of Carol's Antiques and Art in Liverpool, New York, and another daughter of Mary Walrath, came to Fenton with a request. She brought with her sketches she had commissioned artist Paul Mollon to make. I think you will agree that the pieces made for her from those sketches are beautiful in many ways. The Howling is the taller, 12" vase featuring a wolf on a ridge with the moon and a pine tree for a back drop. The shorter, 8" vase is called The Frolic and depicts two wolves walking together with the moon in the sky above them. Favrene glass was a beautiful and fitting choice for the beautiful designs.

In 1998, the full order of these vases was still not filled. Seconds of these were sold in the gift shop with a star that designated them as seconds. They were pieces that Carol Wood personally rejected as being undesirable.

Three more designs were meant to have been made, but the problems in making the Howling wolves made it unlikely that the other three could be made any more successfully than the first pieces.

Favrene The Frolic 8" vase, $300.00 – 350.00.

Favrene Howling Wolf 12" oval vase, $300.00 – 350.00.

McMillen & Husband

McMillen & Husband is a Michigan gift shop that has sold Fenton for 25 years. It is responsible for the beautiful blown eggs pictured here and is now buying special glass for a Yahoo e-group for Fenton collectors. The purple rose is an exclusive decoration used only for that group.

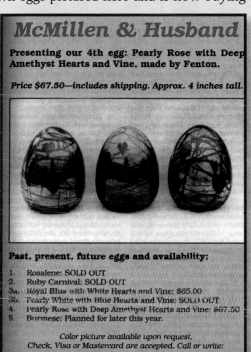
Advertisement for the Pearly Rose blown egg.

Pearly egg with Deep Amethyst Hearts & Vines, $125.00 – 150.00.

Black egg with Opal Hearts & Vines, $125.00 – 150.00.

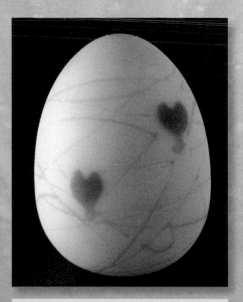

Burmese egg with Hearts and Vines, $175.00 – 200.00.

Cranberry egg with Opal Hearts and Vines, $150.00 – 175.00.

Cranberry egg with Opal Hearts & Vines with a different look, $150.00 – 175.00.

Iridized Ruby egg with Black Hearts & Vines, $175.00 – 200.00.

Milk Glass Blown egg with Black Hearts & Vines, $125.00 – 150.00.

Rosalene egg with Black Hearts & Vines, $175.00 – 200.00.

Royal Blue egg with Opal Hearts & Vines, $150.00 – 175.00.

Topaz egg, struck all over, Black Hearts & Vines, $150.00 – 175.00.

Advertisement for a warehouse find of L.G. Wright lamps made by Fenton: Cranberry Satin, $550.00 – 600.00; Sparkling Cranberry, $550.00 – 600.00; Sparkling Ruby, $550.00 – 600.00; Velvet Ruby and Dark Velvet Ruby, $550.00 – 600.00 each; Satin Milk Glass, $425.00 – 450.00.

Burmese Satin Turtle, $75.00 – 85.00; Burmese Satin Rabbit, $65.00 – 75.00. Both decorated with Purple Rose.

Burmese #5262 Mr. & Mrs. Santa Bunnies, $65.00 – 75.00 each.

Lotus Mist Purple Rose #5165 Cat, $65.00 – 75.00.

Lotus Mist Purple Rose #5251 Small Bear, $65.00 – 75.00; #5151 Sitting Bear, $75.00 – 85.00.

Sea Mist Green oval Fenton logo, $50.00 – 65.00.

Inscription on the back of the logo.

Memories in Glass of Tulsa, Oklahoma, ordered a series of glass ornaments in shapes of Christmas figurines from Fenton. They had some success but not enough, so Fenton bought the moulds and is now making them for QVC. The shapes are very attractive and, if they had been found by more Fenton collectors, I'm sure Memories in Glass would have had more orders.

Description	Value*
Angel	$50.00 – 55.00
Bell	$35.00 – 40.00
Bunny	$40.00 – 45.00
Cross	$35.00 – 40.00
Heart	$35.00 – 40.00
House	$35.00 – 40.00
Jack-O'-Lantern	$45.00 – 50.00
Knight	$45.00 – 50.00
Mouse	$45.00 – 50.00
Santa	$50.00 – 55.00
Snowflake	$35.00 – 40.00
Snowman	$45.00 – 50.00

*Add 20% for Burmese or Vaseline glass.

Amethyst Knight, $45.00 – 50.00.

Amethyst Santa, $50.00 – 55.00.

Topaz Bell and Heart, $42.00 – 48.00; Sea Mist Green Iridized Heart, $35.00 – 40.00.

Blue Heart, $35.00 – 40.00.

Burmese Angel, $60.00 – 65.00.

Burmese Snowflake, $42.00 – 48.00.

Crystal Iridized Snowflake, $35.00 – 40.00.

Green Jack-O'-Lantern on the original base, $65.00 – 70.00.

Green Jack-O'-Lantern on Stand, $65.00 – 70.00; Crystal Santa on Stand, $65.00 – 70.00.

Green Angel, $50.00 – 55.00.

Sea Mist Green Iridized Bunny & Egg, $40.00 – 45.00.

Sea Mist Green Iridized Cross, $35.00 – 40.00.

Pink Angel, $50.00 – 55.00.

Pink Iridized House, $35.00 – 40.00.

Pink Iridized Mouse, $45.00 – 50.00.

Royal Blue Snowman, $45.00 – 50.00.

Ruby Snowman, $45.00 – 50.00.

Topaz Iridized Bell, $42.00 – 48.00.

Topaz Iridized Heart, $42.00 – 48.00.

Metropolitan Museum of Art

The Metropolitan Museum of Art is one of the world's largest and most impressive museums. It has been said that only the Louvre surpasses it in splendor. The museum is located on the eastern side of Central Park in Manhattan. It was created in 1872 by John Taylor Johnston, a railroad executive who had acquired some remarkable pieces of art. It was his collection that composed the nucleus of the art shown in the first years of the museum. Now the museum displays art from every corner of the world, with the European master artists' works being its finest.

While the reason museums exist is to educate the public, they also must have incomes to finance all those works of art and their maintenance, so like other museums, the Metropolitan has a gift shop that sells reproduction art and glassware. Over the years, Fostoria, Imperial, Viking, and Fenton have made glassware to stock the shelves of the gift shop. Every piece of glass made for the MMA is signed using those initials, although on some pieces, the mark is well hidden. In the case of lacy glass, the initials are woven into the pattern, and you must have very good eyes to find them. In the case of Fenton, the pieces are mould blown and, as it is with all blown glass, the initials can fade into the pattern. That is not because the intent is to hide the fact that the pieces are reproductions of old glass, it is because of the difficulty of forcing the molten glass into the bottom of the mould. As with any of Fenton's blown glass, if you look carefully for the correct initials, you will be able to find them.

Of all the glass Fenton has made for MMA, its Stars and Stripes pattern in Cranberry Opalescent is the most popular and the best seller. When you are talking about Fenton, it is hard to find a type of glass that isn't a best seller.

Twilight Blue Thumbprint square-top pitcher, $100.00 – 125.00.

Celeste Blue stretch glass fan vase, $85.00 – 95.00.

Velva Rose stretch glass fan vase, $85.00 – 95.00.

Fan vase written information.

FAN VASE
Fenton Art Glass
America, early 20th century

On May 4, 1905 Frank L. Fenton made a bank deposit of $284.86 and founded Fenton Art Glass. This decorating company began producing handmade glass works from its new factory in Williamstown, West Virginia in 1907.

To create the fan-shaped vase, a gather of molten glass is first dropped into an iron mold. The glass is pressed into the mold with a plunger, and removed while still very hot. It is then reheated and sprayed with metallic salt, which fuses with the glass to create the desired color and texture. The piece is placed in a "glory hole" (the hole in the side of a glass furnace) and reheated a second time, whereupon the fan-shaped form is achieved by working and stretching the vase by hand.

The Museum's Fan Vase reproduction is made by Fenton Art Glass, using the same molds that were used in the original production. To clean, use a mild soap and water.

Proceeds from the sale of all publications and reproductions are used to support the Museum. If you would like information about The Metropolitan Museum of Art, its publications, and the privileges of membership, please write: The Metropolitan Museum of Art Special Service Office, Middle Village, New York 11381-0001 Telephone: 1-800-662-3397   Web site: www.metmuseum.org

THE METROPOLITAN MUSEUM OF ART

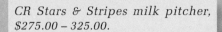
CR Stars & Stripes water tumbler, $75.00 – 85.00; water pitcher, $350.00 – 400.00.

Plum Drapery Optic #1559 vase, $100.00 – 115.00.

CR Stars & Stripes milk pitcher, $275.00 – 325.00.

CR Stars & Stripe ruffled-top vase, $150.00 – 175.00: flared-top vase, $150.00 – 175.00.

CR Stars & Stripes ice tea tumbler, $85.00 – 95.00.

MIMI

I wasn't able to get any information about the man who ordered the first new version of Dugan's Farmyard bowl, but I'll tell you what I can. Sometime in the mid-1980s, this bowl was made by Fenton in two colors, Purple and Ruby Carnival. It is signed "MIMI," which was the name of this man's wife. Eventually, Singleton Bailey bought this mould, and he has had Fenton make it in several colors.

Farmyard Bowl: Purple Carnival, $125.00 – 150.00; Ruby Carnival, $175.00 – 200.00.

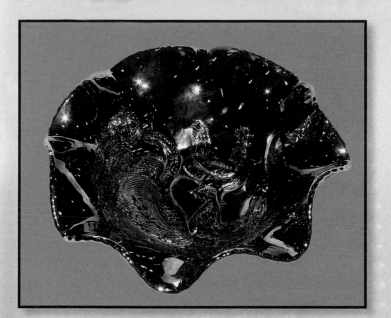

Purple Carnival Farmyard bowl, $150.00 – 175.00.

Purple Carnival Jeweled Heart exterior pattern on Farmyard bowl.

Minerva, Ohio, Sesquicentennial

In 1998, to commemorate Minerva, Ohio's, sesquicentennial, Fenton was commissioned to make bells, plates, and lamps for the Buckeye Town and Country Fenton Finders. Four scenes with special significance to Minerva were chosen, each to be painted on a bell and a plate.

Two lamps were made, with a choice of one scene or, for $50, two scenes. I have no record of which scenes were chosen for the lamps. These were advertised and sold in the *Butterfly Net* and *Glass Review*, a glass collector magazine.

The four scenes of equal value were 1828, The Log Cabin, Minerva's birthplace namesake; 1828, The City Hall; 1828, The Old Mill, Minerva Milling Company; 1871, The Union School, First School in Minerva.

Bell	Plate	Lamp, 1 Scene	Lamp, 2 Scenes
$75.00 – 85.00	$65.00 – 75.00	$400.00 – 450.00	$450.00 – 500.00

Custard City Hall plate, $65.00 – 75.00.

Minerva Milling Company bell, $75.00 – 85.00.

Minerva Milling Company plate, $65.00 – 75.00.

The Log Cabin, Minerva's Birthplace plate, $65.00 – 75.00.

The Log Cabin, Minerva's Birthplace bell, $75.00 – 85.00.

Union School, 1st School in Minerva bell, $75.00 – 85.00.

Union School, 1st School in Minerva plate, $65.00 – 75.00.

#7329 low ftd. comport, Opal with Blue Crest and Milk Glass Crest,
$200.00 – 225.00.

Large Special Hobnail lamp shade, $40.00 –
45.00.

Round Special Hobnail lamp shade, $40.00 –
45.00.

One-of-a-kind blown Globe of World, experimental.
Too rare to price.

Experimental Blue vase with a mirrored interior. Too rare to price.

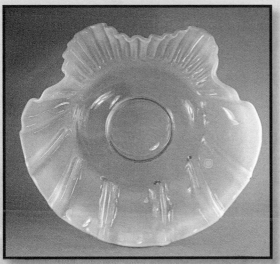

Blue Opalescent #9020 Shell bowl, $125.00 – 150.00.

Crystal Cardinal Head made for Frederick Crawford Museum, Western Reserve Historical Society, Cleveland, Ohio, Crystal, $150.00 – 175.00. Not shown: Crystal Satin, $165.00 – 185.00; Ruby, $200.00 – 225.00.

Opal Clock #8600 with a golfing theme, made for Golf House Collectibles, $175.00 – 200.00.

Signature on the clock.

Blue Iridized Blown Out Hearts bottle made from an original DeVilbiss mould, $125.00 – 150.00.

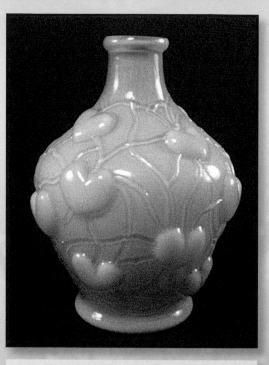

Rose Overlay Blown Out Hearts bottle, $125.00 – 150.00.

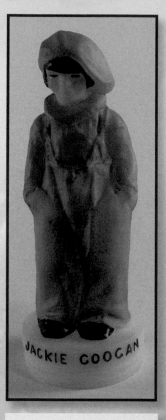

Jackie Coogan candy container, decorated Satin Milk Glass, $125.00 – 150.00.

Jackie Coogan candy container, decorated Crystal, $100.00 – 125.00.

Marigold over Milk Glass Lily of the Valley rose bowl, $100.00 – 125.00.

Burmese Satin Mermaid vase, $250.00 – 275.00.

Opal dental spit bowl made by Fenton for dentists' offices, $35.00 – 40.00.

Royal Blue finger lamp, $75.00 – 85.00.

Teal Overlay finger lamp, $75.00 – 85.00.

Royal Blue Jayhawker made for the Kansas State University Bookstore, $50.00 – 65.00.

Ruby Star paperweight made by Fenton for more than 75 years and sold to special order customers. If decorated, $65.00 – 75.00; without decoration, $35.00 – 40.00.

Vasa Murrhina New World salt and pepper shakers, $100.00 – 125.00 pair either color.

Vasa Murrhina Swirl salt and pepper shakers, $75.00 – 85.00 pair either color.

Monongehela Power Company

In 1995, Monongehela Power Company ordered a lamp with this beautiful farm scene. I have no information concerning how it was distributed. It may have been used as a gift or may have been sold to customers. Either way, it is beautiful.

Fenton's 21" lamp, $450.00 – 500.00.

Nationwide Insurance

Fenton made a beautiful Ruby console set made for Nationwide Insurance in Fenton's Pineapple pattern, one that, in 1986, had not been made for many years. Four pieces were made, two double candlesticks, a console bowl, and a large platter. They were given to Nationwide employees as Christmas presents. Seventy complete sets were made, so they have to be considered rare. They will be signed with the Fenton oval mark and have an "8" under the letters.

Candlestick, $45.00 – 50.00 ea.
Bowl, $125.00 – 150.00
Platter, $75.00 – 95.00

Fenton made this Dusty Rose set using Westmoreland's Paneled Grape moulds. A special plate added the embossed "Nestlé's R&D" in the base of the bowl. It will be signed with a scroll "F," the mark used for items made using non-Fenton moulds.

Dusty Rose Paneled Grape console set: Candlesticks, $35.00 – 40.00 each; console bowl, $65.00 – 75.00.

Northwood Art Glass Company

The name Harry Northwood is closely connected with the Fentons. Frank L. Fenton worked for him, they made the same types of glassware, and they were both geniuses in the artistry required to make beautiful glass.

The man who is responsible for resurrecting this proud name is David McKinley, great-grandson of Harry Northwood's younger brother, Carl. Carl had joined his brother in the glass business in 1886, and he remained at the factory until his death in 1924, just one year before Harry died. Mr. McKinley began the Northwood Art Glass Company in 1998. He introduced a beautiful new design that he called Grape & Cable. It bears a strong resemblance to Dugan's Grape Delight but has many unique features. The top has six points that have a tree of life design.

Fenton also made the dolphin card receiver for him. This is an original mould that had been owned by the L.G. Wright Company. When its moulds were sold in 1999, Northwood's dolphin mould was purchased by Mr. McKinley, who then took it to Island Mould in Wheeling, where it was repaired and made ready for use. Although this is a reproduction, it was never produced in carnival glass until now. In addition to that, the new Northwood script logo was added to the underside of the base. Both the new Grape & Cable pieces and the dolphin card receiver are beautifully made by Fenton.

Plum Carnival Grape & Cable cupped-top vase, total iridization, $150.00 – 175.00.

Plum Carnival straight-top Grape & Cable vase with the background blasted, $150.00 – 175.00.

Blue Carnival flared-top Grape & Cable vase, total iridization, $150.00 – 175.00.

Blue Carnival cupped-top Grape & Cable vase, total iridization, $150.00 – 175.00.

Crystal Satin Carnival blasted details cupped-top vase, background iridized, $150.00 – 175.00.

Crystal Satin Carnival blasted details straight-top vase, background iridized, $150.00 – 175.00.

Plum Carnival Grape & Cable flared-top vase, total iridization, $150.00 – 175.00.

Blue Carnival Dolphin card receiver, $75.00 – 95.00.

Plum Carnival Dolphin cupped-top comport that was sampled for Northwood, $100.00 – 120.00.

Oglebay Institute Glass Museum

The beautiful Oglebay Mansion is located just miles from Wheeling, West Virginia. The eight-room farmhouse was built in 1846 by Hanson Chapline. The home is surrounded by landscaped lawns and rolling hills. The house was sold seven times before it was purchased by Earl W. Oglebay in 1900. Mr. Oglebay renovated and added several more rooms to the home before he passed away in 1926. The mansion and the land was left to the city of Wheeling with the condition that it would be used for educational and recreational purposes. Wheeling's decision to create a museum on the property is a gift to every person who has had the chance to visit this breathtaking estate.

There are two buildings on the site, the mansion and the glass museum. The glass museum is home to the largest piece of cut leaded glass in the world, the Sweeney punch bowl. It is 5' tall and weighs 225 lbs. Can you imagine how hard it would have been to wash this bowl after an evening of entertaining guests?

The museum is also home to 3,000 pieces of Wheeling glass made between 1829 and 1939 that include lead crystal, Depression glass, pattern glass, and Victorian art glass. An enormous collection of glass made by the Northwood Glass Company resides in its own section of the display.

As with every museum, funds must be raised to pay the bills incurred by the daily costs of maintenance. Fenton has made reproductions of the Sweeney punch bowl, and other pieces have been added to its inventory.

Cobalt Blue 6" Sweeney punch bowl replica, $50.00 – 65.00.

Oglebay Institute

6" Sweeney Punch Bowl Replica

A portion of the proceeds benefit
Joseph J. Weishar Glass Fund
to continue education and
research in glass

Moulds made by:
Island Mould & Machine Co., Inc.

Fine Quality Glassware
Made in U.S.A.

Weishar

Oglebay Institute
Sweeney Reproduction

Paperwork for the Cobalt Blue 6" Sweeney punch bowl replica, $50.00 – 65.00.

Cobalt Blue blown pitcher with a Green Crest, $75.00 – 85.00.

Cobalt Blue top piece of 6" Sweeney punch bowl replica, $25.00 – 30.00; 12" Crystal Sweeney punch bowl replica, $65.00 – 85.00; Green 6" replica, $50.00 – 65.00.

Every year on the weekend after Labor Day, a festival is held to celebrate the beautiful old sternwheelers that travel up and down the Ohio River. There is music and theater to entertain the festival goers. It also helps to educate the public that, without help, the sternwheelers could be made obsolete one day. The Historic Sternwheeler Preservation Society promotes awareness of the sternwheelers and their history. The society does not limit itself to the Ohio River boats; it hopes to preserve these magnificent boats that have traveled the rivers as many years as the United States has existed. I'm not certain who ordered these from Fenton, but I do know they were meant for the festival in Marietta, Ohio.

Cobalt Blue #7566 inscribed bell, $65.00 – 85.00.

Brass Lamp with #7204 Opal shade decorated with an Ohio River sternwheeler, $175.00 – 200.00.

Violet Carnival Orange Tree wine, embossed "Sternwheeler Festival 2000," $65.00 – 75.00.

Olde Virginia Glass

Over the years, Fenton has always had a line of glassware that was sold to discounters and mass merchandisers acting as sales agents for smaller stores. The best-known of those lines is the Olde Virginia Glass assortment. The name was first used by Fenton in about 1959. By using a different name, Fenton avoided problems with its regular accounts who were buying the high-end Fenton line. To open an account with Fenton, a store had to be a certain distance, maybe ten miles, from one of Fenton's existing accounts. That would preclude flower shops, hardware stores, and other smaller retailers within that ten miles from selling Fenton. But it would not stop them from selling Olde Virginia Glass, a less expensive line that had no geographical limits. Glass sold in the regular catalog would not be sold in the OVG line. When Fenton Art Glass sold Hobnail, OVG sold Thumbprint, although a small assortment of Hobnail was sold as Olde Virginia Glass in the 1950s. In 1959, Fenton sold its Cactus pattern in Milk Glass and Topaz Opalescent. In 1967, Olde Virginia Glass sold Desert Tree, made using Cactus moulds, in Milk Glass and Amber. Daisy & Button items and Fine Cut & Block pieces were well-known Olde Virginia Glass patterns.

In 1970, the OVG mark was added to those moulds being used for that line, but by 1980, Olde Virginia Glass was no longer being made by Fenton. Even though that division was abandoned, Fenton tried a similar venture in the 1990s called House Warmings.

THUMBPRINT
(Only items priced were made in Topaz Opalescent.)

Description	Ware #	Milk Glass	Topaz Opalescent
Basket, 7"	4437	$25.00 – 30.00	
Basket, 8½"	4438	$35.00 – 45.00	$100.00 – 120.00
Basket, 6½" oval*	4430	$25.00 – 30.00	
Bowl, 12"	4427	$20.00 – 24.00	
Cake plate, high ftd.	4413	$40.00 – 45.00	
Candleholder, low	4474	(ea.) $15.00 – 18.00	
Candleholder, tall	4473	(ea.) $18.00 – 22.00	
Candy & cover	4480	$25.00 – 30.00	
Candy & cover, oval ftd.	4486	$24.00 – 28.00	
Chip & dip	4404	$35.00 – 40.00	
Comport, ftd.	4429	$12.00 – 15.00	
Compote & cover, high ftd.	4484	$40.00 – 45.00	
Creamer		$18.00 – 22.00	
Epergne	4401	$75.00 – 95.00	$225.00 – 275.00
Goblet	4445	$10.00 – 12.00	
Hurricane lamp	4498	$50.00 – 65.00	
Lavabo, 3-pc.	4467	$70.00 – 85.00	

Description	Ware #	Milk Glass	Topaz Opalescent
Planter, hanging bowl	4405	$65.00 – 85.00	
Planter, 4½" square	4497	$20.00 – 22.00	
Planter, 10" rectangular	4490	$35.00 – 45.00	
Punch bowl & stand		$175.00 – 200.00	
Punch cup		$10.00 – 12.00	
Salt & pepper	4408	$22.00 – 24.00	
Sugar, covered		$22.00 – 24.00	
Tidbit, 2-tier	4494	$30.00 – 34.00	
Vase, bud	4456	$18.00 – 22.00	$50.00 – 65.00

*Oval with a handle that opens at the top.

Colonial Amber polka-dot hurricane lamp, OVG label, $65.00 – 75.00. Not Shown: Colonial Blue and Colonial Orange, $75.00 – 100.00 each; Colonial Green, $65.00 – 75.00.

Colonial Amber, top row: *#9158CA Fine Cut small swung vase, $22.00 – 25.00; #9180CA Fine Cut candy box, $25.00 – 30.00; #9137CA Fine Cut 7" basket, $24.00 – 28.00; #1970 D&B candleholders, $24.00 – 30.00 pair; 1930 D&B 10½" basket, $30.00 – 35.00.* **Bottom row:** *#9152CA Fine Cut lg. swung vase, $25.00 – 30.00; #9120CA Fine Cut comport, $20.00 – 24.00; #9172CA Fine Cut candle bowl, $20.00 – 24.00; #1935CA D&B 5" basket, $20.00 – 25.00; #1925CA 10½" D&B bowl, $40.00 – 44.00.* **Colonial Green, top row:** *#1930CG D&B 10½" basket, $30.00 – 35.00; #1970CG D&B candleholders, $24.00 – 30.00 pair; #9180CG candy box, $25.00 – 30.00; #9172CG Fine Cut candle bowl, $20.00 – 24.00; #9158CG small Fine Cut swung vase, $25.00 – 30.00.* **Bottom Row:** *#1925CG D&B 10½" bowl, $40.00 – 44.00; #9137CG 7" basket, $24.00 – 28.00; #9120CG Fine Cut comport, $20.00 – 24.00; #1935CG D&B 5" basket, $20.00 – 25.00; #9152CG large Fine Cut swung vase, $25.00 – 30.00.*

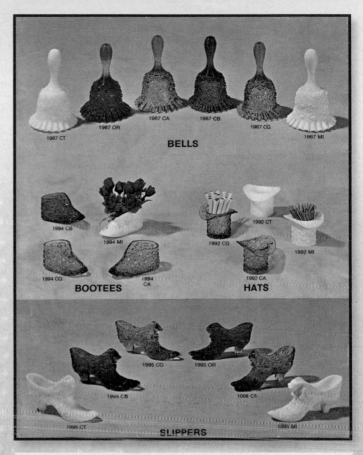

Milk Glass Fine Cut candle bowl: #9172MI, $20.00 – 24.00.
Fine Cut #9102 fairy lights: MI, $30.00 – 34.00; CB, $35.00 – 40.00; CA, $30.00 – 34.00; OR, $35.00 – 40.00; CG, $30.00 – 34.00; CT, $42.00 – 46.00.

Daisy & Button #1967 bells: CT (Custard), $20.00 – 24.00; OR (Orange), $28.00 – 32.00; CA (Colonial Amber), $22.00 – 25.00; CB (Colonial Blue), $28.00 – 32.00; CG (Colonial Green), $22.00 – 25.00; MI (Milk Glass), $22.00 – 25.00.
#1994 booties: MI, $35.00 – 40.00; CB, $40.00 – 45.00; CG, $35.00 – 40.00; CA, $35.00 – 40.00.
#1992 top hat: CT, $15.00 – 18.00; CG, $12.00 – 15.00; CA, $12.00 – 15.00; MI, $12.00 – 15.00.
#1995 Cat slipper: CT, $22.00 – 26.00; CB, $22.00 – 24.00; CG, $18.00 – 20.00; OR, $22.00 – 24.00; CA, $18.00 – 20.00; MI, $18.00 – 20.00.

DAISY & BUTTON

Description	Ware #	Colonial Amber, Milk, Colonial Green	Colonial Blue, Colonial Orange	Carnival
Basket, 5" fan sides	1935	$20.00 – 25.00	$30.00 – 35.00	
Basket, 6" hat	1936	$22.00 – 26.00	$35.00 – 38.00	
Basket, 10½"	1930	$30.00 – 35.00	$40.00 – 45.00	

Description	Ware #	Colonial Amber, Milk, Colonial Green	Colonial Blue, Colonial Orange	Carnival
Bootee	1994	$35.00 – 40.00	$40.00 – 45.00	$50.00 – 55.00
Bowl, oval	1921	$22.00 – 25.00	$25.00 – 28.00	
Bowl, 7" cupped	1927	$38.00 – 44.00	$50.00 – 55.00	
Bowl, 10½"	1925	$40.00 – 44.00	$44.00 – 48.00	
Candleholder, each	1970	$12.00 – 15.00	$14.00 – 18.00	
Creamer	1903a	$12.00 – 15.00	$14.00 – 18.00	
Hat	1992	$12.00 – 15.00	$15.00 – 20.00	$20.00 – 25.00
Salt & pepper	1906	$18.00 – 20.00	$24.00 – 28.00	
Slipper	1995	$18.00 – 20.00	$22.00 – 24.00	$24.00 – 28.00
Sugar	1903b	$10.00 – 12.00	$12.00 – 15.00	
Vase, 8"	1958	$45.00 – 55.00	$65.00 – 75.00	
Vase, 8" fan	1959	$50.00 – 60.00	$70.00 – 80.00	

DESERT TREE/CACTUS

Description	Ware #	Colonial Amber	Milk Glass
Basket, 7"	3437	$25.00 – 28.00	$24.00 – 26.00
Basket, 10"	3430	$30.00 – 34.00	$28.00 – 32.00
Bonbon, handled	3435	$18.00 – 22.00	$15.00 – 20.00
Bowl, 10"	3420	$24.00 – 28.00	$22.00 – 26.00
Butter, ½ lb. covered	3477	$25.00 – 30.00	$25.00 – 30.00
Candleholder, each	3474	$12.00 – 14.00	$10.00 – 12.00
Candy jar*	3480	$65.00 – 75.00	$65.00 – 75.00
Creamer	3468	$15.00 – 18.00	$14.00 – 16.00
Salt & pepper	3406	$24.00 – 28.00	$24.00 – 28.00
Sugar/candy jar w/lid	3488	$24.00 – 28.00	$24.00 – 28.00
Vase, ftd.	3460	$18.00 – 22.00	$15.00 – 18.00
Vase, bud	3450	$15.00 – 18.00	$12.00 – 16.00

*Large cracker jar.

FINE CUT & BLOCK

Description	Ware #	Crystal	Colonial Amber, Milk, Colonial Green	Colonial Blue, Colonial Orange, Carnival
Basket, 7"	9137	$20.00 – 24.00	$24.00 – 28.00	$30.00 – 35.00
Candle bowl	9172	$15.00 – 18.00	$20.00 – 24.00	$25.00 – 30.00
candy box	9180	$22.00 – 25.00	$25.00 – 30.00	$28.00 – 34.00
compote	9120	$15.00 – 18.00	$20.00 – 24.00	$24.00 – 28.00
Fairy light	9102	$25.00 – 28.00	$30.00 – 34.00	$35.00 – 40.00
Nut dish, ftd.	9151	$12.00 – 15.00	$15.00 – 18.00	$20.00 – 24.00
Vase, swung	9152	$22.00 – 28.00	$25.00 – 30.00	$30.00 – 35.00

CUSTARD GLASS

A reproduction of a famous glass treatment originated in 1888 by Harry Northwood. Its soft beauty is compatible with and complimentary to every contemporary decorator color.

Olde Virginia Glass

Handmade "in the age old manner" in three popular early American patterns (Wild Rose and Bow Knot, Daisy & Button and Fine Cut & Block) and three early American colors (Opaque Blue-BG, Custard-CT and Milk Glass-MI).

DAISY & BUTTON

Description	Ware #	Blue Opaque	Custard
Bell	1967	$22.00 – 26.00	$20.00 – 24.00
Bowl, oval	1921	$22.00 – 26.00	$20.00 – 24.00
Candleholder	1970	$20.00 – 24.00	$18.00 – 22.00
Slipper, cat	1995	$24.00 – 28.00	$22.00 – 26.00

FINE CUT & BLOCK

Description	Ware #	Blue Opaque	Custard	Milk Glass
Basket, 7"	9137	$35.00 – 38.00	$30.00 – 35.00	$30.00 – 35.00
Bowl, 7"	9127	$22.00 – 24.00	$20.00 – 22.00	$20.00 – 22.00
Bowl, ftd.	9122	$25.00 – 28.00	$22.00 – 25.00	$20.00 – 24.00

Description	Ware #			
Candy box	9180	$34.00 – 38.00	$32.00 – 35.00	$30.00 – 32.00
Compote	9120	$20.00 – 22.00	$18.00 – 20.00	$14.00 – 16.00
Creamer, ftd.	9103a	$18.00 – 22.00		
Fairy light	9102	$45.00 – 50.00	$42.00 – 46.00	$35.00 – 40.00
Salt & pepper, ftd.	9106	$35.00 – 38.00	$32.00 – 36.00	$30.00 – 34.00
Sugar, ftd. & lid	9103b	$22.00 – 25.00		
Case, 4½"	9157	$20.00 – 24.00	$18.00 – 22.00	$15.00 – 18.00
Vase, swung	9158	$24.00 – 28.00	$22.00 – 25.00	$20.00 – 22.00

WILD ROSE & BOWKNOT

Description	Ware #	Blue Opaque	Custard	Milk Glass
Lamp	2807	$175.00 – 200.00	$150.00 – 175.00	$150.00 – 175.00

CAMEO OPALESCENT DAISY & BUTTON

Description	Ware #	Cameo Opalescent
Bell	1967	$30.00 – 35.00
Bowl, 10½"	1925	$34.00 – 38.00
Bowl, oval	1921	$28.00 – 34.00
Candleholder	1970	(ea.) $24.00 – 28.00
Slipper, cat	1995	$22.00 – 24.00

FINE CUT & BLOCK

Description	Ware #	Cameo Opalescent
Bowl, 7"	9120	$25.00 – 28.00
Candle bowl	9172	$30.00 – 35.00
Candy box	9180	$45.00 – 50.00
Compote	9120	$18.00 – 22.00
Creamer, ftd.	9103a	$20.00 – 22.00
Fairy light	9102	$45.00 – 50.00
Salt & pepper	9106	$38.00 – 44.00
Sugar & lid	9103b	$25.00 – 28.00
Vase, 4½"	9157	$20.00 – 24.00
Vase, swung	9158	$35.00 – 40.00

Olde Virginia Glass CAMEO OPALESCENT

Cameo Opalescent in antique Daisy & Button and Fine Cut & Block patterns. Each functional piece carefully handmade, beautifully polished and authentic in every detail. Sensibly priced for special appeal in the gift market.

ASCAL

Pascal is an extraordinary artist who works in many media, but it is her ability to sculpt glass with a hammer and a chisel that has made her famous. She was the first artist to do that and may be the last. Pascal purchased the Dunbar Glass factory after it burned to the ground and mined an enormous piece of glass that had melted in the fire and sunk into the ground. She then took it back to California, where she began chipping the glass into the form she desired. At the time she was doing this, she realized that figures could be made from the pieces she was chipping off the large glass "rock." Her family saw the chance to reproduce these pieces to make them affordable to the general public. The next problem for them was to find a glass company that had the ability to reproduce these in such a fashion that they would look exactly as the originals. They didn't anticipate the problem they would face until they called Swarovski and several other companies. They were told that none of them could duplicate the chipped look Pascal was seeking.

Then Pascal called Fenton and talked to Don Cunningham. Don believed that there was no piece of glass in any style or treatment that Fenton couldn't duplicate.

The day after the call from her, he received a phone call from Pascal, who was waiting at the local airport. After speaking with Don, Pascal had flown in to Williamstown as soon as she possibly could. Don was very shocked that she would travel there so quickly, but after meeting her, he understood it better. He described her as being a remarkable woman, both in looks and in ability. She definitely turned heads when she walked into the factory. He took her on a tour of the factory before they got down to the business of deciding just how her project could be done. When she left, she gave Don a few of her sculptures, and he took them to a sandcasting company, where the moulds for her pieces were made.

Her sculptures are unique and beautiful. They are all signed "Pascal," making it easy to identify them. These are so unique that I doubt any factory, other than Fenton, would undertake a project of this difficulty. After all, only Fenton was willing to make them. Prices will not vary substantially for any color in any subject. You should expect to pay $150 to 200 for them if they have the embedded colored stones intact. For those without the stones, $125 to $175 will be a bargain.

$\mathscr{P}$ascal was born a deaf child in 1914 and learned to communicate first by drawing, and later through sculpture. At 41, she became the first person to successfully sculpt in glass with hammer and chisel. Pascal's unique medium astounded the art world. Reviews of her exhibits compared her classic forms to Rodin and Michelangelo. She has also become known for her monumental works in stainless steel and her luminescent impressionist oils painted on either wood or lucite. Pascal uses light and its reflective qualities to instill a fourth dimension in her sculptures.

Today, at 76, she is America's preeminent glass and stainless steel sculptor, with her works in many of the world's premier private collections. Below is a partial list.

Pascal.

MAJOR COLLECTIONS

The Honorable & Mrs. Ronald Reagan	Mr. and Mrs. Frank Sinatra	Hebrew Union College,
H.R.H. the Prince and Princess of Wales	Mrs. Paul Trousdale	Skirball Museum, Los Angeles
Mr. and Mrs. Morris Alhadeff	Mrs. Alice Tyler - Museum Collection	Longacres Racetrack, Seattle, WA
Mr. and Mrs. George N. Boone	Ms. Barbara Walters	Los Angeles County Museum of Art,
Ms. Carol Burnett	Mr. and Mrs. Ray Watt	National Center of Contemporary Art,
Mr. Walter Cronkite	American Foundation of the Arts,	Paris, France
Mr. and Mrs. Corwin Denny	Miami, FL	St. Vincent de Paul Church,
Dr. Armand Hammer	Archimedes Plaza,	San Diego, CA
Mr. John Kluge	University of Southern California	United Nations, Geneva, Switzerland
Mr. and Mrs. Henry Mancini	Corcoran Museum, Washington, D.C.	United States Embassy, London
Mr. and Mrs. Morton Phillips	Fox Television Center,	United States Embassy, Tokyo
Mr. and Mrs. Kristoffer Popovich	Los Angeles	United States Embassy, The Vatican

Reproduced and distributed by: Liscot Enterprises, Exclusive Licensee for Pascal. Los Angeles, California   ©1990 Liscot Enterprises

Biography of Pascal.

Liscot Enterprises promotional catalog page displaying two of Pascal's Art-to-Wear sculptures. Amethyst Girl *with* Emeralds, *limited to 375, $3,400.00;* Circus Horse, *limited to 375, $3,400.00.*

Pascal Turns 85!

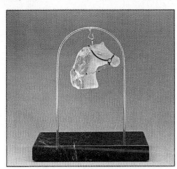

Circus Horse, *limited to 375, $3,400.00.*

Catalog page with amethyst Thoroughbred, *limited to 375, $3,400.00;* Aqua Queen of Cats, *limited to 375, $3,400.00.* Pictured is Pascal sculpting one of her original pieces.

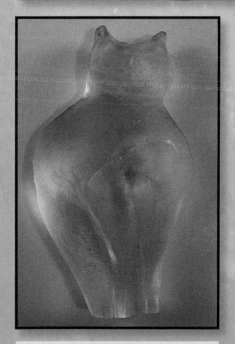

Aquamarine cat used for Queen of Cats, $3,400.00; Blue Cat *(wearing a jeweled necklace), $2,700.00.*

Amethyst Classic Head, *limited to 375, $1,900.00.*

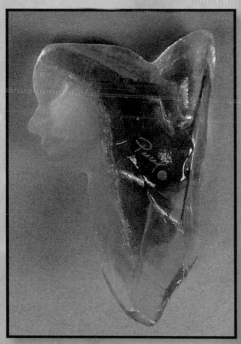

Amethyst Vixen, *used for Girl with Emeralds, $3,400.00.*

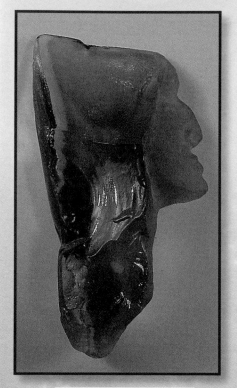

Amber Chief Wapella.

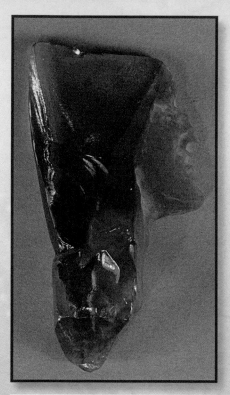

Darker shade of Amber Chief Wapella.

Aquamarine Classic Head.

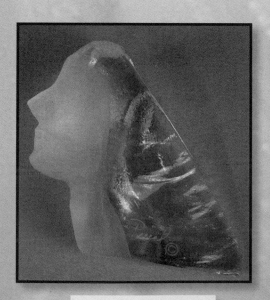

Aquamarine Cleopatra.

Aquamarine Satin Classic Head used for Duchess, $2,700.00.

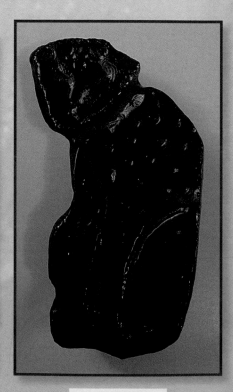

Black Panther.

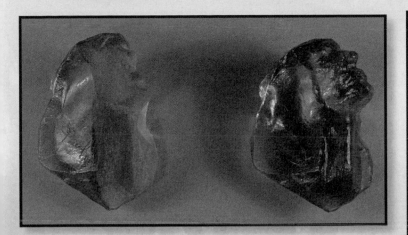

Blue Satin and Shiny Jeune Fillés.

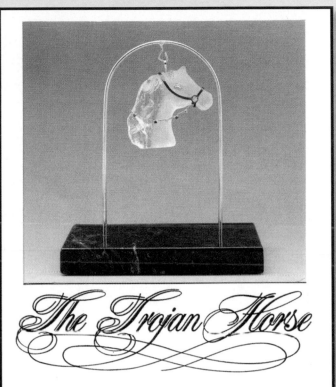

The Trojan Horse

Front page of Liscot catalog.

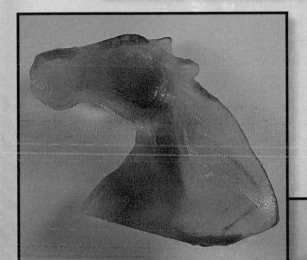

Blue The Winner.

Blue Torso.

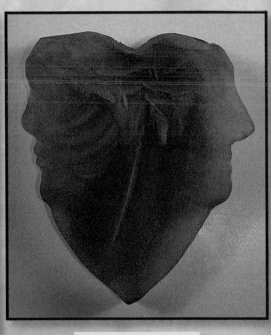

Coral Indian Heart.

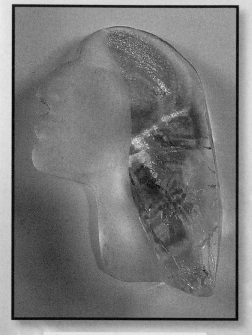

Crystal Young Chochise.

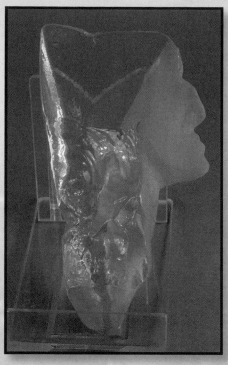

Crystal Chief Wapella.

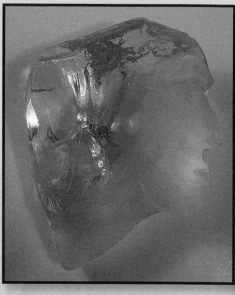

Crystal Classic Head used for Egyptian Head, *$3,400.00.*

Crystal Exotic Bird.

Crystal Jeune Fillé, $950.00.

Opposite view of Jeune Fillé.

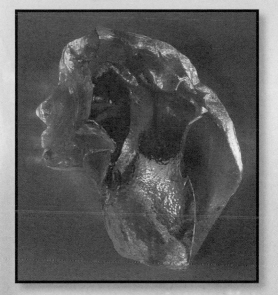

Crystal Girl's Head.

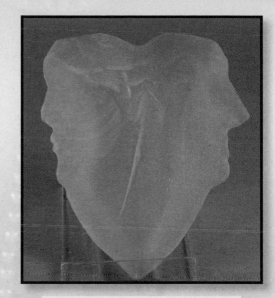

Crystal Satin Indian Head Heart.

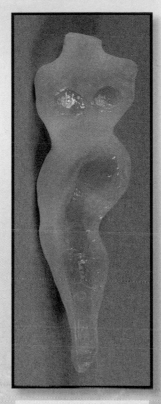

Crystal Satin Torso.

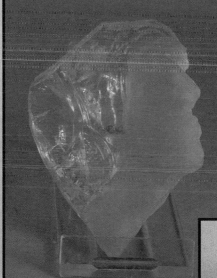

Crystal Satin Classic Head.

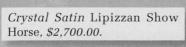

Crystal Satin Lipizzan Show Horse, $2,700.00.

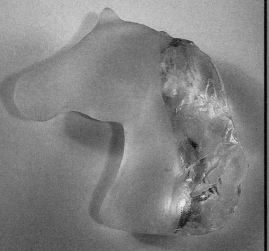

Crystal Thoroughbred (in Amethyst, sold for $2,700.00).

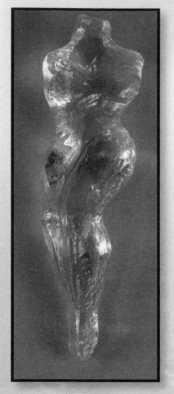

Crystal Torso.

Crystal Vixen.

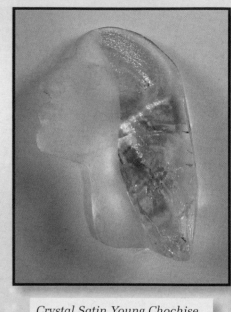

Crystal Satin Young Chochise.

Dusty Rose Vixen used for Girl with Diamonds, $1,900.00.

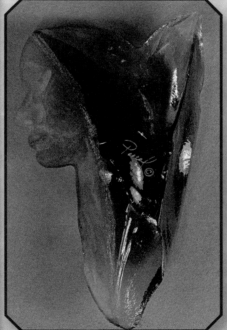

Opposite side of Vixen.

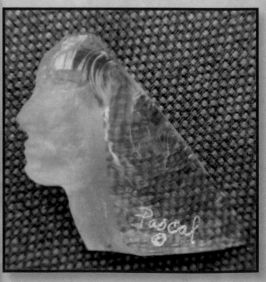

Green Cleopatra.

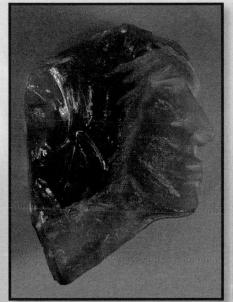

Pink Classic Head.

Pink Sutin Classic Head with the metal piece at top.

Pink Cleopatra.

Opposite view of Cleopatra.

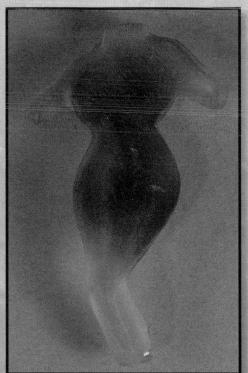

Pink Torso.

Royal Blue Panther.

Ruby-Amberina Torso.

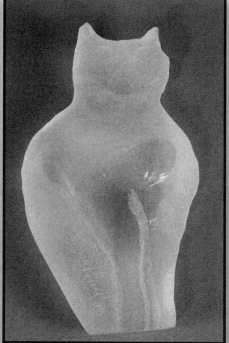

Topaz Cat.

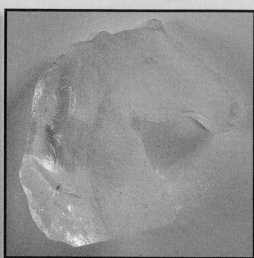

Topaz Thoroughbred used for Jumper, $1,900.00.

Pharmacy Items

Fenton has made these pharmacy items for years. They are bought by several different schools of pharmacy, some of which are represented here. The bowl-style sets were also sold to Martha Stewart.

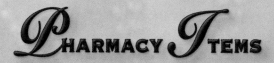

Bowl-style sets, $50.00 – 65.00
Candy base–style sets, $45.00 – 60.00

Milk Glass with Red lettering mortar set, $50.00 – 65.00.

West Virginia University school of pharmacy mortar set, Milk Glass, $50.00 – 65.00.

West Virginia University school of pharmacy mortar set, Black, $45.00 – 60.00.

Publishers Clearing House

I doubt that any person in this country would not recognize this business. It is famous for its mailings declaring that you may have won a million or more dollars. But it also buys glass from Fenton. I was not able to find out where these pieces were sold or if they were gifts for company employees, but I would welcome the information if you have it. Fenton does not keep those types of records.

Angel Girl, #M5114 Empress Rose Iridized, 1/98 and 7,896 made, $75.00 – 85.00.

Angel Girl, #M5114N3 Non-striking Rose Milk, 11/02 and 1,350 made, $75.00 – 85.00.

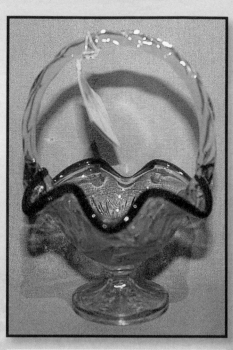

Strawberry basket, #M5939 Aquamarine with Blue Crest, also sold in catalog line. $35.00 – 40.00.

Hobnail bell, #M3368SY Aquamarine, $25.00 – 28.00; Hobnail vase, #M3956SY Aquamarine, $22.00 – 24.00; both 12/01 and limited to 750 sets.

Empress Rose Daffodil vase, #M7652CP, 4/99 and 4,250 pieces made, $75.00 – 85.00.

Christmas Tree, #M5535, Emerald Green, 5/03 and 500 pieces made, $45.00 – 50.00.

Potito Beauty bell, #M7778OE Violet with Rose decoration, 2/02 and 850 pieces made. $18.00 – 22.00.

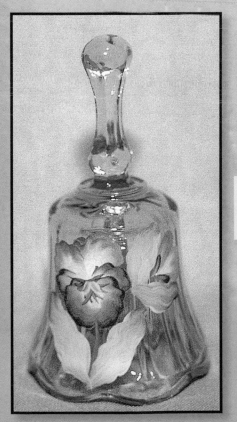

Ribbed bell, #M7662 Aquamarine, also sold in catalog. $18.00 – 22.00.

Lace Edge Shell dish, #M9030OE Violet, 6/02 and 1,750 pieces made. $15.00 – 18.00.

A.L. Randall Company

The A.L. Randall Company of Lincolnshire, Illinois, has been buying glassware from Fenton for as far back as the 1950s. Most of its business is selling to the florist trade, so it has focused its purchases to the container-type glassware. Randall has also bought unusual items like the Frog and Lilies of Fenton's #3800 five-piece epergne set. Some of the most unusual items made for the company were the vases made from the small and medium epergne Lilies, with feet added to the bases. Those, as well as the backward C plate with the metal back added, were all made in the 1950s, but more recent glass has also been added to its catalog line. A few of those items are pictured here. I will apologize up front for the condition of some of the pictures I was able to scan. I have no idea why there is a hole in one of them but, because the items are very scarce, I chose to use the picture anyway.

Blue Pastel Hobnail epergne Block & three Lilies, $75.00 – 95.00.

Black Roses comport, $40.00 – 45.00.

Assortment of Olde Virginia Glass sold by A.L. Randall.

Milk Glass Backward C planter, $65.00 – 70.00

Introducing Randall's Freight Free Fenton Assortments

Olde Virginia Glassware by Fenton

R9451GS $3.75 ea.	R9430GS $5.75 ea.	R9426GS $3.50 ea.	R3327GS $4.00 ea.	R9457GS $4.75 ea.	R8430GS $5.75 ea.	R9439GS $6.50 ea.
R9451RU $3.75 ea.	R9430RU $5.75 ea.	R9426RU $3.50 ea.	R3327RU $4.00 ea.	R9457RU $4.75 ea.	R8430RU $5.75 ea.	R9439RU $6.50 ea.
R9451MI $3.75 ea.	R9430MI $5.75 ea.	R9426MI $3.50 ea.	R3327MI $4.00 ea.	R9457MI $4.75 ea.	R8430MI $5.75 ea.	R9439MI $6.50 ea.

R9481MI $3.75 ea.

24 PC—R0024AS—$112.50 (FREIGHT FREE)

—1982 Prices Apply
—Only Available to A.L. Randall Customers
—Best Handmade Glass in America
—Prompt Delivery
—7 Designs—3 Colors, Ruby, Green, Milk
—No Limit on Assortments R0024AS and R0009AS

Randall A.L. Randall Company
P.O. Box 82, Prairie View, Illinois 60069, 312-634-4300 Toll Free Mercury #91-0463AA

Side view of the Backward C planter.

Catalog page of Milk Glass bud vase, $50.00 – 65.00.

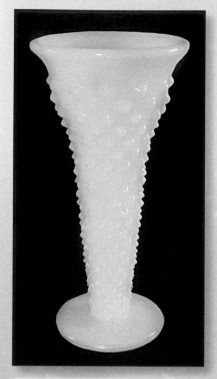

Milk Glass bud vase made from small Hobnail epergne horn, $50.00 – 65.00.

Catalog page of large Milk Glass bud vase, $75.00 – 85.00.

Milk Glass Tulip bud vase made from medium size Hobnail epergne horn, $85.00 – 95.00.

Milk Glass Hobnail planter, $35.00 – 40.00.

America's finest glass in top-selling colors is now available to *all* retail florists from A. L. Randall.

Each piece bears the distinctive Fenton label, assuring your customer of Fenton quality.

These items are lower priced than other comparable Fenton line designs.

A limited number of exclusive Fenton franchise operations are becoming available in select areas. Please check the box on the order blank for more information.

Order any way you choose: as an assortment (see order form for free bonus item) or as individual items.

EXCLUSIVE FENTON CONTAINER DESIGNS AVA

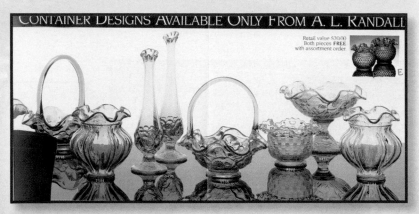

Opal Satin #8226 hexagonal bowl, $75.00 – 05.00; Opal Satin #9538 Water Lily basket, $60.00 – 65.00.

$\mathcal{RCA}$

The Nipper Dog was made in crystal for an RCA company promotion.

Crystal Nipper Dog, $65.00 – 75.00.

Crystal light cover, $65.00 – 85.00.

Side view of light cover.

Rose Presznick

Rose Presznick is a name very well known to carnival glass collectors. She and Marion Hartung were the first of the carnival glass researchers. I have her books and love them. She wrote not only about the glass, but about her adventures finding it, too. If you have the opportunity to read her books, you will understand why she and Marion Hartung are known as the First Ladies of carnival glass. Both of these women had the foresight to recognize the future of glass collecting when others couldn't or wouldn't believe them. Antique shows didn't allow this "cheap" carnival glass, and even the newly formed Depression glass clubs looked down on the brightly colored glass. If only they had known then what we know now. It is normal for a rare piece of carnival to sell for six figures, a price that isn't found in most other categories of glassware.

In 1969, Fenton made a dark carnival Grape & Cable tobacco jar for Rose and Joe Presznick to be sold in their Carnival Glass Museum in Lodi, Ohio. The Presznicks asked Frank to make it with a mark that could not be ground off. The base reads, "Presznick Carnival Museum, Lodi, Ohio, 1969." The Fenton name in an oval is also on the base. This was the very first piece of Fenton to be marked with that logo. Rose Presznick must be credited with the inspiration that eventually caused all glass made by Fenton to be signed. Frank also agreed to her request that the Grape & Cable humidor not be made in Amethyst Carnival again. He kept his word, but the humidor in other colors is a staple of Fenton's product line. The humidors are bringing record prices on eBay, possibly because they are practical as well as beautiful. The heavy lid makes them perfect canisters.

Fenton had been considering reproducing carnival, but until Rose's request, had not done so. Frank and Bill thought that the humidor made for Rose was so beautiful that they decided to put a series of plates made in dark carnival in their catalog line. To assure carnival glass collectors that there would be a way to tell old from new,

Fenton continued signing all carnival as well as all the other glass made by the company after 1970. Carnival glass in a variety of colors has been in the Fenton catalog every year since then.

Rose's great-granddaughter, Kim Myers George, was nice enough to share family information with me for this book. Upon Rose's death, her belongings, including the museum items, were auctioned to the public. Kim kept pieces that meant something to her, as well as the many pieces she was given as gifts. The property that housed the museum in Lodi, Ohio, was divided into several parcels and new homes were built on them.

Photo of Rose Presznick attending a convention.

Dark Carnival Grape & Cable tobacco jar/humidor, $250.00 – 300.00.

Base of the humidor.

JIM MYERS AND KIM MYERS GEORGE, GREAT GRAND-DAUGHTER OF ROSE PRESZNICK

Ruby Carnival Poppy lamp made in 1984 for grandson Jim Myers and great-granddaughter Kim Myers George, $275.00 – 350.00.

Rose and Joe Presznick had one child, a daughter they named Mickey. Mickey gave birth to one child, her son Jim Myers. Jim Myers is the father of Kim Myers George. In 1984, Jim and daughter Kim had a Ruby Carnival Poppy lamp made in the kerosene style. There were samples made in the iridized colors of Plum Opalescent, Crystal, Yellow, and a Marigold-cased carnival called Clambroth. Only three samples of those colors were made. The Ruby Carnival lamp is marked "In Memory of Rose Presznick — 1984-VM." The "VM" was for Von Myers, Mickey's parents' old company name.

I'm certain that Rose would have been very proud of her family for keeping the carnival glass tradition going.

Phil and Helen Rosso started their mail-order business in 1970, when they were selling antique glassware. Their method of selling was to dare customers to buy a bag of glassware not knowing what would be in it. As it became harder to buy antique glass, they moved into the business of buying special-order glassware. They bought from Westmoreland for several years, until Westmoreland closed the factory in 1983. Helen Rosso passed away in 1990. Phil Joseph Jr., called P.J., joined his father in the glass business around that time. They now operate out of a building that houses the company museum as well as its inventory.

Fenton has made a lot of glassware for Rosso, primarily Vaseline glass, but Cranberry Opalescent ware and other colors of glass as well. While glass made for Rosso using moulds that Rosso owns is not signed, it is the policy of Fenton that all glass made in its moulds be signed and dated within 10 years by a decade number under the Fenton name. Even though Fenton always signs glass made from its moulds, it can be difficult to locate the signature. When glass is blown into a mould, often the glass doesn't quite fill in the signature portion of base. If you look hard enough, the oval is usually visible.

CR = Cranberry Opalescent, TO = Topaz Opalescent.

CR Opalescent Dot #1921 hat, $225.00 – 250.00.

CR Coin Dot #1923 basket, $125.00 – 150.00.

CR Coin Dot #1923 basket, $125.00 – 150.00.

CR Coin Dot #1921 hat, $225.00 – 250.00.

CR Coin Dot #1457 7½" vase, $100.00 – 125.00.

CR Coin Dot vase, $175.00 – 200.00.

CR Daisy & Fern #1921 hat, $225.00 – 250.00.

CR Opalescent Dot cruet, $125.00 – 150.00.

Front view of #1921 hat.

CR Fern-pattern decanter, $300.00 – 350.00.

CR Fern cruet, $125.00 – 150.00.

CR Opalescent Dot #1353 jug, $225.00 – 250.00.

CR Opalescent Dot #898 vase, $225.00 – 250.00.

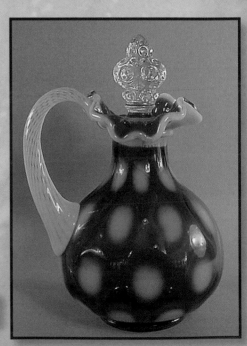

CR Opalescent Dot cruet, $125.00 – 150.00.

CR Opalescent Dot #1921 pitcher, $250.00 – 275.00.

CR Opalescent Dot #1921 basket, $250.00 – 275.00.

CR Opalescent Dot #1457 7½" vase, $100.00 – 125.00.

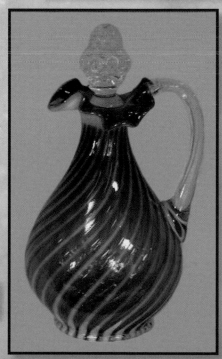

CR Tiny Dot cruet, $125.00 – 150.00.

CR Spiral decanter, $300.00 – 350.00.

CR Spiral #1921 hat, $225.00 – 250.00.

CR Spiral #1921 crimped vase, $175.00 – 200.00.

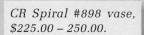

CR Spiral #898 vase, $225.00 – 250.00.

CR Tiny Dot tulip vase, $125.00 – 150.00.

CR Daisy & Fern DC #1921 basket, $250.00 – 275.00.

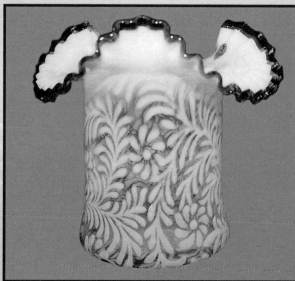

TO with Blue Crest Daisy & Fern #1921 DC vase, $225.00 – 250.00.

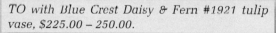

TO with Blue Crest Daisy & Fern #1921 tulip vase, $225.00 – 250.00.

TO with Blue Crest Daisy & Fern #1921 hat smooth edge, $225.00 – 250.00.

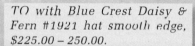

TO with Blue Crest Spiral #1921 hat, crimped edge, $225.00 – 250.00.

TO with Blue Crest Daisy & Fern tulip vase, $125.00 – 150.00.

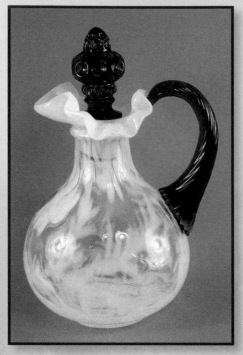

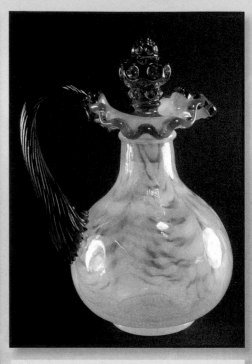

TO Fern Cruet, Blue stopper and handle, $125.00 – 150.00.

TO Coin Dot with Blue Crest #1457 7½" vase, $100.00 – 125.00.

TO Drapery Cruet, Blue stopper and handle, $125.00 – 150.00.

TO Lily of the Valley basket, $75.00 – 85.00.

TO Spiral #6548 vase, $125.00 – 150.00.

TO Hobnail tulip vase, $75.00 – 85.00.

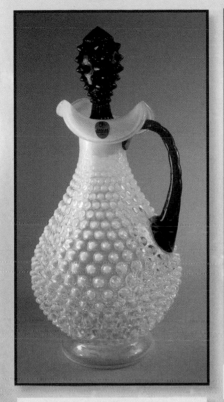

TO Hobnail decanter, Blue stopper and handle, $225.00 – 250.00.

TO Waffle #6137 basket, Blue handle, $75.00 – 85.00.

TO Daisy & Button basket, Blue handle, $65.00 – 75.00.

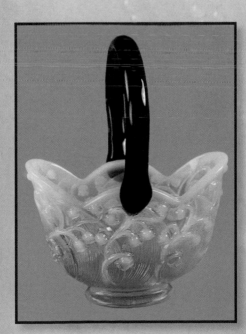

TO Lily of the Valley basket, Blue handle, $75.00 – 85.00.

TO Hobnail 5" basket, Blue handle, $35.00 – 45.00.

FO with Blue Crest Fern tulip vase, $100.00 – 125.00.

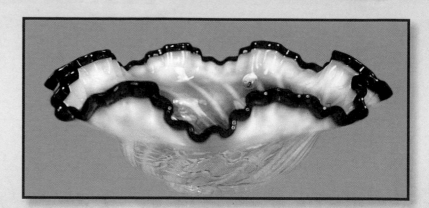

FO with Blue Crest 10" bowl, $65.00 – 75.00.

FO with Blue handle 5" Hobnail basket, $35.00 – 45.00.

FO with Violet Crest tulip vase, $100.00 – 125.00.

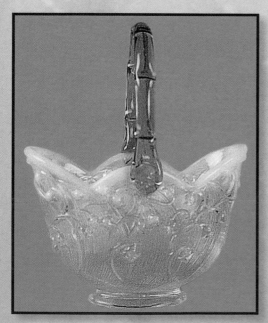

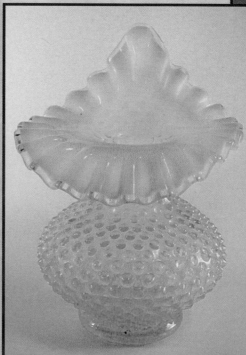

FO Lily of the Valley basket, Pink handle, $65.00 – 75.00.

GO Hobnail tulip vase, $75.00 – 85.00.

GO Hobnail 5" basket, Blue handle, $45.00 – 55.00.

GO Lily of the Valley basket, Blue handle, $75.00 – 85.00.

Iridized Green Hobnail 5" basket, Blue handle, $45.00 – 55.00.

GO with Blue Crest Spiral 10" bowl, $65.00 – 75.00.

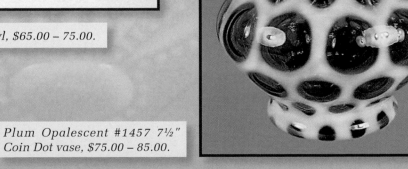

Plum Opalescent #1457 7½" Coin Dot vase, $75.00 – 85.00.

Plum Opalescent tulip vase, $100.00 – 125.00.

Plum Opalescent #1921 Daisy & Fern hat, $225.00 – 250.00.

Plum Opalescent #1457 7½" Daisy & Fern vase, $75.00 – 85.00.

Plum Opalescent #1921 Spiral ruffled hat, $225.00 – 250.00.

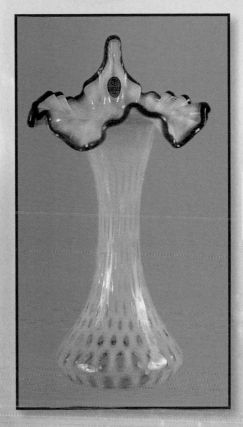

Persian Blue Opalescent Blue Crest Tiny Dot tulip vase, $100.00 – 125.00.

Persian Blue Opalescent Blue Crest Tiny Dot #1457 7½" vase, $85.00 – 95.00.

Persian Blue Opalescent Blue Crest Coin Dot #1457 7½" vase, $85.00 – 95.00.

Royal Blue Lily of the Valley basket, Crystal handle, $75.00 – 85.00.

CR Fern spooner, $50.00 – 65.00.

CR Tiny Dot spooner, unfinished, $50.00 – 65.00 finished.

CR Spiral spooner, $50.00 – 65.00.

All spooner/pickle jars in frames, $150.00 – 175.00.

FO Tiny Dot spooner, $40.00 – 55.00.

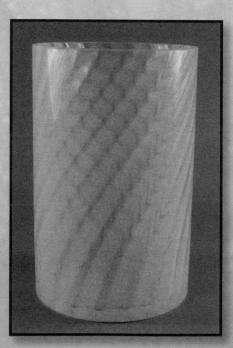

Persian Blue Opalescent Spiral spooner, $50.00 – 65.00.

Persian Blue Opalescent Tiny Dot spooner, $50.00 – 65.00.

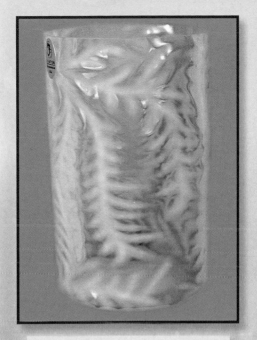

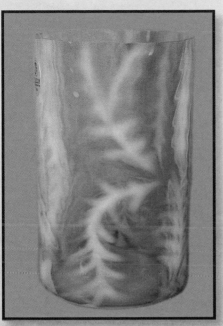

TO Fern spooner, $50.00 – 65.00.

Persian Blue Opalescent Fern spooner, $50.00 – 65.00.

PO Fern spooner, $50.00 – 65.00.

CR Opalescent Dot spooner, $50.00 – 65.00.

Blue Topaz #5165 Sitting Cat, $45.00 – 50.00.

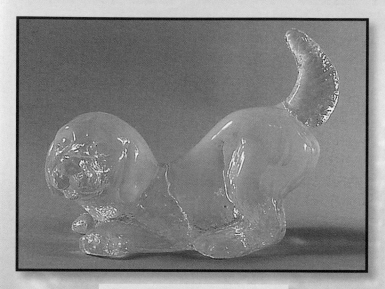

FO #5225 Puppy, $50.00 – 55.00.

Royal Blue #5165 Sitting Cat, $45.00 – 50.00.

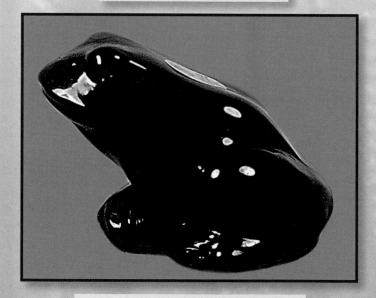

Royal Blue #5166 Frog, $45.00 – 50.00.

Royal Blue #5166 Frog on Stand, $65.00 – 70.00.

Royal Blue #5147 Mallard Duck, $55.00 – 60.00.

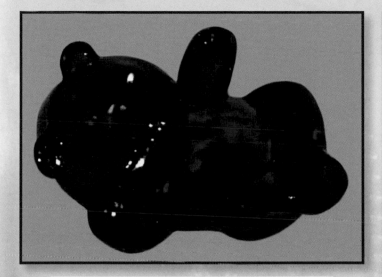

Royal Blue #5233 Reclining Bear, $50.00 – 55.00.

TO #5151 Sitting Bear, $50.00 – 55.00.

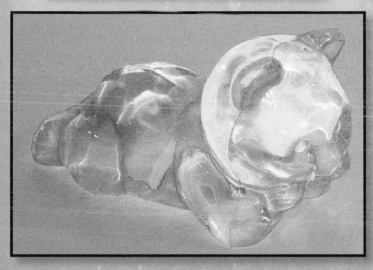

Topaz #5239 Daydreaming Bear, $50.00 – 55.00.

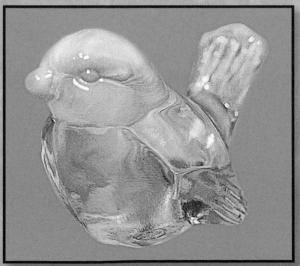

TO #5163 Fat Bird, $45.00 – 50.00.

Topaz #5151 Sitting Bear on Stand, $75.00 – 85.00.

TO #449 8½″ candlesticks, $50.00 – 65.00 pair.

TO #5065 Stylized Cat, $60.00 – 65.00.

TO #5119 Crouching Cat, $45.00 – 50.00.

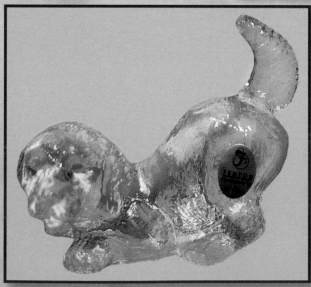

TO #5225 Spaniel with Wagging Tail, $55.00 – 60.00.

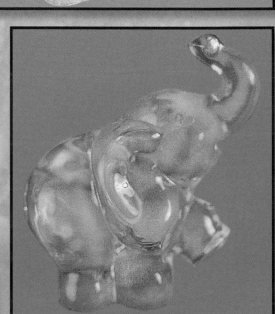

TO #5163 Elephant, foot up, $50.00 – 55.00.

TO #5160 Fawn, $50.00 – 55.00.

Topaz #5274 Frog, $50.00 – 55.00.

TO #5148 Mouse, $45.00 – 50.00.

Topaz #5166 Frog, side view.

Topaz #5166 Frog, decorated with a rose, $50.00 – 55.00.

Topaz 3" #5251 small Bear, $45.00 – 50.00; Topaz #5168 3" Owl, $45.00 – 50.00.

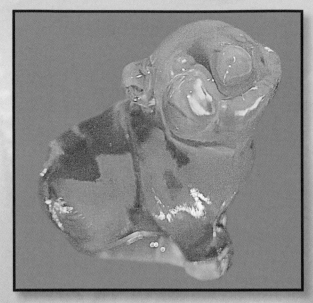

TO #5220 Pig, $45.00 – 50.00.

TO #5225 Puppy on Stand, $75.00 – 85.00.

TO #5142 Raccoon, $50.00 – 55.00.

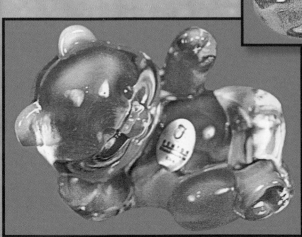

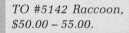

TO #5233 Reclining Bear, $50.00 – 55.00.

TO #5135 Hobby Horse, $45.00 – 50.00.

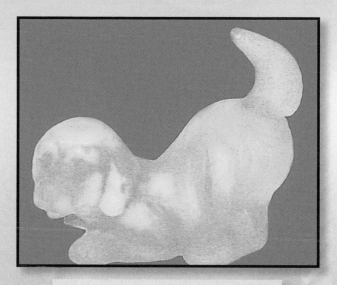

TO Satin #5225 Puppy, $55.00 – 60.00.

Topaz #5214 Scottie, $55.00 – 60.00.

TO #5134 Snail, $55.00 – 60.00.

TO #5159 Entwined Spaniels, $55.00 – 60.00.

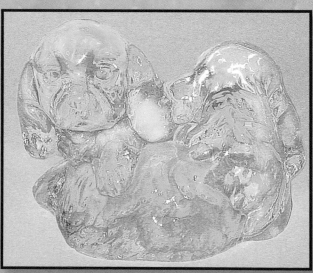

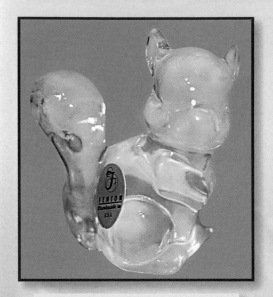

TO #5215 Squirrel, $45.00 – 50.00.

TO #5149 Love Bug, $35.00 – 40.00.

Topaz #5149 Love Bug, $35.00 – 40.00.

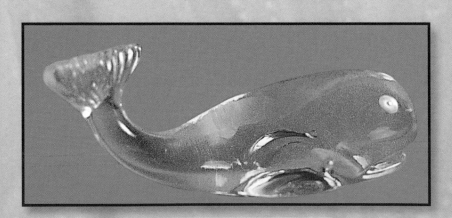

Topaz #5152 Whale, $40.00 – 45.00.

Topaz #5151 Bear on Stand, $65.00 – 75.00.

Topaz #5166 Frog on Stand, $65.00 – 75.00.

Topaz Hen Egg Server, $125.00 – 145.00.

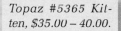

Topaz #5365 Kitten, $35.00 – 40.00.

Topaz #5243 Curious Cat, $35.00 – 40.00.

Topaz #5251 3" Bears on Stand, $85.00 – 95.00.

Topaz #5262 Miniature Rabbit on Stand, $65.00 – 75.00.

Topaz #5065 Stylized Cat on Stand, $75.00 – 85.00.

Topaz #5163 Fat Bird on Stand, $65.00 – 75.00.

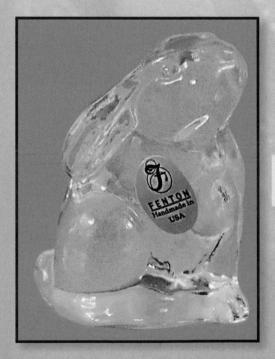

Topaz #5262 Miniature Rabbit, $35.00 – 40.00.

Topaz #5162 Bunny, $45.00 – 50.00.

Topaz Rabbit on Nest, $75.00 – 85.00.

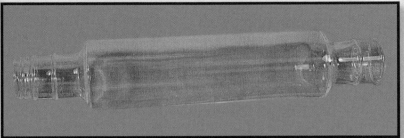

Topaz Rolling Pin, $65.00 – 70.00.

Topaz #5142 Raccoon on Stand, $75.00 – 85.00.

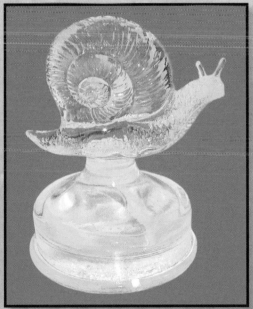

Topaz #5134 Snail on Stand, $65.00 – 75.00.

Topaz #5161 Solid Swan on Stand, $60.00 – 65.00

Topaz #5266 Turtle, $45.00 – 50.00.

Topaz #5109 Polar Bear, $65.00 – 75.00; Topaz #5065 Stylized Cat, $65.00 – 75.00.

Sandwich Historical Society

The Sandwich Historical Society was founded in 1917 to preserve the heritage of the Sandwich, New Hampshire, area. All segments of Sandwich society are preserved, not only the glassware. The museum, in the Elisha Marston house, contains tools, furniture, textiles, and glassware that came from the homes of early Sandwich settlers. The museum also gives historians and collectors the use of its extensive library. As with other museums, the sale of souvenirs helps defray the costs of running it. Many other glass factories have made glass for the historical society, but at this time, Fenton is making glass for it.

The dolphin candlesticks are very popular. The general rule of thumb for telling old from new relates to both the wafer that holds together the base and the cup that holds the candle. Sandwich candlesticks were never made in single pieces. Every candlestick was made by attaching the candle cup to the dolphin with a wafer of glass that was superheated and acted like a glue to hold the pieces in place. Because of that, the mould line running from top to bottom misses the wafer, leaving a gap in the line. Fenton also makes these in two pieces, but it is the joining together of the pieces that is different. Instead of using a wafer, the base of the candle cup and the top of the dolphin base are reheated to a temperature that allows the two pieces to fuse together.

The base is clearly marked with an embossed "SGM." Fenton has also made several colors of the Mayflower salt dip and the button arch pieces that are made using the moulds of the Westlake Ruby Glass Works.

CANDLESTICKS

Pattern	Clear	Ruby, Cobalt Blue, Twilight Blue	Topaz Opalescent
Dolphin candlestick	(ea.) $35.00 – 45.00	(ea.) $60.00 – 70.00	(ea.) $70.00 – 80.00
Mayflower salt dip*	(ea.) $25.00 – 35.00	(ea.) $35.00 – 40.00	

*Mulberry Blue, $45.00 – 65.00.

OTHER PIECES

Pattern	Clear	Color-Stained Tops*
Button Arch toothpick	$15.00 – 18.00	$20.00 – 24.00
Button Arch creamer	$18.00 – 20.00	$22.00 – 26.00

*Color-stained tops are done by Dickie Glass Company.

Twilight Blue Dolphin candlestick, $60.00 – 70.00 each.

Crystal Dolphin candlestick, $35.00 – 40.00 each.

Cobalt Blue Dolphin candlestick, $60.00 – 70.00 each.

Ruby/Amberina Dolphin candlestick, $60.00 – 70.00 each.

Topaz Opalescent Dolphin candlestick, $70.00 – 80.00 each.

Button Arches toothpick, Red-stained top, $18.00 – 20.00.

Button Arches creamer, Red-stained top, $22.00 – 26.00.

Button Arches creamer, Blue-stained top, $22.00 – 26.00.

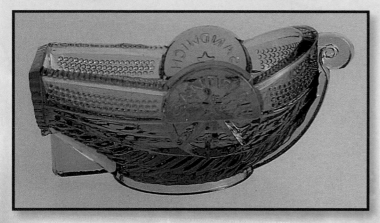

Mulberry Blue Mayflower salt dip, $55.00 – 65.00.

Button Arches toothpick, Green-stained top, $18.00 – 20.00.

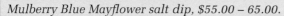

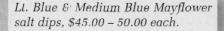

Lt. Blue & Medium Blue Mayflower salt dips, $45.00 – 50.00 each.

Cobalt Blue Mayflower salt dips, $45.00 – 50.00 each.

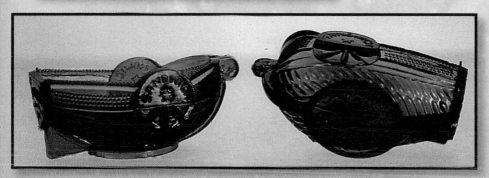

Showcase Dealers

This chapter covers those Fenton dealers who have earned spots as Fenton's Showcase Dealers. Stores who carry Fenton must pass several tests before they can claim to be in that category. First of all, a dealer must be a dealer for more than a year. There is a minimum amount it must buy in one year, and it must carry the majority of Fenton's retail line. The last requirement is that it give a certain amount of space in its stores to Fenton, which then gives it the use of a showcase, hence the name "Fenton Showcase Dealer."

Many of the Showcase dealers buy glass that is designed just for them. More often than not, those pieces are from Fenton's group of creatures. The dealer works with a Fenton designer to create a product that can only be sold by the dealer. When it sells the glass, the price is not much higher than that for pieces in Fenton's catalogs, but as soon as such a piece is gone, it brings double and triple its original price on eBay. These kinds of pieces are usually available in amounts under 100 and are sold regionally, so when they go on the secondary market, the price is set by the old supply and demand scale of value.

I was able to locate several of those dealers and get the information about those items from them. I will expand this chapter as more information becomes available.

CLASSIC GLASS

Steve and Kelly Tonelis are the owners of Classic Glass, located in Gilbertsville, Pennsylvania. In Kelly's words, "Steve and I began our Glass 'obsession' in the early 1990s. By 1995, we had decided to become retailer/dealers because we couldn't find any Fenton Glass locally." They shopped at a local landmark, Zern's Farmers Market, so they decided to take the Fenton product line to the manager of Zerns, and they now have a shop there.

Classic Glass contracted with Fenton for its first special-order glass, a brown puppy named Freckles, in 2003. This dog, a sleeping calico cat named Calli-co, and an elegant calico cat named Callie are each decorated with a red heart. This heart designates that they belong to a collection named Open Your Hearts, unique in that a portion of profit for each sale is donated to Animal Charity.

Its first special-order doll was named Shelley and was issued in 2004. The Black Harvest doll was issued at the same time, December 2004, as the Holiday bridesmaid doll. In 2005, two bridesmaid dolls were developed for the company's "signing event." Customers visiting the website were asked to choose between a Spring Bouquet doll and a Sunflowers doll. There was a tie, so both were made. The Black doll called Mystery was made around the same time in 2005, but was limited to only 55 made. A standard order is for 100 of each.

The pink Celebration Bear and the un-named Favrene labrador were made for the double anniversary of 10 years as Classic Glass and 100 years of Fenton.

ANIMALS				
Name	*Date*	*Color*	*Quantity*	*Value*
Freckles	2003	Opal Satin	100	$65.00 – 85.00
Callie	2003	Opal Satin	100	$75.00 – 95.00
Calli-co	2003	Opal Satin	100	$55.00 – 65.00
Favrene Lab	2005	Favrene	100	$85.00 – 115.00
Celebration Bear	2005	Rosemilk	100	$75.00 – 95.00

BRIDESMAID DOLLS

Name	Date	Color	Quantity	Value
Shelley	2004	Opal Satin	100	$100.00 – 125.00
Harvest	2004	Black	100	$100.00 – 125.00
Holiday	2004	Opal Satin	100	$100.00 – 125.00
Spring Bouquet	2005	Opal	100	$100.00 – 125.00
Sunflower	2005	Opal Satin	100	$100.00 – 125.00
Mystery	2005	Black	55	$125.00 – 150.00

Black Harvest doll, $100.00 – 125.00.

Mystery, Black doll, $125.00 – 150.00.

Side view of Mystery.

Holiday doll, $100.00 – 125.00.

Shelley doll, $100.00 – 125.00.

Spring Bouquet doll, $100.00 – 125.00.

Sunflower doll, $100.00 – 125.00.

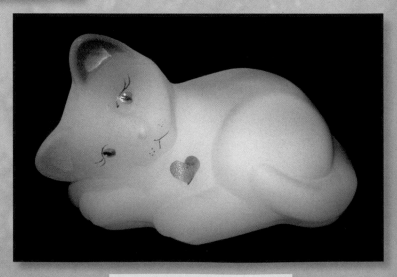

Calli-co, #5064, $55.00 – 65.00.

Freckles, #5225, $65.00 – 85.00.

Callie, #5065, $75.00 – 95.00.

Favrene, #5085 Puppy, Floral decoration, $85.00 – 115.00.

Celebration, Rose Milk #5151, $75.00 – 95.00.

COLLECTABLES UNLIMITED

Collectables Unlimited, of Lewisburg, Pennsylvania, is owned and operated by the Scott family: Jim, Shirley, Jamie, Terry, and Mary Ann. They represent three generations of Fenton dealers and collectors. They have had four of the small baskets made by Fenton especially for their store. All four are miniature baskets with special decorations.

Pink Iridized mini basket decorated with Blue Butterfly, $25.00 – 30.00.

COLLECTORS' SHOWCASE

Marian Thornton has been a Fenton dealer selling both new and old glassware since 1982. She had been a collector for many years and the business just seemed to be a natural progression for her. She has two shops in Washington State, one in Snohomish, north and east of Seattle, and one in Centralia, about halfway between Portland, Oregon, and Seattle, Washington. In Snohomish, Marian, her daughter Jenni and son, BJ, are always available to answer questions and find glass for collectors. Her shop in Centralia, Washington, is managed by very knowledgeable employees. Both shops are packed full with Fenton and with other art glass. Marian always has a large inventory of old and rare glass, as well as the many pieces she has had Fenton make for her exclusively.

When the first Fenton Finders club was formed in Washington State, Marion was one of the biggest supporters of it. Because she kept her shop open later on the weekends, she seldom could make it to the monthly meetings, but she always came to the convention, bringing with her a load of beautiful glassware. Eventually, Fenton began using her shop as an extension of its gift shop, sending her items that had been in the FAGCA Special Glass Room and gift shop exclusives. It has always meant a lot to the collectors in the Northwest who couldn't always travel to West Virginia.

Collectors' Showcase is a popular shop, especially for collectors who specialize in Fenton's animal figurines. Marian regularly orders bears, cats, and other critters decorated in new designs not being made for Fenton's catalog line.

Burmese #5165 Musical Cat, $55.00 – 65.00.

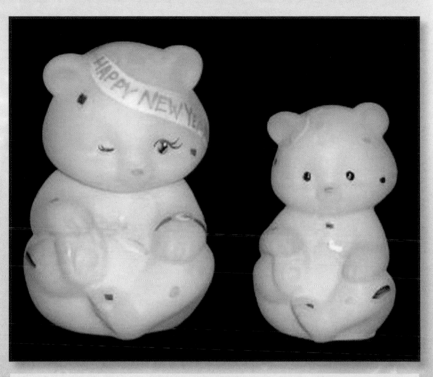

Opal Satin #5151 Sitting Bear and #5251 miniature Bear, New Year's, $100.00 – 125.00 set.

#5151 Baseball Bear, $60.00 – 65.00.

#5151 Black Bear, $65.00 – 85.00.

#5151 Black & Brown Bear, $65.00 – 85.00; #5251 miniature Bear, $45.00 – 55.00.

#5251 Black Panda miniature Bear, $50.00 – 65.00.

Signature on base of Panda Bear.

Collectors' Showcase 2003 B. Hubek

Bridal Set of Bears. #5151 Bears, $60.00 – 65.00 each; #5251 mini Bears, $45.00 – 55.00 each.

Golden Brown #5233 Bear, $45.00 – 55.00.

Burmese #5165 Party Time Cat,
$55.00 – 65.00.

Christmas Bear Set: #5151 Bears, $75.00
– 85.00 each; #5251 mini Bears, $50.00
– 65.00 each.

Easter Bears: #5151 Bear, $55.00 – 65.00;
#5251 miniature Bear, $45.00 – 50.00.

Favrene #5065 decorated Stylized Cat, $75.00 – 95.00.

Fishing Bears: #5151 Bear, $45.00 – 55.00; #5251 miniature Bear, $35.00 – 40.00.

Formal Mice, $45.00 – 50.00 each.

Golden #5151 Bear, $55.00 – 65.00.

Grandparent Mice, $45.00 – 50.00 each.

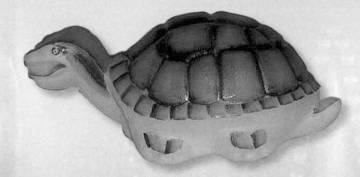

Green & Yellow #5226 Turtle, $45.00 – 50.00.

Halloween Bears: #5151 Bear, $50.00 – 55.00; #5251 miniature Bear, $40.00 – 45.00.

Indian Bears: #5151 Bear, $50.00 – 55.00; #5251 miniature Bear, $40.00 – 45.00.

Military Bears: #5151 Bear, $60.00 – 65.00; #5251 miniature Bear, $50.00 – 55.00.

Burmese #5147 Natural Mallard, $55.00 – 60.00.

Gray Natural #5158 Elephant, $40.00 – 45.00.

New Year's Bears: #5151 Bear, $45.00 – 50.00; #5251 miniature Bear, $30.00 – 35.00.

Patriotic #5225 Puppy, Cobalt Blue, $50.00 – 55.00.

Periwinkle Blue Bears: #5239 Daydreaming Bear, $45.00 – 50.00; #5151 Bear, $45.00 – 50.00; #5251 miniature Bear, $30.00 – 35.00; #5233 Reclining Bear, $45.00 – 50.00.

Pink Iridized blown egg, $100.00 – 125.00.

Pink Iridized blown egg, $100.00 – 125.00.

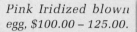

Rose Milk Opalescent Bunny with Blue Butterfly, $45.00 – 50.00.

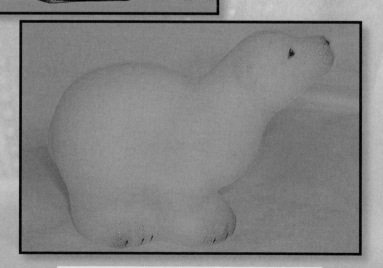

Conductor #5251 miniature Bear, $45.00 – 50.00.

Opal Satin #5109 Polar Bear, $45.00 – 50.00.

Spring set of Bears: #5151 Bear, $50.00 – 55.00; #5251 miniature Bear, $40.00 – 45.00.

Teacher & Student Bears: Teacher #5151 Bear, $60.00 – 65.00; Student #5251 Bear, $50.00 – 55.00.

Topaz Satin #5151 Honey Bear, $60.00 – 65.00.

Topaz Satin #5151 decorated Bear, $60.00 – 65.00.

Tropical #5151 Panda Bear, $60.00 – 65.00.

Valentine Bears: #5151 Bear, $50.00 – 55.00; #5251 miniature Bear, $40.00 – 45.00.

DREAMS & RAINBOWS

Dreams and Rainbows, of Kingman, Arizona, was the first Fenton Showcase Dealer in the state of Arizona. It is located between Las Vegas, Nevada, and Laughlin, Arizona, two cities that are famous for their gambling casinos. It had the bell that is pictured here and a cat with a rainbow on the back made by Fenton. Both are exclusive to its store. The Lotus Mist bell features a dragonfly on the front and is inscribed with the store's name inside.

Lotus Mist bell, Dragonfly decoration, $65.00 – 75.00.

Lotus Mist bell, $75.00 -$85.00.
French Opalescent Cat, $35.00 – $40.00.
Opal Iridized Cat, $35.00 – $40.00.

RANDY'S ANTIQUES AND GIFTS

Randy Bradshaw, former board member of the FAGCA, has owned and operated his Showcase Dealer shop, Randy's Antiques and Gifts, located in St Paul, Minnesota, for several years now. He carries so much Fenton that he is called the Fenton Man of the Twin Cities area. Like many other Showcase Dealers, Randy has purchased several pieces of Fenton that were made to be sold exclusively in his shop.

Each of the Opal Satin animals are signed by the artist and have a logo, "Minnesota's Own." The bottom of the butterfly is signed "Minnesota's Seasons — 2002." The epergne is signed with the "100th Anniversary" logo for Fenton as well as a "Randy's Antiques & Gifts" logo, but is not numbered. The base of the Rosalene pitcher and the Black fan vase reads "Minnesota Seasons — 2002" and is also signed by the artist.

Opal Satin tinted Pink #5265 Cats decorated with Lady Slippers, $50.00 – 75.00 each.

FENTON EXCLUSIVES MADE FOR RANDY'S ANTIQUES & GIFTS

Decorated Glassware

Shape	Ware #	Color	Decoration	Edition	Value
Elephant	5058	Opal Satin	Lady Slipper	100	$50.00 – 75.00
Floppy Ear Bunny	5293	Opal Satin	Lady Slipper	100	$50.00 – 75.00
Sitting Cat	5165	Opal Satin	Lady Slipper	100	$50.00 – 75.00
Butterfly	5271	Green Burmese	Morning Glory	68	$65.00 – 95.00
Pitcher		Rosalene	Tulips		$135.00 – 165.00
Vase, Fan		Black	Sunflowers	72	$100.00 – 125.00

RUBY SILVER CREST

Shape	Ware #	Pattern	Edition	Value
Epergne	4808*	Diamond Lace	109	$325.00 – 375.00

*The smaller #4801 Diamond Lace epergne has no crest; with a crest, it is #4808.

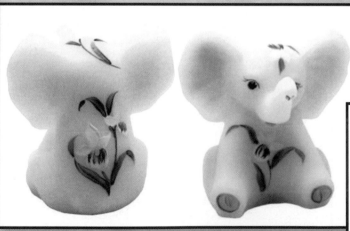

Opal Satin tinted Pink #5058 Baby Elephants, Lady Slipper decoration, $50.00 – 75.00 each.

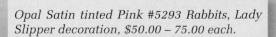

Opal Satin tinted Pink #5293 Rabbits, Lady Slipper decoration, $50.00 – 75.00 each.

Lotus Mist Burmese #5721 Butterfly, Morning Glory decorated, $65.00 – 95.00.

Ruby Silver Crest Diamond Lace #4808 epergne, $325.00 – 375.00.

Black Sunflower #1259 decorated fan vase, $100.00 – 125.00.

Rosalene pitcher, Tulip decorated, $135.00 – 165.00.

Singleton Bailey lives in the small town of Loris, South Carolina, a town that was originally built on tobacco farming. It was surrounded by fields of tobacco, but most of those fields grow corn and soybeans these days. They are not as profitable as tobacco, but Loris has found a way to re-energize its economy, not a small feat for a town that boomed during the tobacco days. Loris consists of many family-owned businesses that have been passed down from one generation to the next. Singleton's drug store is one of those businesses. Singleton's father retired about 15 years ago, leaving Singleton in charge. The drug store includes a working antique soda fountain, something that attracts tourists.

In 1965, Singleton discovered a love of carnival glass. It was that carnival glass that drew him to the Fenton Art Glass Company. It was still producing glass and, in 1970, it began reproducing carnival glass that it signed, making it easy for collectors to distinguish the old from the new. When I met Singleton and his wife, Cheryl, he was also collecting Peacock vases and Dancing Lady items, the same items I was trying to add to my collection. When Singleton sold that part of his collection, I was able to buy a few of his pieces.

In 1986, Singleton had a mould made for a mug that used the design of Dugan's Stork & Rushes mug but replaced the stork with a swan. It was a perfect design in that it had the look of old glass without actually reproducing it. As his success with those pieces grew, Singleton branched out with Poppy (original Imperial mould), Heavy Iris (original Dugan mould), and Milady (original Fenton mould) vases. When the Westmoreland Glass Company went out of business, he bought the Swan & Cattails mould. He added the Farmyard pieces using a mould that was originally marked "Mimi" but was now marked "DSB." Most of the glass made for him is iridized, but there are exceptions to that rule, such as the Cranberry Opalescent, Burmese, Rosalene, and Topaz Satin pieces.

Singleton currently has many colors and styles of glass available.

ATLANTIS PATTERN

Year	Color	Shape	Price
1988	Rosalene	Vase	$175.00 – 200.00
1988	Ruby Marigold	Vase	$150.00 – 175.00
1988	Ruby Marigold	Basket	$175.00 – 200.00
1993	Twilight Blue Iridized	Vase	$125.00 – 150.00

BUTTERFLY & BERRY

Year	Color	Shape	Price
1988	Topaz Opalescent Carnival	Bowl, plain edge	$125.00 – 150.00
1988	Topaz Opalescent Carnival	Plate	$175.00 – 195.00
1988	Topaz Opalescent Carnival	Basket	$200.00 – 225.00
2000	Black Carnival	Bowl, ftd.	$100.00 – 125.00

CAPRICE (CAMBRIDGE MOULD)

Color	Basket	Bowl	Vase w/Bow
Country Cranberry	$100.00 – 125.00	$65.00 – 75.00	$100.00 – 125.00

FARMYARD

Year	Color	9" Basket Pl. Hndl.	Basket Loop Hndl.	11" Chop Plate	Cuspidor	Rose Bowl	Bowl
1990	Ruby Irid.	$65.00 – 85.00	$75.00 – 100.00	$65.00 – 85.00	$75.00 – 100.00	$65.00 – 85.00	$45.00 – 65.00
1990	Green Irid.	$65.00 – 85.00		$65.00 – 85.00	$75.00 – 100.00	$65.00 – 85.00	$45.00 – 65.00
1991	Black Irid. (6")	$65.00 – 85.00		$65.00 – 85.00	$75.00 – 100.00	$65.00 – 85.00	$45.00 – 65.00
1991	Burmese				$100.00 – 125.00		$65.00 – 85.00
1991	Burmese Irid.				$100.00 – 125.00		$65.00 – 85.00
1991	Rosalene				$100.00 – 125.00	$85.00 – 100.00	
1992	Electric Blue Irid.	$65.00 – 85.00		$65.00 – 85.00	$75.00 – 100.00	$65.00 – 85.00	
1992	Ruby Iridized	$65.00 – 85.00					
1993	Sea Mist Green Irid.			$100.00 – 125.00	$100.00 – 125.00		$65.00 – 85.00
1993	Rose Magnolia Iridized			$65.00 – 85.00			$45.00 – 65.00
1995	Off-color Custard Irid.			$75.00 – 95.00			$50.00 – 65.00
1997	Burmese Irid.			$100.00 – 125.00			$65.00 – 85.00
1997	Topaz Irid.			$100.00 – 125.00			$65.00 – 85.00
1999	Lt. Gold Irid.			$75.00 – 95.00			$50.00 – 65.00
2001	Green Burmese Iridized			$75.00 – 100.00			$50.00 – 65.00
2001	Blue Burmese Irid.			$100.00 – 125.00			$65.00 – 85.00

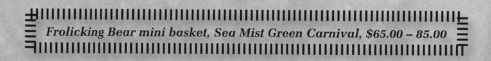

Frolicking Bear mini basket, Sea Mist Green Carnival, $65.00 – 85.00

GLASS ANIMALS

Description	Color	Item #	Value
Alley cat*	Ruby Carnival	5177IR	$175.00 – 225.00
Bear, sitting	Ruby Carnival	5151IR	$65.00 – 84.00

Description	Color	Item #	Value
Bear, sitting	Crystal Marigold	5151IX	$45.00 – 65.00
Bear, reclining	White Carnival	5233CYR	$45.00 – 65.00
Bear, reclining	Crystal Marigold	5233IX	$45.00 – 65.00
Cat, sitting	Ocean Blue, decorated	5119	$45.00 – 65.00
Swan	Ruby Carnival		$55.00 – 70.00

*In 1999, the Alley Cat was made for Singleton in Ruby Carnival; it was later made to be sold in the 2003 catalog in Ruby Amberina Stretch #5177UR.

HEAVY IRIS VASE

2001 Black Carnival	2002 Topaz, Ball Struck All Over Irid.	2003 Blue Carnival	2003 Ruby Carnival
$175.00 – 200.00	$225.00 – 250.00	$175.00 – 200.00	$225.00 – 250.00

PEACOCK VASE

Color	Cupped Edge	Flared Neck	Straight Edge
Ruby Marigold	$75.00 – 95.00	$75.00 – 85.00	$75.00 – 85.00
Topaz Opal. Carnival	$95.00 – 115.00	$95.00 – 115.00	
Black Carnival	$65.00 – 85.00		
Chocolate	$75.00 – 95.00		
Celeste Blue	$75.00 – 95.00		

PERSIAN MEDALLION CUSPIDOR

Color	Value
Black Iridized	$50.00 – 65.00
Topaz Opalescent Iridized	$60.00 – 75.00

POPPY VASE
(All iridized unless noted.)

Color	6-pt. Crimped	Tulip/Jack-In-Pulpit
Aquamarine	$150.00 – 175.00	
Blue Burmese	$150.00 – 175.00	
Blue Topaz	$165.00 – 185.00	
Burmese	$125.00 – 150.00	$125.00 – 150.00
Celeste Blue	$150.00 – 175.00	
Champagne	$145.00 – 165.00	
Cranberry Opalescent*	$135.00 – 165.00	$140.00 – 180.00

Color	6-pt. Crimped	Tulip/ Jack In Pulpit
Emerald Green	$120.00 – 145.00	
Emerald Green over MG core	$140.00 – 160.00	
Gold (Amber)	$100.00 – 125.00	$100.00 – 125.00
Green Burmese	$120.00 – 140.00	
Ice Blue	$120.00 – 140.00	
Martha Stewart Green	$100.00 – 125.00	
Milk Glass	$75.00 – 95.00	
Mint Green	$100.00 – 125.00	
Mulberry Blue	$125.00 – 150.00	$125.00 – 150.00
Opaline	$125.00 – 150.00	
Pink Chiffon	$145.00 – 165.00	
Plum	$125.00 – 145.00	
Royal Blue	$125.00 – 145.00	$125.00 – 150.00
Ruby	$140.00 – 155.00	
Ruby*	$100.00 – 120.00	
Sea Green	$100.00 – 120.00	
Shell Pink	$125.00 – 145.00	
Special Milk Glass	$75.00 – 95.00	
Spruce Green	$100.00 – 120.00	
Topaz Opalescent	$150.00 – 175.00	
Topaz Opalescent Satinized*	$150.00 – 175.00	
Violet	$100.00 – 120.00	
Yellow Topaz over MG	$150.00 – 175.00	

*Not iridized.

POPPY
(Fenton mould used for lamps.)

Color	Cuspidor	Rose Bowl
Provincial Blue Iridized	65.00 – 85.00	50.00 – 70.00

POULTRY
(Mini baskets.)

Aquamarine Iridized	Violet Iridized	Willow Green Iridized
50.00 – 65.00	$50.00 – 65.00	$50.00 – 65.00

REGENCY

Color	Pitcher	Tumbler
Ruby Marigold	$65.00 – 80.00	$30.00 – 35.00

SUNBURST

Color	7" Basket	Cuspidor
Green Opalescent Iridized	$65.00 – 75.00	$65.00 – 75.00
Topaz Opalescent Iridized	$65.00 – 75.00	$65.00 – 75.00
Black Iridized	$65.00 – 75.00	$65.00 – 75.00

MISCELLANEOUS

Hobnail, Cat Slipper, Ruby Carnival, $25.00 – 30.00

Hobnail, Cuspidor, Ruby Carnival, $45.00 – 55.00

Tiny Rose, Basket, Ruby Carnival, $45.00 – 55.00

SWAN MUG

Color	Value
Amethyst Carnival	$50.00 – 65.00
Black Carnival	$50.00 – 65.00
Burmese*	$65.00 – 85.00
Burmese Carnival	$65.00 – 85.00
Cobalt Blue Carnival	$50.00 – 65.00
Green Carnival	$50.00 – 65.00
Pink Carnival	$50.00 – 65.00
Provincial Blue Carnival	$50.00 – 65.00
Rosalene*	$65.00 – 85.00
Ruby Carnival	$60.00 – 75.00
Shell Pink Carnival	$50.00 – 75.00
Teal Marigold	$50.00 – 75.00
Topaz Carnival	$65.00 – 85.00

SWAN AND CATTAILS VASE

Color	Value
Provincial Blue Opalescent	$65.00 – 75.00
Ruby Carnival	$75.00 – 85.00
Topaz Opalescent	$75.00 – 85.00

Provincial Blue Carnival Poppy rose bowl, $50.00 – 70.00.

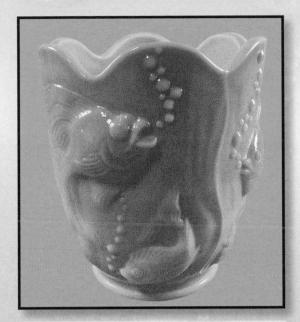

Atlantis vase, Peachalene. The Peachalene Atlantis vase was made for Singleton but was sold in the Convention Special Glass Room. $225.00 – 250.00.

Rosalene Atlantis vase, $175.00 – 200.00.

Topaz Opalescent Carnival Basketweave cuspidor, $65.00 – 75.00.

***Black Carnival assortment, top row:** Farm-yard basket, $65.00 – 85.00; Farmyard chop plate, $65.00 – 85.00; Farmyard cuspidor, $75.00 – 100.00.*
***Bottom row:** Swan & Cat Tails vase, $65.00 – 75.00; Swan mug, $50.00 – 65.00; Farm-yard rose bowl, $65.00 – 85.00; Farmyard double-crimped bowl, $45.00 – 65.00.*

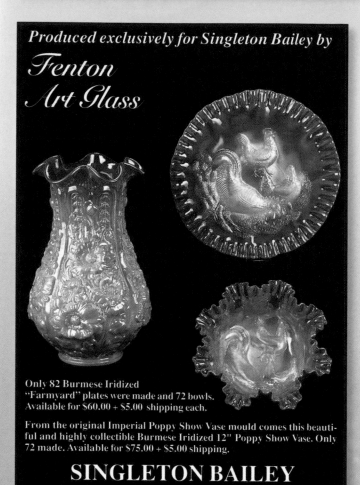
Burmese Carnival: Poppy vase, $125.00 – 150.00; Farmyard chop plate, $85.00 – 100.00; Farmyard double-crimped bowl, $65.00 – 85.00.

Black Carnival Butterfly & Berry bowl, $100.00 – 125.00.

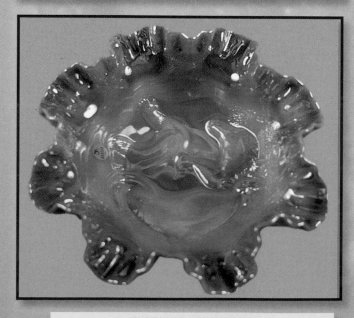

Blue Burmese Carnival DC bowl, $65.00 – 85.00.

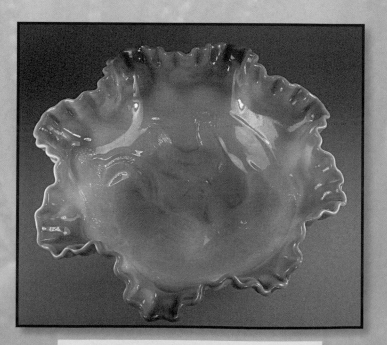

Burmese Farmyard DC bowl, $65.00 – 85.00.

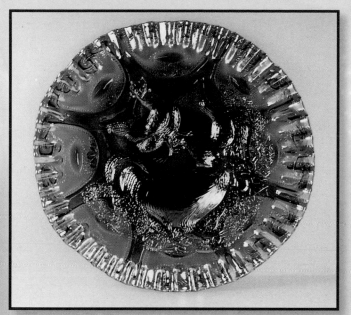

Plum Carnival Farmyard plate, $75.00 – 95.00.

Plum Carnival Farmyard DC bowl, $65.00 – 85.00.

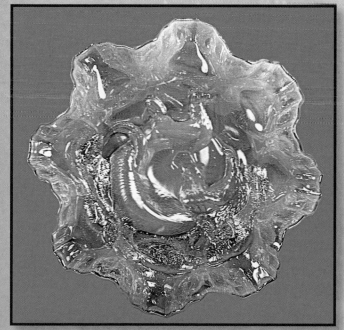

Topaz Opalescent Carnival Farmyard DC bowl, $65.00 – 85.00.

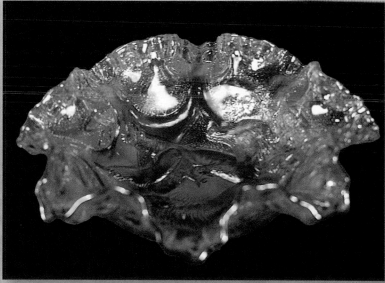

Smoky Iridescent Farmyard bowl, $65.00 – 85.00. The color code for this bowl is GJ, but I wasn't able to get the correct color name for this piece. It may be a off-color Misty Blue, or it could be an experimental color, but it is very pretty.

Blue Burmese Iridized Farmyard chop plate, $100.00 – 125.00.

Burmese Iridized Farmyard chop plate, $100.00 – 125.00.

Topaz Opalescent Iridized Farmyard chop plate, $100.00 – 125.00.

Lt. Gold Iridized Farmyard chop plate, $75.00 – 95.00.

Sea Mist Green Iridized Farmyard chop plate, $100.00 – 125.00.

Rosalene Farmyard smooth-rim rose bowl, Jeweled Heart exterior, $85.00 – 100.00.

Rosalene Farmyard smooth-rim cuspidor, Jeweled Heart exterior, $100.00 – 125.00.

Electric Blue assortment: *Farmyard chop plate, $65.00 – 85.00; Farmyard basket, $65.00 – 85.00; 7" whimsey bowl/ruffled-edge cuspidor, $75.00 – 100.00; 6" smooth-edge rose bowl, $65.00 – 85.00; Ruby Iridized Farmyard basket, $65.00 – 85.00.*

Sea Mist Green assortment: Farmyard chop plate, $100.00 – 125.00; Farmyard cuspidor, $100.00 – 125.00; Farmyard pie-crimped 9" bowl, $65.00 – 85.00; Frolicking Bear miniature basket, $65.00 – 85.00.

Emerald Green Good Luck cupped bowl, $65.00 – 75.00.

Emerald Green Good Luck pie-crimped plate, $75.00 – 85.00.

Black Carnival Heart & Vine plate, $85.00 – 95.00.

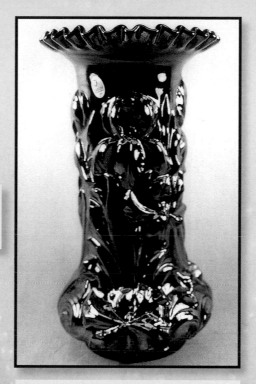

Blue Carnival Hobnail swung vase, $65.00 – 75.00.

Black Carnival Iris vase, $150.00 – 175.00.

Cobalt Blue Iris vase, $150.00 – 175.00.

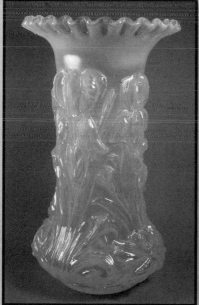

Topaz Opalescent ball-struck Iris vase. Topaz Opalescent glass is usually reheated to achieve opalescence after the glass has been moulded. Ball-struck Topaz Opalescent glass is reheated before it has been dropped into the mould, which gives the piece an opalescent effect evenly throughout it. $165.00 – 195.00.

Ruby Iridized Iris vase, $175.00 – 200.00.

Cobalt Blue Iridized Milady vase, $175.00 – 200.00.

*Celeste Blue Peacock vase, fan top,
$75.00 – 95.00.*

*Chocolate Glass Peacock vase,
$75.00 – 95.00.*

*Topaz Opalescent Iridized Persian Medal-
lion cuspidor, $60.00 – 75.00.*

*Black Iridized Persian Medallion cuspidor,
$50.00 – 65.00.*

*Cranberry Iridized Poppy tulip/
JIP vase, $140.00 – 180.00.*

*Lt. Gold Iridized Poppy tulip vase,
$125.00 – 150.00.*

Black Iridized Poppy tulip vase, $125.00 – 150.00.

Burmese Iridized Poppy tulip vase, $150.00 – 175.00.

Mulberry Blue Iridized Poppy tulip vase, $125.00 – 150.00.

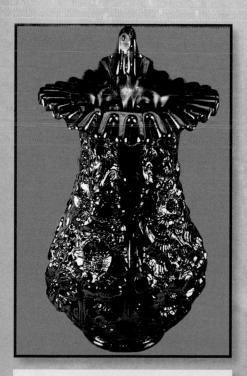

Cobalt Blue Iridized Poppy tulip vase, $125.00 – 150.00.

Blue Burmese Iridized Poppy crimped vase, $150.00 – 175.00.

Mint Green Iridized Poppy vase, $100.00 – 125.00.

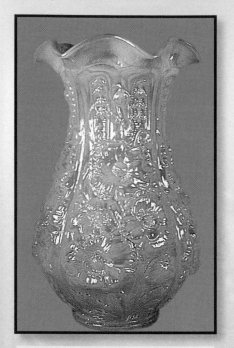

Shell Pink Iridized Poppy vase,
$125.00 – 145.00.

Lt. Amber Iridized Poppy vase,
$100.00 – 125.00.

Aquamarine Iridized Poppy vase,
$150.00 – 175.00.

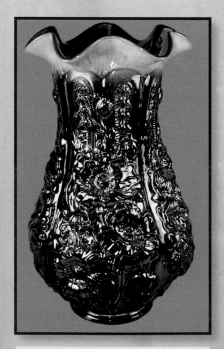

Black Opalescent Iridized Poppy
vase, $165.00 – 185.00.

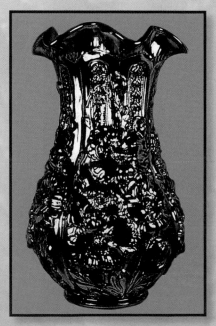

Black Iridized Poppy vase,
$100.00 – 125.00.

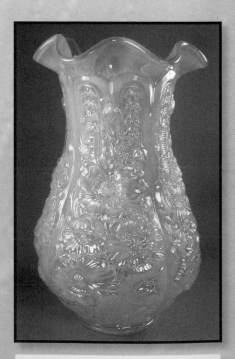

Blue Topaz Iridized Poppy vase,
$165.00 – 185.00.

Cobalt Blue Iridized Poppy vase,
$125.00 – 145.00.

Cranberry Opalescent Iridized
Poppy vase, $135.00 – 165.00.

Cranberry Opalescent Poppy vase,
$135.00 – 165.00.

Emerald Green over Milk Glass Iridized Poppy vase, $140.00 – 160.00.

Emerald Green Iridized Poppy vase,
$120.00 – 145.00.

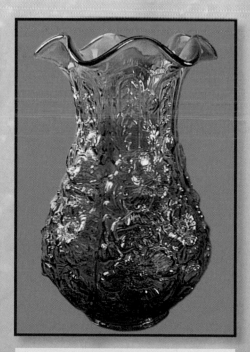

Mulberry Blue Iridized Poppy vase,
$125.00 – 150.00.

Lotus Mist Green Burmese Iridized Poppy vase, $120.00 – 140.00.

Off-color Pink Chiffon Iridized Poppy vase, $145.00 – 165.00.

Topaz cased over Cloud White Iridized Poppy vase, $150.00 – 175.00.

Violet Iridized Poppy vase, $150.00 – 175.00.

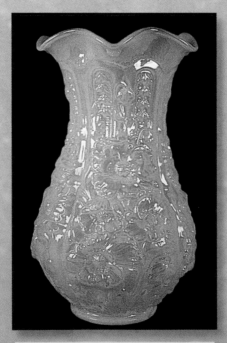

Opal Iridized Poppy vase, $100.00 – 125.00.

Topaz Opalescent Iridized Poppy vase, $150.00 – 175.00.

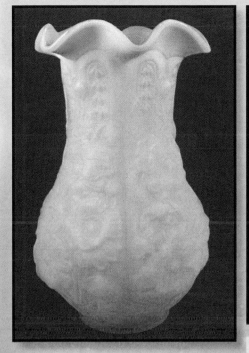

Topaz Opalescent Satin Poppy vase, $150.00 – 175.00.

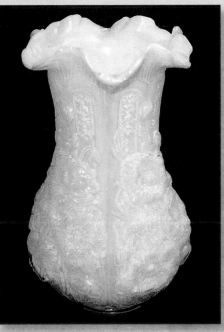

Topaz cased with Opal Iridized Poppy whimsey vase, $200.00 – 225.00.

Black Iridized Poppy whimsey pitcher, $200.00 – 225.00.

Poultry miniature baskets: Aquamarine Iridized, $50.00 – 65.00; Willow Green Opalescent Iridized, $60.00 – 75.00.

Violet Iridized Poultry miniature basket, $50.00 – 65.00.

Burmese by Fenton

Fenton Swan Vase—Iridized
Limited offering of 107
$50.00 each postpaid
(9458IE)

Fenton Swan Vase—Satin
Limited offering of 107
$50.00 each postpaid
(9458BR)

Singleton Bailey   P.O. Box 95, Loris, SC 29569

Rosalene Swan vase, $125.00 – 150.00.

Black Iridized Sunburst cuspidor, $65.00 – 75.00.

Cobalt Blue Iridized Swan mug, $50.00 – 65.00.

Topaz Opalescent Iridized cuspidor, $65.00 – 75.00.

Cobalt Blue Iridized Swan mug, $50.00 – 65.00.

Provincial Blue Iridized Swan mug, $50.00 – 65.00.

Limited Edition

GREEN CARNIVAL SWAN MUG

By FENTON

IGHT—3¾"   PRICE $28.50 post pa

Singleton Bailey

P.O. Box 95, Loris, S.C. 29569

Advertisement. Green Iridized Swan mug, $50.00 – 65.00.

Limited Edition

Carnival Swan Mugs

Height—3⅜"   Price = $28.50 each Postpaid

Made by Fenton for

Singleton Bailey

P.O. Box 95, Loris, SC 29569

Swan Mugs advertisement: Provincial Blue Iridized, $50.00 – 65.00; Shell Pink Iridized, $60.00 – 75.00; Teal Marigold, $60.00 – 75.00; Topaz Opalescent Iridized, $65.00 – 85.00.

Snyder's Vaughn-Haven

Snyder's Vaughn-Haven is a Rushville, Illinois, support group for patients suffering from Alzheimer disease. It is associated with the Snyder's Vaughn-Haven rest home in the same location. I wasn't able to get more information about this little turtle. It may have been used as a gift, or it may have been sold in the gift shop of the facility.

Opal Decorated #5266 Turtle with "Snyder's Vaughn-Haven Soc." on the side, $45.00 – 50.00.

Sports Awards

How could you ask for a more unique piece of glass to be made for a little league or for high school and college teams? The backside of each piece has the qualities you see in a baseball or football, but the front of the piece is flat so that it can be personalized for a school, sports team, or college.

Not only do these shapes work well for awards, they are also perfect pieces to use as promotional items sold to raise money for those associations.

Vases and other shapes, like the piece that has been sandcarved with basketball players, have also been used as presentation awards.

Cobalt Blue Baseball paperweight, $35.00 – 40.00.

Ruby Overlay Spiral Optic cylinder vase, sample only.

Plum Football paperweight with "Purple Riders," $35.00 – 40.00.

Cobalt Blue Football paperweight, "Erickson All-Sports Facility," $35.00 – 40.00.

Cobalt Blue backside of Football paperweight.

Stevenson's Apple Orchard Restaurant

Stephenson's Apple Orchard Restaurant is one of Kansas City's best. It has been in business since the 1960s and continues to be popular with its customers. The Ruby Thumbprint ice tea tumblers were made for it in the 1970s.

Ruby Thumbprint ice tea glass, $22.50 – 25.00.

The first mention of these little bell-shaped paperweights was in 1948. They were sold to Western Electric, and a small size was embossed with "Save Time Telephone" and a larger size with "Save Steps Telephone." These bells have been made for telephone companies ever since that first order, but I think you will agree, no one would have identified them as Fenton. The business in these boomed after AT&T was split into numerous smaller telephone companies. These may have been made for employees, or they may have been sold as promotional items. Either way, they are very attractive paperweights, and the Crystal with the blue core is a perfect demonstration of the talent of Fenton's glassmakers.

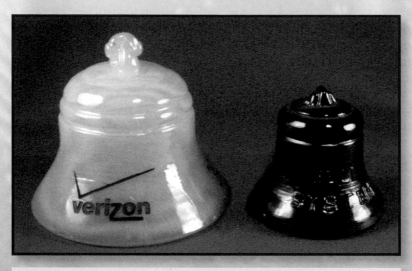

Opal Iridized lg. Bell paperweight, $35.00 – 40.00; Ruby Iridized small Bell paperweight, $20.00 – 25.00.

Black Pacific Bell paperweight, large size, $35.00 – 40.00.

Large Crystal with Blue top, Bell South paperweight, $40.00 – 45.00.

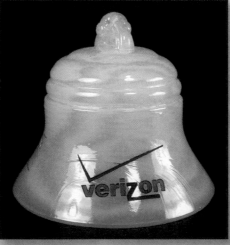

Opal Iridized lg. Verizon paperweight, $35.00 – 40.00.

Topaz small Telephone paperweight, $20.00 – 25.00.

Group of small Telephone paper-weights, $20.00 – 25.00 each.

Group of large Telephone paper-weights, $35.00 – 40.00 each.

Tiara Exclusives

Tiara Exclusives was a home party plan developed by its parent company, Indiana Glass Company, in 1970. The Tiara division of Indiana was developed to compete in the home party business made popular by companies like Princess House, Tupperware, and Home Interiors. Catalogs were produced and sent to a Tiara associate, who booked parties with hostesses who would be rewarded with a piece of glass commensurate with the dollar value sold at the party. Sales associates were paid a commission for the glass sold, but they could also earn special pieces of glass. Pieces like the Stagecoach and Pie Wagon, pictured in this chapter, were only available to successful associates and are quite rare for that reason.

The Indiana Glass Co. began in 1896 as the Beatty Brady Glass Company and became Indiana Glass in 1908. Then, in the 1970s, Indiana was sold to Lancaster Colony.

In 1983, Lancaster Colony bought moulds from the Imperial Company that included moulds once owned by Cambridge, Heisey and Central Glass. When Fostoria went out of business, Lancaster bought almost all of its moulds, and those were added to the long list of moulds available to the Tiara Company. To make all this more difficult, none of the Tiara moulds owned by Lancaster are signed, with the exception of the baskets. The baskets made by Indiana when it was making handmade glass have a handler mark at the base of the handle where it attaches to the bowl. The handler mark consisted of the initials of the man who added the handle.

Don Cunningham, who came from the Viking Glass Company, was hired by Fenton in 1986 to work in its special products division. One of the first accounts he handled was that of the Tiara Company. This was one of Fenton's largest special-order accounts. Fenton agreed to supply articles for Tiara at only a small margin over cost. It did this to give the employees steady work, and it certainly did that. When Fenton began making glass for QVC, the demands of producing glass for the catalog line and for QVC left little time for the production of Tiara items. Tiara was having a great deal of success with the products supplied by Fenton. Dusty Rose and opalescent items were steady sellers for the company, just as they were in Fenton's own product line. Some of Tiara's best sellers were the beautiful handled baskets made for it by Fenton. It was the success of those baskets that finally caused the partnership between the two companies to end. There simply weren't enough artisans available to put handles on all those baskets. Don Cunningham sent the Tiara business to L.E. Smith, who made glass for it, although Fenton continued to do some of its work for a few more years.

Tiara Exclusives went out of business in 1998, possibly due to the fact that it was no longer able to find a factory that could produce the handmade glass sold by it in its catalogs. The moulds it had been using for the Tiara line were put up for sale, and Fenton bought most of them. You will probably recognize the Plume vase in Tea Rose. Fenton has made it in several colors, including Periwinkle Blue. Originally, it was a Central Glass mould, but was then purchased by Imperial, whose moulds were eventually sold to Lancaster Colony, the parent company of Tiara.

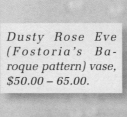

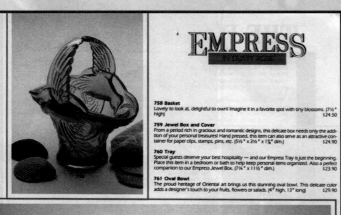

Dusty Rose Eve (Fostoria's Baroque pattern) vase, $50.00 – 65.00.

Dusty Rose Boudoir (Imperial's Spun pattern) 7¼" vase, $35.00 – 40.00.

Dusty Rose Empress pattern: *Basket, $40.00 – 45.00; tray, 11½" x 7¼", $25.00 – 30.00; jewel box, 5½" x 3½", $40.00 – 45.00; bowl, 13" x 4¼", $35.00 – 40.00.*

Dusty Rose Eve ice bucket/console bowl, $60.00 – 65.00.

Dusty Rose assortment: Baroness bowl, $25.00 – 30.00; 10½" Baroness basket, $70.00 – 85.00; Lady Rebecca figurine, $50.00 – 65.00.

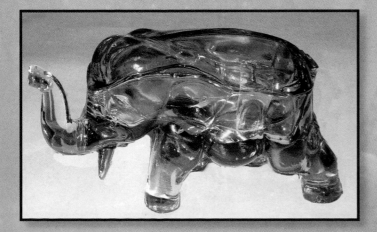

Dusty Rose Elephant box, $65.00 – 75.00.

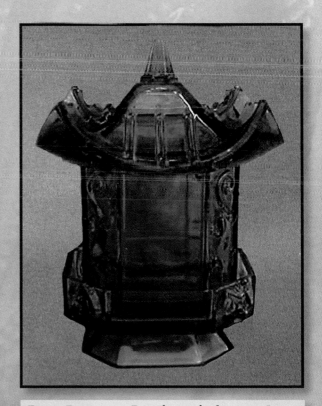

Dusty Rose 3-pc. Pagoda made from an Imperial Glass Company Cathey mould. This was never sold by Tiara; it was an incentive award. Very rare. $175.00 – 200.00.

Dusty Rose fan box and cover also made from an Imperial Glass Company Cathey mould, $75.00 – 85.00.

Dusty Rose Stagecoach made from a Fostoria mould. This was never sold and was used as an incentive gift. Very rare. $250.00 – 300.00; also made in Platinum, $200.00 – 250.00.

Dusty Rose open rose bowl (Imperial Glass Co. mould), $45.00 – 50.00.

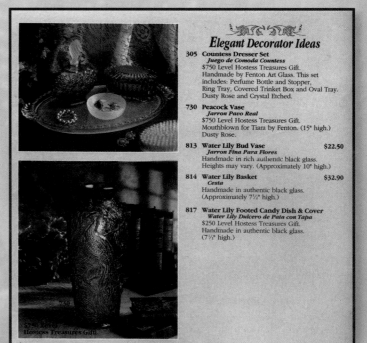

Elegant Decorator Ideas

305 Countess Dresser Set
Juego de Comoda Countess
$750 Level Hostess Treasures Gift.
Handmade by Fenton Art Glass. This set
includes: Perfume Bottle and Stopper,
Ring Tray, Covered Trinket Box and Oval Tray.
Dusty Rose and Crystal Etched.

730 Peacock Vase
Jarron Pavo Real
$750 Level Hostess Treasures Gift.
Mouthblown for Tiara by Fenton. (15" high.)
Dusty Rose.

813 Water Lily Bud Vase $22.50
Jarron Fina Para Flores
Handmade in rich authentic black glass.
Heights may vary. (Approximately 10" high.)

814 Water Lily Basket $32.90
Cesta
Handmade in authentic black glass.
(Approximately 7½" high.)

817 Water Lily Footed Candy Dish & Cover
Water Lily Dulcero de Pata con Tapa
$250 Level Hostess Treasures Gift.
Handmade in authentic black glass.
(7½" high.)

Dusty Rose 5½" Imperial ashtray (Imperial Glass Co. Cathey mould), $20.00 – 25.00.

Dusty Rose assortment: Countess dresser set, $125.00 – 150.00 set; blown Peacock vase, $75.00 – 85.00.

$500 Level
(Values up to $70.00)

619 Windmill Basket
White Lace Crystal

864 Colony Gardens Bowl & Plate
Wisteria

Or Your Choice

403 Crown Starter Set
16 pcs., imperial blue

406 Ponderosa Pine Starter Set
16 pcs., crystal
(Includes: Dinner Plates; Salad Plates;
Coffee Mugs and Water Goblets)

961 Sandwich Starter Set
16 pc., peach
(Includes Dinner Plates, Salad Bowls,
Cups, and Saucers)

$750 Level
(Values up to $100.00)

463 Westclair Lamp
Handpainted

746 Primrose Vase
Dusty Rose

819 Branch Vase
Handpainted, black

Impressions

White lace crystal selections in our Impressions giftware offer a blend of romantic opalescence and timeless style. Each piece is carefully crafted and shaped by hand for your discerning decorating pleasure.

086 Laurel Comport (8¼" dia.) $34.90
Compota

613 Swan (3" high) $14.50
Cisne

615 Laurel Basket (11½" high) $44.50
Cesta con disenos de lauros grabados

617 3-Toed Bowl (6" dia.) $24.90
Cuenco con base de tres pies

Upper right side: *White Lace Crystal Windmill basket (Imperial Glass mould), $65.00 – 75.00; Wisteria Colony bowl and underplate, $30.00 – 35.00 set.*

Bottom photos: *Black Branch 17½" vase, $75.00 – 85.00; Dusty Rose 17½" Primrose vase, $70.00 – 80.00.*

White Lace Crystal assortment: *Laurel 8¼" comport/ftd. bowl, $55.00 – 65.00; 3" open Swan, $20.00 – 24.00; 11½" Laurel basket, $85.00 – 95.00; 3-toed bowl, $18.00 – 22.00.*

Impressions

Soft romantic shades of pink are tipped with a milky opalescence and finished by hand for Tiara's "Impressions Collection" in tea rose. A grouping of nostalgic decorator and accent items you'll enjoy for a lifetime! All handmade by American craftsmen, especially for Tiara Exclusives.

125 Laurel Basket (11½" high) $39.90

126 Crimped 3 Toed Bowl (6" dia.) $19.50

127 Laurel Marmalade Jar (5½" high) $24.90

Tea Rose assortment: *11½" basket, $100.00 – 115.00; crimped 6" 3-toed bowl, $24.00 – 26.00; Laurel marmalade, $50.00 – 65.00.*

Limited edition Black vase decorated with Blue Florals, $65.00 – 85.00.

Water Lily

Crisp provincial blue, tipped in milky white opalescence by master craftsmen, that's Tiara's new Water Lily! The rich floral pattern takes on new dimensions in your decorating scheme. The captivating shapes of handmade glassware offer a myriad of gift possibilities. Choose your occasion, then choose from our Water Lily Collection.

692	Fruit Bowl (11" dia.)	$38.50
693	Bud Vase (10½" high)	$39.90
694	Candle Holders, pair (3" high)	$28.50
695	Basket (7½" high)	$25.90

Provincial Blue Water Lily assortment, left side: *7" basket, $45.00 – 50.00; 10¼" bud vase, $35.00 – 40.00.*
Right side: *11" fruit bowl/comport, $75.00 – 85.00; 3" candlesticks, $40.00 – 50.00 pair.*

Provincial Blue Dewdrop basket, $65.00 - 75.00.

Impressions

White lace crystal selections in our Impressions giftware offer a blend of romantic opalescence and timeless style. Each piece is carefully crafted and shaped by hand for your discerning decorating pleasure.

086	Laurel Comport (8¼" dia.)	$34.90
	Compota	
613	Swan (3" high)	$14.50
	Cisne	
615	Laurel Basket (11½" high)	$44.50
	Cesta con diseños de lauros grabados	
617	3-Toed Bowl (6" dia.)	$24.90
	Cuenco con base de tres pies	

Sage Mist Desert Blossoms assortment: *2-light candleholder, $40.00 - 45.00; single ftd. candlestick, $25.00 - 30.00; 8¼" vase, $50.00 - 65.00.*

Sage Mist Desert Blossom 11½" crimped basket, $100.00 – 125.00.

Wisteria Colony Gardens assortment, left side: *Colonial Lady bell, $45.00 – 50.00; console bowl, $60.00 – 70.00; square 9½" Antique Daisy bowl, $40.00 – 45.00.*
Right side: *9¾" tall basket, $75.00 – 95.00; 6½" powder box & lid, $50.00 – 65.00; 4" ftd. tray, $25.00 – 30.00.*

Hostess Treasures assortment, left side: *wall sconces were not made by Fenton; decorated Black Adore 8½" bud vase, $55.00 – 65.00; White Lace Crystal Laurel cake plate, $55.00 – 65.00; Peach Paradise vase, $45.00 – 55.00; Provincial Blue Dewdrop 11" basket, $75.00 – 85.00.*
Right side: *Wisteria Colony Gardens bowl & plate set, $30.00 – 35.00 set; White Lace Crystal Windmill basket, $65.00 – 75.00; Sage Mist Desert Blossom console bowl, $45.00 – 50.00; Baroness 15¾" candle lamp, $65.00 – 75.00; Imperial Blue 10" dinner plate, $15.00 – 18.00; Imperial Blue 8" salad plate, $12.00 – 15.00; Imperial Blue cup & saucer, $12.00 - 15.00 set; Ruby Crown ftd. chalice & lid (Fostoria Mould), $65.00 – 70.00.*

$750.00 Level
(Values up to $100.00)

240 Branch Vase
amber (17½" high)

381 Rose Vase
pink (13" high)

424 Primrose Vase
amethyst (17½" high)

825 Branch Vase
black, handpainted (17½" high)

Top level hostess gifts: Pink 13" Rose vase, $75.00 – 85.00; Black 17½" Branch vase, $75.00 – 85.00; Amethyst 17½" Primrose vase, $70.00 – 80.00; Amber 17½" Branch vase, $55.00 – 65.00.

Black ftd. 8¼" Conquistador bowl, $35.00 – 40.00.

Black 7¼" Marquis vase, $45.00 – 50.00.

$250 Level
Hostess Treasures Gift!

Black Water Lily assortment: 10¼" bud vase, $35.00 – 40.00; 7½" ftd. candy w/lid, $50.00 – 60.00; 7" basket, $40.00 – 50.00.

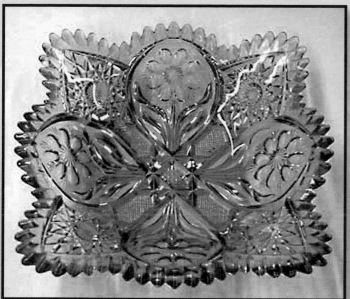

Ice Blue Antique Daisy 9" square bowl, $40.00 – 45.00.

Imperial Blue Crown cup & saucer, $25.00 – 30.00 set.

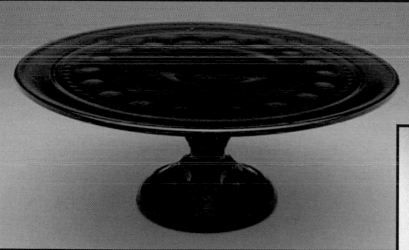

Imperial Blue Crown cake plate, $65.00 – 75.00; also made in Provincial Blue, $85.00 – 100.00.

Imperial Blue 64 oz. pitcher, $75.00 – 85.00.

Imperial Blue 7½" ftd. covered candy, $50.00 – 65.00.

Colorful Creations

Selecting a truly unique gift item is easy with Tiara's assortment of colors and styles. Our timeless Empress pattern in azure blue is a handcrafted collection with a distinct flair. Hand-pressed Floral Medley Trays in pink are perfect for your dresser or vanity.

387	**Floral Medley Tray,** pink	$19.90
	Bandeja de color rosa	
	(10¼"x7¾" w.)	
396	**Floral Medley Tray,** pink	$28.90
	Bandeja de color rosa	
	(12¼"x8½" w.)	
602	**Empress Jewel Box & Cover,** azure blue	$24.50
	Joyero con tapadera, azulado	
	(5½"x3½" w.)	
604	**Empress Tray,** azure blue	$25.90
	Bandeja, azulado	
	(11½"x7¼" w.)	
605	**Empress Oval Bowl,** azure blue	$34.90
	Cuenco ovalado, azulado	
	(13" long, 4¼" high)	

Left side: Pink Floral Medley tray, 12¼" x 8¾", $35.00 – 40.00; Pink Floral Medley tray, 10¼" x 7¾", 35.00 – 40.00.
Right side: Azure Blue Empress bowl, 13" x 4¼" tall, $35.00 – 40.00; Empress tray, 11½" x 7¼", $25.00 – 30.00; Empress jewel box, 5½" x 3½", $40.00 – 45.00.

Azure Blue Swallows bowl, $75.00 – 85.00.

Coral Empress 9½" vase, $75.00 – 85.00.

Peach Sandwich assortment: *Butter dish, $40.00 – 45.00; cream & covered sugar, $24.00 – 28.00 set; napkin holder, $30.00 – 35.00.*

Sea Mist Antique Daisy assortment: *8" oval relish, $20.00 – 25.00; 9½" square bowl, $40.00 – 15.00; 7" round bowl, $40.00 – 45.00; 3½" crimped sherbet, $14.00 – 16.00.*

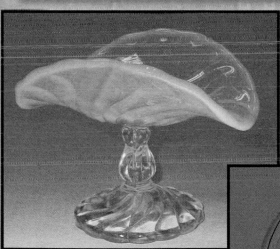

Teal Mist 4½" ftd. tray, $25.00 – 30.00.

Teal Mist Water Lily 7" basket, $45.00 – 55.00.

Teal Mist Water Lily jardiniere, $75.00 – 85.00.

Tom Collins and Audrey and Joe Humphrey purchased a turn of these beautiful Black Crest one-piece fairy lights from Fenton in the late 1980s. They were sold without decoration in the beginning, but some can also be found decorated with a floral design.

Black Crest 1-pc. fairy light, $200.00 – 225.00.

VIP Antiques

This cute little #5158 elephant was decorated for VIP Antiques in 2000.

Opal Satin #5158 Elephant decorated with a Red flower, $35.00 – 40.00.

Virginia's Gift Shop, Knott's Berry Farm

Knott's Berry Farm, founded by Walter Knott, has been an amusement park for 72 years. In 1934, Walter Knott's daughter, Virginia, began selling souvenirs in the company's Chicken Dinner restaurant. That was the beginning of Virginia's Gift Shop. Virginia was still in charge of the gift shop in the 1990s, after 67 years of business. Visitors to the amusement park look forward to shopping in the beautiful shop that stocks a variety of unique giftware items.

Fenton has been sold in Virginia's since as far back as the 1950s. One of the designs made exclusively for it is a blackberry decoration put on vases, animals, and bells.

Blue Topaz decorated with Berries: #1145 bell, $50.00 – 65.00; Blue Topaz #5238 Bird on a Log decorated with Berries, $50.00 – 65.00; Blue Topaz over Opal #3071 vase decorated with Berries, $75.00 – 95.00.

Westlake Ruby Glass Works

The Westlake Ruby Glass Works was a customer of the Fenton Art Glass Company in 1954 and 1955. If I could have found the pieces, or photos of the pieces, made for it, I would have included this company in *Fenton, Glass Made for Other Companies, 1907 – 1980* but I couldn't and didn't. It wasn't until I poured through pictures of special-order glass that are stored at the Fenton offices that I found examples that I am including in this book.

The only pieces I can place with any of the circa-1800s glass factory are the toothpick and the mug shown here. From those, I've been able to say with some certainty that Westlake Ruby Glass Works owned moulds used by the Jefferson Glass Company. After searching through all my pattern glass books and old Butler Brothers catalogs, I was unable to find any advertisement for

these items. I will list all of them with the hopes that one of our readers will find archive material for these in the future. I am listing, but not pricing, the 1950s production until more information can be located.

The following moulds were left at, and eventually bought by, Fenton:

1 square jewel box	1 square jewel box cover
1 #39 toothpick	1 #39 2 oz. mug
1 #39 4 oz. mug	2 #39 6 oz. mug
1 #25 toy basket	1 card table ashtray
1 #39 individual creamer	1 #39 salt
1 toy Hatchet (double)	2 #45 whiskey
1 Boot mould	2 slippers
1 #5 toothpick	

Button Arches Ruby-stained creamer, $22.00 – 26.00.

Button Arches Blue-stained creamer, $22.00 – 26.00.

Ruby-stained Button Arches toothpick holder, $18.00 – 20.00.

Crystal Button Arches toothpick holder, $15.00 – 18.00.

Ruby-stained Button Arches toothpick holder, $18.00 – 20.00.

West Virginia Parkway Authority

The West Virginia Parkway Authority is responsible for the promotion and development of tourism issues. With its help, rest areas were transformed into travel plazas where West Virginia products and crafts could be sold. Eventually, state parks and specialty shops joined in this project. After a few years, the Tamarack Craft Center was built by the state for the purpose of coordinating the effort to promote the West Virginia–made products. These are Fenton's contributions to that effort.

Country Cranberry #3271 6½" bell decorated with a winter scene, $75.00 – 95.00.

Country Cranberry Thumbprint #6435 7" basket decorated with a winter scene, $150.00 – 175.00.

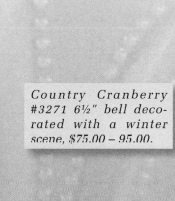

Country Cranberry #1685 7½" tulip vase, $125.00 – 150.00.

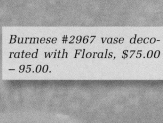

Burmese #2967 vase decorated with Florals, $75.00 – 95.00.

Wheaton Village

Southern New Jersey is the site of some of America's very earliest glass factories, one of which is the Wheaton Glass Factory. In 1789, Caspar Wistar opened the first glass factory in Millville, NJ. But he was quickly followed in 1888, when Theodore Wheaton opened a factory in which he made his own pharmaceutical bottles. From this humble beginning, Wheaton Glass Company became Wheaton Industries, and it continues to make glass, but it also preserves the history of the region.

In 1960, Frank Wheaton, grandson of Theodore, made a visit to the Corning Museum, located in Bath, New York, and found that it was displaying a large group of Jersey Glass. He decided that a collection of Jersey Glass should reside in New Jersey, the area where it was made, so he came home and began to plan for the museum of his dreams. To open this museum, he sought out a collection that would be worthy of the grand museum he was planning. He found that collection in the Bucks County Museum in Pennsylvania. The collection resided in the Wheaton family home until, in 1970, the first building in what was to become Wheaton Village was opened to the public.

The present-day Wheaton Village is home to the museum, the gift shop, the glass factory, and a furnace that is used by glass artists who demonstrate the art of glass-making for the public. There are 20 buildings, built on 60 acres of land, that house restaurants, crafts, and many other interesting displays. The gift shop sells new Fenton, mostly glass sold through Fenton's retail catalog, but a few special-order items are purchased every year. I was only able to confirm and photograph two pieces but, in the future, I will do my best to add to this chapter.

Ruby Iridized #8200 heart-shaped box, decorated with Florals, $100.00 – 125.00.

Amethyst Iridized Golden Daisy bell, $50.00 – 65.00.

Zeta & Charles Todd

Zeta and Charles Todd lived in Aurora, Colorado, and were members of both the FAGCA and the Fenton Finders of Mile High City. In the mid-1980s, Zeta bought several orders of glass made exclusively for her.

Item	Color	Item #	Value
Basket, miniature	Plum Opalescent	7567	$75.00 – 95.00
Basket, miniature	Ruby, Snow Crest	7567	$65.00 – 80.00
Basket, miniature	Cobalt, Silver Crest	7567	$65.00 – 80.00
Basket, miniature	Black, Peach Crest	7567	$65.00 – 80.00
Basket, miniature	Milk Glass, Orange Crest	7567	$65.00 – 80.00
Basket, small	Black Rose	7436	$75.00 – 95.00
Basket, small	Ebony Crest	7436	$75.00 – 95.00
Basket, small	Rosalene	7436	$100.00 – 120.00
Epergne, one-horn	Black Rose	9308	$125.00 – 175.00
Epergne, one-horn	Rosalene	9309	$125.00 – 175.00

**FENTON
4" MINI-BASKETS**
(No. 289 Heacock's Book 2)

**Limited Series of Five
made exclusively for us by
Fenton Art Glass**

•

Plum Opalescent - Sold Out
Ruby with snowcrest petticoat & hdl.
$19.50 - 375 made
Cobalt with silvercrest pettitcoat & hdl.
$16.50 - 396 made
Black with peachcrest petticoat & hdl.
$19.50 - 601 made
White milkglass with orange
petticoat & hdl.
(available April 15)

•

**POSTAGE & HANDLING
$2.00 Each**
(4 or more, $1.50 each)
Dealers write for quantity discounts

**CHARLES & ZETA TODD
12822 E. ALASKA PLACE
AURORA, CO 80012
(303) 343-7899**

Advertisement for Charles and Zeta Todd's miniature baskets.

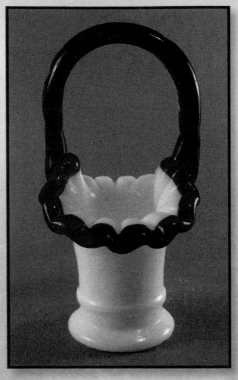

Orange Crest on Milk Glass #7567 miniature basket, $65.00 – 80.00.

Plum Opalescent #7567 miniature basket, $75.00 – 95.00.

Cobalt Blue with Crystal Crest #7567 miniature basket, $65.00 – 80.00.

Ruby Snow Crest #7567 miniature basket, $65.00 – 80.00.

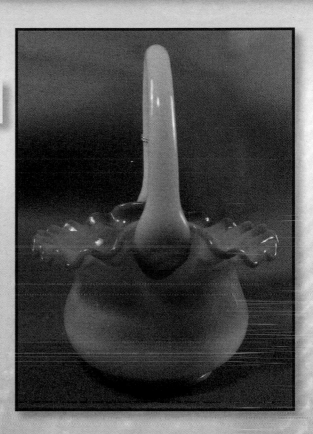

Rosalene #7436 small basket, $100.00 – 120.00.

Black with Peach Crest #7567 miniature basket, $65.00 – 80.00.

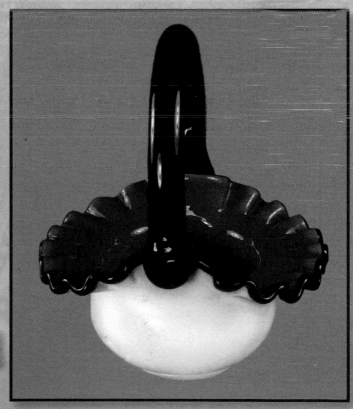

Black Rose #7436 small basket, $75.00 – 95.00.

Black Rose #9308 one-horn epergne, $125.00 – 175.00.

Black Crest on Milk Glass #7436 small basket, $75.00 – 95.00.